HONDA
ACCORD & PRELUDE
1976-1985
SHOP MANUAL

ALAN AHLSTRAND
Editor

JEFF ROBINSON
Publisher

CLYMER PUBLICATIONS

*World's largest publisher of books
devoted exclusively to automobiles and motorcycles*

12860 MUSCATINE STREET • P.O. BOX 4520 • ARLETA, CALIFORNIA 91333-4520

FIRST EDITION
First Printing July, 1978

SECOND EDITION
Revised by Jim Combs to include 1978-1979 models
First Printing January, 1980

THIRD EDITION
Revised by Jim Combs to include 1980 models
First Printing March, 1981

FOURTH EDITION
Revised by Ron Wright to include 1981 models
First Printing April, 1983

FIFTH EDITION
Revised by Alan Ahlstrand to include 1982-1984 models ;
First Printing May, 1985

SIXTH EDITION
Revised by Ed Scott to include 1985 models
First Printing December, 1985
Second Printing July, 1986
Third Printing December, 1986

Printed in U.S.A.

ISBN: 0-89287-201-2

Production Coordinator, Janet Alice Long

*COVER: Photographed by Michael Brown Photographic Productions, Los Angeles, California. Assisted by Ned
Quick and Dennis Miller. Cars courtesy of American Honda Motor Corporation.*

Technical illustrations by Steve Amos.
Technical assistance by Joe Hennessey, Hennesey Jaguar, Costa Mesa, California, and Ansel Darrow.

CONTENTS

QUICK REFERENCE DATA

MAINTENANCE SCHEDULE (1976-1979)

Every 5,000 miles
- Check idle speed and idle mixture[1]
- Change engine oil and filter
- Check throttle controlling unit
- Check ignition timing and adjust if required[1]
- Check valve clearances and adjust if required[1]
- Adjust rear brake (Accord)
- Adjust parking brake
- Check the brake hoses and lines
- Check master cylinder brake fluid level
- Check front brake pads and caliper
- Check play of clutch release arm and adjust if required
- Check play of clutch pedal and adjust if required
- Check clutch master cylinder fluid level
- Check condition of radiator fan
- Check condition of exhaust system and repair if required
- Check tightness of all suspension mounting bolts
- Check the steering, tie rod ends and steering gearbox for correct operation. Adjust if required
- Check rack guides for grease
- Inspect all power steering components and repair as required
- Adjust the power steering belt
- Check the power steering fluid level

Every 10,000 miles
- Clean the disc brake vacuum booster air cleaner [2]
- Check the condition of the rear brake linings and replace if required
- Check front wheel alignment[3]

Every 15,000 miles
- Check the tension of the alternator drive belt and adjust if required
- Change the transaxle oil
- Check the condition of all water hoses and replace/or tighten connections as required
- Replace the engine coolant[2]
- Clean the radiator exterior of all dirt, bugs, etc.
- Replace the air filter
- Replace the fuel filter
- Inspect the air temperature control system
- Inspect the start control system
- Check the choke operation
- Check condition of all vacuum lines and hoses and repair as required
- Inspect the condition of the charcoal canister
- Inspect the idle cutoff valve
- Inspect the 2 way valve
- Replace the contact points (if so equipped) and set the ignition timing[1]
- Replace the spark plugs[1]
- Inspect the ignition timing control system
- Check resistance of the spark plug wires and replace if required
- Clean the condensation chamber, hoses and fixed orifice in the crankcase emission system

(continued)

MAINTENANCE SCHEDULE (1976-1979) (continued)

Every 20,000 miles	• Replace the brake fluid[4]
Every 30,000 miles	• Replace the charcoal canister • Replace the distributor cap and rotor (see notes 1 and 5)

1. Tune-up task.
2. Every 30,000 miles or 34 months on 1977-1979 models.
3. Every 25,000 miles on 1978-1979 models.
4. Every 25,000 miles on 1978-1979 models.
5. Breaker point ignition systems only. Replace parts on transistorized ignition systems if required.

MAINTENANCE SCHEDULE (1979-1981)

Every 7,500 miles	• Change engine oil and filter • Adjust rear brakes (Accord) • Adjust parking brake • Check tightness of suspension mounting bolts • Check exhaust system components and fasteners for condition and tightness. Repair as required • Check steering operation • Check steering rack for grease and adjustment • Inspect tension and condition of the power steering belt • Inspect the power steering system • Check the power steering reservoir fluid level • Inspect the brake lines and hoses • Check the brake master cylinder fluid level • Check the clutch master cylinder fluid level • Check the clutch release arm adjustment • Check the clutch pedal free play
Every 15,000 miles	• Check front wheel alignment • Replace the automatic transaxle fluid • Inspect the front brake pad thickness • Check the condition of the front brake rotor • Check the valve clearances[1]
Every 30,000 miles	• Replace the manual transaxle fluid • Inspect the rear brake adjustment (Accord) • Replace the brake fluid • Inspect the cooling system hoses and connections • Replace the engine coolant (see notes 2 and 3) • Check the alternator belt tension • Replace the spark plugs[1] • Replace the air filter • Check the choke coil tension and linkage
Every 45,000 miles	• Change the engine coolant[4]
Every 60,000 miles	• Repack the rear wheel bearings • Replace the fuel filter • Replace the fuel hose • Clean the condensation chamber, hoses and fixed orifice in the crankcase emission system • Inspect the distributor cap and rotor[1] • Check resistance of the spark plug wires and replace if required

(continued)

Every 60,000 miles	• Check the choke opener operation • Check the intake air control system (cold and hot) • Check the ignition timing control[6] • Check the fast idle unloader (cold and hot)[6] • Check purge control unloader solenoid valve • Inspect the EGR system (see notes 4 and 5) • Check the choke coil tension and heater • Check the ignition timing[1] • Check the fast idle • Check the throttle controller diaphragm • Check the throttle controller dashpot • Check the throttle controller control valve • Check the throttle controller speed sensor • Check idle speed and idle mixture[1] • Check idle control system on air conditioned models • Check anti-afterburn valve (see notes 4 and 6) • Inspect purge control/unloader solenoid valve (hot) • Inspect bypass solenoid valve (hot) (see notes 4 and 7) • Check power valve (see notes 4 and 6) • Check air vent cutoff diaphragm • Check 2-way valve • Inspect catalytic converter heat shield[5]

1. Tune-up task.
2. 1980 models only.
3. Replace every 30,000 miles or 24 months, whichever occurs first.
4. 1981 models only.
5. California manual transaxle only.
6. 1980 California automatic transaxle only.
7. Except 1980 California vehicles with automatic transaxle.

MAINTENANCE SCHEDULE (1982-ON)

Every 7,500 miles	• Change engine oil and filter • Inspect front brake pads and discs • Check clutch pedal and release arm play • Inspect power steering system and check power steering fluid
Every 15,000 miles	• Check automatic transaxle fluid • Check suspension mounting bolt tightness[1] • Inspect exhaust system[1] • nspect brake lines and hoses[1] • Adjust valve clearance[2] • Check front wheel alignment
Every 30,000 miles	• Check manual transaxle oil • Inspect rear brake linings • Inspect parking brake[1] • Inspect steering system and check operation[1] • Change brake fluid • Inspect cooling system hoses and connections • Inspect and adjust alternator belt • Inspect and adjust power steering pump belt • Inspect crankcase emission control system • Replace spark plugs[2] • Replace air cleaner element • Clean and inspect choke linkage

(continued)

MAINTENANCE SCHEDULE (1982-ON) (continued)

Every 60,000 miles	• Lubricate rear wheel bearings • Inspect fuel lines and connections • Replace fuel filters and engine compartment fuel hoses • Inspect distributor cap and rotor[2] • Inspect ignition wiring[2] • Check ignition timing • Adjust carburetor(s)[3] • Inspect emission control systems[3]

1. First inspection @ 7,500 miles.
2. Described under Tune-up in this chapter.
3. Have done by a Honda dealer or mechanic familiar with Honda emission controls.

APPROXIMATE REFILL CAPACITIES

1976-1981
Engine oil	3.2 qt.
Manual transaxle	2.8 qt.
Automatic transaxle	2.6 qt.
Cooling system	1.3 gal.

1979-1981
Engine oil	
Without filter change	3.2 qt.
With filter change	3.7 qt.
Manual transaxle	2.5 qt.
Automatic transaxle	2.6 qt.
Cooling system	1.6 gal.

1982
Engine oil	
Without filter change	3.2 qt.
With filter change	3.7 qt.
Manual transaxle	2.5 qt.
Automatic transaxle	2.6 qt.
Cooling system	
Accord	1.3 gal.
Prelude	1.6 gal.

1983-on Accord
Engine oil	
Without filter change	3.2 qt.
With filter change	3.7 qt.
Manual transaxle	2.5 qt.
Automatic transaxle	3.0 qt.
Cooling system	
1983	1.3 gal.
1984-on	1.8 gal.

1983-on Prelude
Engine oil	
Without filter change	3.2 qt.
With filter change	3.7 qt.
Manual transaxle	2.5 qt.
Automatic transaxle	3.0 qt.
Cooling system	
Manual	1.8 gal.
Automatic	2.0 gal.

HONDA
ACCORD & PRELUDE
1976-1985
SHOP MANUAL

INTRODUCTION

This detailed, comprehensive manual covers all 1976-1985 Honda Accords and 1979-1985 Honda Preludes. The expert text gives complete information on maintenance, repair and overhaul. Hundreds of photos and drawings guide you through every step. The book includes all you need to know to keep your car running right.

Where repairs are practical for the owner/mechanic, complete procedures are given. Equally important, difficult jobs are pointed out. Such operations are usually more economically performed by a dealer or independent garage.

A shop manual is a reference. You want to be able to find information fast. As in all Clymer books, this one is designed with this in mind. All chapters are thumb tabbed. Important items are indexed at the rear of the book. Finally, all the most frequently used specifications and capacities are summarized on the *Quick Reference* pages at the front of the book.

Keep the book handy. Carry it in your glove box. It will help you to better understand your Honda, lower repair and maintenance costs, and generally improve your satisfaction with your vehicle.

CHAPTER ONE

GENERAL INFORMATION

The troubleshooting, tune-up, maintenance, and step-by-step repair procedures in this book are written for the owner and home mechanic. The text is accompanied by useful photos and diagrams to make the job as clear and correct as possible.

Troubleshooting, tune-up, maintenance, and repair are not difficult if you know what tools and equipment to use and what to do. Anyone not afraid to get their hands dirty, of average intelligence, and with some mechanical ability can perform most of the procedures in this book.

In some cases, a repair job may require tools or skills not reasonably expected of the home mechanic. These procedures are noted in each chapter and it is recommended that you take the job to your dealer, a competent mechanic, or machine shop.

MANUAL ORGANIZATION

This chapter provides general information and safety and service hints. Also included are lists of recommended shop and emergency tools as well as a brief description of troubleshooting and tune-up equipment.

Chapter Two provides methods and suggestions for quick and accurate diagnosis and repair of problems. Troubleshooting procedures discuss typical symptoms and logical methods to pinpoint the trouble.

Chapter Three explains all periodic lubrication and routine maintenance necessary to keep your vehicle running well. Chapter Three also includes recommended tune-up procedures, eliminating the need to constantly consult chapters on the various subassemblies.

Subsequent chapters cover specific systems such as the engine, transmission, and electrical systems. Each of these chapters provides disassembly, repair, and assembly procedures in a simple step-by-step format. If a repair requires special skills or tools, or is otherwise impractical for the home mechanic, it is so indicated. In these cases it is usually faster and less expensive to have the repairs made by a dealer or competent repair shop. Necessary specifications concerning a particular system are included at the end of the appropriate chapter.

When special tools are required to perform a procedure included in this manual, the tool is illustrated either in actual use or alone. It may be possible to rent or borrow these tools. The inventive mechanic may also be able to find a suitable substitute in his tool box, or to fabricate one.

The terms NOTE, CAUTION, and WARNING have specific meanings in this manual. A NOTE provides additional or explanatory information. A CAUTION is used to emphasize areas where equipment damage could result if proper precautions are not taken. A WARNING is used to stress those areas where personal injury or death could result from negligence, in addition to possible mechanical damage.

SERVICE HINTS

Observing the following practices will save time, effort, and frustration, as well as prevent possible injury.

Throughout this manual keep in mind two conventions. "Front" refers to the front of the vehicle. The front of any component, such as the transmission, is that end which faces toward the front of the vehicle. The "left" and "right" sides of the vehicle refer to the orientation of a person sitting in the vehicle facing forward. For example, the steering wheel is on the left side. These rules are simple, but even experienced mechanics occasionally become disoriented.

Most of the service procedures covered are straightforward and can be performed by anyone reasonably handy with tools. It is suggested, however, that you consider your own capabilities carefully before attempting any operation involving major disassembly of the engine.

Some operations, for example, require the use of a press. It would be wiser to have these performed by a shop equipped for such work, rather than to try to do the job yourself with makeshift equipment. Other procedures require precision measurements. Unless you have the skills and equipment required, it would be better to have a qualified repair shop make the measurements for you.

Repairs go much faster and easier if the parts that will be worked on are clean before you begin. There are special cleaners for washing the engine and related parts. Brush or spray on the cleaning solution, let it stand, then rinse it away with a garden hose. Clean all oily or greasy parts with cleaning solvent as you remove them.

WARNING
Never use gasoline as a cleaning agent. It presents an extreme fire hazard. Be sure to work in a well-ventilated area when using cleaning solvent. Keep a fire extinguisher, rated for gasoline fires, handy in any case.

Much of the labor charge for repairs made by dealers is for the removal and disassembly of other parts to reach the defective unit. It is frequently possible to perform the preliminary operations yourself and then take the defective unit in to the dealer for repair, at considerable savings.

Once you have decided to tackle the job yourself, make sure you locate the appropriate section in this manual, and read it entirely. Study the illustrations and text until you have a good idea of what is involved in completing the job satisfactorily. If special tools are required, make arrangements to get them before you start. Also, purchase any known defective parts prior to starting on the procedure. It is frustrating and time-consuming to get partially into a job and then be unable to complete it.

Simple wiring checks can be easily made at home, but knowledge of electronics is almost a necessity for performing tests with complicated electronic testing gear.

During disassembly of parts keep a few general cautions in mind. Force is rarely needed to get things apart. If parts are a tight fit, like a bearing in a case, there is usually a tool designed to separate them. Never use a screwdriver to pry apart parts with machined surfaces such as cylinder head and valve cover. You will mar the surfaces and end up with leaks.

Make diagrams wherever similar-appearing parts are found. You may think you can remember where everything came from — but mistakes are costly. There is also the possibility you may get sidetracked and not return to work for days or even weeks — in which interval, carefully laid out parts may have become disturbed.

Tag all similar internal parts for location, and mark all mating parts for position. Record number and thickness of any shims as they are removed. Small parts such as bolts can be identified by placing them in plastic sandwich bags that are sealed and labeled with masking tape.

Wiring should be tagged with masking tape and marked as each wire is removed. Again, do not rely on memory alone.

When working under the vehicle, do not trust a hydraulic or mechanical jack to hold the vehicle up by itself. Always use jackstands. See **Figure 1**.

Disconnect battery ground cable before working near electrical connections and before disconnecting wires. Never run the engine with the battery disconnected; the alternator could be seriously damaged.

Protect finished surfaces from physical damage or corrosion. Keep gasoline and brake fluid off painted surfaces.

Frozen or very tight bolts and screws can often be loosened by soaking with penetrating oil like Liquid Wrench or WD-40, then sharply striking the bolt head a few times with a hammer and punch (or screwdriver for screws). Avoid heat unless absolutely necessary, since it may melt, warp, or remove the temper from many parts.

Avoid flames or sparks when working near a charging battery or flammable liquids, such as brake fluid or gasoline.

No parts, except those assembled with a press fit, require unusual force during assembly. If a part is hard to remove or install, find out why before proceeding.

Cover all openings after removing parts to keep dirt, small tools, etc., from falling in.

When assembling two parts, start all fasteners, then tighten evenly.

The clutch plate, wiring connections, brake shoes, drums, pads, and discs should be kept clean and free of grease and oil.

When assembling parts, be sure all shims and washers are replaced exactly as they came out.

Whenever a rotating part butts against a stationary part, look for a shim or washer. Use new gaskets if there is any doubt about the condition of old ones. Generally, you should apply gasket cement to one mating surface only, so the parts may be easily disassembled in the future. A thin coat of oil on gaskets helps them seal effectively.

Heavy grease can be used to hold small parts in place if they tend to fall out during assembly. However, keep grease and oil away from electrical, clutch, and brake components.

High spots may be sanded off a piston with sandpaper, but emery cloth and oil do a much more professional job.

Carburetors are best cleaned by disassembling them and soaking the parts in a commercial carburetor cleaner. Never soak gaskets and rubber parts in these cleaners. Never use wire to clean out jets and air passages; they are easily damaged. Use compressed air to blow out the carburetor, but only if the float has been removed first.

Take your time and do the job right. Do not forget that a newly rebuilt engine must be broken in the same as a new one. Refer to your owner's manual for the proper break-in procedures.

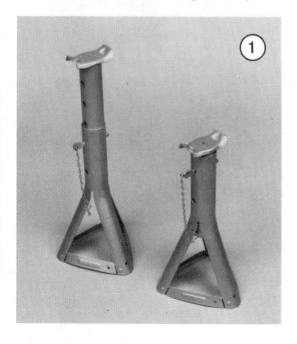

SAFETY FIRST

Professional mechanics can work for years and never sustain a serious injury. If you observe a few rules of common sense and safety, you can enjoy many safe hours servicing your vehicle. You could hurt yourself or damage the vehicle if you ignore these rules.

1. Never use gasoline as a cleaning solvent.

2. Never smoke or use a torch in the vicinity of flammable liquids such as cleaning solvent in open containers.

3. Never smoke or use a torch in an area where batteries are being charged. Highly explosive hydrogen gas is formed during the charging process.

4. Use the proper sized wrenches to avoid damage to nuts and injury to yourself.

5. When loosening a tight or stuck nut, be guided by what would happen if the wrench should slip. Protect yourself accordingly.

6. Keep your work area clean and uncluttered.

7. Wear safety goggles during all operations involving drilling, grinding, or use of a cold chisel.

8. Never use worn tools.

9. Keep a fire extinguisher handy and be sure it is rated for gasoline (Class B) and electrical (Class C) fires.

EXPENDABLE SUPPLIES

Certain expendable supplies are necessary. These include grease, oil, gasket cement, wiping rags, cleaning solvent, and distilled water.

Also, special locking compounds, silicone lubricants, and engine cleaners may be useful. Cleaning solvent is available at most service stations and distilled water for the battery is available at most supermarkets.

SHOP TOOLS

For proper servicing, you will need an assortment of ordinary hand tools (**Figure 2**).

As a minimum, these include:

a. Combination wrenches

b. Sockets

c. Plastic mallet

d. Small hammer

e. Snap ring pliers

f. Gas pliers

g. Phillips screwdrivers

h. Slot (common) screwdrivers

i. Feeler gauges

j. Spark plug gauge

k. Spark plug wrench

Special tools necessary are shown in the chapters covering the particular repair in which they are used.

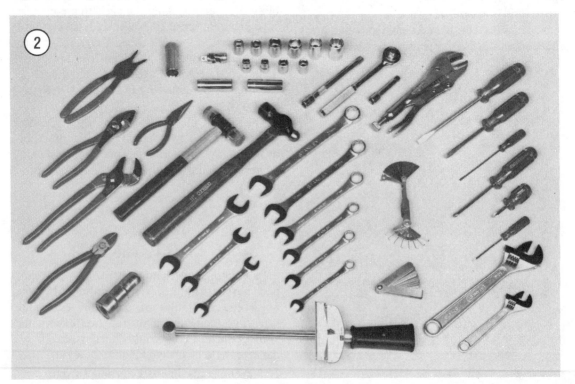

Engine tune-up and troubleshooting procedures require other special tools and equipment. These are described in detail in the
following sections.

EMERGENCY TOOL KIT

A small emergency tool kit kept in the trunk
is handy for road emergencies which otherwise
could leave you stranded. The tools listed below
and shown in **Figure 3** will let you handle most
roadside repairs.

a. Combination wrenches

b. Crescent (adjustable) wrench

c. Screwdrivers — common and Phillips

d. Pliers — conventional (gas) and needle
nose

e. Vise Grips

f. Hammer — plastic and metal

g. Small container of waterless hand cleaner

h. Rags for clean up

i. Silver waterproof sealing tape (duct tape)

j. Flashlight

k. Emergency road flares — at least four

l. Spare drive belts (water pump, alternator,
etc.)

TROUBLESHOOTING AND TUNE-UP EQUIPMENT

Voltmeter, Ohmmeter, and Ammeter

For testing the ignition or electrical system, a
good voltmeter is required. For automotive use,
an instrument covering 0-20 volts is satisfac-

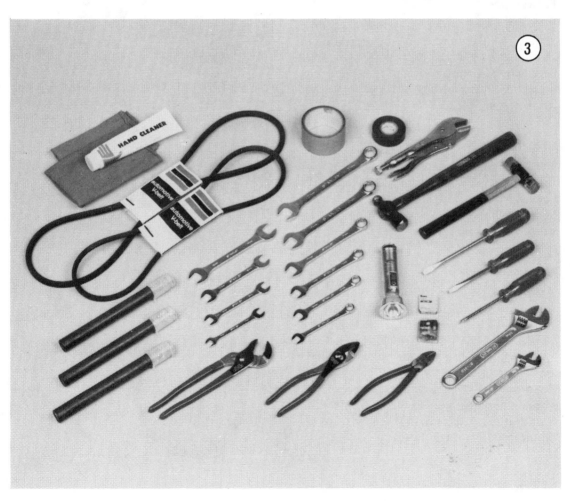

tory. One which also has a 0-2 volt scale is necessary for testing relays, points, or individual contacts where voltage drops are much smaller. Accuracy should be ± ½ volt.

An ohmmeter measures electrical resistance. This instrument is useful for checking continuity (open and short circuits), and testing fuses and lights.

The ammeter measures electrical current. Ammeters for automotive use should cover 0-50 amperes and 0-250 amperes. These are useful for checking battery charging and starting current.

Several inexpensive VOM's (volt-ohm-milliammeter) combine all three instruments into one which fits easily in any tool box. See **Figure 4**. However, the ammeter ranges are usually too small for automotive work.

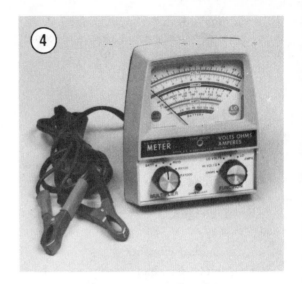

Hydrometer

The hydrometer gives a useful indication of battery condition and charge by measuring the specific gravity of the electrolyte in each cell. See **Figure 5**. Complete details on use and interpretation of readings are provided in the electrical chapter.

Compression Tester

The compression tester measures the compression pressure built up in each cylinder. The results, when properly interpreted, can indicate general cylinder and valve condition. See **Figure 6**.

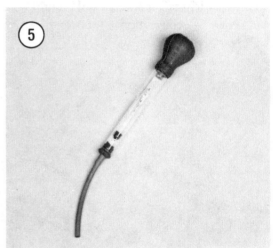

Vacuum Gauge

The vacuum gauge (**Figure 7**) is one of the easiest instruments to use, but one of the most difficult for the inexperienced mechanic to interpret. The results, when interpreted with other findings, can provide valuable clues to possible trouble.

To use the vacuum gauge, connect it to a vacuum hose that goes to the intake manifold. Attach it either directly to the hose or to a T-fitting installed into the hose.

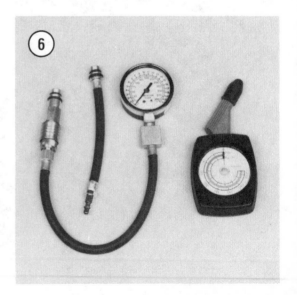

NOTE: *Subtract one inch from the reading for every 1,000 ft. elevation.*

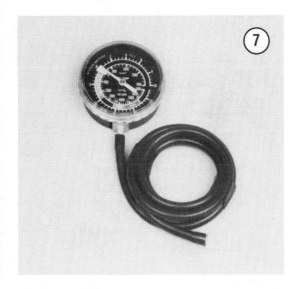

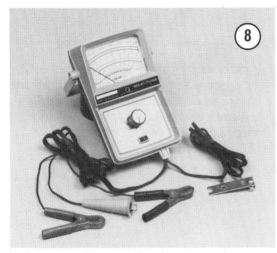

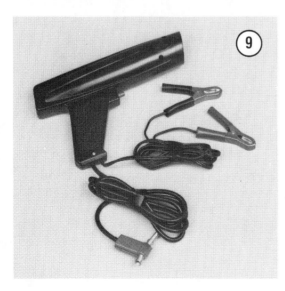

Fuel Pressure Gauge

This instrument is invaluable for evaluating fuel pump performance. Fuel system trouble-shooting procedures in this manual use a fuel pressure gauge. Usually a vacuum gauge and fuel pressure gauge are combined.

Dwell Meter (Contact Breaker Point Ignition Only)

A dwell meter measures the distance in degrees of cam rotation that the breaker points remain closed while the engine is running. Since this angle is determined by breaker point gap, dwell angle is an accurate indication of breaker point gap.

Many tachometers intended for tuning and testing incorporate a dwell meter as well. See **Figure 8**. Follow the manufacturer's instructions to measure dwell.

Tachometer

A tachometer is necessary for tuning. See **Figure 8**. Ignition timing and carburetor adjustments must be performed at the specified idle speed. The best instrument for this purpose is one with a low range of 0-1,000 or 0-2,000 rpm for setting idle, and a high range of 0-4,000 or more for setting ignition timing at 3,000 rpm. Extended range (0-6,000 or 0-8,000 rpm) instruments lack accuracy at lower speeds. The instrument should be capable of detecting changes of 25 rpm on the low range.

Strobe Timing Light

This instrument is necessary for tuning, as it permits very accurate ignition timing. The light flashes at precisely the same instant that No. 1 cylinder fires, at which time the timing marks on the engine should align. Refer to Chapter Three for exact location of the timing marks for your engine.

Suitable lights range from inexpensive neon bulb types ($2-3) to powerful xenon strobe lights ($20-40). See **Figure 9**. Neon timing lights are difficult to see and must be used in dimly lit areas. Xenon strobe timing lights can be used outside in bright sunlight. Both types work on this vehicle; use according to the manufacturer's instructions.

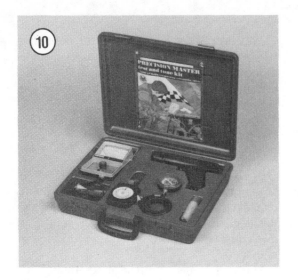

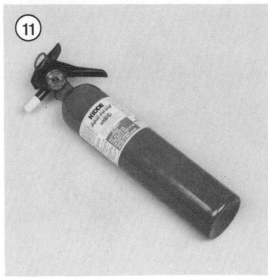

Tune-up Kits

Many manufacturer's offer kits that combine several useful instruments. Some come in a convenient carry case and are usally less expensive than purchasing one instrument at a time. **Figure 10** shows one of the kits that is available. The prices vary with the number of instruments included in the kit.

Fire Extinguisher

A fire extinguisher is a necessity when working on a vehicle. It should be rated for both *Class B* (flammable liquids—gasoline, oil, paint, etc.) and *Class C* (electrical—wiring, etc.) type fires. It should always be kept within reach. See **Figure 11**.

TROUBLESHOOTING

Troubleshooting can be a relatively simple matter if it is done logically. The first step in any troubleshooting procedure must be defining the symptoms as closely as possible. Subsequent steps involve testing and analyzing areas which could cause the symptoms. A haphazard approach may eventually find the trouble, but in terms of wasted time and unnecessary parts replacement, it can be very costly.

The troubleshooting procedures in this chapter analyze typical symptoms and show logical methods of isolation. These are not the only methods. There may be several approaches to a problem, but all methods must have one thing in common — a logical, systematic approach.

STARTING SYSTEM

The starting system consists of the starter motor and the starter solenoid. The ignition key controls the starter solenoid, which mechanically engages the starter with the engine flywheel, and supplies electrical current to turn the starter motor.

Starting system troubles are relatively easy to find. In most cases, the trouble is a loose or dirty electrical connection. **Figures 1 and 2** provide routines for finding the trouble.

CHARGING SYSTEM

The charging system consists of the alternator (or generator on older vehicles), voltage regulator, and battery. A drive belt driven by the engine crankshaft turns the alternator which produces electrical energy to charge the battery. As engine speed varies, the voltage from the alternator varies. A voltage regulator controls the charging current to the battery and maintains the voltage to the vehicle's electrical system at safe levels. A warning light or gauge on the instrument panel signals the driver when charging is not taking place. Refer to **Figure 3** for a typical charging system.

Complete troubleshooting of the charging system requires test equipment and skills which the average home mechanic does not possess. However, there are a few tests which can be done to pinpoint most troubles.

Charging system trouble may stem from a defective alternator (or generator), voltage regulator, battery, or drive belt. It may also be caused by something as simple as incorrect drive belt tension. The following are symptoms of typical problems you may encounter.

1. *Battery dies frequently, even though the warning lamp indicates no discharge* — This can be caused by a drive belt that is slightly too

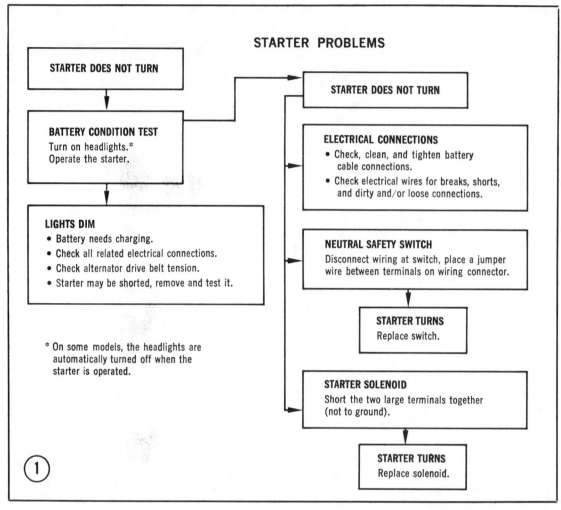

STARTER PROBLEMS

STARTER DOES NOT TURN

BATTERY CONDITION TEST
Turn on headlights.*
Operate the starter.

LIGHTS DIM
- Battery needs charging.
- Check all related electrical connections.
- Check alternator drive belt tension.
- Starter may be shorted, remove and test it.

* On some models, the headlights are automatically turned off when the starter is operated.

STARTER DOES NOT TURN

ELECTRICAL CONNECTIONS
- Check, clean, and tighten battery cable connections.
- Check electrical wires for breaks, shorts, and dirty and/or loose connections.

NEUTRAL SAFETY SWITCH
Disconnect wiring at switch, place a jumper wire between terminals on wiring connector.

STARTER TURNS
Replace switch.

STARTER SOLENOID
Short the two large terminals together (not to ground).

STARTER TURNS
Replace solenoid.

①

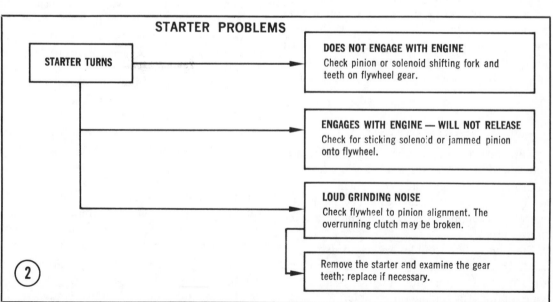

STARTER PROBLEMS

STARTER TURNS

DOES NOT ENGAGE WITH ENGINE
Check pinion or solenoid shifting fork and teeth on flywheel gear.

ENGAGES WITH ENGINE — WILL NOT RELEASE
Check for sticking solenoid or jammed pinion onto flywheel.

LOUD GRINDING NOISE
Check flywheel to pinion alignment. The overrunning clutch may be broken.

Remove the starter and examine the gear teeth; replace if necessary.

②

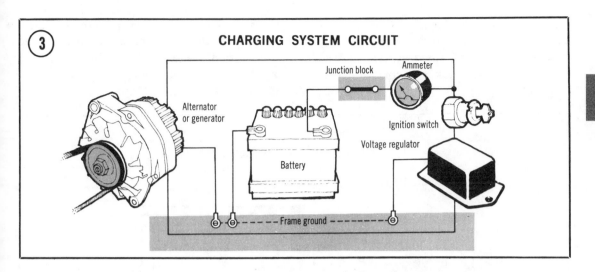

CHARGING SYSTEM CIRCUIT

③ Alternator or generator — Junction block — Ammeter — Ignition switch — Voltage regulator — Battery — Frame ground

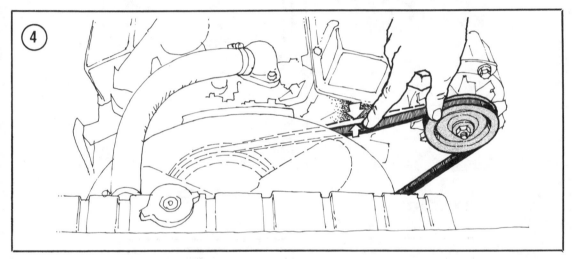

④

loose. Grasp the alternator (or generator) pulley and try to turn it. If the pulley can be turned without moving the belt, the drive belt is too loose. As a rule, keep the belt tight enough that it can be deflected about ½ in. under moderate thumb pressure between the pulleys (**Figure 4**). The battery may also be at fault; test the battery condition.

2. *Charging system warning lamp does not come on when ignition switch is turned on* — This may indicate a defective ignition switch, battery, voltage regulator, or lamp. First try to start the vehicle. If it doesn't start, check the ignition switch and battery. If the car starts, remove the warning lamp; test it for continuity with an ohmmeter or substitute a new lamp. If the lamp is good, locate the voltage regulator

and make sure it is properly grounded (try tightening the mounting screws). Also the alternator (or generator) brushes may not be making contact. Test the alternator (or generator) and voltage regulator.

3. *Alternator (or generator) warning lamp comes on and stays on* — This usually indicates that no charging is taking place. First check drive belt tension (**Figure 4**). Then check battery condition, and check all wiring connections in the charging system. If this does not locate the trouble, check the alternator (or generator) and voltage regulator.

4. *Charging system warning lamp flashes on and off intermittently* — This usually indicates the charging system is working intermittently.

Check the drive belt tension (**Figure 4**), and check all electrical connections in the charging system. Check the alternator (or generator). *On generators only*, check the condition of the commutator.

5. *Battery requires frequent additions of water, or lamps require frequent replacement* — The alternator (or generator) is probably overcharging the battery. The voltage regulator is probably at fault.

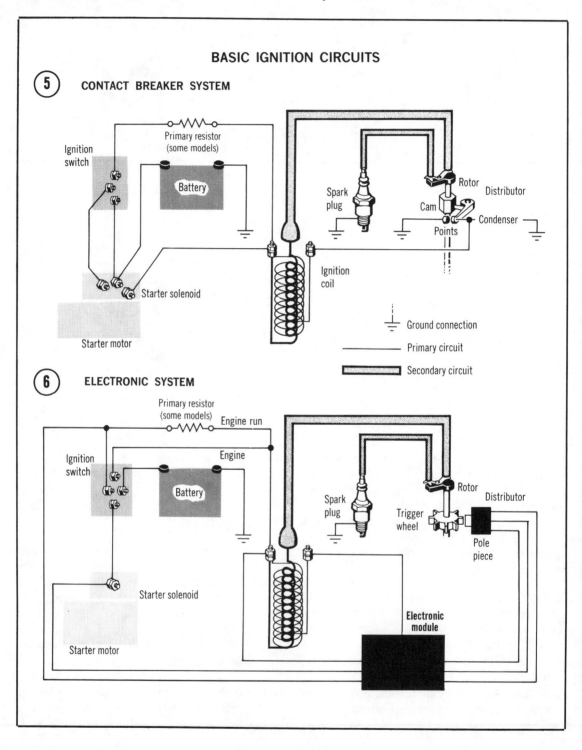

BASIC IGNITION CIRCUITS

5 CONTACT BREAKER SYSTEM

Primary resistor (some models)

Ignition switch

Battery

Spark plug

Rotor

Distributor

Cam

Condenser

Points

Ignition coil

Starter solenoid

Starter motor

Ground connection

Primary circuit

Secondary circuit

6 ELECTRONIC SYSTEM

Primary resistor (some models)

Engine run

Ignition switch

Engine

Battery

Spark plug

Rotor

Distributor

Trigger wheel

Pole piece

Starter solenoid

Electronic module

Starter motor

6. *Excessive noise from the alternator (or generator)* — Check for loose mounting brackets and bolts. The problem may also be worn bearings or the need of lubrication in some cases. If an alternator whines, a shorted diode may be indicated.

IGNITION SYSTEM

The ignition system may be either a conventional contact breaker type or an electronic ignition. See electrical chapter to determine which type you have. **Figures 5 and 6** show simplified diagrams of each type.

Most problems involving failure to start, poor performance, or rough running stem from trouble in the ignition system, particularly in contact breaker systems. Many novice troubleshooters get into trouble when they assume that these symptoms point to the fuel system instead of the ignition system.

Ignition system troubles may be roughly divided between those affecting only one cylinder and those affecting all cylinders. If the trouble affects only one cylinder, it can only be in the spark plug, spark plug wire, or portion of the distributor associated with that cylinder. If the trouble affects all cylinders (weak spark or no spark), then the trouble is in the ignition coil, rotor, distributor, or associated wiring.

The troubleshooting procedures outlined in **Figure 7** (breaker point ignition) or **Figure 8**

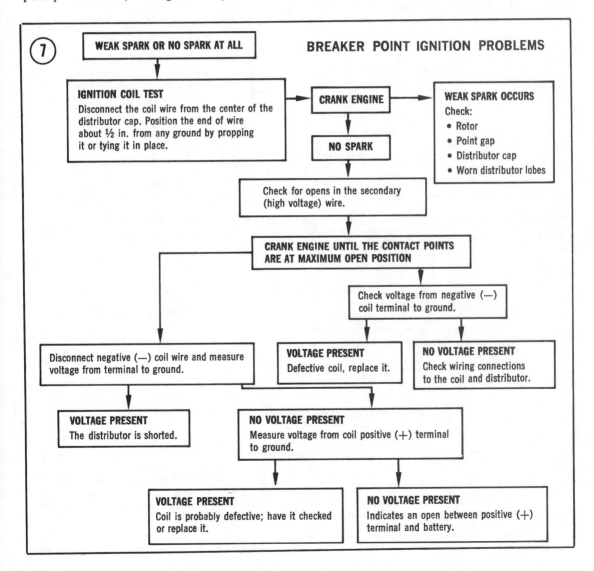

7 **WEAK SPARK OR NO SPARK AT ALL**   **BREAKER POINT IGNITION PROBLEMS**

IGNITION COIL TEST
Disconnect the coil wire from the center of the distributor cap. Position the end of wire about ½ in. from any ground by propping it or tying it in place.

CRANK ENGINE

WEAK SPARK OCCURS
Check:
• Rotor
• Point gap
• Distributor cap
• Worn distributor lobes

NO SPARK

Check for opens in the secondary (high voltage) wire.

CRANK ENGINE UNTIL THE CONTACT POINTS ARE AT MAXIMUM OPEN POSITION

Check voltage from negative (—) coil terminal to ground.

Disconnect negative (—) coil wire and measure voltage from terminal to ground.

VOLTAGE PRESENT
Defective coil, replace it.

NO VOLTAGE PRESENT
Check wiring connections to the coil and distributor.

VOLTAGE PRESENT
The distributor is shorted.

NO VOLTAGE PRESENT
Measure voltage from coil positive (+) terminal to ground.

VOLTAGE PRESENT
Coil is probably defective; have it checked or replace it.

NO VOLTAGE PRESENT
Indicates an open between positive (+) terminal and battery.

(electronic ignition) will help you isolate ignition problems fast. Of course, they assume that the battery is in good enough condition to crank the engine over at its normal rate.

ENGINE PERFORMANCE

A number of factors can make the engine difficult or impossible to start, or cause rough running, poor performance and so on. The majority of novice troubleshooters immediately suspect the carburetor or fuel injection system. In the majority of cases, though, the trouble exists in the ignition system.

The troubleshooting procedures outlined in **Figures 9 through 14** will help you solve the majority of engine starting troubles in a systematic manner.

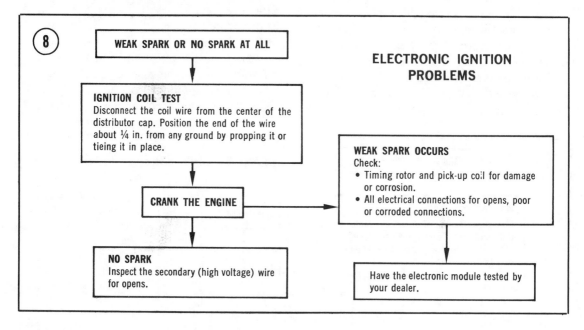

⑧ WEAK SPARK OR NO SPARK AT ALL

ELECTRONIC IGNITION PROBLEMS

IGNITION COIL TEST
Disconnect the coil wire from the center of the distributor cap. Position the end of the wire about ¼ in. from any ground by propping it or tieing it in place.

CRANK THE ENGINE

NO SPARK
Inspect the secondary (high voltage) wire for opens.

WEAK SPARK OCCURS
Check:
• Timing rotor and pick-up coil for damage or corrosion.
• All electrical connections for opens, poor or corroded connections.

Have the electronic module tested by your dealer.

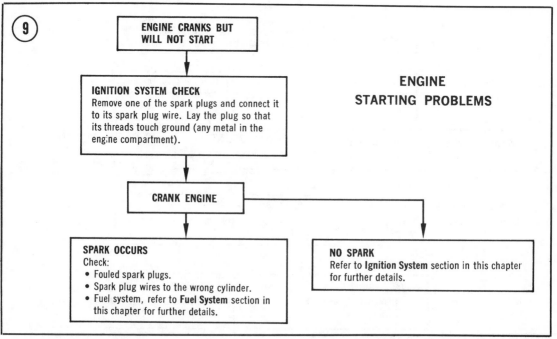

⑨ ENGINE CRANKS BUT WILL NOT START

ENGINE STARTING PROBLEMS

IGNITION SYSTEM CHECK
Remove one of the spark plugs and connect it to its spark plug wire. Lay the plug so that its threads touch ground (any metal in the engine compartment).

CRANK ENGINE

SPARK OCCURS
Check:
• Fouled spark plugs.
• Spark plug wires to the wrong cylinder.
• Fuel system, refer to **Fuel System** section in this chapter for further details.

NO SPARK
Refer to **Ignition System** section in this chapter for further details.

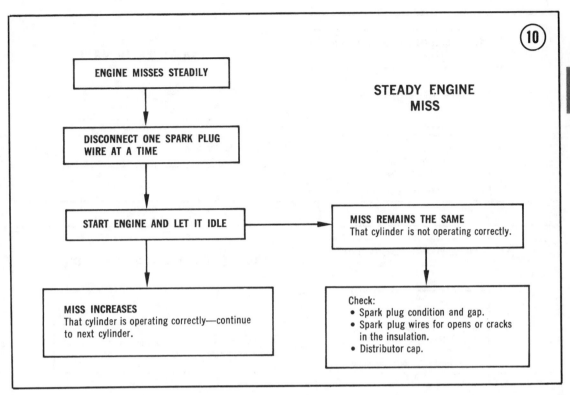

10

ENGINE MISSES STEADILY

STEADY ENGINE
MISS

DISCONNECT ONE SPARK PLUG
WIRE AT A TIME

START ENGINE AND LET IT IDLE → MISS REMAINS THE SAME
That cylinder is not operating correctly.

MISS INCREASES
That cylinder is operating correctly—continue
to next cylinder.

Check:
• Spark plug condition and gap.
• Spark plug wires for opens or cracks
  in the insulation.
• Distributor cap.

2

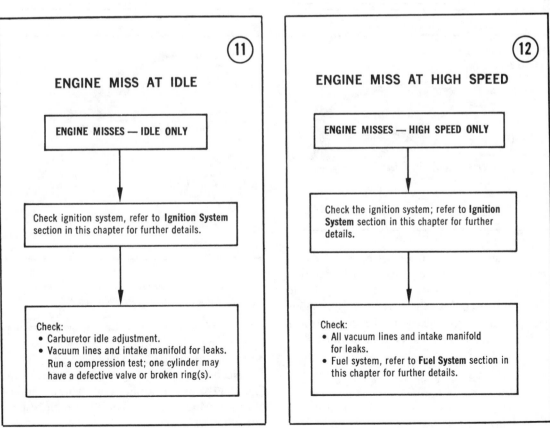

11

ENGINE MISS AT IDLE

ENGINE MISSES — IDLE ONLY

Check ignition system, refer to **Ignition System**
section in this chapter for further details.

Check:
• Carburetor idle adjustment.
• Vacuum lines and intake manifold for leaks.
  Run a compression test; one cylinder may
  have a defective valve or broken ring(s).

12

ENGINE MISS AT HIGH SPEED

ENGINE MISSES — HIGH SPEED ONLY

Check the ignition system; refer to **Ignition
System** section in this chapter for further
details.

Check:
• All vacuum lines and intake manifold
  for leaks.
• Fuel system, refer to **Fuel System** section in
  this chapter for further details.

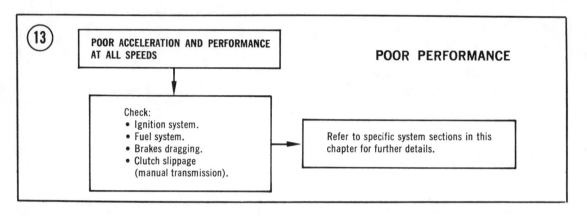

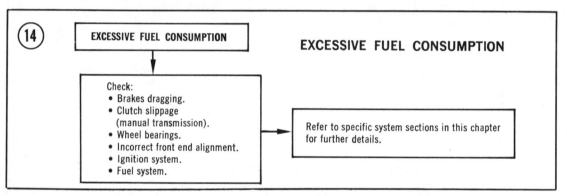

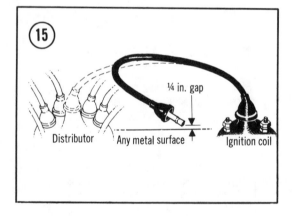

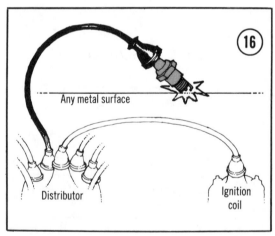

Some tests of the ignition system require running the engine with a spark plug or ignition coil wire disconnected. The safest way to do this is to disconnect the wire with the engine stopped, then prop the end of the wire next to a metal surface as shown in **Figures 15 and 16**.

WARNING
Never disconnect a spark plug or ignition coil wire while the engine is running. The high voltage in an ignition system, particularly the newer high-

energy electronic ignition systems could cause serious injury or even death.

Spark plug condition is an important indication of engine performance. Spark plugs in a properly operating engine will have slightly pitted electrodes, and a light tan insulator tip. **Figure 17** shows a normal plug, and a number of others which indicate trouble in their respective cylinders.

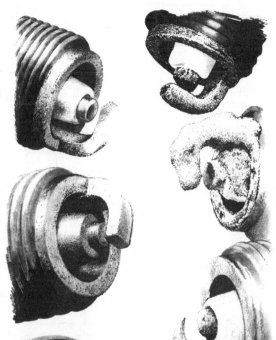

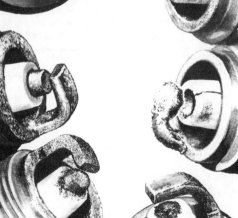

2

• Appearance—Firing tip has deposits of light gray to light tan.
• Can be cleaned, regapped and reused.

• Appearance—Dull, dry black with fluffy carbon deposits on the insulator tip, electrode and exposed shell.
• Caused by—Fuel/air mixture too rich, plug heat range too cold, weak ignition system, dirty air cleaner, faulty automatic choke or excessive idling.
• Can be cleaned, regapped and reused.

• Appearance—Wet black deposits on insulator and exposed shell.
• Caused by—Excessive oil entering the combustion chamber through worn rings, pistons, valve guides or bearings.
• Replace with new plugs (use a hotter plug if engine is not repaired).

• Appearance — Yellow insulator deposits (may sometimes be dark gray, black or tan in color) on the insulator tip.
• Caused by—Highly leaded gasoline.
• Replace with new plugs.

• Appearance—Yellow glazed deposits indicating melted lead deposits due to hard acceleration.
• Caused by—Highly leaded gasoline.
• Replace with new plugs.

• Appearance—Glazed yellow deposits with a slight brownish tint on the insulator tip and ground electrode.
• Replace with new plugs.

• Appearance — Brown colored hardened ash deposits on the insulator tip and ground electrode.
• Caused by—Fuel and/or oil additives.
• Replace with new plugs.

• Appearance — Severely worn or eroded electrodes.
• Caused by—Normal wear or unusual oil and/or fuel additives.
• Replace with new plugs.

• Appearance — Melted ground electrode.
• Caused by—Overadvanced ignition timing, inoperative ignition advance mechanism, too low of a fuel octane rating, lean fuel/air mixture or carbon deposits in combustion chamber.

• Appearance—Melted center electrode.
• Caused by—Abnormal combustion due to overadvanced ignition timing or incorrect advance, too low of a fuel octane rating, lean fuel/air mixture, or carbon deposits in combustion chamber.
• Correct engine problem and replace with new plugs.

• Appearance—Melted center electrode and white blistered insulator tip.
• Caused by—Incorrect plug heat range selection.
• Replace with new plugs.

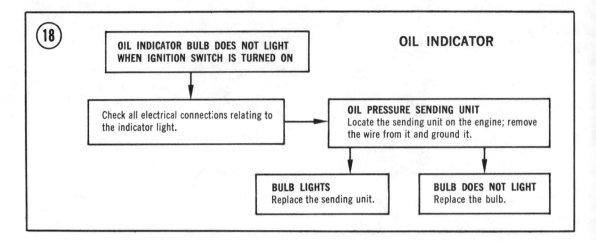

ENGINE OIL
PRESSURE LIGHT

Proper oil pressure to the engine is vital. If oil pressure is insufficient, the engine can destroy itself in a comparatively short time.

The oil pressure warning circuit monitors oil pressure constantly. If pressure drops below a predetermined level, the light comes on.

Obviously, it is vital for the warning circuit to be working to signal low oil pressure. Each time you turn on the ignition, but before you start the car, the warning light should come on. If it doesn't, there is trouble in the warning circuit, not the oil pressure system. See **Figure 18** to troubleshoot the warning circuit.

Once the engine is running, the warning light should stay off. If the warning light comes on or acts erratically while the engine is running there is trouble with the engine oil pressure system. *Stop the engine immediately*. Refer to **Figure 19** for possible causes of the problem.

FUEL SYSTEM
(CARBURETTED)

Fuel system problems must be isolated to the fuel pump (mechanical or electric), fuel lines, fuel filter, or carburetor. These procedures assume the ignition system is working properly and is correctly adjusted.

1. *Engine will not start* — First make sure that fuel is being delivered to the carburetor. Remove the air cleaner, look into the carburetor throat, and operate the accelerator

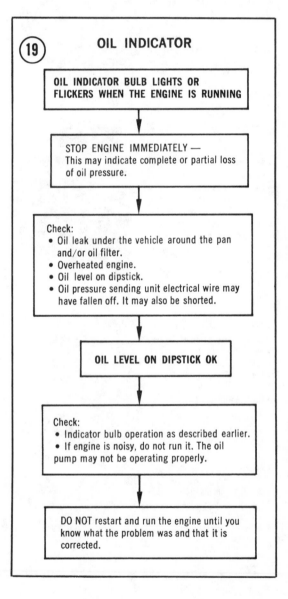

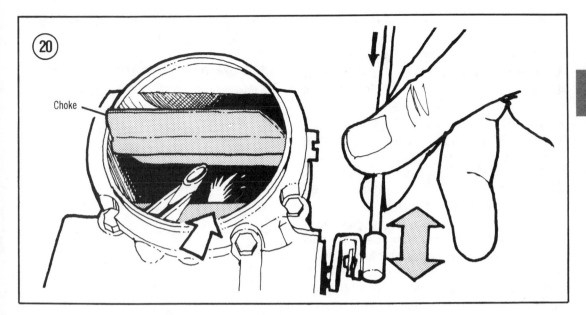

Choke

linkage several times. There should be a stream of fuel from the accelerator pump discharge tube each time the accelerator linkage is depressed (**Figure 20**). If not, check fuel pump delivery (described later), float valve, and float adjustment. If the engine will not start, check the automatic choke parts for sticking or damage. If necessary, rebuild or replace the carburetor.

2. *Engine runs at fast idle* — Check the choke setting. Check the idle speed, idle mixture, and decel valve (if equipped) adjustment.

3. *Rough idle or engine miss with frequent stalling* — Check idle mixture and idle speed adjustments.

4. *Engine "diesels" (continues to run) when ignition is switched off* — Check idle mixture (probably too rich), ignition timing, and idle speed (probably too fast). Check the throttle solenoid (if equipped) for proper operation. Check for overheated engine.

5. *Stumbling when accelerating from idle* — Check the idle speed and mixture adjustments. Check the accelerator pump.

6. *Engine misses at high speed or lacks power* — This indicates possible fuel starvation. Check fuel pump pressure and capacity as described in this chapter. Check float needle valves. Check for a clogged fuel filter or air cleaner.

7. *Black exhaust smoke* — This indicates a badly overrich mixture. Check idle mixture and idle speed adjustment. Check choke setting. Check for excessive fuel pump pressure, leaky floats, or worn needle valves.

8. *Excessive fuel consumption* — Check for overrich mixture. Make sure choke mechanism works properly. Check idle mixture and idle speed. Check for excessive fuel pump pressure, leaky floats, or worn float needle valves.

FUEL SYSTEM (FUEL INJECTED)

Troubleshooting a fuel injection system requires more thought, experience, and know-how than any other part of the vehicle. A logical approach and proper test equipment are essential in order to successfully find and fix these troubles.

It is best to leave fuel injection troubles to your dealer. In order to isolate a problem to the injection system make sure that the fuel pump is operating properly. Check its performance as described later in this section. Also make sure that fuel filter and air cleaner are not clogged.

FUEL PUMP TEST (MECHANICAL AND ELECTRIC)

1. Disconnect the fuel inlet line where it enters the carburetor or fuel injection system.

2. Fit a rubber hose over the fuel line so fuel can be directed into a graduated container with about one quart capacity. See **Figure 21**.

3. To avoid accidental starting of the engine, disconnect the secondary coil wire from the coil or disconnect and insulate the coil primary wire.

4. Crank the engine for about 30 seconds.

5. If the fuel pump supplies the specified amount (refer to the fuel chapter later in this book), the trouble may be in the carburetor or fuel injection system. The fuel injection system should be tested by your dealer.

6. If there is no fuel present or the pump cannot supply the specified amount, either the fuel pump is defective or there is an obstruction in the fuel line. Replace the fuel pump and/or inspect the fuel lines for air leaks or obstructions.

7. Also pressure test the fuel pump by installing a T-fitting in the fuel line between the fuel pump and the carburetor. Connect a fuel pressure gauge to the fitting with a short tube **(Figure 22)**.

8. Reconnect the coil wire, start the engine, and record the pressure. Refer to the fuel chapter later in this book for the correct pressure. If the pressure varies from that specified, the pump should be replaced.

9. Stop the engine. The pressure should drop off very slowly. If it drops off rapidly, the outlet valve in the pump is leaking and the pump should be replaced.

EMISSION CONTROL SYSTEMS

Major emission control systems used on nearly all U.S. models include the following:

   a. Positive crankcase ventilation (PCV)

   b. Thermostatic air cleaner

   c. Air injection reaction (AIR)

   d. Fuel evaporation control

   e. Exhaust gas recirculation (EGR)

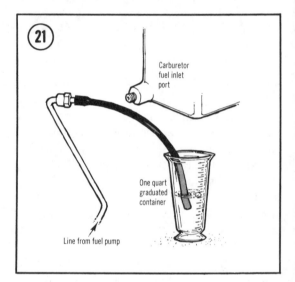

(21)

Carburetor fuel inlet port

One quart graduated container

Line from fuel pump

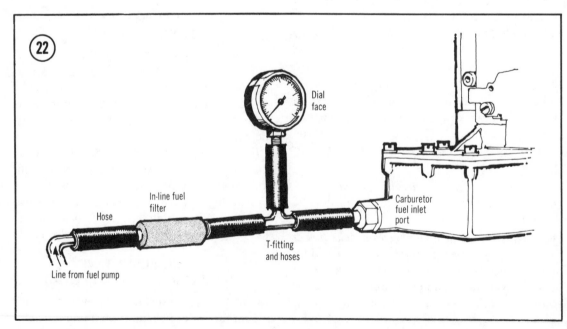

(22)

Dial face

In-line fuel filter

Hose

Carburetor fuel inlet port

T-fitting and hoses

Line from fuel pump

Emission control systems vary considerably from model to model. Individual models contain variations of the four systems described here. In addition, they may include other special systems. Use the index to find specific emission control components in other chapters.

Many of the systems and components are factory set and sealed. Without special expensive test equipment, it is impossible to adjust the systems to meet state and federal requirements.

Troubleshooting can also be difficult without special equipment. The procedures described below will help you find emission control parts which have failed, but repairs may have to be entrusted to a dealer or other properly equipped repair shop.

With the proper equipment, you can test the carbon monoxide and hydrocarbon levels.

Figure 23 provides some sources of trouble if the readings are not correct.

Positive Crankcase Ventilation

Fresh air drawn from the air cleaner housing scavenges emissions (e.g., piston blow-by) from the crankcase, then the intake manifold vacuum draws emissions into the intake manifold. They can then be reburned in the normal combustion process. **Figure 24** shows a typical system. **Figure 25** provides a testing procedure.

Thermostatic Air Cleaner

The thermostatically controlled air cleaner maintains incoming air to the engine at a predetermined level, usually about 100°F or higher. It mixes cold air with heated air from the exhaust manifold region. The air cleaner in-

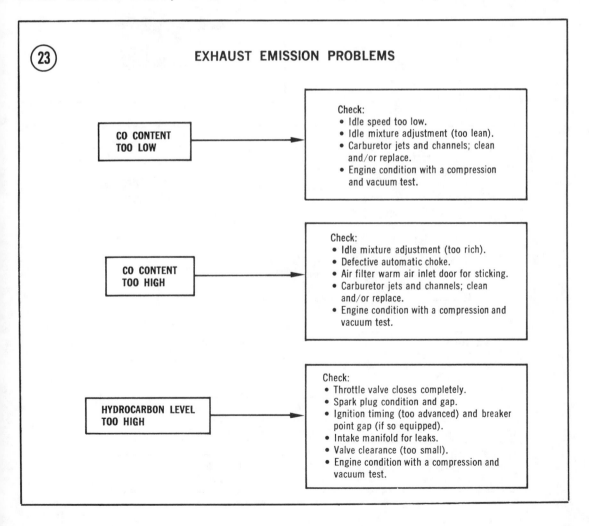

(23) **EXHAUST EMISSION PROBLEMS**

CO CONTENT TOO LOW

Check:
• Idle speed too low.
• Idle mixture adjustment (too lean).
• Carburetor jets and channels; clean and/or replace.
• Engine condition with a compression and vacuum test.

CO CONTENT TOO HIGH

Check:
• Idle mixture adjustment (too rich).
• Defective automatic choke.
• Air filter warm air inlet door for sticking.
• Carburetor jets and channels; clean and/or replace.
• Engine condition with a compression and vacuum test.

HYDROCARBON LEVEL TOO HIGH

Check:
• Throttle valve closes completely.
• Spark plug condition and gap.
• Ignition timing (too advanced) and breaker point gap (if so equipped).
• Intake manifold for leaks.
• Valve clearance (too small).
• Engine condition with a compression and vacuum test.

cludes a temperature sensor, vacuum motor, and a hinged door. See **Figure 26**.

The system is comparatively easy to test. See **Figure 27** for the procedure.

Air Injection Reaction System

The air injection reaction system reduces air pollution by oxidizing hydrocarbons and carbon monoxide as they leave the combustion chamber. See **Figure 28**.

The air injection pump, driven by the engine, compresses filtered air and injects it at the exhaust port of each cylinder. The fresh air mixes with the unburned gases in the exhaust and promotes further burning. A check valve prevents exhaust gases from entering and damaging the air pump if the pump becomes inoperative, e.g., from a fan belt failure.

Figure 29 explains the testing procedure for this system.

Fuel Evaporation Control

Fuel vapor from the fuel tank passes through the liquid/vapor separator to the carbon canister. See **Figure 30**. The carbon absorbs and

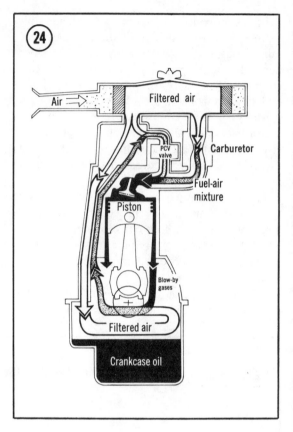

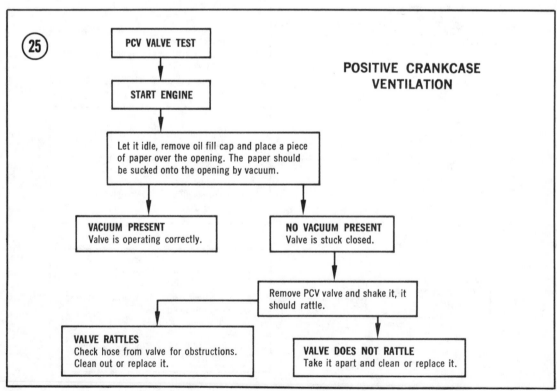

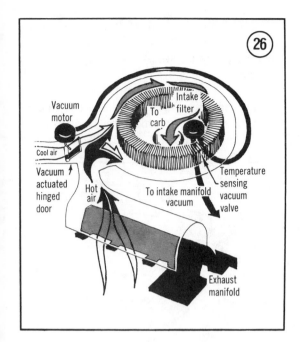

(26)

Vacuum motor

Intake filter

To carb

Cool air

Vacuum actuated hinged door

Hot air

Temperature sensing vacuum valve

To intake manifold vacuum

Exhaust manifold

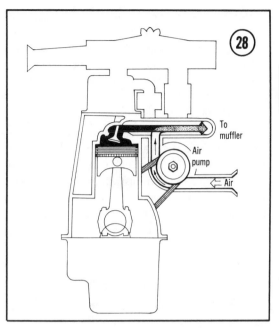

(28)

To muffler

Air pump

Air

2

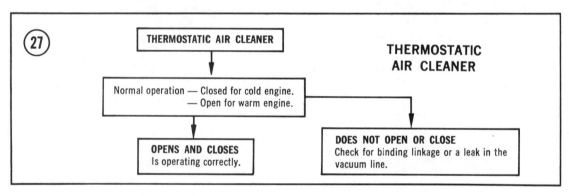

(27)

THERMOSTATIC AIR CLEANER

THERMOSTATIC AIR CLEANER

Normal operation — Closed for cold engine.
— Open for warm engine.

OPENS AND CLOSES
Is operating correctly.

DOES NOT OPEN OR CLOSE
Check for binding linkage or a leak in the vacuum line.

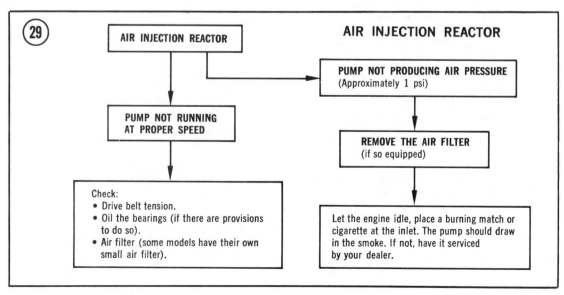

(29)

AIR INJECTION REACTOR

AIR INJECTION REACTOR

PUMP NOT PRODUCING AIR PRESSURE
(Approximately 1 psi)

PUMP NOT RUNNING AT PROPER SPEED

REMOVE THE AIR FILTER
(if so equipped)

Check:
• Drive belt tension.
• Oil the bearings (if there are provisions to do so).
• Air filter (some models have their own small air filter).

Let the engine idle, place a burning match or cigarette at the inlet. The pump should draw in the smoke. If not, have it serviced by your dealer.

stores the vapor when the engine is stopped. When the engine runs, manifold vacuum draws the vapor from the canister. Instead of being released into the atmosphere, the fuel vapor takes part in the normal combustion process.

Exhaust Gas Recirculation

The exhaust gas recirculation (EGR) system is used to reduce the emission of nitrogen oxides (NOx). Relatively inert exhaust gases are introduced into the combustion process to slightly reduce peak temperatures. This reduction in temperature reduces the formation of NOx.

Figure 31 provides a simple test of this system.

ENGINE NOISES

Often the first evidence of an internal engine trouble is a strange noise. That knocking, clicking, or tapping which you never heard before may be warning you of impending trouble.

While engine noises can indicate problems, they are sometimes difficult to interpret correctly; inexperienced mechanics can be seriously misled by them.

Professional mechanics often use a special stethoscope which looks similar to a doctor's stethoscope for isolating engine noises. You can do nearly as well with a "sounding stick" which can be an ordinary piece of doweling or a section of small hose. By placing one end in contact with the area to which you want to listen and the other end near your ear, you can hear

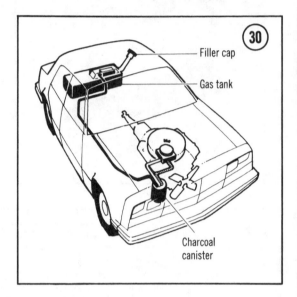

Filler cap

Gas tank

Charcoal canister

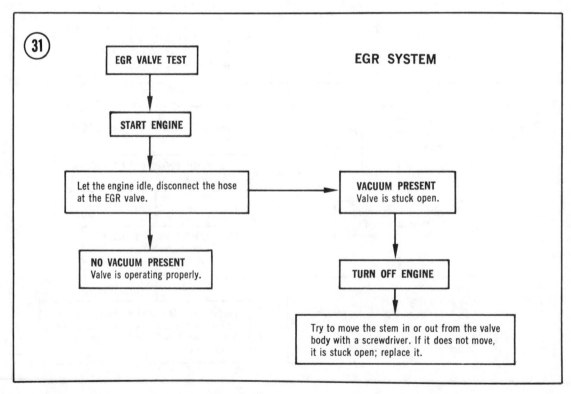

EGR VALVE TEST

EGR SYSTEM

START ENGINE

Let the engine idle, disconnect the hose at the EGR valve.

VACUUM PRESENT
Valve is stuck open.

NO VACUUM PRESENT
Valve is operating properly.

TURN OFF ENGINE

Try to move the stem in or out from the valve body with a screwdriver. If it does not move, it is stuck open; replace it.

sounds emanating from that area. The first time you do this, you may be horrified at the strange noises coming from even a normal engine. If you can, have an experienced friend or mechanic help you sort the noises out.

Clicking or Tapping Noises

Clicking or tapping noises usually come from the valve train, and indicate excessive valve clearance.

If your vehicle has adjustable valves, the procedure for adjusting the valve clearance is explained in Chapter Three. If your vehicle has hydraulic lifters, the clearance may not be adjustable. The noise may be coming from a collapsed lifter. These may be cleaned or replaced as described in the engine chapter.

A sticking valve may also sound like a valve with excessive clearance. In addition, excessive wear in valve train components can cause similar engine noises.

Knocking Noises

A heavy, dull knocking is usually caused by a worn main bearing. The noise is loudest when the engine is working hard, i.e., accelerating hard at low speed. You may be able to isolate the trouble to a single bearing by disconnecting

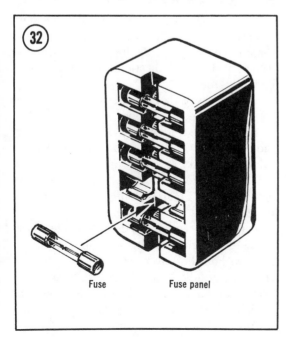

Fuse   Fuse panel

the spark plugs one at a time. When you reach the spark plug nearest the bearing, the knock will be reduced or disappear.

Worn connecting rod bearings may also produce a knock, but the sound is usually more "metallic." As with a main bearing, the noise is worse when accelerating. It may even increase further just as you go from accelerating to coasting. Disconnecting spark plugs will help isolate this knock as well.

A double knock or clicking usually indicates a worn piston pin. Disconnecting spark plugs will isolate this to a particular piston, however, the noise will *increase* when you reach the affected piston.

A loose flywheel and excessive crankshaft end play also produce knocking noises. While similar to main bearing noises, these are usually intermittent, not constant, and they do not change when spark plugs are disconnected.

Some mechanics confuse piston pin noise with piston slap. The double knock will distinguish the piston pin noise. Piston slap is identified by the fact that it is always louder when the engine is cold.

ELECTRICAL ACCESSORIES

Lights and Switches (Interior and Exterior)

1. *Bulb does not light* — Remove the bulb and check for a broken element. Also check the inside of the socket; make sure the contacts are clean and free of corrosion. If the bulb and socket are OK, check to see if a fuse has blown or a circuit breaker has tripped. The fuse panel (**Figure 32**) is usually located under the instrument panel. Replace the blown fuse or reset the circuit breaker. If the fuse blows or the breaker trips again, there is a short in that circuit. Check that circuit all the way to the battery. Look for worn wire insulation or burned wires.

If all the above are all right, check the switch controlling the bulb for continuity with an ohmmeter at the switch terminals. Check the switch contact terminals for loose or dirty electrical connections.

2. *Headlights work but will not switch from either high or low beam* — Check the beam selector switch for continuity with an ohmmeter

at the switch terminals. Check the switch contact terminals for loose or dirty electrical connections.

3. *Brake light switch inoperative* — On mechanically operated switches, usually mounted near the brake pedal arm, adjust the switch to achieve correct mechanical operation. Check the switch for continuity with an ohmmeter at the switch terminals. Check the switch contact terminals for loose or dirty electrical connections.

4. *Back-up lights do not operate* — Check light bulb as described earlier. Locate the switch, normally located near the shift lever. Adjust switch to achieve correct mechanical operation. Check the switch for continuity with an ohmmeter at the switch terminals. Bypass the switch with a jumper wire; if the lights work, replace the switch.

Directional Signals

1. *Directional signals do not operate* — If the indicator light on the instrument panel burns steadily instead of flashing, this usually indicates that one of the exterior lights is burned out. Check all lamps that normally flash. If all are all right, the flasher unit may be defective. Replace it with a good one.

2. *Directional signal indicator light on instrument panel does not light up* — Check the light bulbs as described earlier. Check all electrical connections and check the flasher unit.

3. *Directional signals will not self-cancel* — Check the self-cancelling mechanism located inside the steering column.

4. *Directional signals flash slowly* — Check the condition of the battery and the alternator (or generator) drive belt tension (**Figure 4**). Check the flasher unit and all related electrical connections.

Windshield Wipers

1. *Wipers do not operate* — Check for a blown fuse or circuit breaker that has tripped; replace or reset. Check all related terminals for loose or dirty electrical connections. Check continuity of the control switch with an ohmmeter at the switch terminals. Check the linkage and arms

for loose, broken, or binding parts. Straighten out or replace where necessary.

2. *Wiper motor hums but will not operate* — The motor may be shorted out internally; check and/or replace the motor. Also check for broken or binding linkage and arms.

3. *Wiper arms will not return to the stowed position when turned off* — The motor has a special internal switch for this purpose. Have it inspected by your dealer. Do not attempt this yourself.

Interior Heater

1. *Heater fan does not operate* — Check for a blown fuse or circuit breaker that has tripped. Check the switch for continuity with an ohmmeter at the switch terminals. Check the switch contact terminals for loose or dirty electrical connections.

2. *Heat output is insufficient* — Check the heater hose/engine coolant control valve usually located in the engine compartment; make sure it is in the open position. Ensure that the heater door(s) and cable(s) are operating correctly and are in the open position. Inspect the heat ducts; make sure that they are not crimped or blocked.

COOLING SYSTEM

The temperature gauge or warning light usually signals cooling system troubles before there is any damage. As long as you stop the vehicle at the first indication of trouble, serious damage is unlikely.

In most cases, the trouble will be obvious as soon as you open the hood. If there is coolant or steam leaking, look for a defective radiator, radiator hose, or heater hose. If there is no evidence of leakage, make sure that the fan belt is in good condition. If the trouble is not obvious, refer to **Figures 33 and 34** to help isolate the trouble.

Automotive cooling systems operate under pressure to permit higher operating temperatures without boil-over. The system should be checked periodically to make sure it can withstand normal pressure. **Figure 35** shows the equipment which nearly any service station has for testing the system pressure.

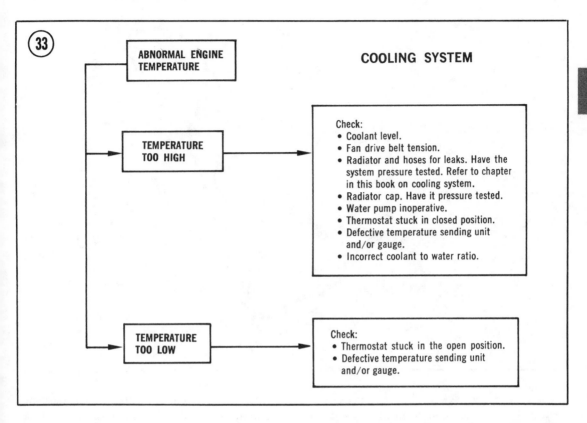

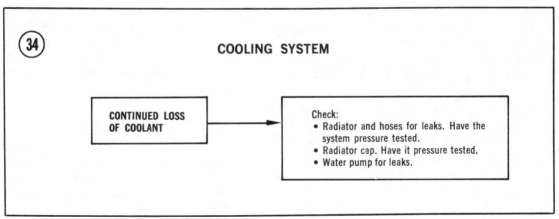

CLUTCH

All clutch troubles except adjustments require transmission removal to identify and cure the problem.

1. *Slippage* — This is most noticeable when accelerating in a high gear at relatively low speed. To check slippage, park the vehicle on a level surface with the handbrake set. Shift to 2nd gear and release the clutch as if driving off. If the clutch is good, the engine will slow and stall. If the clutch slips, continued engine speed will give it away.

Slippage results from insufficient clutch pedal free play, oil or grease on the clutch disc, worn pressure plate, or weak springs.

2. *Drag or failure to release* — This trouble usually causes difficult shifting and gear clash, especially when downshifting. The cause may be excessive clutch pedal free play, warped or bent pressure plate or clutch disc, broken or

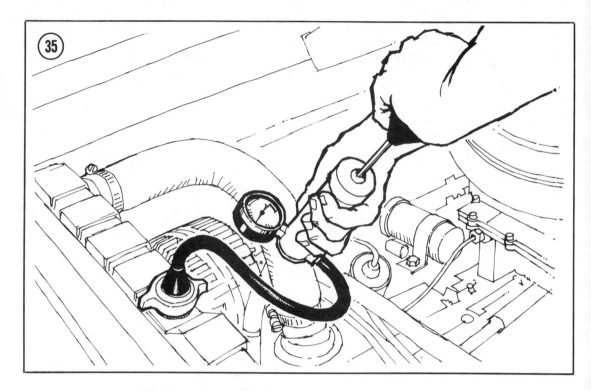

loose linings, or lack of lubrication in pilot bearing. Also check condition of transmission main shaft splines.

3. *Chatter or grabbing* — A number of things can cause this trouble. Check tightness of engine mounts and engine-to-transmission mounting bolts. Check for worn or misaligned pressure plate and misaligned release plate.

4. *Other noises* — Noise usually indicates a dry or defective release or pilot bearing. Check the bearings and replace if necessary. Also check all parts for misalignment and uneven wear.

MANUAL TRANSMISSION/TRANSAXLE

Transmission and transaxle troubles are evident when one or more of the following symptoms appear:

   a. Difficulty changing gears

   b. Gears clash when downshifting

   c. Slipping out of gear

   d. Excessive noise in NEUTRAL

   e. Excessive noise in gear

   f. Oil leaks

Transmission and transaxle repairs are not recommended unless the many special tools required are available.

Transmission and transaxle troubles are sometimes difficult to distinguish from clutch troubles. Eliminate the clutch as a source of trouble before installing a new or rebuilt transmission or transaxle.

AUTOMATIC TRANSMISSION

Most automatic transmission repairs require considerable specialized knowledge and tools. It is impractical for the home mechanic to invest in the tools, since they cost more than a properly rebuilt transmission.

Check fluid level and condition frequently to help prevent future problems. If the fluid is orange or black in color or smells like varnish, it is an indication of some type of damage or failure within the transmission. Have the transmission serviced by your dealer or competent automatic transmission service facility.

BRAKES

Good brakes are vital to the safe operation of the vehicle. Performing the maintenance speci-

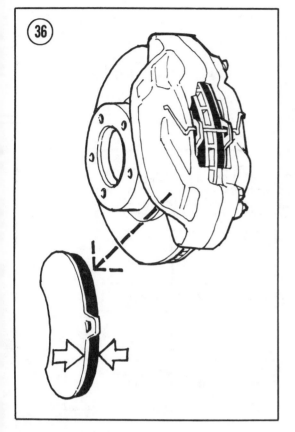

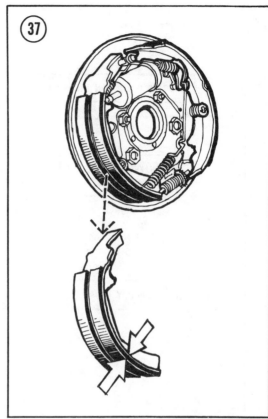

fied in Chapter Three will minimize problems with the brakes. Most importantly, check and maintain the level of fluid in the master cylinder, and check the thickness of the linings on the disc brake pads (**Figure 36**) or drum brake shoes (**Figure 37**).

If trouble develops, **Figures 38 through 40** will help you locate the problem. Refer to the brake chapter for actual repair procedures.

STEERING AND SUSPENSION

Trouble in the suspension or steering is evident when the following occur:

a. Steering is hard

b. Car pulls to one side

c. Car wanders or front wheels wobble

d. Steering has excessive play

e. Tire wear is abnormal

Unusual steering, pulling, or wandering is usually caused by bent or otherwise misaligned suspension parts. This is difficult to check without proper alignment equipment. Refer to the suspension chapter in this book for repairs that you can perform and those that must be left to a dealer or suspension specialist.

If your trouble seems to be excessive play, check wheel bearing adjustment first. This is the most frequent cause. Then check ball-joints (refer to Suspension chapter). Finally, check tie rod end ball-joints by shaking each tie rod. Also check steering gear, or rack-and-pinion assembly to see that it is securely bolted down.

TIRE WEAR ANALYSIS

Abnormal tire wear should be analyzed to determine its causes. The most common causes are the following:

a. Incorrect tire pressure

b. Improper driving

c. Overloading

d. Bad road surfaces

e. Incorrect wheel alignment

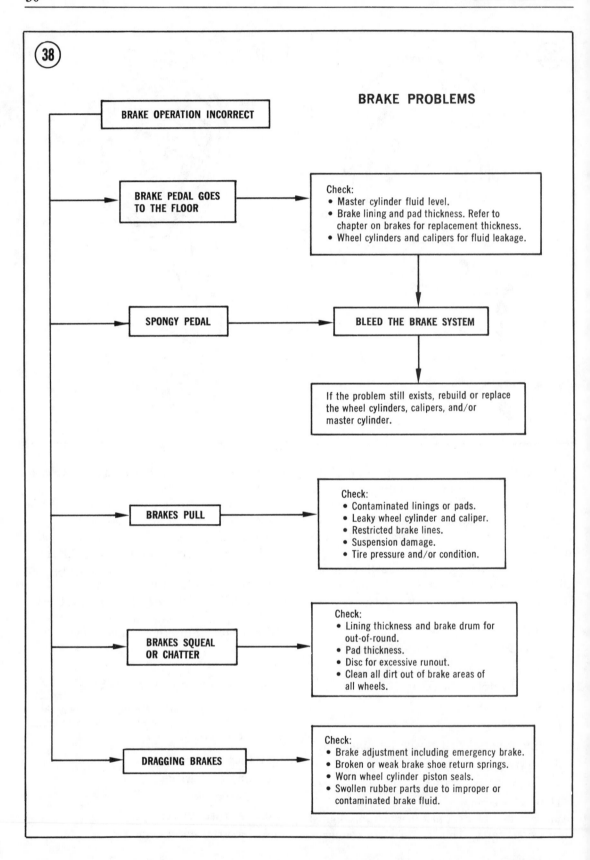

(38)

BRAKE PROBLEMS

BRAKE OPERATION INCORRECT

BRAKE PEDAL GOES
TO THE FLOOR

Check:
• Master cylinder fluid level.
• Brake lining and pad thickness. Refer to
  chapter on brakes for replacement thickness.
• Wheel cylinders and calipers for fluid leakage.

SPONGY PEDAL

BLEED THE BRAKE SYSTEM

If the problem still exists, rebuild or replace
the wheel cylinders, calipers, and/or
master cylinder.

BRAKES PULL

Check:
• Contaminated linings or pads.
• Leaky wheel cylinder and caliper.
• Restricted brake lines.
• Suspension damage.
• Tire pressure and/or condition.

BRAKES SQUEAL
OR CHATTER

Check:
• Lining thickness and brake drum for
  out-of-round.
• Pad thickness.
• Disc for excessive runout.
• Clean all dirt out of brake areas of
  all wheels.

DRAGGING BRAKES

Check:
• Brake adjustment including emergency brake.
• Broken or weak brake shoe return springs.
• Worn wheel cylinder piston seals.
• Swollen rubber parts due to improper or
  contaminated brake fluid.

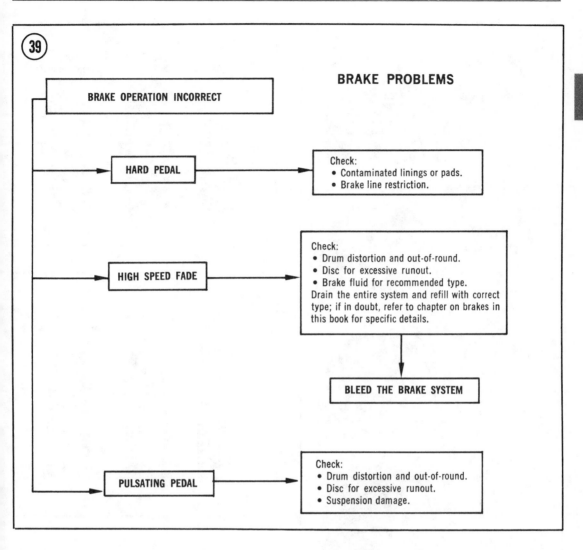

39

BRAKE PROBLEMS

BRAKE OPERATION INCORRECT

HARD PEDAL

Check:
- Contaminated linings or pads.
- Brake line restriction.

HIGH SPEED FADE

Check:
- Drum distortion and out-of-round.
- Disc for excessive runout.
- Brake fluid for recommended type.
Drain the entire system and refill with correct type; if in doubt, refer to chapter on brakes in this book for specific details.

BLEED THE BRAKE SYSTEM

PULSATING PEDAL

Check:
- Drum distortion and out-of-round.
- Disc for excessive runout.
- Suspension damage.

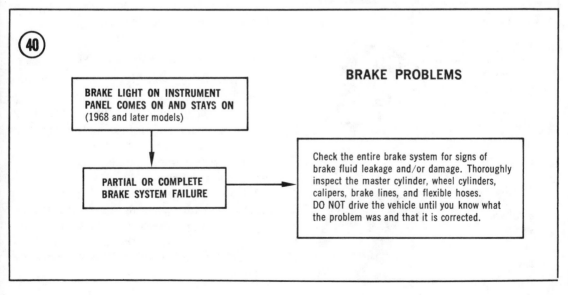

40

BRAKE PROBLEMS

BRAKE LIGHT ON INSTRUMENT PANEL COMES ON AND STAYS ON
(1968 and later models)

PARTIAL OR COMPLETE BRAKE SYSTEM FAILURE

Check the entire brake system for signs of brake fluid leakage and/or damage. Thoroughly inspect the master cylinder, wheel cylinders, calipers, brake lines, and flexible hoses.
DO NOT drive the vehicle until you know what the problem was and that it is corrected.

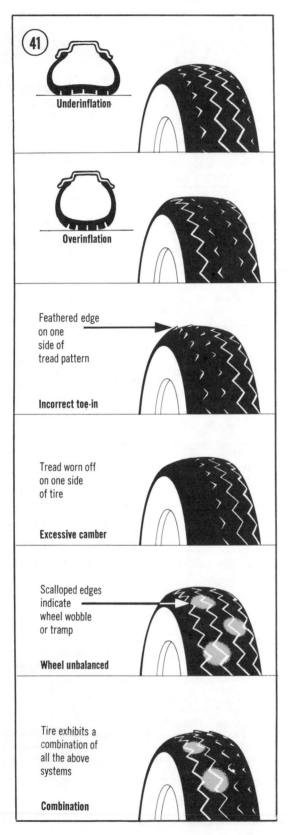

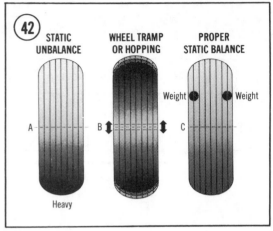

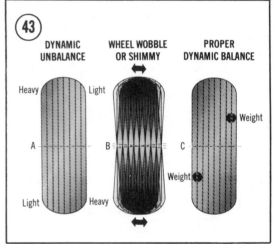

Figure 41 identifies wear patterns and indicates the most probable causes.

WHEEL BALANCING

All four wheels and tires must be in balance along two axes. To be in static balance (Figure 42), weight must be evenly distributed around the axis of rotation. (A) shows a statically unbalanced wheel; (B) shows the result — wheel tramp or hopping; (C) shows proper static balance.

To be in dynamic balance (Figure 43), the centerline of the weight must coincide with the centerline of the wheel. (A) shows a dynamically unbalanced wheel; (B) shows the result — wheel wobble or shimmy; (C) shows proper dynamic balance.

CHAPTER THREE

3

LUBRICATION, MAINTENANCE
AND TUNE-UP

This chapter deals with the normal maintenance necessary to keep your car running properly.

Tables 1-3 list maintenance intervals for cars given normal use. Cars driven in severe conditions require more frequent maintenance. These conditions include:

a. Frequent short trips.
b. Rough or muddy roads.
c. Salted roads.
d. Severe dust.
e. Extremely cold weather.

Some maintenance procedures are included in the *Tune-up* section of this chapter and detailed instructions will be found there. Other steps are described in the following chapters. Chapter references are included with these steps.

> *NOTE*
> *Honda's warranty requirements (as well as additional warranty packages) state that the vehicle must be maintained and serviced in accordance with Honda specifications. When performing maintenance procedures, keep accurate records as well as dated bills for parts (and service performed by independent garages) to serve as proof that the services were performed when required.*

ROUTINE CHECKS

The following checks should be performed at each fuel stop.

1. *Check engine oil*—Shut off the engine and allow a few moments for the oil to return to the crankcase. Remove the dipstick, wipe it off and reinsert, making sure it is seated in the tube. See **Figure 1** (1976-1983 Accord, 1979-1982 Prelude) or **Figure 2** (1984 Accord, 1983-on Prelude). Remove it again and inspect; add oil if the level is near the lower mark on the dipstick. See **Table 4** and **Table 5** for recommended oil grades.

> *CAUTION*
> *Do not fill past the higher mark on the dipstick.*

2. *Check battery condition*—On translucent batteries, check fluid level with the scale on the

side of the battery. See **Figure 3**. Level should be maintained between the "UPPER" and "LOWER" marks. Top up with distilled water only; never add electrolyte to a battery in service. Do not overfill. On 1983-on models, the battery may be equipped with a built-in condition indicator. See **Figure 4** and **Figure 5**. If the indicator is red, the electrolyte level is low. Since water cannot be added to this type of battery, the battery must be replaced. If the indicator is white, the battery needs to be recharged.

3. *Check drive belt condition and tension*— Measure tension by pressing on each belt midway between pulleys. See **Figure 6**. Compare with specifications in **Table 10**. If tension is not correct, adjust as described under *Drive Belts* in this chapter.

4. *Check tire pressures*—Check when tires are cold. Maximum pressure is imprinted on each tire.

5. *Check windshield washer container level*—It should be kept full. See **Figure 7**.

6. *Check coolant level*—Note markings on reservoir indicating correct level for hot and cold engine. See **Figure 8**. See Chapter Seven if coolant level is not correct.

SCHEDULED MAINTENANCE

All of the following procedures are done at specified intervals of miles or time, except for coolant replacement which is done every 24 months regardless of mileage.

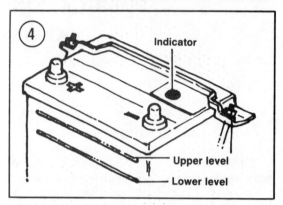

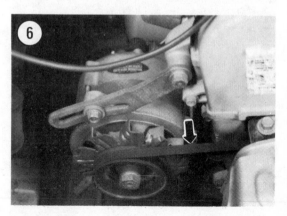

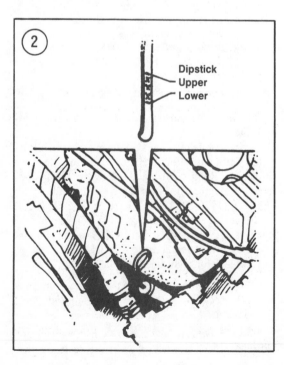

Engine Oil and Filter Change

The oil and filter change interval varies depending on the type of driving you do. For normal driving, including some city traffic, change oil and filter at the intervals specified in **Tables 1-3**. If driving is primarily stop-and-go traffic or includes trailer pulling or short trips in cold climates, change oil and filter every 3,000 miles or 3 months. Change oil and filter at least twice a year if the car is driven only a few hundred miles each month.

Any oil used must be rated SF. Non-detergent oils are not recommended. See **Table 4** and **Table 5** for recommended oil grades. The oil rating is usually printed on the can (**Figure 9**).

NOTE
The rating SF is designed for use in all 1980 and later models and its use is required to meet the manufacturer's warranty standards. At the time of their introduction, all 1976-1979 models were required to use oil rated SE. However, to benefit from the added protection that SF oils offer against engine deposits, rust and corrosion, its use is recommended in all models covered in this manual.

To drain the oil and change the filter, you will need the following (**Figure 10**):
   a. Drain pan.
   b. Funnel.
   c. Can opener or pour spout.
   d. Filter wrench.
   e. Ratchet and socket.
   f. 4 quarts of oil.
   g. Oil filter.
   h. New aluminum gasket for drain plug.

NOTE
Some oil manufacturers package motor oil in plastic containers which eliminate the need for a funnel or spout. The plastic containers can be resealed, so leftover oil can be conveniently stored.

There are a number of ways to discard the old oil safely. The easiest is to pour it from the drain pan into a gallon bleach bottle. Many service stations accept used oil for recycling. Check local regulations before disposing of oil in your household trash. Never let oil drain onto the ground.

1. Warm the engine to normal operating temperature, then shut it off.

> *WARNING*
> *During the next step, hot oil will spurt from the drain hole. Be ready to move your hand away quickly so hot oil does not run down your arm.*

2. Place the drain pan under the drain plug, then remove the plug. See **Figure 11**. Discard the drain plug gasket.

3. Let the oil drain for at least 10 minutes.

4. Turn the oil filter counterclockwise to remove. See **Figure 12** (1976-1983 Accord, 1979-1982 Prelude) or **Figure 13** (1984 Accord, 1983-on Prelude). If the filter is hard to remove, use a filter wrench.

5. Wipe the gasket surface on the engine block with a clean, lint-free cloth.

6. Coat the gasket on the new filter with clean engine oil. See **Figure 14**.

7. Screw the filter onto the engine *by hand* until the filter gasket just touches the mounting surface (until you feel a slight resistance when turning the filter). Then tighten the filter *by hand*, following instructions printed on the filter.

> *CAUTION*
> *Do not overtighten and do not use a filter wrench or the filter will leak.*

8. Install the oil pan drain plug, using a new gasket, and tighten securely.

9. Remove the oil filler cap. See **Figure 15** (1976-1983 Accord, 1979-1982 Prelude) or **Figure 16** (1984 Accord, 1983-on Prelude).

10. Pour in the amount of oil recommended in **Table 6**, then reinstall the filler cap.

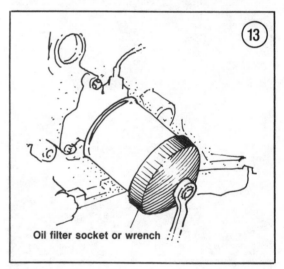

Oil filter socket or wrench

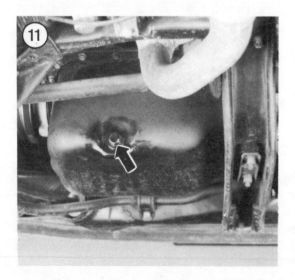

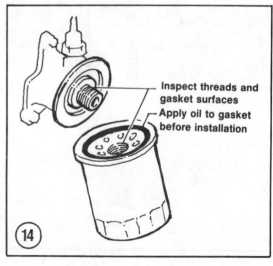

Inspect threads and gasket surfaces
Apply oil to gasket before installation

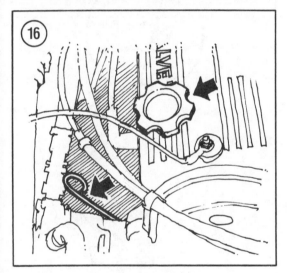

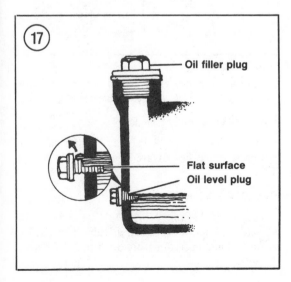

Oil filler plug

Flat surface
Oil level plug

11. Start the engine and let it idle. The oil pressure light on the instrument panel will remain on for 15-30 seconds, then go out.

CAUTION
Do not rev the engine to make the oil light go out. It takes time for oil to reach all areas of the engine and excessive speed could damage dry parts.

12. While the engine is running, make sure the oil filter and drain plug are not leaking.

13. Turn the engine off. Give the oil a few moments to settle back into the crankcase, then check oil level with the dipstick. See **Figure 1** or **Figure 2**. Add oil if necessary to bring the level up to the higher mark on the dipstick, but do not overfill.

Manual Transaxle Oil Check

At the specified intervals, check the oil level in manual transaxles as follows.

1. *1976-1978*:
   a. Drive the car to warm the oil to normal operating temperature.
   b. With the car sitting level, unscrew the level plug (**Figure 17**). Oil should begin to run out of the transaxle. If it does not, turn the level plug so that the flat side faces up (**Figure 17**).
   c. Remove the filler plug and add oil until it begins to seep past the level plug. Tighten the level plug and the filler plug securely and wipe any oil from the side of the transaxle.

2. *1979-on*:
   a. Drive the car to warm the oil to operating temperature.
   b. With the car sitting level, loosen the level plug (**Figure 18**). Oil should begin to run out of the transaxle. If it does not, remove the level plug and add oil until it begins to run out the plug hole. Then install the level plug and tighten securely.

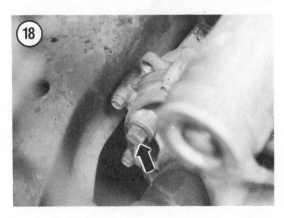

Manual Transaxle Oil Change

The oil in the manual transaxle should be changed at the intervals specified in **Tables 1-3**. Use only a quality oil recommended in **Table 4**.

1. Prior to draining the transaxle, drive the car for several miles to warm the oil so that it will flow freely.
2. Remove the level plug. See **Figure 17** (1976-1978) or **Figure 18** (1979-on). Discard the plug gasket.
3. Place a pan beneath the drain plug (**Figure 19**). Remove the drain plug and discard the gasket.
4. Allow the oil to drain for several minutes, then install the drain plug, using a new gasket.
5. Fill the transaxle with an oil recommended in **Table 4**. Approximate capacity is listed in **Table 6**. Fill as described under *Manual Transaxle Oil Check* in this chapter.

Automatic Transaxle Fluid Check

Check automatic transaxle fluid at the intervals specified in **Tables 1-3**.

1. Drive the car several miles to warm the transaxle fluid to operating temperature, then park the transaxle on a level surface.
2. Unscrew the dipstick (**Figure 20**), wipe it with a clean cloth and reinsert it. Do *not* screw the dipstick back in.
3. Pull the dipstick out and check the level. See **Figure 20**. Fluid must be maintained between the upper and lower marks. If necessary, add fluid through the dipstick hole, but do not overfill. See **Table 4** for fluid recommendations.

CAUTION
Overfilling can cause the fluid to foam, resulting in wear or damage.

4. After checking transaxle fluid level, screw the dipstick back into the transaxle by hand. Do not use a wrench to tighten.

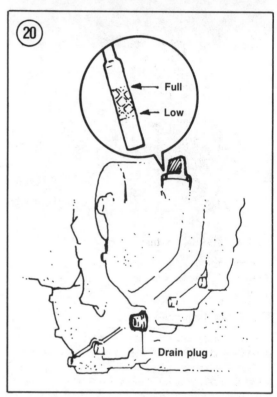

Automatic Transaxle Fluid Change

1. Drive the car several miles to warm the transaxle fluid to operating temperature, then park the transaxle on a level surface.
2. Place a drain pan beneath the transaxle. Remove the drain plug (**Figure 20**) and discard the gasket.
3. Let the fluid drain for several minutes.
4. Install the drain plug, using a new gasket, and tighten securely.
5. Fill the transaxle with a fluid recommended in **Table 4**. Capacity is listed in **Table 6**. Check fluid level on the dipstick as described under *Automatic Transaxle Fluid Check* in this chapter.

Power Steering Fluid Check

Procedures for inspecting and maintaining the power steering system are described in Chapter Ten.

Rear Brake Adjustment

The rear brakes on 1976-1981 Accords should be adjusted at intervals specified in **Table 1** and **Table 2**. Adjustment procedures are described in Chapter Twelve.

Parking Brake Adjustment

Adjust the parking brake at intervals specified in **Tables 1-3**. The procedure is described in Chapter Twelve.

Disc Brake Inspection

Disc brakes are used at the front wheels on all models and at the rear wheels on 1984 Preludes.

The thickness of the disc brake pads and condition of the brake discs should be inspected at intervals specified in **Tables 1-3**. Procedures are described in Chapter Twelve.

Brake Fluid

Brake fluid should be checked (or replaced) at intervals specified in **Tables 1-3**, as well as at any time the brake pedal can be pushed within a couple of inches of the floor. The level should be maintained between the upper and lower marks in both reservoirs (**Figure 21**). If the level is below the lower mark, clean the area around the master cylinder cover(s) and remove them. Add DOT 3 or DOT 4 brake fluid to bring the level up to the top mark in both reservoirs. Install the caps and check pedal movement.

WARNING
If the pedal feels soft or can be pushed close to the floor, there is a problem in the brake system. Do not drive the car until the problem has been found and corrected.

To replace brake fluid, bleed the brake system as described in Chapter Twelve. Continue adding fluid at the master cylinder and bleeding it at the wheels until the fluid leaving the system is clean and free of air bubbles.

Brake Lines and Hoses

Brake lines and hoses should be routinely checked for signs of deterioration, chafing and kinks each time the brake pad and lining condition is checked. Any line or hose that is less than perfect should be replaced immediately.

Check all connections for tightness and look for signs of leakage which may indicate a cracked or otherwise unserviceable fitting. As with lines and hoses, any connections or fittings that are less than perfect should be replaced immediately. When a line has been replaced or in any situation where a brake line or hose has been disconnected, refer to Chapter Twelve and fill and bleed the brake hydraulic system before driving the car.

Vacuum Booster Filter Inspection/Cleaning

1. From inside the driver's compartment, check the filter condition by observing it through the breather holes in the bellows next to the firewall.
2. If the filter is dirty, refer to Chapter Twelve, *Vacuum Booster Removal/Installation,* and loosen the booster just enough to slide it off the bellows. Remove the filter, clean in solvent and reinstall.

Clutch Fluid Level

This procedure applies to 1976-1981 Accords and 1979-1982 Preludes equipped with a manual transaxle.

The clutch fluid level should be checked whenever the brake fluid level is checked. It should also be checked if you experience gear clash or difficulty shifting gears. If the level is low, add DOT 3 or DOT 4 brake fluid. Bring the fluid level to the upper mark (**Figure 22**).

CAUTION
Clean the area around the cap before removing.

If the level is extremely low, it may be necessary to bleed the system to remove air. See Chapter Nine.

Clutch Adjustment

Clutch release arm adjustment and clutch pedal free play should be checked at intervals specified in **Tables 1-3**. Adjustment procedures are described in Chapter Nine.

Engine Compartment Check

Every 5,000 to 7,500 miles, check the entire engine compartment for leaking or deteriorated oil or fuel lines. Check electrical wiring for breaks in the insulation caused by deterioration or chafing. Check the radiator and hose connections for coolant residue or rust. Check for loose or missing bolts, nuts and screws. On cars with automatic transaxles, check fluid cooler lines at the radiator and transaxle for leakage.

Rear Wheel Bearing Service

At intervals specified in **Tables 1-3**, the rear wheel bearings should be removed, inspected and packed with new grease as described in Chapter Eleven.

Exhaust System

Every 7,500 miles or 6 months, examine mufflers, tailpipes, exhaust header and system

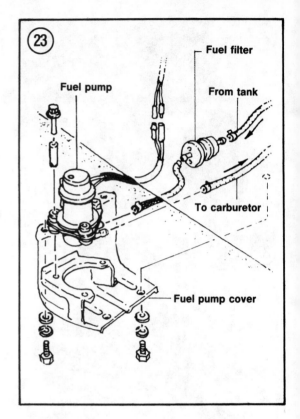

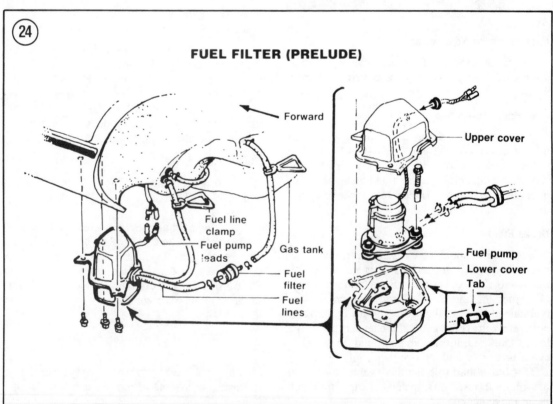

FUEL FILTER (PRELUDE)

fasteners for rust, holes and other damage. Replace any damaged parts. See Chapter Six.

> *WARNING*
> *Replacement of damaged exhaust system components is necessary to prevent the entry of exhaust fumes into the passenger compartment. In addition, damaged fasteners which are not replaced can eventually allow exhaust components to fall off the car and become a potential hazard to other drivers.*

Fuel Filter

The fuel filter(s) should be replaced at the intervals specified in **Tables 1-3**. The 1976-1981 Accords and 1979-1982 Preludes use a single fuel filter. The 1982-on Accords and 1983-on Preludes

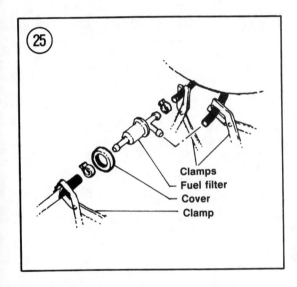

Clamps
Fuel filter
Cover
Clamp

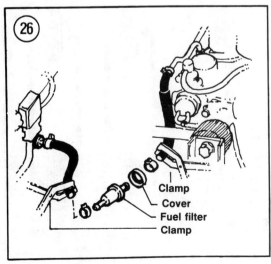

Clamp
Cover
Fuel filter
Clamp

use 2 filters, one at the front of the car and one at the rear.

> *NOTE*
> *If the car is operated for long periods of time in dusty or sandy areas, it may be necessary to change the filter more often.*

> *NOTE*
> *If the engine loses power or "stumbles" at high speed or when accelerating or climbing long hills, the problem may be caused by a clogged fuel filter.*

1976-1981 Accord, 1979-1982 Prelude

Refer to **Figure 23** (Accord) or **Figure 24** (Prelude). The fuel filter is located near the fuel pump at the rear of the car.
1. Place the transaxle in FIRST (manual) or PARK (automatic).
2. Securely block both front wheels so the car will not roll in either direction.
3. Jack up the rear end of the car and place it on jackstands.
4. Loosen the fuel filter attaching clamps and remove the filter from the fuel line.
5. Installation is the reverse of removal. After installation, drive the car a short distance and check the fuel filter for leakage.

1982-on Accord, 1983-on Prelude

1. Disconnect the lines from the engine compartment filter, take it out and install a new one. See **Figure 25** (Accord) or **Figure 26** (Prelude).
2. Place the transaxle in FIRST (manual) or PARK (automatic). Securely block both front wheels so the car will not roll in either direction.
3. Jack up the rear end of the car and place it on jackstands.
4. Push in on the rear fuel filter tab to release the holder. See **Figure 27**. Remove the rear fuel filter

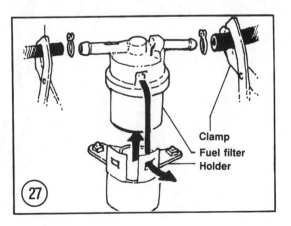

Clamp
Fuel filter
Holder

from its bracket, disconnect the lines and install a new filter.

5. Drive the car a short distance and check to be sure the fuel filters are not leaking.

Steering Gear and Tie Rods

Check the steering gear and linkage for looseness or damage. Repair as needed. See Chapter Ten.

Tire and Wheel Inspection

Routinely check the condition of all tires. Check local traffic regulations concerning minimum tread depth. Most recommend replacing tires when tread depth is less than 1/32 inch. Original equipment tires have tread wear indicators molded into the bottom of the tread grooves. Tread wear indicators appear as 1/2-inch bands (**Figure 28**) when tread depth becomes 1/16 inch. Tires should be replaced at this point.

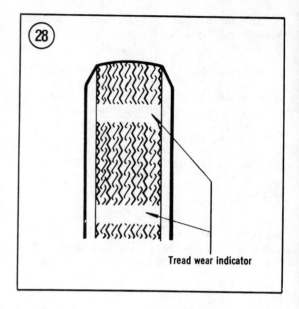

Tread wear indicator

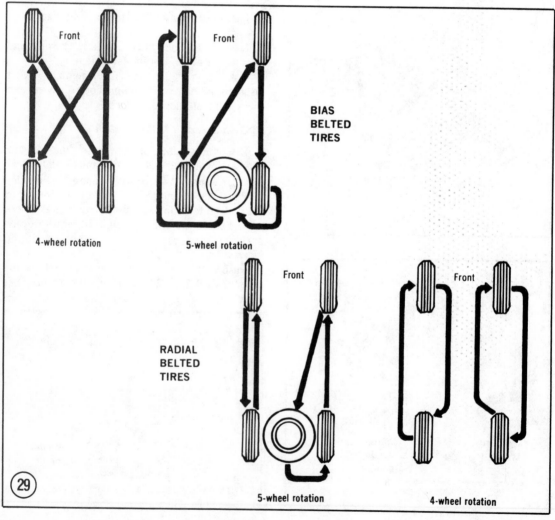

4-wheel rotation

5-wheel rotation

BIAS BELTED TIRES

RADIAL BELTED TIRES

5-wheel rotation

4-wheel rotation

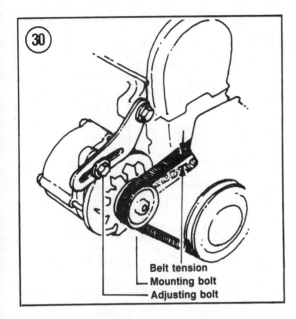

Belt tension
Mounting bolt
Adjusting bolt

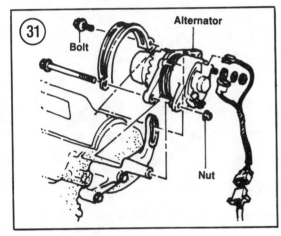

Bolt

Alternator

Nut

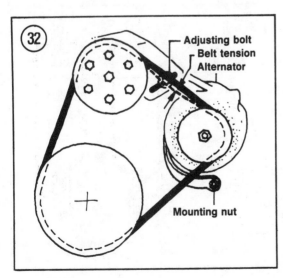

Adjusting bolt
Belt tension
Alternator

Mounting nut

Honda recomends rotating radial tires initially at 6,000 miles. **Figure 29** shows how this should be done. Inspect front disc brakes (and rear disc brakes on 1984 Preludes) as described in Chapter Twelve while the tires are off for rotation.

Windshield Wiper Blades

Exposure to weather and road film hardens the rubber wiper blades and destroys their effectiveness. When blades smear or otherwise fail to clean the windshield, they should be replaced.

Drive Belts

The drive belts drive the water pump, alternator, air conditioning compressor and power steering pump. A belt in poor condition or improperly adjusted can cause serious cooling or battery charging problems.

1. At the specified time or mileage, check the belts for wear, fraying or cracking. If any of these conditions exist, replace the belt as described in this chapter.

NOTE
On models equipped with air conditioning or power steering, the air conditioning compressor belt and power steering pump belt must be removed before the alternator belt can be removed.

2. If belts are in good condition, check belt tension and adjust if necessary. To check tension, press on the belt midway between pulleys and note how far the belt deflects. Compare the deflection with **Table 10** at the end of the chapter. If belt deflection is not within specifications, adjust it as described in the following paragraphs.

Alternator belt
(1976-1983 Accord, 1979-1982 Prelude)

1. Loosen the alternator mounting and adjusting bolts. See **Figure 30** (with air conditioning) or **Figure 31** (without air conditioning). Push the alternator toward the engine to loosen the belt, then take the belt off.
2. Install the new belt on the pulleys. Pry the alternator away from the belt to set tension. When tension is set correctly, tighten the adjusting bolt, then the mounting bolt.

Alternator belt (1984 Accord)

1. Loosen the alternator adjusting bolt and mounting nut. See **Figure 32**.
2. Push the alternator toward the engine to loosen the belt, then take the belt off the pulleys.

3. Install the new belt on the pulleys. Pry the alternator away from the engine until tension is as specified in **Table 10**, then tighten the mounting nut and adjusting bolt.

Alternator belt (1983-on Prelude)

1. Loosen the mounting nut at the bottom of the alternator and the mounting bolt at the top. See **Figure 33**.
2. Loosen the adjusting nut, push the alternator toward the engine to loosen the belt, then take the belt off the pulleys.
3. Install a new belt on the pulleys.
4. Tighten the adjusting nut until belt deflection is as specified in **Table 10** at the end of the chapter. Then tighten the mounting nut and mounting bolt.

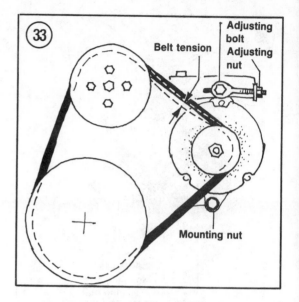

Power steering belt (1978-1981 Accord)

1. Loosen the pump adjusting bolt (**Figure 34**) and the pivot bolt at the bottom of the pump.
2. Push the pump toward the engine to loosen the belt. Take the belt off the pulleys.
3. Place the new belt on the pulleys.
4. Pry the pump away from the engine until belt tension is as specified in **Table 10**. Tighten the adjusting bolt, then the pivot bolt.

> *NOTE*
> *If the adjusting bolt can be pulled out to the bump on the adjusting bracket, the belt is stretched beyond use and must be replaced.*

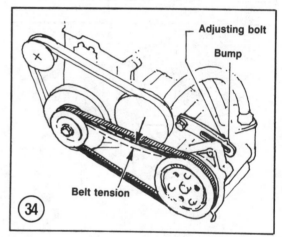

Power steering belt (1982-1983 Accord, 1982 Prelude)

1. Loosen the pivot bolt and adjusting bolt (**Figure 35**). Push the pump toward the engine to loosen the belt, then take the belt off the pulleys.
2. Install the new belt on the pulleys.
3. Pry the pump away from the engine to tighten the belt. When belt tension is as specified in **Table 10**, tighten the adjusting bolt, then the pivot bolt.

Power steering belt (1984 Accord, 1983-on Prelude)

1. Loosen the pivot bolt and adjusting bolt (**Figure 36**). Push the pump toward the engine to loosen the belt, then take the belt off the pulleys.
2. Install the new belt on the pulleys.
3. Pry the pump away from the engine to tighten the belt. When belt tension is as specified in **Table 10**, tighten the adjusting bolt, then the pivot bolt.

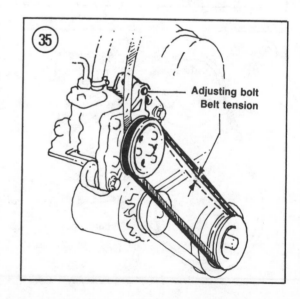

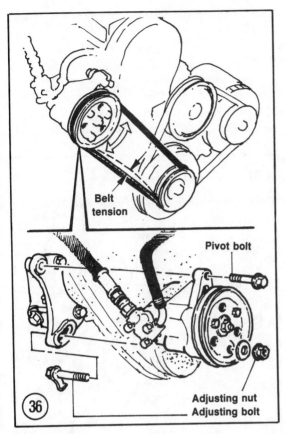

Belt
tension

Pivot bolt

Adjusting nut
Adjusting bolt

36

Air conditioner belt
(1978-1981 Accord, 1979-1982 Prelude)

Refer to **Figure 37** for this procedure.

1. Loosen the compressor mounting bolt, adjusting bolt locknut and adjusting bolt. Push the compressor toward the engine to loosen the belt, then take it off the pulleys.

2. Install a new belt on the pulleys.

3. Tighten the adjusting bolt until belt tension is as specified in **Table 10**. Then tighten the adjusting bolt locknut and compressor mounting bolt.

Air conditioner belt
(1982-1983 Accord)

Refer to **Figure 38** for this procedure.

1. Loosen the compressor mounting and adjusting bolts and nuts. Push the compressor toward the engine to loosen the belt, then take it off the pulleys.

2. Install a new belt on the pulleys.

3. Tighten the adjusting bolt until belt tension is as specified in **Table 10**. Then tighten the adjusting bolt locknut and compressor mounting bolt.

Air conditioner belt (1984 Accord)

Refer to **Figure 39** (Honda/Keihin type compressor) or **Figure 40** (Sanden type compressor).

3

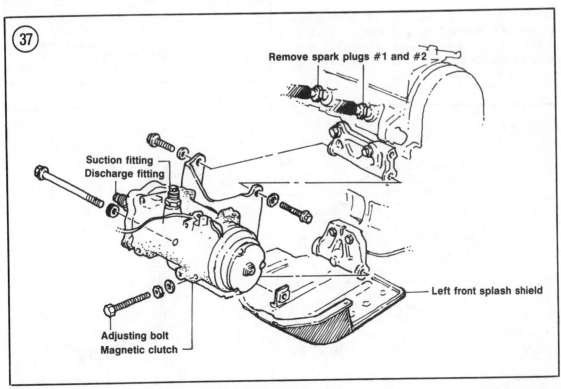

37

Remove spark plugs #1 and #2

Suction fitting
Discharge fitting

Left front splash shield

Adjusting bolt
Magnetic clutch

1. Loosen the compressor mounting and adjusting bolts. Push the compressor toward the engine to loosen the belt, then take it off the pulleys.

2. Install a new belt on the pulleys.

3. Tighten the adjusting bolt until belt tension is as specified in **Table 10**. Then tighten the mounting and adjusting bolts.

Air conditioner belt (1983-on Prelude)

Refer to **Figure 41** and **Figure 42** for this procedure.

1. Loosen the compressor mounting bolt and adjusting bolt nut. Push the compressor toward the engine to loosen the belt, then take it off the pulleys.

2. Install a new belt on the pulleys.

3. Tighten the adjusting bolt until belt tension is as specified in **Table 10**. Then tighten the adjusting bolt locknut and compressor mounting bolt.

Cooling System Service

At specified intervals, service the cooling system as follows.

WARNING
Do not remove the radiator cap when the engine is warm or hot. You could be seriously burned by escaping coolant and steam which is under considerable pressure.

1. With the engine cool, turn the radiator cap **(Figure 43)** counterclockwise without pushing down. When residual pressure (if any) has been relieved (hissing will stop), press the cap down and turn it counterclockwise to remove.

2. Wash the radiator cap and filler neck with clean water.

NOTE
Step 3 and Step 4 require special equipment available at most service stations or dealerships.

3. Test freeze protection with a coolant hydrometer. These are available inexpensively at

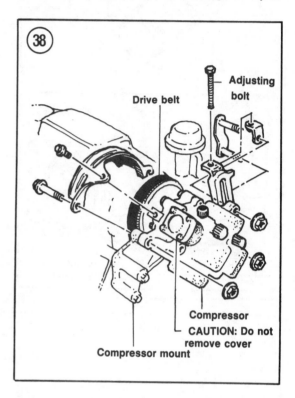

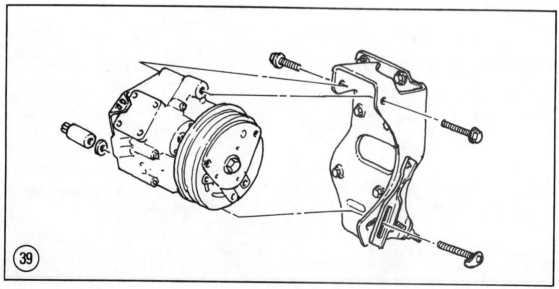

auto parts stores. The system must be protected to at least -34° F (-37° C) to provide corrosion protection, but protection must exceed the lowest anticipated temperature in your area.

4. Pressure test the cooling system and radiator cap with a pressure tester. Have this done by a Honda dealer or service station if you don't have the necessary equipment.

5. Check condition of hoses. Replace hoses if they are cracked, deteriorated, mildewed or extremely soft. See Chapter Seven.

6. Check tightness of hose clamps. Replace questionable clamps with adjustable stainless steel clamps.

7. Clean bugs and dirt from the front of the radiator and air conditioning condenser. If a compressor is available, blow compressed air through the back side of the radiator to clean the front side. If not, use a garden hose and soft brush.

Coolant Change

At specified intervals, drain, flush and refill the cooling system as described in Chapter Seven.

Air Cleaner

At specified intervals, replace the air cleaner element as described in Chapter Six.

Vacuum Fittings and Hoses

Check the vacuum fittings and connections to make sure they are tight. Inspect the hoses for cracks, kinks or deterioration. Tighten loose connections and replace defective hoses.

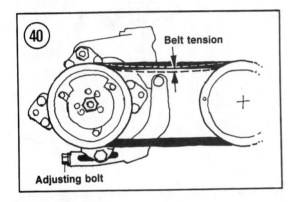

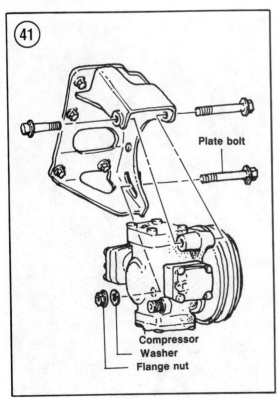

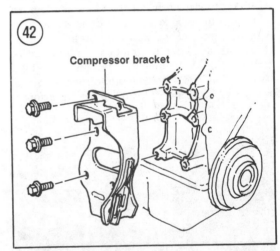

Emission Controls

Emission control systems and components which can be inspected by the owner/mechanic are described in Chapter Six. Periodic inspection intervals for emission control systems are in **Tables 1-3**. The following paragraphs describe crankcase emission control servicing.

Crankcase Emission Control

The crankcase emission control system should be inspected and cleaned at intervals specified in **Tables** 1-3.

1976-1977 models

1. Disconnect the drain tube from the condensation chamber under the air cleaner housing (**Figure 44**).
2. If the tube has a slit end (**Figure 44**), squeeze the end of the tube to open and drain it. If not, remove and invert the tube to open and drain it.
3. Disconnect the outside hose from the joint (**Figure 45**) and clean the joint end with the shank end of a No. 65 (1976) or No. 59 (1977) drill bit.
4. Inspect all hoses for deterioration and replace as necessary. Reconnect all hoses previously disconnected.

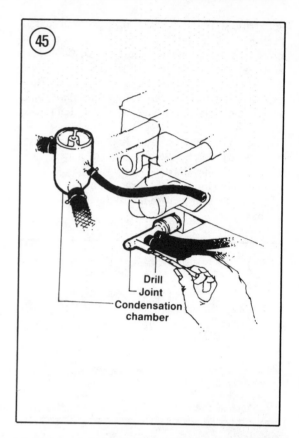

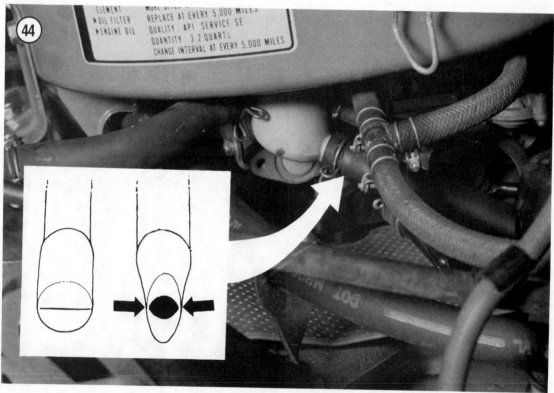

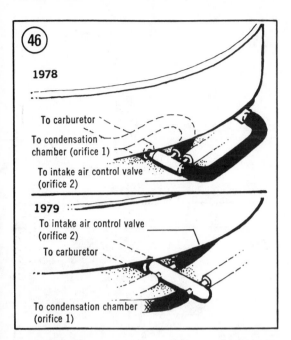

1978-1979 models

1. Disconnect the condensation chamber-to-joint breather hose (1, **Figure 46**). Clean the joint end with the shank end of a No. 59 drill bit.

2. Inspect all hoses for deterioration and replace as necessary. Reconnect all hoses.

1980-1983 Accord, 1980-1982 Prelude

1. Disconnect the breather hose at the carburetor insulator. See **Figure 47**. Clean the joint end (**Figure 48**) with the shank end of a No. 57 drill bit.

2. Inspect all hoses for deterioration and replace as necessary. Reconnect the breather hose.

3

Condensation chamber inspection (1976-1983 Accord, 1979-1982 Prelude)

On 1976-1983 Accords and 1979-1982 Preludes, the condensation chamber (**Figure 49**) must be inspected and cleaned of all sludge and varnish buildup. To do so, remove the air cleaner. Remove the top rubber gasket (**Figure 50**) and clean the

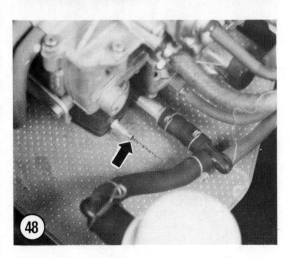

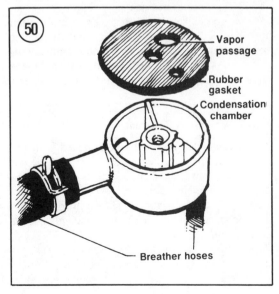

inside of the chamber with contact cleaner. Reverse these steps to install; make sure the rubber gasket is properly installed to prevent breather restriction.

1984 Accord, 1983-on Prelude

1. Check the system hoses for cracks, deterioration, clogging or looseness. Replace, clean or tighten as needed.
2. Remove the PCV valve from the valve cover. See **Figure 51**.
3. Start the engine and let it idle. While the engine idles, plug the bottom of the PCV valve with a finger as shown in **Figure 51**. A click should be heard as the valve is plugged:
   a. If a click is heard, the valve is good.
   b. If there is no click, replace the valve and repeat Step 3.
4. Check the PCV valve's grommet in the valve cover for cracks or deterioration. Replace it if these conditions are found.
5. Reinstall the PCV valve in the valve cover.
6. Remove the PCV filter from the air cleaner. See **Figure 52** (Accord) or **Figure 53** (Prelude).
7. Inspect the filter and replace it if it is contaminated with dirt or oil.

TUNE-UP

A complete tune-up consists of the following:
a. Valve clearance adjustment.
b. Compression test.
c. Ignition system work.
d. Carburetor adjustment.

Some tune-up procedures are done more often than others. Some procedures apply only to specific models. Service intervals and model applications for each tune-up procedure are listed in the maintenance schedules at the end of the chapter.

Valve Clearance Adjustment

The valve clearance must be adjusted with the engine cold. An accepted practice is to let the car stand overnight and adjust the valves the following day before the engine is run. Valve clearances are in **Table 7**. Valve location is shown in **Figure 54**.
1. Disconnect the breather hose at the valve cover (**Figure 55**).
2. Referring to **Figure 56**, remove the air cleaner-to-valve cover bracket bolts and remove the bracket.

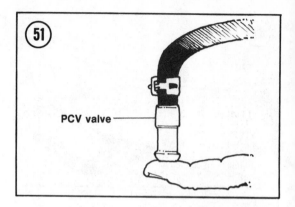

PCV valve

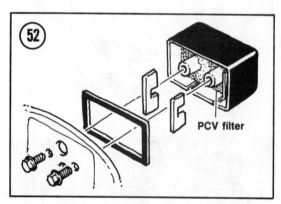

PCV filter

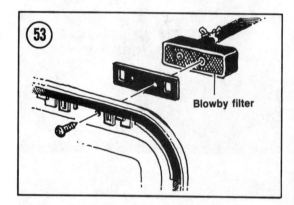

Blowby filter

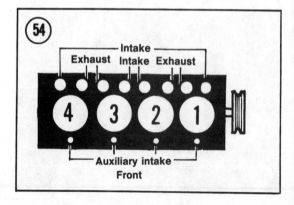

Intake
Exhaust   Intake   Exhaust

4   3   2   1

Auxiliary intake
Front

CAUTION
During the next step, refer to **Spark**
Plugs *in this chapter for correct*
removal procedures.

3. Remove the spark plugs.
4. Remove the spark plug wires from the bracket at the left side of the valve cover (**Figure 57**) and remove the bracket.
5. Remove the valve cover attaching bolts and remove the valve cover.
6. Identify valves, referring to **Figure 54**. Continue with the proper procedure for your specific model.

1976-1978 models

1. Remove the upper belt cover attaching screws and remove the belt cover (**Figure 58**).
2. Place a wrench on the crankshaft pulley bolt. Turn the engine by hand (counterclockwise, viewed from the timing belt end of the engine) so the timing mark on the camshaft pulley aligns with the arrow on the cylinder head (**Figure 59**). Make sure the word "UP" on the pulley and keyway on the camshaft are pointing up.
3. Refer to **Figure 54** and identify the following valves:
   a. Intake 1 and 2.
   b. Exhaust 1 and 3.
   c. Auxiliary intake 1 and 2.
   Adjust these valves during Steps 4-7.
4. Find valve clearance for your engine in **Table 7**. Select a flat feeler gauge of the same thickness and insert it between the stem of the valve being adjusted and the rocker arm adjuster screw. See **Figure 60**. Slide the feeler gauge in and out. There should be a slight drag:

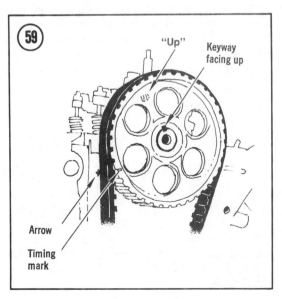

a. If so, that valve's clearance is correct. Go to the next valve.

b. If the feeler gauge is too easy or too hard to pull, adjust as described in Step 5 and Step 6.

5. If the feeler gauge is too easy or too hard to pull, loosen the adjuster locknut and turn the adjuster screw in or out (**Figure 61**) until a slight drag can be felt when the feeler gauge is pulled between the adjuster and the stem.

6. When the clearance is correct, hold the adjuster screw to keep it from turning farther and tighten the locknut. Then recheck the clearance with the feeler gauge to make sure the adjuster hasn't moved.

7. Turn the crankshaft one full turn. The camshaft keyway and the word "UP" should now be facing down. The timing mark should be 180° away from the arrow. See **Figure 62**.

8. Refer to **Figure 54** and identify the following valves:

a. Intake 3 and 4.

b. Exhaust 2 and 4.

c. Auxiliary valves 3 and 4.

Adjust these valves as described in Steps 4-6.

9. Once all valves are adjusted, reinstall the timing belt upper cover and valve cover.

1979-1981 models

1. Place a wrench on the crankshaft pulley bolt. Turn the engine by hand so the top dead center timing grooves on the back of the camshaft pulley align with the cylinder head surface. The word "UP" on the pulley should point upward. See **Figure 63**.

2. Remove the distributor cap and make sure the rotor points to the No. 1 spark plug terminal. This is identified by a vertical line on the cap (**Figure 64**).

> *NOTE*
> *Distributor cap terminals are numbered 1-3-4-2 in the counterclockwise direction around the cap.*

3. Refer to **Figure 54** and identify the following valves:

a. No. 1 intake.

b. No. 1 exhaust.

c. No. 1 auxiliary intake.

4. Find valve clearance for your engine in **Table 7**. Select a flat feeler gauge of the same thickness and insert it between the stem of the valve being adjusted and the rocker arm adjuster screw. See **Figure 60**. Slide the feeler gauge in and out. There should be a slight drag:

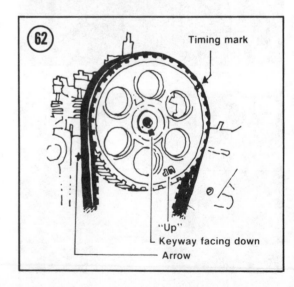

Timing mark

"Up"

Keyway facing down

Arrow

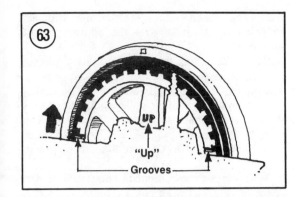

"Up" Grooves

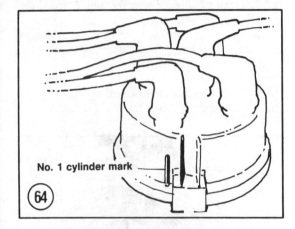

No. 1 cylinder mark

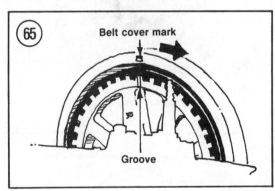

Belt cover mark

Groove

a. If so, that valve's clearance is correct. Go to the next valve.

b. If the feeler gauge is too easy or too hard to pull, adjust as described in Step 5 and Step 6.

5. If the feeler gauge is too easy or too hard to pull, loosen the adjuster locknut and turn the adjuster screw in or out (**Figure 61**) until a slight drag can be felt when the feeler gauge is pulled between the adjuster and the stem.

6. When the clearance is correct, hold the adjuster screw to keep it from turning farther and tighten the locknut. Then recheck the clearance with the feeler gauge to make sure the adjuster hasn't moved.

7. Turn the crankshaft 180° counterclockwise (viewed from the timing belt end of the engine). The camshaft pulley will rotate 90°. The timing grooves on the back of the pulley should align with the belt cover mark as shown in **Figure 65**. The word "UP" should not be visible. The distributor rotor should point to the No. 3 spark plug wire terminal.

8. With the engine positioned as described in Step 7, adjust all 3 valves for No. 3 cylinder.

9. Turn the crankshaft another 180°. Again, the camshaft pulley will rotate 90°. The timing grooves on the back of the camshaft pulley should move to align with the cylinder head surface. See **Figure 66**. The distributor rotor should point to No. 4 spark plug wire terminal.

10. With the engine positioned as described in Step 9, adjust all 3 valves for No. 4 cylinder.

11. Turn the crankshaft another 180°. The timing grooves on the back of the camshaft pulley should move to align with the belt cover mark and the word "UP" should become visible. See **Figure 67**. The distributor rotor should point to No. 2 spark plug terminal.

12. With the engine positioned as described in Step 11, adjust all 3 valves for No. 2 cylinder.

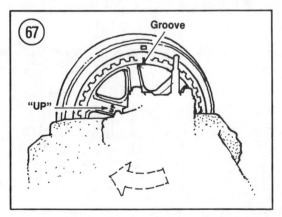

Groove

"UP"

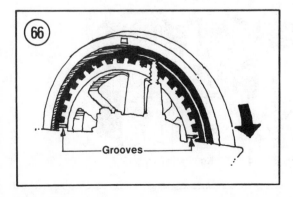

Grooves

1982 models

1. Place a wrench on the crankshaft pulley bolt. Turn the engine by hand so the top dead center timing grooves on the back of the camshaft pulley align with the cylinder head surface. The word "UP" on the pulley should point upward. See **Figure 63**.

2. Remove the distributor cap and make sure the rotor points to the No. 1 spark plug terminal. This is identified by a vertical line on the cap (**Figure 64**).

> *NOTE*
> *Distributor cap terminals are numbered 1-3-4-2 in the counterclockwise direction around the cap.*

3. Refer to **Figure 68** and identify the following valves:
   a. No. 1 intake.
   b. No. 1 exhaust.
   c. No. 1 auxiliary intake.

4. Find valve clearance for your engine in **Table 7**. Select a flat feeler gauge of the same thickness and insert it between the stem of the valve being adjusted and the rocker arm adjuster screw. See **Figure 60**. Slide the feeler gauge in and out. There should be a slight drag:
   a. If so, that valve's clearance is correct. Go to the next valve.
   b. If the feeler gauge is too easy or too hard to pull, adjust as described in Step 5 and Step 6.

5. If the feeler gauge is too easy or too hard to pull, loosen the adjuster locknut and turn the adjuster screw in or out (**Figure 61**) until a slight drag can be felt when the feeler gauge is pulled between the adjuster and the stem.

6. When the clearance is correct, hold the adjuster screw to keep it from turning farther and tighten the locknut. Then recheck the clearance with the feeler gauge to make sure the adjuster hasn't moved.

7. Turn the crankshaft 180° counterclockwise (viewed from the timing belt end of the engine). The camshaft pulley will rotate 90°. The timing grooves on the back of the pulley should align with the belt cover mark as shown in **Figure 65**. The word "UP" should not be visible. The distributor rotor should point to the No. 3 spark plug wire terminal.

8. With the engine positioned as described in Step 7, adjust all 3 valves for No. 3 cylinder.

9. Turn the crankshaft another 180°. Again, the camshaft pulley will rotate 90°. The timing grooves on the back of the camshaft pulley should move to align with the cylinder head surface. See **Figure 66**. The distributor rotor should point to No. 4 spark plug wire terminal.

10. With the engine positioned as described in Step 9, adjust all 3 valves for No. 4 cylinder.

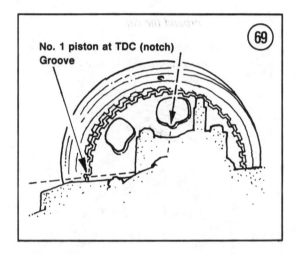

No. 1 piston at TDC (notch) Groove

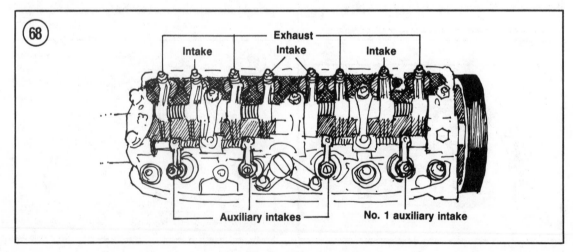

11. Turn the crankshaft another 180°. The timing grooves on the back of the camshaft pulley should move to align with the belt cover mark and the word "UP" should become visible. See **Figure 67**. The distributor rotor should point to No. 2 spark plug terminal.

12. With the engine positioned as described in Step 11, adjust all 3 valves for No. 2 cylinder.

1983 Accord

1. Place a wrench on the crankshaft pulley bolt. Turn the engine by hand so the cutaway in the pulley is at the top and the top dead center groove in the back of the pulley aligns with the cylinder head surface. See **Figure 69**.

2. Remove the distributor cap and make sure the rotor points to the No. 1 spark plug terminal. This is identified by a vertical line on the cap (**Figure 64**).

NOTE
Distributor cap terminals are numbered 1-3-4-2 in the counterclockwise direction around the cap.

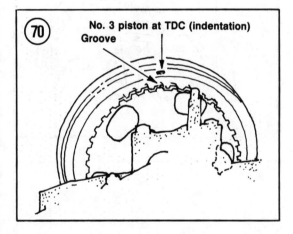

⑦⓪ No. 3 piston at TDC (indentation)
Groove

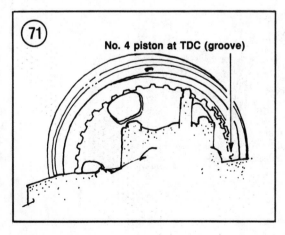

⑦① No. 4 piston at TDC (groove)

3. Refer to **Figure 68** and identify the following valves:
   a. No. 1 intake.
   b. No. 1 exhaust.
   c. No. 1 auxiliary intake.

4. Find valve clearance for your engine in **Table 7**. Select a flat feeler gauge of the same thickness and insert it between the stem of the valve being adjusted and the rocker arm adjuster screw. See **Figure 60**. Slide the feeler gauge in and out. There should be a slight drag:
   a. If so, that valve's clearance is correct. Go to the next valve.
   b. If the feeler gauge is too easy or too hard to pull, adjust as described in Step 5 and Step 6.

5. If the feeler gauge is too easy or too hard to pull, loosen the adjuster locknut and turn the adjuster screw in or out (**Figure 61**) until a slight drag can be felt when the feeler gauge is pulled between the adjuster and the stem.

6. When the clearance is correct, hold the adjuster screw to keep it from turning farther and tighten the locknut. Then recheck the clearance with the feeler gauge to make sure the adjuster hasn't moved.

7. Turn the crankshaft 180° counterclockwise (viewed from the timing belt end of the engine). The camshaft pulley will rotate 90°. The top dead center groove on the back of the pulley should align with the indentation in the belt cover (**Figure 70**). The distributor rotor should point to the No. 3 spark plug wire terminal.

8. With the engine positioned as described in Step 7, adjust all 3 valves for No. 3 cylinder.

9. Turn the crankshaft another 180°. Again, the camshaft pulley will rotate 90°. The top dead center groove on the back of the camshaft pulley should move to align with the cylinder head surface. See **Figure 71**. The distributor rotor should point to No. 4 spark plug wire terminal.

10. With the engine positioned as described in Step 9, adjust all 3 valves for No. 4 cylinder.

11. Turn the crankshaft another 180°. The timing groove on the back of the camshaft pulley should be downward and the cutaway in the pulley should be visible. See **Figure 72**. The distributor rotor should point to No. 2 spark plug terminal.

12. With the engine positioned as described in Step 11, adjust all 3 valves for No. 2 cylinder.

1984 Accord, 1983-on Prelude

1. Place a wrench on the crankshaft pulley bolt. Turn the engine by hand so the round mark in the pulley is at the top and the grooves in the back of

the pulley align with the cylinder head surface. See **Figure 73**.

2. Identify the valves for No. 1 cylinder. To do this, refer to the following illustrations:
a. **Figure 74**—1984 Accord, 1983 Prelude.
b. **Figure 75**—1984 Prelude.

NOTE
Cylinders are numbered 1 through 4, counting from the timing belt end of the engine.

3. Adjust the valves for No. 1 cylinder. To do this, find valve clearance for your engine in **Table 7**. Select a flat feeler gauge of the same thickness and insert it between the stem of the valve being adjusted and the rocker arm adjuster screw. See **Figure 76**. Slide the feeler gauge in and out. There should be a slight drag.
a. If so, that valve's clearance is correct. Go to the next valve.
b. If the feeler gauge is too easy or too hard to pull, adjust as described in Step 4 and Step 5.

4. If the feeler gauge is too easy or too hard to pull, loosen the adjuster locknut and turn the adjuster screw in or out (**Figure 76**) until a slight drag can be felt when the feeler gauge is pulled between the adjuster and the stem. The slight drag means the valve's clearance is correct.

5. When the clearance is correct, hold the adjuster screw to keep it from turning farther and tighten the locknut. Then recheck the clearance with the feeler gauge to make sure the adjuster hasn't moved.

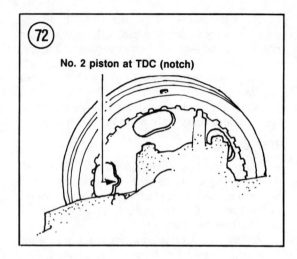

No. 2 piston at TDC (notch)

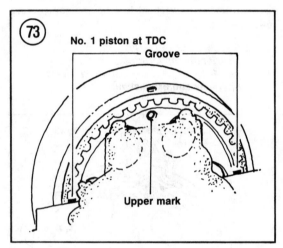

No. 1 piston at TDC
Groove
Upper mark

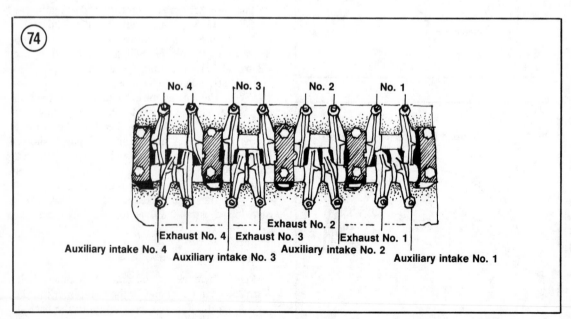

No. 4   No. 3   No. 2   No. 1

Exhaust No. 2
Exhaust No. 4   Exhaust No. 3   Exhaust No. 1
Auxiliary intake No. 4   Auxiliary intake No. 2
Auxiliary intake No. 3   Auxiliary intake No. 1

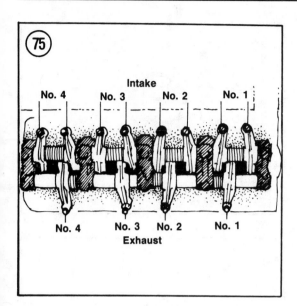

Intake

No. 4   No. 3   No. 2   No. 1

No. 4   No. 3 No. 2   No. 1
Exhaust

6. Turn the crankshaft 180° counterclockwise (viewed from the timing belt end of the engine). The camshaft pulley will rotate 90°. The groove on the back of the pulley should align with the indentation in the belt cover (**Figure 77**).

7. With the engine positioned as described in Step 6, adjust all valves for No. 3 cylinder.

8. Turn the crankshaft another 180°. Again, the camshaft pulley will rotate 90°. The grooves on the back of the camshaft pulley should align with the cylinder head surface. See **Figure 78**.

9. With the engine positioned as described in Step 8, adjust all valves for No. 4 cylinder.

10. Turn the crankshaft another 180°. The groove on the back of the camshaft pulley should align with the belt cover mark and the round mark in the pulley should be visible. See **Figure 79**.

11. With the engine positioned as described in Step 10, adjust all valves for No. 2 cylinder.

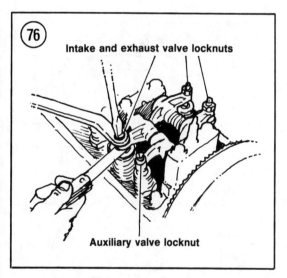

Intake and exhaust valve locknuts

Auxiliary valve locknut

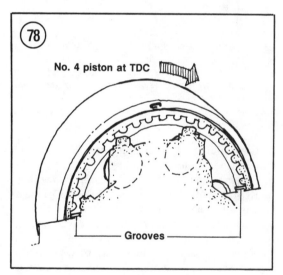

No. 4 piston at TDC

Grooves

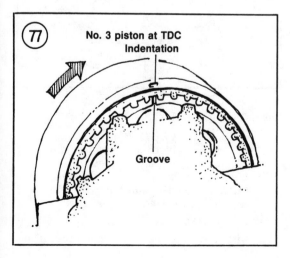

No. 3 piston at TDC
Indentation

Groove

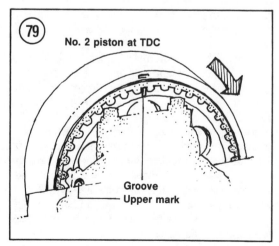

No. 2 piston at TDC

Groove
Upper mark

Compression Test

The compression test need not be done periodically. Compression should be tested if performance is poor, oil consumption is high or the cooling system requires repeated topping up and there is no visible leak.

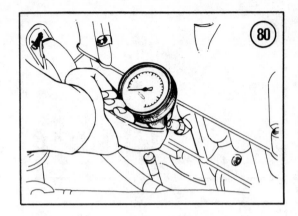

There are 2 types of compression test: "wet" and "dry." These tests are interpreted together to isolate problems in cylinders and valves. The dry compression test is done first. Test as follows.

1. Warm the engine to normal operating temperature.

2. Remove the spark plugs.

3. Connect the compression tester to one cylinder following manufacturer's instructions. **Figure 80** shows a hand-held compression tester in use. You can also use the screw-in type described in Chapter One.

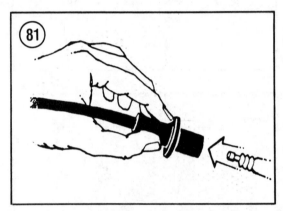

NOTE
Hand-held compression testers require 2 people, one to hold the compression tester and one to crank the engine. Screw-in compression testers require only one person.

4. Crank the engine over until there is no further increase in compression reading.

5. Remove the tester and write down the reading.

6. Repeat Steps 3-5 for each cylinder. Compare results with **Table 7** in this chapter.

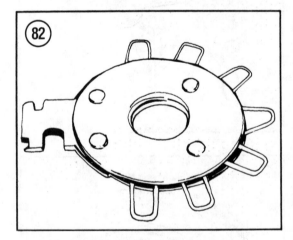

When interpreting the results, actual readings are not as important as the differences in readings. Low readings, although they may be even, are a sign of wear. Low readings in 2 adjacent cylinders may indicate a defective head gasket. An excessive difference in readings indicates worn or broken rings, leaky or sticking valves, a defective head gasket or a combination of all.

If the dry compression test indicates a problem, isolate the cause with a wet compression test. This is done in the same way as the dry compression test, except that about one tablespoon of oil is poured down the spark plug holes before performing Steps 3-6. If the wet compression readings are much greater than the dry readings, the trouble is probably due to worn or broken rings. If there is little difference between wet and dry readings, the trouble is probably due to leaky or sticking valves. If 2 adjacent cylinders are low and the wet and dry readings are close, the head gasket may be damaged.

Spark Plug Removal

CAUTION
When spark plugs are removed, dirt from around the plugs can fall into the spark plug holes. This can cause expensive engine damage. For this reason, be sure to perform the first step.

1. Blow out any foreign matter from around spark plugs with compressed air. Use a compressor if you

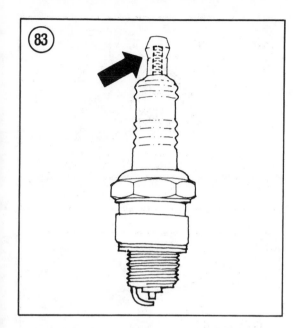

3. Disconnect spark plug wires. Pull off by grasping the connector, *not* the wire. See **Figure 81**. Pulling on the wire may break it.

NOTE
If the boots seem to be stuck, twist them 1/2 turn to break the seal. Do not pull on boots with pliers. The pliers could cut the insulation and allow the spark to arc to ground.

4. Remove the plugs with a 13/16 in. spark plug socket. Keep the plugs in order so you know which cylinder they came from.
5. Examine each spark plug. Compare its condition with the illustrations in Chapter Two. Spark plug condition indicates engine condition and can warn of developing trouble.
6. Discard the plugs. Although they could be cleaned, regapped and reused if in good condition, they seldom last very long; new plugs are inexpensive and far more reliable.

Spark Plug Gapping and Installation

New plugs should be carefully gapped to ensure a reliable, consistent spark. Use a special spark plug tool with a wire gauge. See **Figure 82**.
1. Remove the plugs from the boxes. See if the small end pieces (**Figure 83**) are screwed on. If not, install them.
2. Find the correct spark plug gap for your car in **Table 7**. Insert the correct diameter wire gauge between the spark plug electrodes. See **Figure 84**. If the gap is correct, there will be a slight drag as the wire is pulled through. If there is no drag or if the wire won't pull through, bend the side electrode with the gapping tool (**Figure 85**) to change the gap.
3. Apply aluminum anti-seize compound to the threads of each spark plug.
4. Crank the starter for about 5 seconds to blow away any dirt around the spark plug holes.
5. Screw each plug in by hand until it seats. Very little effort is required. If force is necessary, the plug is cross-threaded. Unscrew it and try again.

CAUTION
Do not overtighten the plugs during the next step. This prevents the plugs from seating.

6. Tighten the spark plugs. If you have a torque wrench, tighten to 1.5-2.0 mkg (11-14 ft.-lb.). If not, tighten the plug with fingers, then tighten an additional 1/4-1/2 turn with the plug wrench.
7. If you plan to inspect the distributor, leave the plug wires disconnected. If not, reconnect the wires to the spark plugs. Spark plugs are numbered from

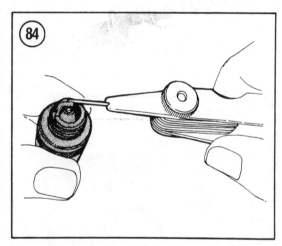

have one. Another method is to use a can of compressed inert gas, available from photo stores.

NOTE
If the engine is very dirty or greasy, clean it with engine cleaner. Highly effective engine cleaners which can be rinsed off with water are available at auto parts stores.

2. Mark spark plug wires with the cylinder numbers so you can reconnect them properly. Cylinders are numbered one through 4, counting from the timing belt end of the engine.

NOTE
To make labels, wrap a small strip of masking tape around each wire.

1 through 4, counting from the timing belt end of the engine (nearest the driver's side of the car). Distributor cap terminals are numbered 1-3-4-2 counterclockwise around the cap. To identify No. 1 terminal, refer to the following illustrations:

a. 1976 manual—**Figure 86**.
b. 1976 automatic—**Figure 87**.
c. 1977-1978 manual and 49-state automatic—**Figure 86**.
d. 1977-1978 California and high altitude automatic—**Figure 88**.
e. 1979-1981—**Figure 89**.
f. All 1982, 1983 Accord—**Figure 89** (Hitachi type) or **Figure 90** (Toyo Denso type).
g. 1984 Accord—**Figure 91** (Hitachi type) or **Figure 92** (Toyo Denso type).
h. 1983-on Prelude—**Figure 93**.

Distributor Inspection (1976-1978)

Refer to **Figure 94** and **Figure 95** for this procedure.

1. Remove the distributor cap. Clean it carefully to remove grease and dirt.

2. Examine the inside of the cap for dirt and wear. Look for signs of carbon tracks (arcing) from contact to contact inside the distributor cap. If any are found, replace the cap and rotor as a set.

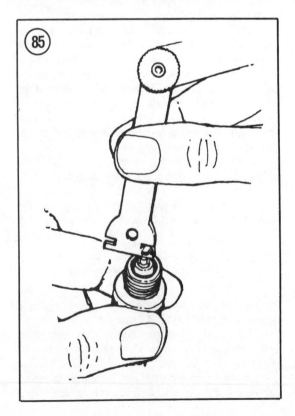

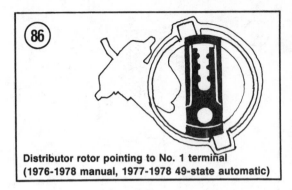

Distributor rotor pointing to No. 1 terminal
(1976-1978 manual, 1977-1978 49-state automatic)

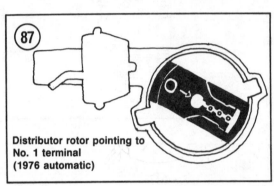

Distributor rotor pointing to
No. 1 terminal
(1976 automatic)

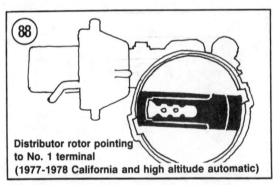

Distributor rotor pointing
to No. 1 terminal
(1977-1978 California and high altitude automatic)

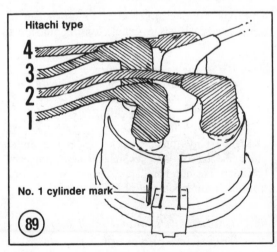

Hitachi type

4
3
2
1

No. 1 cylinder mark

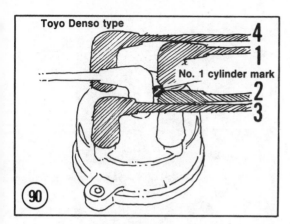

Toyo Denso type

4
1
No. 1 cylinder mark
2
3

90

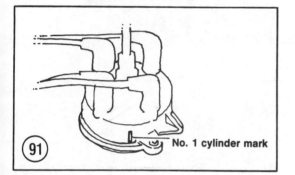

No. 1 cylinder mark

91

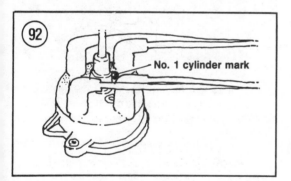

92

No. 1 cylinder mark

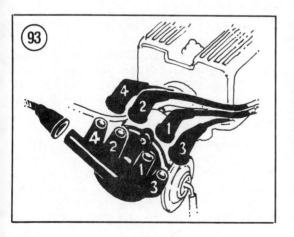

93

4
2
1
3
4
2
1
3

3

94

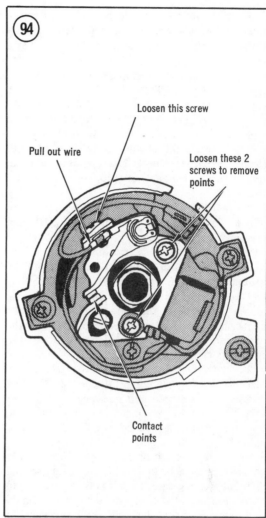

Loosen this screw

Pull out wire

Loosen these 2
screws to remove
points

Contact
points

95

3. Remove the rotor and check it for excessive wear or burning around the top metal contact surface. If defective, replace the rotor and cap as a set.

4. Gently open the contact points with a screwdriver and check their condition. If the points are only slightly pitted or irregular, they are acceptable. If they are badly pitted they must be replaced. If the points show signs of wear or pitting, remove the contact point assembly and clean or replace the points. Use a point file to clean the contacts. Do not attempt to remove all roughness.

5. To remove the points, note the position of the ground lead connector and unscrew the contact breaker mounting screws (**Figure 94**). Remove the contact breaker assembly (and internal condenser, if so equipped) and disconnect the lead from the moveable contact.

6. On distributors with external condensers, loosen the screw in the condenser contact block and disconnect the condenser lead. Unscrew the condenser mounting screw and remove the condenser (**Figure 95**).

7. Check the movement of the centrifugal advance mechanism by carefully turning the contact breaker cam by hand and releasing it. It should snap back against spring tension. If it does not, have the distributor repaired by a Honda dealer or automotive electrical shop.

8. Wipe the cam and breaker plate clean. Lightly coat the contact breaker cam with special distributor cam grease. This is available from auto parts stores. Never use oil or ordinary multipurpose grease; they will break down under the high frictional load and find their way onto the contacts.

9. Install the new contact breaker assembly and condenser by reversing the removal steps. Make certain the ground wire and condenser-to-contact wire are installed exactly as they were before; double check the connections and screws to ensure that they are tight.

10. Rotate the crankshaft using a wrench on the crankshaft pulley nut until the contacts are at their maximum opening. Check the gap with a flat feeler gauge and compare to the specifications in **Table 7**. To adjust the contact gap, loosen the retaining screws in the fixed contact plate and turn the eccentric adjuster screw to increase or decrease the gap as necessary (**Figure 96**). Then tighten the retaining screws.

11. If a dwell meter is available, connect it in accordance with the manufacturer's instructions. Disconnect the coil wire from the distributor and

ground it to nearby bare metal. Crank the engine with the starter and check the dwell angle. It should be $52 \pm 3°$. If it is incorrect, readjust the points gap to change it.

NOTE
Increasing points gap decreases dwell angle. Decreasing points gap increases dwell angle.

12. Inspect the insulation on all wires leading to or within the distributor. Replace damaged wires.

13. Install the rotor and distributor cap. Connect the spark plug wires to the distributor cap and spark plugs. See *Spark Plug Gapping and Installation* for distributor terminal identification.

Distributor Inspection (1979-on)

The inspection procedure for 1979-on models is the same as for 1976-1978 models, except for Steps 4-11 which deal with contact breaker points. As with 1976-1978 models, spark plug wire terminals are numbered one through 4, counting from the timing belt end of the engine. Distributor cap

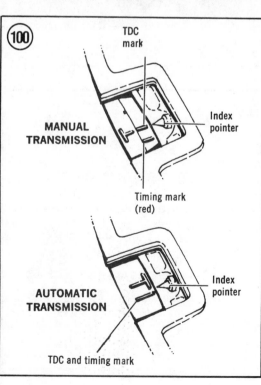

TDC mark

Index pointer

MANUAL TRANSMISSION

Timing mark (red)

Index pointer

AUTOMATIC TRANSMISSION

TDC and timing mark

terminals are numbered 1-3-4-2, counting counterclockwise around the distributor cap. To identify the No. 1 distributor cap terminal, refer to *Spark Plug Gapping and Installation*.

Ignition Timing

The distributor must be aligned to fire each plug precisely at the right moment. The emission control decal under the hood specifies this time for different combinations of engine and optional equipment and for different points of sale. See **Figure 97**. Due to varying state and federal regulations, your decal may differ from the one shown. Always use the specifications on the decal on your own car. If the decal is missing or illegible, use the specifications in **Table 7**.

1. Connect a timing light to the engine, following the timing light manufacturer's instructions.

2. Remove the rubber timing plug cover from the engine, near the point where it mates to the transaxle. See **Figure 98**.

3. Make sure the timing light wires are out of the way of all drive belts and pulleys, then start the engine.

4. Refer to the emission control decal and make sure idle speed is correct:

   a. On all Accords and 1979-1982 Preludes, adjust idle speed if necessary with the throttle stop screw. **Figure 99** shows a typical throttle stop screw.

NOTE
Figure 99 shows the air cleaner removed for clarity. Idle speed must be adjusted with the air cleaner installed.

   b. On 1983 and later Preludes, idle speed is not adjustable by home mechanics. If idle speed is incorrect, refer further service to a Honda dealer or mechanic familiar with Honda emission controls.

5. Point the timing light at the timing scale. The timing mark on the flywheel will appear to stand still (it may waver occasionally) opposite the pointer. **Figure 100** shows typical timing marks. On 1976-1981 engines, the timing mark is indicated by a color. **Table 8** describes the ignition timing marks and pointer colors for different 1976-1981 engines:

   a. If the timing marks indicated on your emission decal align, no further adjustment is necessary.

   b. If not, adjust as described in the following steps.

6. If adjustment is required, turn off the engine and loosen the distributor hold-down clamp. Refer to the following illustrations:
  a. 1979-1983 Accord, 1979-1982 Prelude—**Figure 101**.
  b. 1984 Accord—**Figure 102**.
  c. 1983-on Prelude—**Figure 103**.
7. Start the engine, point the timing light at the scale and slowly rotate the distributor body until the notch on the pulley aligns with the proper timing mark. When this happens, shut off the engine and tighten the distributor hold-down clamp.
8. Restart the engine and recheck timing. If timing has changed, repeat Step 6 and Step 7 to adjust it.
9. Turn off the engine.
10. Disconnect the timing light and tachometer.

Idle Speed Adjustment

This procedure applies to all models except 1983 and later Preludes. Carburetor adjustments on 1983 and later Preludes should be done by a Honda dealer or mechanic familiar with Honda emission controls.
1. Securely block the front and rear wheels so the car will not roll in either directon.
2. Start the engine and warm it to normal operating temperature (the fan will come on).
3. Connect a tachometer to the engine, following manufacturer's instructions.
4. On 1980 and later models, disconnect the vacuum hose from the intake air control diaphragm on the air cleaner tunnel and plug the end of the hose (**Figure 104**). A golf tee works well for this.
5A. *1976-1979 models:* Turn the headlights on. In addition, either the cooling fan or high-speed heater fan must be on, but not both. Proceed to Step 5.
5B. *1980 and later models*: The headlights, cooling fan and air conditioner must be off. If the cooling fan is turned on, stop the engine and disconnect the cooling fan wiring connector at the fan (**Figure 105**). Restart the engine and proceed to Step 6.
6. Check the idle speed (manual transaxle in NEUTRAL; automatic transaxle in DRIVE). Compare with specifications on your car's emission decal or in **Table 6**. Adjust the idle speed, if necessary, by turning the throttle stop screw (**Figure 99**). Turn the engine off.

> *NOTE*
> *The air cleaner is shown removed for clarity in **Figure 99**. Idle speed must be adjusted with the air cleaner installed.*

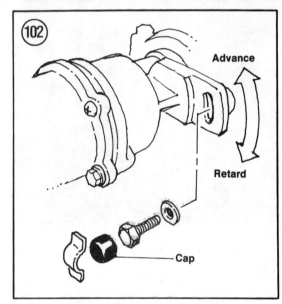

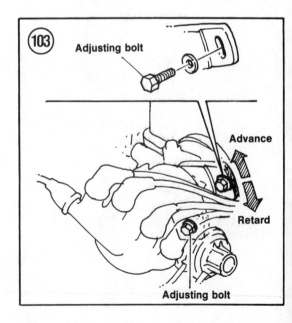

7. Reconnect the cooling fan connector, if necessary. Remove the tachometer from the engine.

Idle Mixture Adjustment (1976-1979)

1. Perform *Idle Speed Adjustment* in this chapter. Leave the headlights and either the heater fan or cooling fan on. Leave the shift lever in NEUTRAL (manual) or DRIVE (automatic).

> *CAUTION*
> *When performing the following procedure with an automatic transaxle in DRIVE, make sure to block the front and rear wheels to prevent the car from moving forward.*

2. Remove the limiter cap from the idle mixture screw. Turn the idle mixture screw counterclockwise until the highest engine speed is reached.

> *NOTE*
> *The idle mixture screw is located directly under the primary main fuel cutoff valve in **Figure 106**.*

3. Adjust idle speed with the throttle stop screw to "best idle" speed shown in **Table 8**.
4. Turn the mixture screw in (clockwise) to bring the final idle speed to that specified in **Table 8**. Install the limiter cap with the pointer set 180° from the top lug.
5. On 1979 models with air conditioning, turn the air conditioner on and recheck the idle speed. It should still be within specifications (Step 3). If not, remove the rubber cap from the idle boost diaphragm and turn the adjusting screw as required.

Idle Mixture Adjustment (1980-on)

A propane enrichment kit is required for this procedure. In addition, a special mixture adjustment tool is required on some models. As this adjustment is normally required only at 60,000-mile intervals, it is more economical to have the adjustment done by a Honda dealer or mechanic familiar with Honda emission controls.

After every engine tune-up, have a Honda dealer or qualified specialist check carbon monoxide (CO content) of exhaust gas.

Tables are on the following pages.

Table 1 MAINTENANCE SCHEDULE (1976-1979)

Every 5,000 miles	• Check idle speed and idle mixture[1] • Change engine oil and filter • Check throttle controlling unit • Check ignition timing and adjust if required[1] • Check valve clearances and adjust if required[1] • Adjust rear brake (Accord) • Adjust parking brake • Check the brake hoses and lines • Check master cylinder brake fluid level • Check front brake pads and caliper • Check play of clutch release arm and adjust if required • Check play of clutch pedal and adjust if required • Check clutch master cylinder fluid level • Check condition of radiator fan • Check condition of exhaust system and repair if required • Check tightness of all suspension mounting bolts • Check the steering, tie rod ends and steering gearbox for correct operation. Adjust if required • Check rack guides for grease • Inspect all power steering components and repair as required • Adjust the power steering belt • Check the power steering fluid level
Every 10,000 miles	• Clean the disc brake vacuum booster air cleaner [2] • Check the condition of the rear brake linings and replace if required • Check front wheel alignment[3]

Every 15,000 miles	• Check the tension of the alternator drive
	  belt and adjust if required
	• Change the transaxle oil
	• Check the condition of all water hoses and
	  replace/or tighten connections as required
	• Replace the engine coolant[2]
	• Clean the radiator exterior of all dirt, bugs, etc.
	• Replace the air filter
	• Replace the fuel filter
	• Inspect the air temperature control system
	• Inspect the start control system
	• Check the choke operation
	• Check condition of all vacuum lines and hoses
	  and repair as required
	• Inspect the condition of the charcoal canister
	• Inspect the idle cutoff valve
	• Inspect the 2 way valve
	• Replace the contact points (if so equipped)
	  and set the ignition timing[1]
	• Replace the spark plugs[1]
	• Inspect the ignition timing control system
	• Check resistance of the spark plug wires
	  and replace if required
	• Clean the condensation chamber, hoses and fixed orifice
	  in the crankcase emission system

(continued)

Table 1 MAINTENANCE SCHEDULE (1976-1979) (continued)

Every 20,000 miles	• Replace the brake fluid[4]
Every 30,000 miles	• Replace the charcoal canister • Replace the distributor cap and rotor (see notes 1 and 5)

1. Tune-up task.
2. Every 30,000 miles or 34 months on 1977-1979 models.
3. Every 25,000 miles on 1978-1979 models.
4. Every 25,000 miles on 1978-1979 models.
5. Breaker point ignition systems only. Replace parts on transistorized ignition systems if required.

3

Table 2 MAINTENANCE SCHEDULE (1979-1981)

Every 7,500 miles	• Change engine oil and filter • Adjust rear brakes (Accord) • Adjust parking brake • Check tightness of suspension mounting bolts • Check exhaust system components and fasteners for condition and tightness. Repair as required • Check steering operation • Check steering rack for grease and adjustment • Inspect tension and condition of the power steering belt • Inspect the power steering system • Check the power steering reservoir fluid level • Inspect the brake lines and hoses • Check the brake master cylinder fluid level • Check the clutch master cylinder fluid level • Check the clutch release arm adjustment • Check the clutch pedal free play
Every 15,000 miles	• Check front wheel alignment • Replace the automatic transaxle fluid • Inspect the front brake pad thickness • Check the condition of the front brake rotor • Check the valve clearances[1]
Every 30,000 miles	• Replace the manual transaxle fluid • Inspect the rear brake adjustment (Accord) • Replace the brake fluid • Inspect the cooling system hoses and connections • Replace the engine coolant (see notes 2 and 3) • Check the alternator belt tension • Replace the spark plugs[1] • Replace the air filter • Check the choke coil tension and linkage

(continued)

Table 2 MAINTENANCE SCHEDULE (1979-1981) (continued)

Every 45,000 miles	• Change the engine coolant[4]
Every 60,000 miles	• Repack the rear wheel bearings • Replace the fuel filter • Replace the fuel hose • Clean the condensation chamber, hoses and fixed orifice in the crankcase emission system • Inspect the distributor cap and rotor[1] • Check resistance of the spark plug wires and replace if required • Check the choke opener operation • Check the intake air control system (cold and hot) • Check the ignition timing control[6] • Check the fast idle unloader (cold and hot)[6] • Check purge control unloader solenoid valve • Inspect the EGR system (see notes 4 and 5) • Check the choke coil tension and heater • Check the ignition timing[1] • Check the fast idle • Check the throttle controller diaphragm • Check the throttle controller dashpot • Check the throttle controller control valve • Check the throttle controller speed sensor • Check idle speed and idle mixture[1] • Check idle control system on air conditioned models • Check anti-afterburn valve (see notes 4 and 6) • Inspect purge control/unloader solenoid valve (hot) • Inspect bypass solenoid valve (hot) (see notes 4 and 7) • Check power valve (see notes 4 and 6) • Check air vent cutoff diaphragm • Check 2-way valve • Inspect catalytic converter heat shield[5]

1. Tune-up task.
2. 1980 models only.
3. Replace every 30,000 miles or 24 months, whichever occurs first.
4. 1981 models only.
5. California manual transaxle only.
6. 1980 California automatic transaxle only.
7. Except 1980 California vehicles with automatic transaxle.

Table 3 MAINTENANCE SCHEDULE (1982-ON)

Every 7,500 miles	• Change engine oil and filter • Inspect front brake pads and discs • Check clutch pedal and release arm play • Inspect power steering system and check power steering fluid
Every 15,000 miles	• Check automatic transaxle fluid • Check suspension mounting bolt tightness[1] • Inspect exhaust system[1] • Inspect brake lines and hoses[1] • Adjust valve clearance[1] • Check front wheel alignment

(continued)

Table 3 MAINTENANCE SCHEDULE (1982-ON) (continued)

Every 30,000 miles	• Check manual transaxle oil • Inspect rear brake linings • Inspect parking brake[1] • Inspect steering system and check operation[1] • Change brake fluid • Inspect cooling system hoses and connections • Inspect and adjust alternator belt • Inspect and adjust power steering pump belt • Inspect crankcase emission control system • Replace spark plugs[2] • Replace air cleaner element • Clean and inspect choke linkage
Every 60,000 miles	• Lubricate rear wheel bearings • Inspect fuel lines and connections • Replace fuel filters and engine compartment fuel hoses • Inspect distributor cap and rotor[2] • Inspect ignition wiring[2] • Check ignition timing • Adjust carburetor(s)[3] • Inspect emission control systems[3]

1. First inspection @ 7,500 miles.
2. Described under Tune-up in this chapter.
3. Have done by a Honda dealer or mechanic familiar with Honda emission controls.

Table 4 RECOMMENDED LUBRICANTS AND FLUIDS

Application	Lubricant or fluid
Engine	API service SF, fuel-efficient type
Transaxle	
Manual	SAE 10W-30 or 10W-40 engine oil
Automatic	Dexron ATF
Brake fluid	DOT 3 or DOT 4
Clutch fluid	DOT 3 or DOT 4 brake fluid
Power steering	Honda power steering fluid only
Wheel bearings, steering ball-joints, steering gear box, shift lever ball, brake master cylinder pushrod, battery terminals, parking brake equalizer, hatch side strikers, pedal linkage, shinges, latches, locks	Multipurpose grease

Table 5 ENGINE OIL VISCOSITY

Temperature range*	Viscosity
Below 15° F	SAE 5W-20
Below 30° F	SAE 5W-30
0-90° F	10W-30
Above 0° F	10W-40
Above 15° F	20W-40, 20W-50

* Temperatures anticipated until next oil change.

Table 6 APPROXIMATE REFILL CAPACITIES

1976-1978
Engine oil	3.2 qt.
Manual transaxle	2.8 qt.
Automatic transaxle	2.6 qt.
Cooling system	1.3 gal.

1979-1981
Engine oil	
Without filter change	3.2 qt.
With filter change	3.7 qt.
Manual transaxle	2.5 qt.
Automatic transaxle	2.6 qt.
Cooling system	1.6 gal.

1982
Engine oil	
Without filter change	3.2 qt.
With filter change	3.7 qt.
Manual transaxle	2.5 qt.
Automatic transaxle	2.6 qt.
Cooling system	
Accord	1.3 gal.
Prelude	1.6 gal.

1983-on Accord
Engine oil	
Without filter change	3.2 qt.
With filter change	3.7 qt.
Manual transaxle	2.5 qt.
Automatic transaxle	3.0 qt.
Cooling system	
1983	1.3 gal.
1984	1.8 gal.

1983-on Prelude
Engine oil	
Without filter change	3.2 qt.
With filter change	3.7 qt.
Manual transaxle	2.5 qt.
Automatic transaxle	3.0 qt.
Cooling system	
Manual	1.8 gal.
Automatic	2.0 gal.

Table 7 TUNE-UP SPECIFICATIONS

1976-1977			
Ignition timing (1976)		Idle mixture CO%	0.4%
Manual transaxle	2° BTDC @ 800 rpm	Distributor	
		Point gap	0.45-0.55 mm
			(0.018-0.022 in.)
Automatic transaxle	0° BTDC @ 680 rpm	Dwell angle	52 ±3°
		Spark plug type (1976)	
Ignition timing (1977)		Standard	NGK B-6ES; ND W-20ES
Manual transaxle		Cold type	NGK B-7ES; ND W-22ES
49-state	6° BTDC @ 800 rpm	Spark plug type (1977)	
Calif. & high altitude	2° BTDC @ 800 rpm	Standard	NGK B-6EB; ND W-20ES-L
		Cold type	NGK B-7EB; ND W-22ES-L
		Spark plug gap	0.7-0.8 mm
			(0.028-0.032 in.)
(continued)			

Table 7 TUNE-UP SPECIFICATIONS (continued)

1976-1977 (continued)			
Automatic transaxle		Valve clearance	0.12-0.18 mm
49-state	6° BTDC @ 680 rpm		(0.006-0.007 in.)
Calif. & high altitude	0° BTDC @ 680 rpm		
		Compression	
Idle speed		Minimum	136 psi
Manual transaxle	750-850 rpm	Maximum	192 psi
Automatic transaxle	630-680 rpm	Maximum variation	20 psi

1978			
Ignition timing		Spark plug type	
Manual transaxle		Standard	NGK B-6EB; ND W-20ES-L
49-state	6° BTDC @ 700 rpm	Cold type	NGK B-5EB; ND W-16ES-L
Calif. & high altitude	2° BTDC @ 700 rpm	Hot type	NGK B-7EB; ND W-22ES-L
Automatic transaxle		Spark plug gap	0.7-0.8 mm
49-state	6° BTDC @ 650 rpm		(0.028-0.032 in.)
Calif. & high altitude	2° BTDC @ 650 rpm	Valve clearance	
Idle speed		Intake & auxiliary	0.12-0.18 mm
Manual transaxle	650-750 rpm		(0.006-0.007 in.)
Automatic transaxle	600-700 rpm	Exhaust	0.17-0.23 mm
Idle mixture CO%	0.4%		(0.007-0.009 in.)
Distributor		Compression	
Point gap	0.45-0.55 mm	Minimum	142 psi
	(0.018-0.022 in.)	Maximum	198 psi
Dwell angle	52 ±3°	Maximum variation	20 psi

1979			
Ignition timing		Spark plug type	
Manual transaxle		Standard	NGK B-7EB
49-state	6° BTDC @ 700 rpm	Cold type	NGK B-6EB
Calif. & high altitude	0° BTDC @ 700 rpm	Spark plug gap	0.7-0.8 mm
			(0.028-0.032 in.)
Automatic transaxle		Valve clearance	
49-state	4° BTDC @ 700 rpm	Intake & auxiliary	0.12-0.17 mm
Calif. & high altitude	2° BTDC @ 700 rpm		(0.006-0.007 in.)
		Exhaust	0.25-0.30 mm
			(0.010-0.011 in.)
Idle speed		Compression	
Manual transaxle	650-750 rpm	Normal	156 psi
Automatic transaxle	650-750 rpm	Minimum	128 psi
Idle mixture CO%	0.4%	Maximum variation	20 psi

1980			
Ignition timing (Accord)		All others	
Manual transaxle		Standard	NGK B-7EB
All (except Calif. sedan)	0° TDC @ 800 rpm	Cold type	NGK B-6EB
Calif. sedan	4° ATDC @ 800 rpm	Spark plug gap	0.7-0.8 mm
Automatic transaxle	0° TDC @		(0.028-0.032 in.)
Ignition timing (Prelude)	0° TDC @ 800 rpm		
Idle speed			
Manual transaxle	750-850 rpm	Valve clearance	
Automatic transaxle	750-850 rpm	Intake & auxiliary	0.12-0.17 mm
			(0.006-0.007 in.)

(continued)

Table 7 TUNE-UP SPECIFICATIONS (continued)

1980 (continued)	

Idle mixture CO%	Exhaust	0.25-0.30 mm
Calif. with automatic		(0.010-0.012 in.)
transaxle	0.1%	
All others	0.4%	Compression
Spark plugs		Normal	156 psi
Calif. with automatic transaxle		
Required	NGK B-7EB11	Minimum	128 psi
Spark plug gap	1.0-1.1 mm	Maximum variation	20 psi
	(0.039-0.043 in.)	

1981	

Ignition timing	0° TDC @ 800 rpm	Valve clearance
Idle speed	800 rpm	Intake & auxiliary	0.12-0.17 mm
Idle mixture CO%	See dealer		(0.006-0.007 in.)
Spark plugs		
Standard	NGK B-6EB-11;	Exhaust	0.25-0.30 mm
	ND W21 ES-L11		(0.010-0.012 in.)
Cold type	NGK B-7EB-11;	Compression
	ND W22ES-L11	Normal	156 psi
Spark plug gap	1.0-1.1 mm	Minimum	128 psi
	(0.039-0.043 in.)	Maximum variation	20 psi

1982	

Ignition timing	
California 5-speed	12° BTDC @ 750 rpm
49-state, high altitude	16° BTDC @ 750 rpm
3-speed (automatic)	16° BTDC @ 700 rpm
Idle speed	
Manual	750 ±50 rpm
Automatic	700 ±50 rpm (in gear)
Idle mixture CO%	See dealer
Spark plug type	NGK BR6EB-L-11; ND W21ESR-L11
Spark plug gap	1.0-1.1 mm (0.039-0.043 in.)
Valve clearance	
Intake and auxiliary	0.12-0.17 mm (0.005-0.007 in.)
Exhaust (Accord)	0.17-0.22 mm (0.007-0.008 in.)
Exhaust (Prelude)	0.25-0.30 mm (0.010-0.012 in.)
Compression	
Normal	185 psi
Minimum	156 psi
Maximum variation	28 psi

1983 Accord	

Ignition timing	
California 5-speed	12° BTDC @ 750 rpm
49-state, high altitude	16° BTDC @ 750 rpm
4-speed (automatic)	16° BTDC @ 700 rpm
Idle speed	
Manual	750 ±50 rpm
Automatic	700 ±50 rpm (in gear)
Idle mixture CO%	See dealer
Spark plug type	NGK BR6EB-L-11; ND W21ESR-L11
Spark plug gap	1.0-1.1 mm (0.039-0.043 in.)

(continued)

Table 7 TUNE-UP SPECIFICATIONS (continued)

1983 Accord (continued)

Valve clearance	
Intake and auxiliary	0.12-0.17 mm (0.005-0.007 in.)
Exhaust	0.17-0.22 mm (0.007-0.008 in.)
Compression	
Normal	185 psi
Minimum	156 psi
Maximum variation	28 psi

1983 Prelude

Ignition timing	
California, high altitude	12° BTDC @ 800 rpm
49-state manual	10° BTDC @ 800 rpm
Automatic	12° BTDC @ 750 rpm
Idle speed	
Manual	800 ±50 rpm
Automatic	750 ±50 rpm (in gear)
Idle mixture CO%	See dealer
Spark plug type	NGK BUR6EB-11; ND W20EKR-S11
Spark plug gap	1.0-1.1 mm (0.039-0.043 in.)
Valve clearance	
Intake and auxiliary	0.12-0.17 mm (0.005-0.007 in.)
Exhaust	0.25-0.30 mm (0.010-0.012 in.)
Compression	
Normal	192 psi
Minimum	163 psi
Maximum variation	28 psi

1984 Accord

Ignition timing	
California, high altitude	18° BTDC @ 750 rpm
49-state manual	22° BTDC @ 750 rpm
Automatic	18° BTDC @ 700 rpm
Idle speed	
Manual	750 ±50 rpm
Automatic	700 ±50 rpm (in gear)
Idle mixture CO%	See dealer
Spark plug type	NGK BUR6EB-11; ND W20EKR-S11
Spark plug gap	1.0-1.1 mm (0.039-0.043 in.)
Valve clearance	
Intake and auxiliary	0.12-0.17 mm (0.005-0.007 in.)
Exhaust	0.25-0.30 mm (0.010-0.012 in.)
Compression	
Normal	184 psi
Minimum	156 psi
Maximum variation	28 psi

(continued)

3

Table 7 TUNE-UP SPECIFICATIONS (continued)

1984 Prelude	
Ignition timing	
California	20° BTDC @ 800 rpm
49-state manual	20° BTDC @ 800 rpm
Automatic	12° BTDC @ 800 rpm
Idle speed	800 ±50 rpm
Idle mixture CO%	See dealer
Spark plug type	NGK BPR6EY-11; ND W20EXR-U11
Spark plug gap	1.0-1.1 mm (0.039-0.043 in.)
Valve clearance	
Intake	0.12-0.17 mm (0.005-0.007 in.)
Exhaust	0.25-0.30 mm (0.010-0.012 in.)
Compression	
Normal	185 psi
Minimum	156 psi
Maximum variation	28 psi

Table 8 IGNITION TIMING MARKS

	Timing mark color	
Year	Manual	Automatic
1976-1978		
1978 49-state	Yellow	Red
All others	Red	Red
1979		
49-state	Yellow	Blue
Calif. & high alt.	White	Black
1980-1981		
1980 Calif. Accord sedan, automatic transaxle		Red
All others	White	White

Table 9 FINAL IDLE SPEED (1976-1979)

	Idle speed[1]	
Model*	Best idle (rpm)	Final idle (rpm)
1976		
Manual	880	800
Automatic	730	680
1977		
High altitude		
Manual	920[2]	800
Automatic	760[3]	680
49-state		
Manual	850	800
Automatic	720	680
California		
Manual	850	800
Automatic	710	680

(continued)

Table 9 FINAL IDLE SPEED (1976-1979) (continued)

Model*	Idle speed[1]	
	Best idle (rpm)	Final idle (rpm)
1978		
High altitude		
Manual	810[4]	700
Automatic	730[3]	650
49-state		
Manual	790	700
Automatic	710	650
California		
Manual	810	700
Automatic	730	650
1979 Accord		
High altitude		
Manual	770[5]	700
Automatic	750[6]	700
49-state		
Manual	780	700
Automatic	750	700
California		
Manual	770	700
Automatic	750	700

1. With headlights on. Also turn on either high-speed heater fan or cooling fan (but not both) on 1978 and later models. Automatic transaxle in gear (block drive wheels).
2. 970 rpm at sea level.
3. 780 rpm at sea level.
4. 910 rpm at sea level.
5. 880 rpm at sea level.
6. 810 rpm at sea level.

Table 10 BELT DEFLECTION SPECIFICATIONS

Belt	mm	in.
Accord		
1976-1981		
Alternator	12-17	0.5-0.7
Power steering pump		
New belt	10-12	7/16
Used belt	12-14	9/16
1982-1983		
Alternator	14-17	0.6-0.7
Power steering pump	18-22	3/4-7/8
Air conditioning compressor	12-16	0.47-0.63
1984		
Alternator	6-9	0.2-0.4
Power steering pump	18-22	3/4-7/8
Air conditioning compressor	10-12	3/8-1/2
Prelude		
1979-1982		
Alternator	12-17	0.5-0.7
Power steering pump	18-22	3/4-7/8
Air conditioning compressor	8-10	5/16-3/8
1983-on		
Alternator (1983)	14-17	0.6-0.7
Alternator (1984)		
New belt	5-7	0.2-0.3
Used belt	7-10	0.3-0.4
Power steering pump	18-22	3/4-7/8
Air conditioning compressor	10-12	3/8-1/2

3

CHAPTER FOUR

CVCC ENGINE

The 1976-1983 Accord and 1979-1982 Prelude are powered by a single overhead cam engine that has an extra intake valve for each cylinder to provide stratified charge combustion. This design is referred to as the CVCC engine. The initials stand for compound vortex controlled combustion.

In the CVCC design, 2 chambers are used—a main combustion chamber and an auxiliary chamber. The chambers are connected by an opening. The main combustion chamber has one intake and one exhaust valve. The auxiliary chamber has only one intake valve. A single overhead camshaft operates all valves. Except for the auxiliary valve, valve train and cylinder head design, the CVCC engine is similar to other 4-cylinder, inline, single overhead cam engines.

The engine is transversely mounted and uses a cast aluminum cylinder head. The cylinder block is cast iron. The camshaft is driven by the crankshaft through a toothed belt. Helical gears on the camshaft drive the distributor and the sump-mounted oil pump. The crankshaft is supported by 5 main bearings.

Engine displacement is 1600 cc (1976-1978) or 1751 cc (1979 and later). Engine specifications are listed in **Table 1** (1976-1978) and **Table 2** (1979-on). Tightening torques are listed in **Table 3**. **Tables 1-5** are at the end of the chapter.

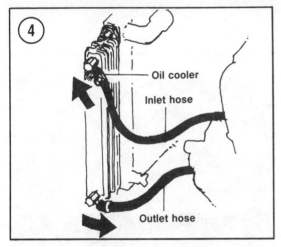

Oil cooler

Inlet hose

Outlet hose

ENGINE REMOVAL

NOTE
Before disconnecting and/or removing wires, hoses and tubes, be sure to identify each connection with either tape or small cardboard tags. Tag each side of a connection with identical numbers. Use a permanent-type marker as the tag may be subjected to oil, grease, etc.

1. Remove the headlight trim and grille to provide access to the hood bolts (**Figure 1**). Remove the hood bolts and lift the hood off. Place the hood in a protected area.

2A. *Accord:* Disconnect the negative cable from the battery. See **Figure 2**.

2B. *Prelude:* Disconnect the negative cable from the battery. Then disconnect the positive battery cable and remove the battery, battery tray and mount.

WARNING
Before removing the radiator cap (next step), make sure the engine is cold to avoid scalding by the coolant or steam.

3. Remove the radiator cap (**Figure 3**), open the drain valve at the radiator and drain the coolant into a suitable container. If the coolant is to be reused, make sure the container is clean.

4. On 1979 and later models, disconnect the upper and lower oil cooler hoses at the radiator and allow oil to drain from hoses. Then cap end of hoses to prevent contamination and position hoses back and out of way. See **Figure 4**.

5. Remove the air cleaner assembly as described in Chapter Six.

6. Identify and disconnect the ignition primary and secondary wires at the distributor (**Figure 5**).

7. Disconnect the engine ground wire at the transaxle and also the starter wires. See **Figure 6**.

8. Remove the engine ground wire (**Figure 7**) and disconnect the alternator harness (**Figure 8**).

9. Disconnect the vacuum line from the brake booster (**Figure 9**). Cap end of hose.

10. Remove the carburetor as described in Chapter Six.

11. On vehicles equipped with automatic transaxle, disconnect the fluid cooler hoses from the transaxle (**Figure 10**). Plug hoses and fittings and position hoses back and out of way.

12. Remove the radiator and heater hoses at the engine (**Figure 11**).

13. Identify and disconnect the vacuum lines from the emission control box. Remove the control box attaching screws and remove the box. **Figure 12** shows a typical emission control box. The 1981 California models use 3 emission control boxes.

14. On high-altitude models, label and disconnect the tubes from the air jet controller unit. **Figure 13** shows the 1981 unit. The 1982 unit is similar.

15. On 1976-1981 models with manual transaxle, remove the clutch spring and 2 attaching bolts (**Figure 14**). Remove the clutch slave cylinder with the hydraulic line still attached. Place the cylinder out of the way.

NOTE
Step 16A and Step 16B describe removal of the speedometer cable or speedometer sensor assembly.

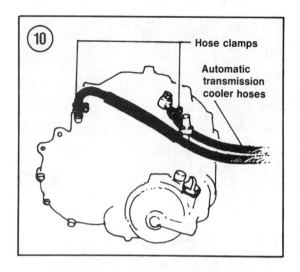

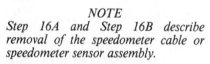

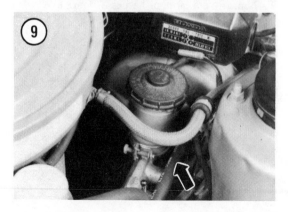

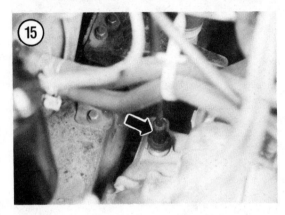

16A. *Non-power steering models:* Pull up the speedometer cable rubber boot (**Figure 15**) to provide access to the cable clip attachment. Then remove the clip (7, **Figure 16**) and pull the speedometer cable from the gear fitting on the transaxle.

CAUTION
Do not remove the speedometer gear holder or the speedometer gear may fall into the transaxle housing. **Figure 17** *and* **Figure 18** *show different methods of attaching the speedometer gear holder assembly to the transaxle housing.*

16B. *Power steering models:* Remove the speed sensor securing bolt, then remove the sensor by pulling it upward along with the hose and speedometer cable. Set the speed sensor assembly

4

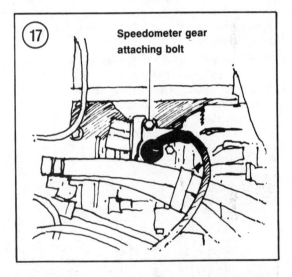

Speedometer gear attaching bolt

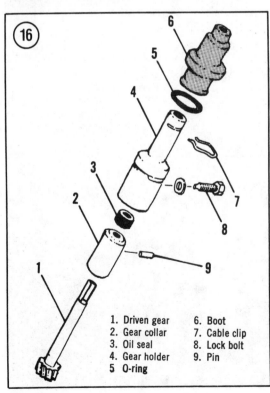

1. Driven gear
2. Gear collar
3. Oil seal
4. Gear holder
5 O-ring
6. Boot
7. Cable clip
8. Lock bolt
9. Pin

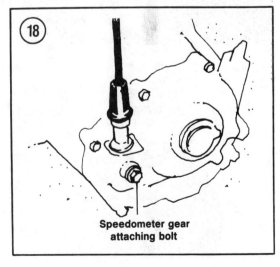

Speedometer gear attaching bolt

aside. See **Figure 19** (manual transaxle) or **Figure 20** (automatic transaxle).

> *NOTE*
> *Do not remove the hose or attaching bolts from the speed sensor or power steering fluid will spill out.*

17. *Power steering models:* Remove the upper and lower power steering pump attaching/adjusting bolts (**Figure 21**). Then remove the power steering pump without detaching any hoses. Set the power steering pump aside.

18. Remove the anti-afterburn valve on 1981-1982 models.

19. *Air-conditioned vehicles:* Remove the alternator and bracket. Disconnect the idle control solenoid. On 1982 models, remove the compressor and bracket and tie them back out of the way.

> *WARNING*
> *Do not disconnect any air conditioning hoses unless the system has been discharged.*

20. Securely block both rear wheels so the car will not roll in either direction. Jack up the front end of the car and place it on jackstands. Remove the front wheels.

21. Drain the engine oil (**Figure 22**). If equipped with a manual transaxle, drain the oil (**Figure 23**).

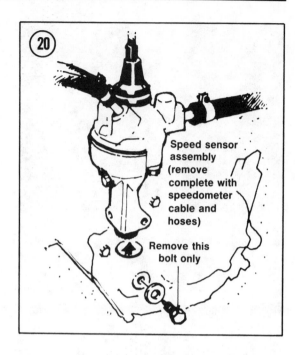

Speed sensor assembly (remove complete with speedometer cable and hoses)

Remove this bolt only

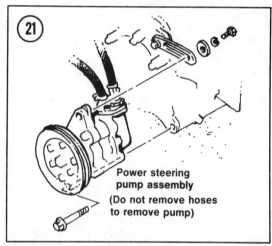

Power steering pump assembly (Do not remove hoses to remove pump)

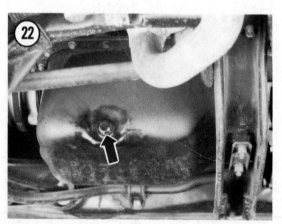

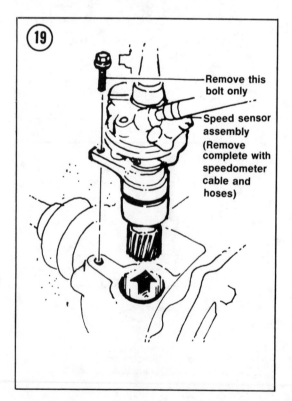

Remove this bolt only

Speed sensor assembly (Remove complete with speedometer cable and hoses)

If equipped with an automatic transaxle, drain the fluid (**Figure 24**).

22. Attach an engine lifting sling to the engine at the points shown in **Figure 25**. Using a suitable lifting device, remove all slack and place slight tension on the lifting sling. Make sure the tension on both legs of the sling is approximately equal. Adjust the sling, if required.

23. Remove the cotter pin and locknut from the tie rod ball-joint (**Figure 26**) and the lower arm ball-joint (**Figure 27**). Then, using Honda tool part No. 07941-6710000, separate the joints as shown in **Figure 28**.

24A. *1976-1978 models:* Pry the circlips from the grooves in the inboard ends of the drive axles. Then pull the shafts from the transaxle.

24B. *1979 and later models:* Using a screwdriver between the drive axle housing and the transaxle housing (**Figure 29**), pry the inboard drive axle joints out of the transaxle about 1/2 in., then pull the shafts from the transaxle.

25. Remove the center beam attaching bolts (**Figure 30**) and remove the center beam.

26. On 1976-1978 models, use a pin punch to drive out the retaining pin and remove the shift rod positioner (**Figure 31**). On 1979 and later

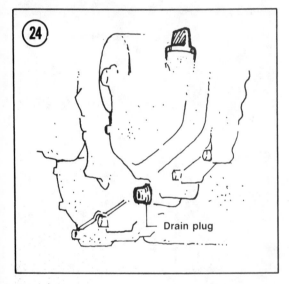

Drain plug

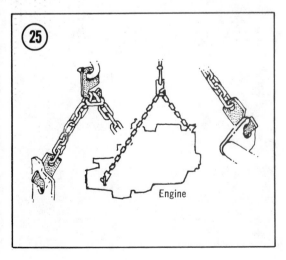

Engine

models, remove the shift rod yoke attaching bolt as shown in **Figure 32**.

27. Disconnect the shift rod positioner at the transaxle. See **Figure 33**.

28. On 1980 Accord and all Prelude models equipped with automatic transaxle, remove the center console as shown in **Figure 34**. Then remove the shift cable adjuster pin and separate the shift cable from the adjuster. Remove the shift cable mounting bolts and remove the shift cable holder. See **Figure 35**. After loosening the cable inside the car, remove the shift cable holder bolts from underneath the car (**Figure 36**) and remove the cable together with the cable holder.

29. On 1976-1980 models equipped with automatic transaxle, remove the splash guard (**Figure 37**) and the control cable (**Figure 38**).

30. On 1980 and later models with automatic transaxle, loosen locknut A, **Figure 39**, and remove the throttle control cable from the throttle lever and bracket. Do not loosen locknut B in **Figure 39** as this will change the transaxle shift points.

31. Remove the attaching nuts and bolts and remove the exhaust pipe as shown in **Figure 40**.

32. Remove the 3 engine support bolts shown in **Figure 41**. Then push the left engine support into

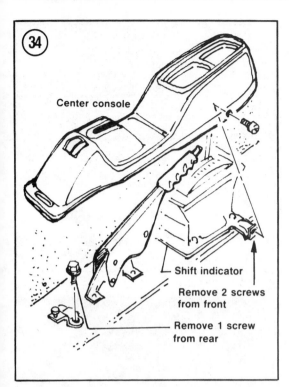

34

Center console

Shift indicator

Remove 2 screws
from front

Remove 1 screw
from rear

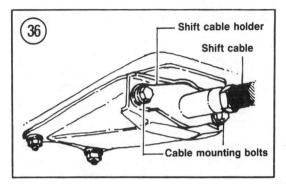

36

Shift cable holder

Shift cable

Cable mounting bolts

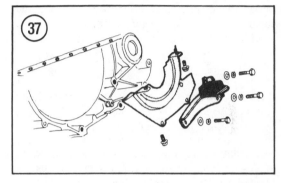

37

4

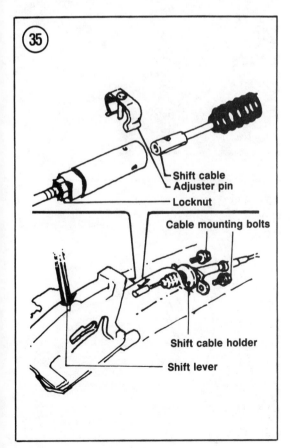

35

Shift cable
Adjuster pin

Locknut

Cable mounting bolts

Shift cable holder

Shift lever

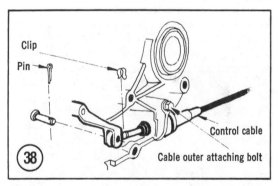

Clip

Pin

38

Control cable

Cable outer attaching bolt

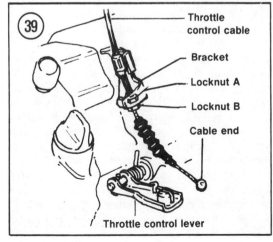

39

Throttle
control cable

Bracket

Locknut A

Locknut B

Cable end

Throttle control lever

the left shock absorber bracket as shown in **Figure 42**.

> *CAUTION*
> *At this point, there should not be any wires, hoses, tubes or linkages attaching the engine and transaxle to the car. Recheck this to be sure nothing can hamper engine removal.*

33. Raise the engine slightly to remove the weight from the engine mounts. Then remove the front and rear engine mounts. See **Figure 43**.

34. Slowly raise the engine with the hoist and remove it from the car (**Figure 25**). Place the engine on a suitable stand or workbench.

> *CAUTION*
> *Coat all finished and precision metal surfaces with grease and cover them with plastic bags.*

ENGINE INSTALLATION

Installation is the reverse of the removal procedure (Steps 1-34). In addition to retracing the removal steps, carefully study the following installation/adjustment procedures.

1. When installing the drive axles, push them as far as they will go into the transaxle to make sure the spring clips or circlips click into place in the differential gear grooves. See **Figure 44**. Otherwise, the drive axles could work loose while the car is being driven.

2A. On 1976-1979 models with automatic transaxle, insert the retaining pin from the torque converter side when installing the transaxle control cable. Secure the pin with a clip. See **Figure 38**.

2B. On 1980 and later models with automatic transaxle, adjust the shift cable as described in Chapter Nine.

3. On 1976-1978 models, when installing the shift rod, use a new spring pin and slide the cover over the pin after installation as shown in **Figure 45**.

4. On 1979 and later models, replace the exhaust flange gasket before installing the exhaust pipe.

5. Take care not to interchange inlet and outlet hoses when reconnecting heater and radiator hoses.

6. When refilling the radiator, open the air bleed bolt (**Figure 46**) and open the heater valve to make sure all air is bled from the system. Be sure to retighten the bolt after the system is bled.

7. Make sure all wires are reconnected to their proper places. Make sure that wires and hoses are not pinched and do not interfere with other parts.

8. Use new washers when installing the engine and transaxle drain plugs.

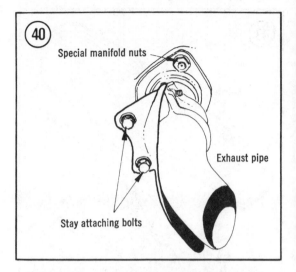

Special manifold nuts

Exhaust pipe

Stay attaching bolts

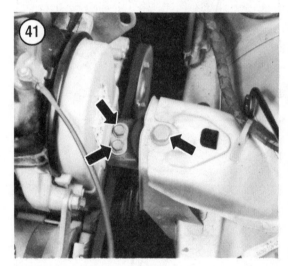

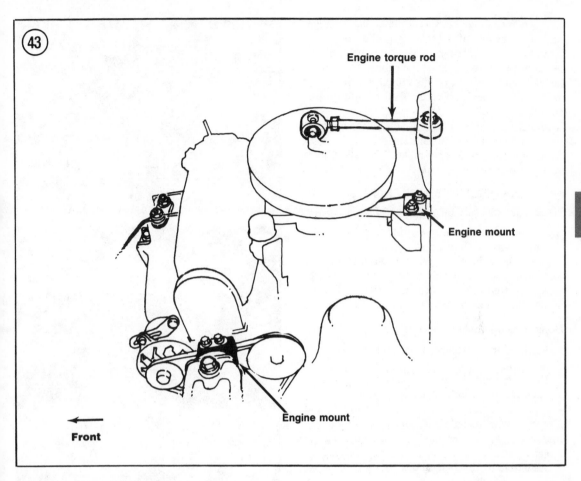

Engine torque rod

Engine mount

Engine mount

Front

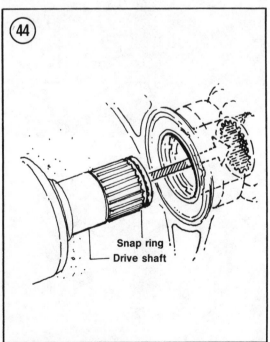

Snap ring
Drive shaft

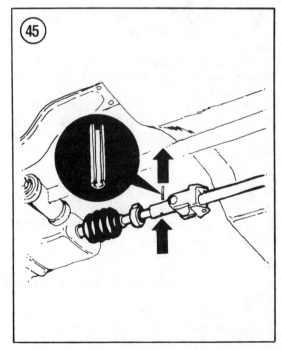

9. When installing the speedometer cable, align the tab on the end of the cable with the slot in the fixture. After installation, make sure the cable is secure by pulling on it. Slide the rubber boot down the cable and secure it on the clutch housing.

10. Install a new oil filter before filling the crankcase.

11. Refer to Chapter Three and check the ignition timing and carburetor adjustment.

12. If equipped with a manual transaxle, check clutch adjustment as described in Chapter Nine.

DISASSEMBLY CHECKLISTS

The following checklists tell how much of the engine to remove and disassemble to do a specific type of service, such as a valve job.

To use these checklists, remove and inspect each part mentioned. Then go through the checklists backwards to install the parts. Each part is covered in detail in this chapter, unless otherwise noted.

Decarbonizing or Valve Service

1. Remove the exhaust and intake manifolds (Chapter Six).

2. Remove the rocker arms and camshaft.

3. Remove the cylinder head.

4. Have a professional mechanic remove and inspect valves (including auxiliary intake valves). Inspect valve guides and seats, repairing or replacing as necessary.

5. Assemble by reversing Steps 1-4.

Valve and Ring Service

1. Perform Steps 1-4 of *Decarbonizing or Valve Service*.

2. Remove the oil pan and oil pump.

3. Remove the pistons together with the connecting rods.

4. Remove the piston rings. It is not necessary to separate the pistons from the connecting rods unless a piston, connecting rod or piston pin needs repair or replacement.

5. Assemble by reversing Steps 1-4.

General Overhaul

1. Remove the engine from the car.

2. Remove the alternator and distributor (Chapter Eight).

3. Remove the fuel pump, carburetor and manifolds.

4. Remove the water pump and thermostat (Chapter Seven).

5. Remove the rocker arms and camshaft.

6. Remove the front covers and timing belt.

7. Remove the cylinder head.

8. Remove the flywheel or torque converter drive plate.
9. Remove the oil pan and oil pump.
10. Remove the piston/connecting rod assemblies.
11. Remove the crankshaft.
12. Inspect the cylinder block.
13. Assembly is the reverse of these steps.

CAMSHAFT AND ROCKER ARMS

Rocker Arm/Camshaft Removal

1. Remove the valve cover.
2. Unscrew the bolts from the upper front cover and remove it. See **Figure 47**.
3. Rotate the crankshaft with a wrench on the crankshaft pulley bolt and bring No. 1 piston to TDC on the compression stroke (both valves closed).

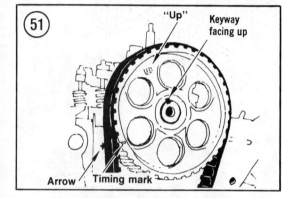

NOTE
*If the engine is installed in the car during this procedure, the crankshaft bolt can be turned with a ratchet, extension and socket through the access hole in the left wheel well. See **Figure 48**.*

CAUTION
During the next step, do not twist or bend the timing belt. Do not use sharp instruments to remove it. Do not let grease or oil touch the belt.

4. Loosen (do not remove) the timing belt pivot bolt and lockbolt (**Figure 49**). Then slip the timing belt off the pulley as shown in **Figure 50**.
5. Align the camshaft pulley timing mark with the arrow on the cylinder head as shown in **Figure 51**.
6. Remove the camshaft pulley retaining bolt and washer. Then remove the camshaft pulley (**Figure 52**).

7. Attach a dial indicator with a plunger touching the end of the camshaft as shown in **Figure 53**. Then using a screwdriver (**Figure 53**), pry the camshaft forward and rearward and measure camshaft end play. Compare with **Table 1** or **Table 2**. If end play exceeds specifications, remove the rocker arms and camshaft. Then refer to *Camshaft Inspection*.
8. Loosen the camshaft and rocker shaft holder bolts in the pattern shown in **Figure 54**. When all bolts are loose, take them out and remove the rocker arms and holders as an assembly.
9. Remove the camshaft from the head. See **Figure 55**.

4

Rocker Arm Disassembly

Refer to **Figure 56** for this procedure.

1. Lay the rocker assembly on a workbench. See **Figure 57**.

2. Pull the pin from the right end of the camshaft holder. See **Figure 58**.

3. Disassemble the rocker arm assembly. Be sure to keep all parts in order so they can be reassembled in their original positions. See **Figure 56**.

Rocker Arm Inspection

1. Measure rocker shaft outside diameter at each rocker arm location. See **Figure 59**. Write the measurements down.

2. Measure the inside diameter of each rocker arm with a bore gauge and micrometer (**Figure 60** and **Figure 61**).

3. Calculate the difference between rocker shaft outside diameter and rocker arm inside diameter to determine rocker arm clearance.

4. If rocker arm-to-shaft clearance is not within specifications (end of chapter), replace the rocker arm or shaft, whichever is worn.

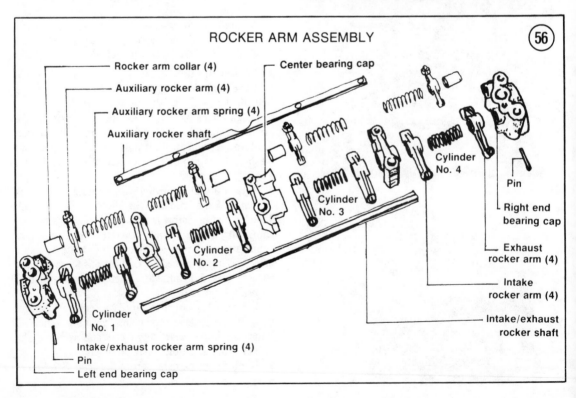

ROCKER ARM ASSEMBLY

Rocker arm collar (4)

Auxiliary rocker arm (4)

Auxiliary rocker arm spring (4)

Auxiliary rocker shaft

Center bearing cap

Cylinder No. 4

Cylinder No. 3

Cylinder No. 2

Cylinder No. 1

Intake/exhaust rocker arm spring (4)

Pin

Left end bearing cap

Pin

Right end bearing cap

Exhaust rocker arm (4)

Intake rocker arm (4)

Intake/exhaust rocker shaft

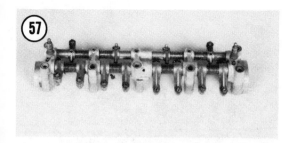

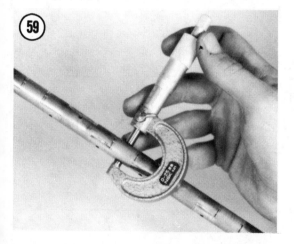

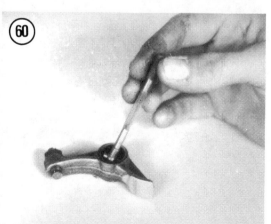

Camshaft Inspection

1. If camshaft end play exceeds specifications, inspect the right-end bearing cap and camshaft thrust areas indicated in **Figure 62**. If the right-end bearing cap is worn in the thrust area, replace it with a new one and recheck camshaft end play during assembly.

2. Place the camshaft in position on the cylinder head. See **Figure 55**.

3. Cut a piece of Plastigage the width of each camshaft journal. Place a piece of Plastigage on each camshaft journal as shown in **Figure 63**, then install the rocker assembly.

NOTE
Do not rotate the camshaft while the Plastigage is in place.

4. Tighten the rocker arm assembly to the specifications in **Figure 64**.

5. Remove the rocker arm assembly. Bearing clearance is determined by comparing the width of the flattened Plastigage to the markings on the envelope (**Figure 65**). If the clearance of any bearing exceeds specifications at the end of the chapter, measure camshaft journal diameter as shown in **Figure 66**:

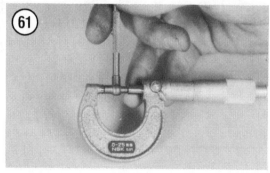

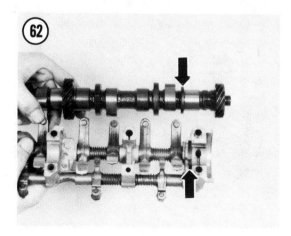

a. If camshaft journal diameter is not within specifications, replace the camshaft.

b. If camshaft journal diameter is within specifications, replace the cylinder head.

6. Measure camshaft bend. Rotate the camshaft between accurate centers (V-blocks or a lathe) with a dial indicator contacting the center journal. See **Figure 67**. Actual bend is half the reading shown on the gauge when the camshaft is rotated one full turn. Replace the camshaft if bend exceeds specifications at the end of the chapter.

Rocker Arm/Camshaft Installation

1. Coat the camshaft journals and bearing surfaces with clean engine oil. Turn the camshaft in the bearings until the key groove is facing upward (indicating No. 1 cylinder is at TDC).

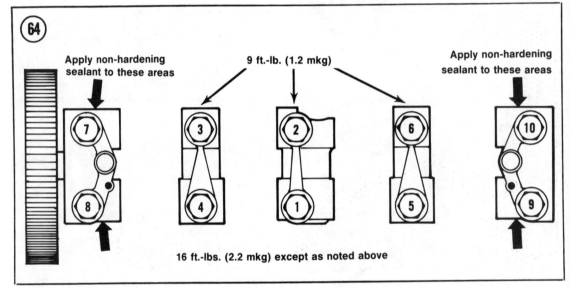

Apply non-hardening sealant to these areas

9 ft.-lb. (1.2 mkg)

Apply non-hardening sealant to these areas

16 ft.-lbs. (2.2 mkg) except as noted above

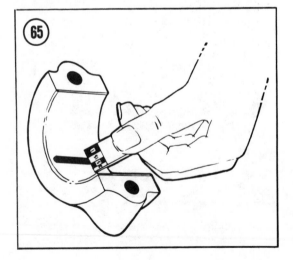

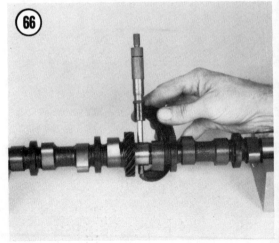

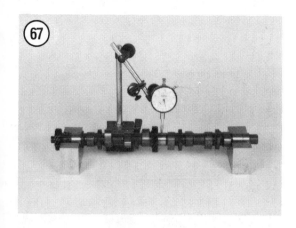

2. Assemble the rocker arm assembly, making sure all parts are installed in their original order. Line up the notches in the rocker shafts with their respective bolt holes. When the bolts are installed, the rocker shafts are locked in place so there is an adequate flow of lubricating oil through the system.

3. Install a new pin into the right-end bearing cap (**Figure 58**). Then check the movement of the rocker arms to make sure there is no binding or stiffness.

4. Loosen each valve locknut and back off each valve adjusting screw.

5. Coat the left-end and right-end bearing caps with silicone rubber sealant. See **Figure 64**.

6. Set the rocker assembly into place on the cylinder head. Install the bolts finger-tight.

NOTE
After tightening rocker arm bolts finger-tight, make sure each valve aligns with its rocker arm. In addition, make sure none of the rocker arms is binding on its valve. If so, the valve adjustment screw must be backed out further.

7. Tighten the rocker assembly bolts in the sequence shown in **Figure 64**. Tighten bolts to specifications in **Figure 64**.

8. Coat the inside of a new camshaft seal with engine oil. Then install the seal into the left-end bearing cap with a suitable drift (**Figure 68**). Make sure when installing that the spring faces in. See **Figure 69**.

9. Set the Woodruff key in the camshaft (**Figure 70**). Line up the keyway in the camshaft sprocket with the key and push the pulley onto the shaft

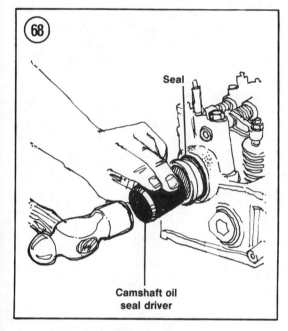

Seal

Camshaft oil
seal driver

(**Figure 71**). Install the washer and bolt on the end of the shaft and tighten the bolt to specifications at the end of the chapter.

10. Line up the marks on sprocket and head, with the keyway facing up. See **Figure 72**.

11. Turn the crankshaft bolt counterclockwise with a 17 mm wrench and align the flywheel TDC mark with the crankcase pointer. **Figure 73** shows typical timing marks.

> *NOTE*
> *If the engine is in the car during this procedure, the crankshaft bolt can be turned with a ratchet, extension and socket through the access hole in the left wheel well.*

12. Install the timing belt on the top pulley without changing the position of the pulley (**Figure 74**). Do not twist the belt any more than necessary.

13. Adjust the valves as described in Chapter Three.

> *NOTE*
> *Step 14 describes timing belt tension adjustment.*

14. Loosen the cam tensioner pivot and adjustment bolts (**Figure 75**). Pivot bolt is top bolt in **Figure 75**. Rotate the crankshaft counterclockwise 90° (1/4 turn). This puts tension adjustment on the timing belt. Tighten the adjustment bolt to specifications (end of chapter). Then tighten the pivot bolt to specifications.

15. Install the upper front cover (**Figure 76**).

16. Install the valve cover.

17. Run the engine and check for leaks.

FRONT COVER, TIMING BELT AND TENSIONER

Figure 77 shows the front cover/camshaft drive assembly. Refer to it as needed for the following procedures.

Front Cover Removal/Installation

Two covers (upper and lower) are used to protect the cam drive mechanism. See **Figure 78**.

1. Remove the front left-hand side engine mount. See **Figure 79**.

2. Remove the drive belts as described in Chapter Three.

3. Remove the attaching bolts and remove the water pump pulley (**Figure 80**).

4. Remove the crankshaft pulley bolt plug from the left wheel well. See **Figure 48**. Then, using a socket with ratchet and extension, turn the crankshaft counterclockwise to align the flywheel timing marks as shown in **Figure 73**.

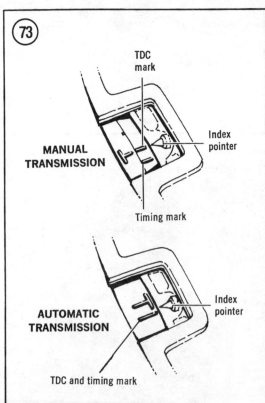

MANUAL TRANSMISSION — TDC mark, Index pointer, Timing mark

AUTOMATIC TRANSMISSION — Index pointer, TDC and timing mark

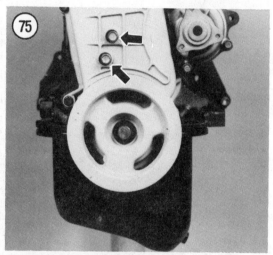

5. Remove the crankshaft bolt and slide the pulley off the end of the crankshaft.

6. Loosen the attaching bolts and remove the upper cover (**Figure 77**).

7. Slide the rubber washers from behind the timing belt pivot bolt and adjusting bolt (**Figure 77**). Then remove the lower cover bolts and remove the lower cover.

8. Installation is the reverse of these steps. After installing the front cover, install the rubber washers behind the timing belt pivot and adjusting bolts (**Figure 77**).

9. Adjust the drive belts as described in Chapter Three.

Timing Belt Replacement

The timing belt is made of fiberglass and should be handled with care. When removing the belt, do not use sharp objects to pry the belt off the sprockets and do not bend or twist the belt. Do not let oil or grease touch the belt.

1. Remove the upper and lower front covers as described in this chapter.

2. Remove the crankshaft pulley bolt plug from the left wheel well. See **Figure 48**. Then using a socket with a ratchet and extension, turn the crankshaft counterclockwise to align the flywheel timing marks as shown in **Figure 73**.

3. Draw an arrow on the timing belt with chalk, pointing in the direction of rotation.

4. Slide the timing belt off the camshaft pulley and remove the belt from the engine. See **Figure 77**. Do not nick the belt during removal.

5. Inspect the timing belt for cracks, excessive wear marks and oil stains. Replace the belt if any of these problems is found.

6. Check the flywheel timing marks to make sure they are aligned with the index pointer at the TDC position shown in **Figure 73**. Then position the camshaft sprocket so the word "UP" on the pulley is facing upward and the timing mark on the sprocket is aligned with the arrow on the cylinder head. See **Figure 72**.

7. Position the timing belt on the crankshaft sprocket and then slide the belt onto the camshaft sprocket.

8. Install the upper and lower front covers as described in this chapter.

9. Loosen the cam tensioner pivot and adjustment bolts (**Figure 75**). Pivot bolt is top bolt in **Figure 75**. Rotate the crankshaft counterclockwise 90° (1/4 turn). This puts tension on the timing belt. Tighten the adjustment bolt to specifications at the end of the chapter. Then tighten the pivot bolt to the same torque.

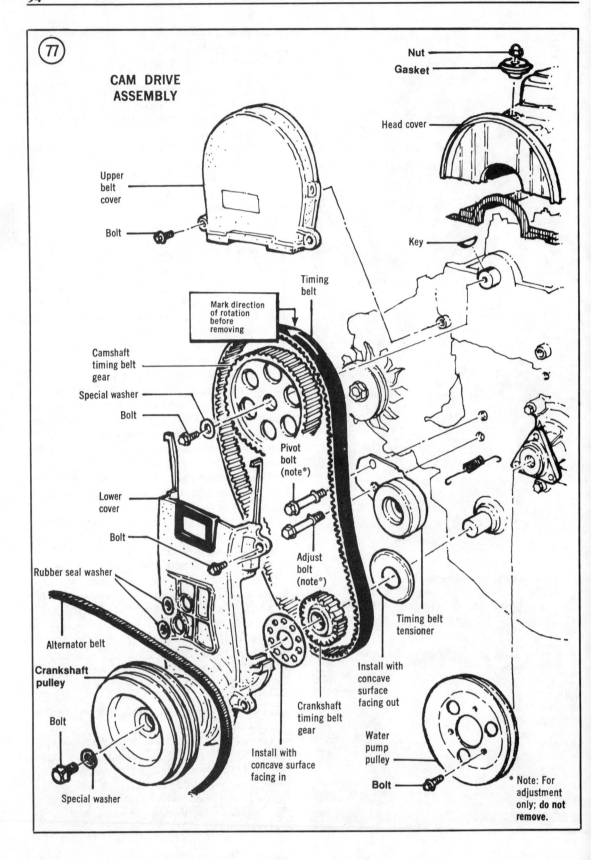

(77)

CAM DRIVE
ASSEMBLY

Nut
Gasket

Head cover

Upper belt cover

Bolt

Key

Timing belt

Mark direction of rotation before removing

Camshaft timing belt gear

Special washer

Bolt

Pivot bolt (note*)

Lower cover

Bolt

Adjust bolt (note*)

Rubber seal washer

Timing belt tensioner

Alternator belt

Install with concave surface facing out

Crankshaft pulley

Bolt

Crankshaft timing belt gear

Water pump pulley

Install with concave surface facing in

Special washer

Bolt

* Note: For adjustment only; do **not** remove.

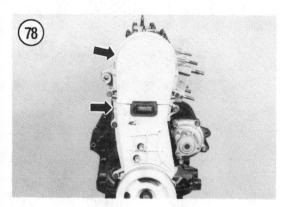

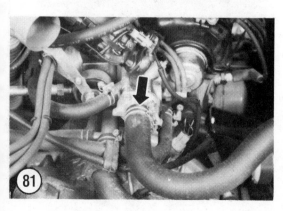

Lower Front Cover
Oil Seal Replacement

1. Remove the lower front cover.
2. Carefully pry out the old oil seal. Do not gouge the cover.
3. Tap in a new oil seal. Coat the seal lip with multipurpose grease.
4. Install the lower front cover.

CYLINDER HEAD

Removal

To prevent warping, the cylinder head should be removed only when engine temperature is below 100° F.

1. Disconnect the negative cable from the battery.
2. Drain the radiator and disconnect the top hose from the thermostat cover (**Figure 81**).
3. Remove the spark plugs as described in Chapter Three.
4. Refer to Chapter Six and perform the following:
   a. Remove the air cleaner.
   b. Disconnect the fuel line, choke cable (if so equipped) and throttle cable at the carburetor.

5A. *Cars without air conditioning:* Loosen the alternator bracket bolts. Then remove the upper alternator bracket-to-cylinder head bolt (top arrow, **Figure 82**).

5B. *Cars with air conditioning:* Remove the upper alternator bracket and alternator. See Chapter Eight.

6. Remove the distributor as described in Chapter Eight.
7. Unscrew the nuts from the exhaust pipe flange at the bottom of the manifold.

8. Remove the bolts from the engine torque rod and remove it. See **Figure 83**.

9. Label and disconnect or remove any emission control devices or hoses which will interfere with cylinder head removal.

10. Remove the valve cover.

11. Remove the upper front cover (**Figure 77**).

12. Turn the crankshaft with a wrench on the crankshaft pulley bolt to bring No. 1 piston to top dead center on its compression stroke. When this occurs, both rocker arms for No. 1 cylinder (**Figure 84**) will be loose. If the rocker arms are tight, No. 4 cylinder is at TDC compression. Turn the crankshaft another full turn and recheck to make sure the No. 1 rocker arms are loose.

13. Loosen the timing belt pivot and adjusting bolts (**Figure 77**). Then slip the timing belt off the pulley (**Figure 75**).

CAUTION
Do not bend or twist the belt or use sharp instruments when removing it. Do not let oil or grease touch the belt.

14. Remove the bolts fom the oil pump gear housing (**Figure 85**), then remove the housing, gear (**Figure 86**) and shaft.

15. Remove the cylinder head bolts in the pattern shown in **Figure 87**. Remove the cylinder head with the intake and exhaust manifolds attached. Cover the top of the block with a clean shop cloth.

16. Remove the intake and exhaust manifolds as described in Chapter Six.

Inspection

1. Check the cylinder head for coolant leaks before cleaning.

2. Clean the cylinder head thoroughly with solvent. While cleaning, check for cracks or other visible damage. Look for corrosion or foreign material in oil or water passages. Clean the passages with a stiff spiral wire brush, then blow them out with compressed air.

3. Check the cylinder head bottom (block mating) surface for flatness. Place an accurate straightedge along the surface. See **Figure 88**. If there is any gap between the straightedge and cylinder head surface, measure it with a feeler gauge. If warpage exceeds specifications at the end of the chapter, have the cylinder head resurfaced by a machine shop. If more than 0.2 mm (0.008 in.) would have to be removed from the head to straighten it, replace the head.

4. Check studs in the cylinder head for general condition.

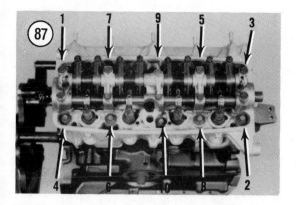

Decarbonizing

1. Without removing valves, remove all deposits from combustion chambers, intake ports and exhaust ports. Use a wire brush dipped in solvent or make a scraper out of hardwood. Be careful not to scratch or gouge the combustion chambers.

2. After all carbon is removed from the combustion chambers and ports, clean the entire head with solvent.

3. Clean away all carbon on the piston tops. Do not remove the carbon ridge at the top of the cylinder bore.

Installation

1. Clean the cylinder head mating surfaces and the engine block, intake manifold and valve cover surfaces to which the cylinder head mounts. Be sure the cylinder bores are clean and check all visible oil and water passages for cleanliness.

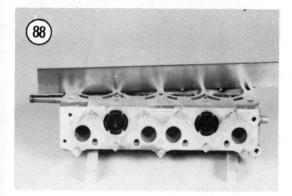

> *CAUTION*
> *Be sure all head bolt threads and all head bolt holes in the cylinder block are completely clean. Dirt on the threads or in the holes will give inaccurate torque readings.*

2. If any dowel pins remained in the cylinder head, reinstall them in the cylinder block to help position the cylinder head gasket (**Figure 89**).

3. Install the camshaft and rocker arm assembly on the cylinder head if they were removed. See *Rocker Arm/Camshaft Installation* in this chapter.

> *NOTE*
> *Do not install the oil pump gear shaft and cover at this time.*

4. Install the exhaust and intake manifolds as described in Chapter Six.

5. Make sure No. 1 piston is at TDC by viewing the flywheel timing marks (**Figure 73**). The stationary index pointer must align with the flywheel timing mark.

6. Place a new cylinder head gasket onto the cylinder block. Make sure the gasket aligns correctly with the dowel pins and bolt holes (**Figure 90**).

7. Place the cylinder head on the cylinder block.

8. With the engine cool, tighten the head bolts in the order shown in **Figure 87**. Tighten in 2 stages to specifications at the end of the chapter.

9. Insert the oil pump gear and shaft into the cylinder head. Tighten the gear housing bolts to specifications (end of chapter).

10. Install the timing belt, camshaft sprocket and front covers as described in this chapter.

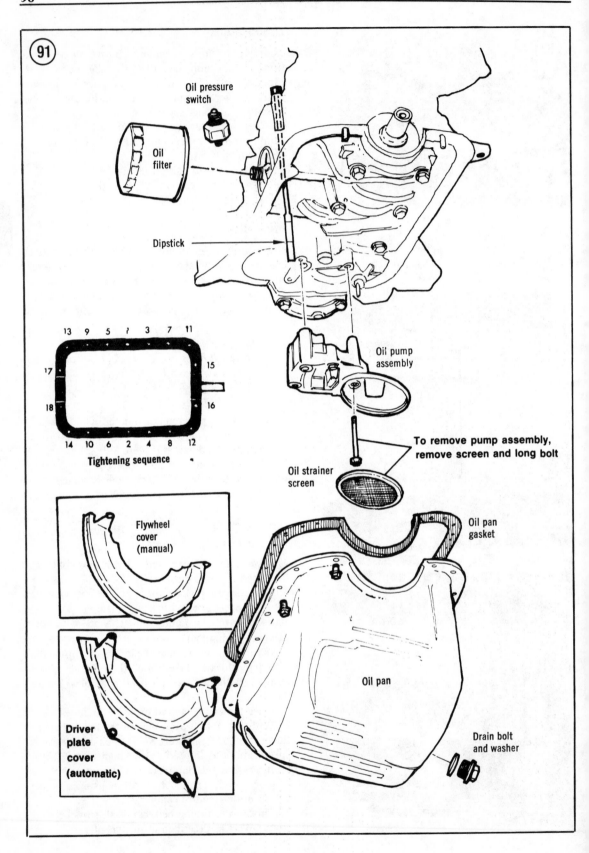

91

Oil pressure switch

Oil filter

Dipstick

Oil pump assembly

13 9 5 1 3 7 11

17   15

18   16

14 10 6 2 4 8 12

Tightening sequence

To remove pump assembly, remove screen and long bolt

Oil strainer screen

Flywheel cover (manual)

Oil pan gasket

Oil pan

Driver plate cover (automatic)

Drain bolt and washer

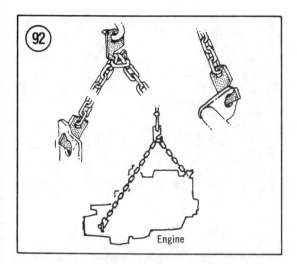

Engine

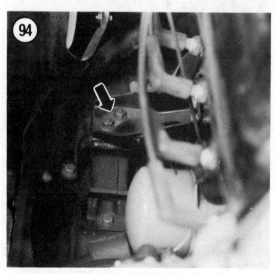

11. Adjust the valve clearances as described in Chapter Three.

12. Install the spark plugs and valve cover.

13. Run the engine and check for leaks.

VALVES AND VALVE SEATS

General practice among those who do their own service is to remove the cylinder head and take it to a machine shop for inspection and service. Valve and valve seat service requires special knowledge and expensive machine tools. Since the cost of a professional valve job is low in relation to the required effort and equipment, this is usually the best approach, even for experienced mechanics. Valve specifications are listed in **Table 1** and **Table 2** for your mechanic's use.

OIL PAN AND PUMP

The lubrication system is shown in **Figure 91**. Refer to it as needed for the following procedures.

Oil Pan Removal/Installation

1. Set the handbrake. Securely block both rear wheels so the car will not roll in either direction.

2. Jack up the front end of the car and place it on jackstands.

3. Drain the engine oil.

4. Hook a chain hoist to the engine lifting brackets (**Figure 92**) and lift the engine just enough to remove the engine's weight from the center beam mount. Then remove the center beam (**Figure 93**) and lower engine mount. **Figure 94** shows the lower mount for the Accord; the one for the Prelude is similar.

5. Remove the oil pan bolts in the pattern shown in **Figure 91**, then remove the oil pan and the flywheel or drive plate cover from the clutch housing. It may be necessary to tap on the corners of the oil pan with a soft mallet to break the pan loose.

6. Clean the oil pan thoroughly. If it is difficult to clean, have the pan boiled out by a machine shop. Check for cracks, dents, bent gasket surfaces and damaged drain hole threads. Replace the oil pan if damage is found.

7. Check for a clogged oil strainer screen (**Figure 91**). Remove the strainer and clean it if necessary.

8. Installation is the reverse of these steps. Coat the gasket surface with sealer except where the

gasket fits around the crankshaft oil seal. Tighten the oil pan bolts in the pattern shown in **Figure 91** a little at a time to prevent warping the pan.

Oil Pump Removal/Installation

1. Remove the oil pan as described in this chapter.
2. Remove the oil pump mounting screws on the outside of the pump (**Figure 95**). Then remove the oil strainer screen and remove the one hidden bolt (**Figure 96**).
3. Remove the oil pump.
4. Installation is the reverse of these steps.

PISTON/CONNECTING ROD ASSEMBLY

CAUTION
Handle the piston/connecting rod assemblies with care during the following procedures. Do not clamp the piston in a vise or allow it to hit against another object. This can ruin the piston.

Removal

1. Remove the cylinder head as described in this chapter.
2. Remove the oil pan as described in this chapter.
3. Check the big-end play between the crankshaft and each connecting rod as shown in **Figure 97**. Compare with specifications at the end of the chapter. Replace the connecting rod if big-end play is excessive.

CAUTION
The next step is necessary to prevent damage to the pistons during removal.

4. Check for carbon ridges at the tops of the cylinder bores. If these are present, remove the ridges from the tops of the bores with a ridge reamer. These are available from tool rental dealers.

CAUTION
Do not cut into the ring travel area when using the ridge reamer.

5. Rotate the crankshaft until the piston is all the way to the bottom of its travel and the connecting rod is centered in the cylinder bore.
6. Check the rods and bearing caps for cylinder number markings. If there are no marks visible, scribe your own with a sharp tool. Make the marks on the same side of rod and cap so they can be

reassembled in the same relative positions. See **Figure 98**.

CAUTION
Wrap the connecting rod studs with tape so they won't damage the crankshaft during the next step.

7. Unbolt the connecting rod cap and remove the rod cap and bearing from the crankshaft.
8. Free the connecting rod from the crankshaft by tapping gently with a wooden hammer handle.

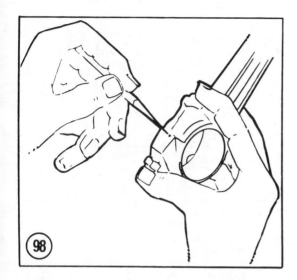

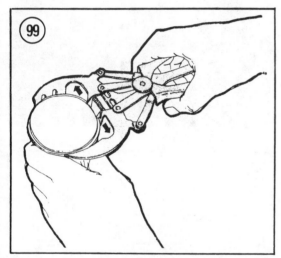

Push the piston/connecting rod assembly out the top of the bore with the hammer handle.

9. Remove the rings with a ring expander tool. See **Figure 99**.

Piston Pin Removal/Installation

The piston pins are installed with a tight press fit. Removal and installation require a hydraulic press and special fixture. This is a job for a Honda dealer or machine shop equipped to fit the pistons and pins and align the pistons with the connecting rods. When reassembling a piston assembly, make sure the mark on the piston crown is assembled on the same side as the oil jet in the connecting rod. See **Figure 100**. During piston installation, these marks must face toward the intake manifold.

Piston Cleaning and Inspection

CAUTION
Do not soak pistons in dip-type parts cleaner. Do not clean pistons with a wire brush.

1. Clean the pistons thoroughly in solvent. Scrape carbon deposits from the piston tops with a flat blunt-edged scraper (plastic or hardwood). The ring grooves can be cleaned with a ring groove cleaner or with a squared-off piece of broken piston ring.

CAUTION
Do not cut the ring grooves deeper when cleaning.

2. Check the pistons for cracks at the skirts, ring grooves, pin or bushing bosses and top. Any noticeable fault requires that the piston be replaced.

NOTE
The following steps should be done at room temperature. The cylinder walls must be clean and dry.

3. Measure the cylinder bore as described under *Cylinder Block Inspection* in this chapter.

4. Measure piston diameter with a micrometer at the point indicated in **Figure 101**. See **Table 1** or **Table 2** for specifications. If the piston diameter is less than the service limit, replace the piston.

NOTE
Piston diameter must be measured at the point shown in **Figure 101** *because it is the point of maximum piston wear.*

5. Determine the difference between the cylinder bore and piston diameter taken in Step 3 and Step 4. This gives the piston clearance. Compare this figure with specifications in **Table 1** or **Table 2**. If clearance is excessive, the cylinders must be bored to the next oversize and new pistons installed. New pistons are available 0.25 mm (0.010 in.) oversize.

> *NOTE*
> *The new pistons should be obtained before the cylinders are bored so they can be measured; slight manufacturing tolerances must be taken into account to determine the actual bore size and working clearance.*

6. Repeat this procedure for the other 3 cylinders and pistons.

Piston Ring Fit/Installation

1. Check the ring gap of each piston ring. To do this, position the ring at the top or bottom of the ring travel area and square it by tapping gently with an inverted piston.

> *NOTE*
> *If the cylinders have not been rebored, check the gap at the bottom of the ring travel, where the cylinder is least worn.*

2. Measure ring gap with a feeler gauge as shown in **Figure 102**. Compare with specifications at the end of the chapter. If the ring gap is not within specifications, use another set of rings.

3. Check side clearance of the rings as shown in **Figure 103**. Place the feeler gauge alongside the ring all the way into the groove. Specifications are listed at the end of the chapter. The feeler gauge should slide all the way around the pistons without binding. Any wear that occurs will form a step at the inner portion of the groove's lower edge. If large steps are detected (**Figure 104**), the pistons should be replaced.

4. Using a ring expander tool, carefully install the oil ring assembly, then the compression rings. Refer to **Figure 105** and note the following:

   a. Be sure to stagger the oil ring rails so they are 20-30 mm (25/32-1 3/16 in.) apart. See **Figure 106**.
   b. Identify the top compression and second compression ring by their chamfers (**Figure 107**).
   c. Make sure the manufacturer's marks on the compression rings face upward when the rings are installed. See **Figure 105**.
   d. Stagger the compression rings as shown in **Figure 106**. None of the gaps should be lined up with the piston pin ends or at 90° to the

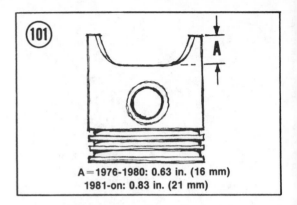

A=1976-1980: 0.63 in. (16 mm)
1981-on: 0.83 in. (21 mm)

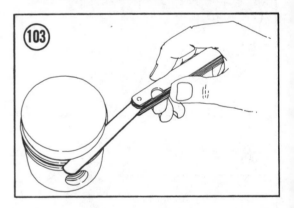

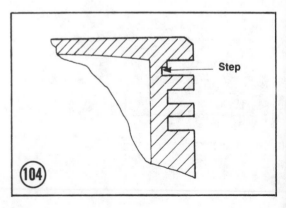

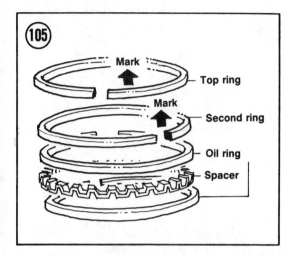

(105)

Mark — Top ring
Mark — Second ring
Oil ring
Spacer

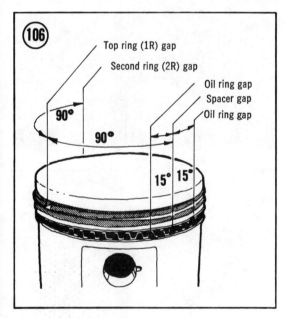

(106)

Top ring (1R) gap
Second ring (2R) gap
Oil ring gap
Spacer gap
Oil ring gap
90°
90°
15° 15°

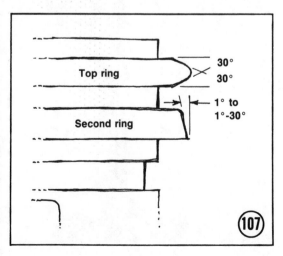

Top ring
30°
30°
1° to
1°-30°
Second ring

(107)

piston pin ends. The gap in the oil ring expander should be used for reference when installing the oil ring rails.

Connecting Rod Inspection

1. Check the pistons for shiny, scuffed areas above the piston pin on one side and below the piston pin on the other. This indicates a bent connecting rod.
2. Have the connecting rods checked by a dealer or machine shop for twisting or bending.

Connecting Rod Bearing Clearance Measurement

1. Assemble connecting rods with bearing inserts on the proper crankshaft journals.
2. Place a piece of Plastigage the width of the bearing on each crankshaft journal.

NOTE
Do not place the Plastigage over the crankshaft journal oil hole.

3. Install the connecting rod cap together with its bearing insert and tighten to specifications at the end of the chapter. Do not rotate the crankshaft while the Plastigage is in place.
4. Remove the connecting rod cap. Bearing clearance is determined by comparing the width of the flattened Plastigage with the scale markings on the Plastigage envelope (**Figure 108**). Compare actual clearance with specified clearance in **Table 1** or **Table 2**. If the clearance is not within specifications, replace the bearing inserts. Remove the Plastigage strips.
5. If the bearing clearance is greater than specified, use the following steps for new bearing selection.
6. The connecting rods are marked with numbers (1, 2, 3 or 4) which are the connecting rod bore identification number. Any combination of numbers can be used in any one engine. See **Table 4**. The crankshaft is marked with letters (A, B, C or D; see **Figure 109**) on the counterbalance weights. These letters indicate the rod journal diameter for that journal. See **Table 4**. Any combination of letters can be used on any one crankshaft.
7. Select new bearings by cross-referencing the crankpin journal diameter letters (**Figure 109**) to the connecting rod identification numbers in **Table 4**. Where the 2 columns intersect, the new bearing replacement color is indicated. **Table 4** gives the dimensions for each bearing color.
8. After new bearings have been installed, use Plastigage to recheck clearance with the specifications listed in **Table 1** or **Table 2**. If the clearance is not within specifications, then either the connecting rod or the crankshaft journal is

4

worn beyond tolerance. Take the parts to a Honda dealer or qualified specialist for further service.

9. Repeat Steps 1-8 for the other cylinders.

Installing Piston/ Connecting Rod Assembly

1. Make sure the pistons are correctly installed on the connecting rods. The piston crown marks and oil jets must face toward the intake manifold when the assemblies are installed in the engine.

2. Be sure the ring gaps are positioned correctly (**Figure 106**).

3. Install the bearing halves in connecting rod and cap. Be sure the locating tangs in the bearing halves are in the notches in connecting rod and cap. See **Figure 110**. Be sure the bearing oil hole aligns with the oil hole in the connecting rod.

4. Immerse the entire piston in clean engine oil. Coat the cylinder wall with oil. Coat the connecting rod journal on the crankshaft with oil.

5. Place pieces of hose over the connecting rod studs. This will prevent the studs from scratching the crankshaft during installation.

> *NOTE*
> *If you don't have the right size hose, wrap the studs with tape.*

6. Position the piston/connecting rod assembly over the bore. Be sure the piston notch and connecting rod oil jet face the intake manifold side of the engine.

7. Slide a ring compressor over the rings. Compress the rings into the grooves. See **Figure 111**.

8. Be sure the connecting rod number mark corresponds with the cylinder number (counting from the front of the engine). Install the piston/connecting rod assembly in the cylinder. Tap lightly with a wooden hammer handle to insert the piston.

> *CAUTION*
> *Use extreme care not to let the connecting rod nick the crankpin.*

9. Install the connecting rod cap. Make sure the rod and cap number marks are on the same side. Tighten the cap nuts to specifications (end of chapter).

10. Recheck connecting rod big-end play as described under *Piston Removal*.

CRANKSHAFT, MAIN BEARINGS AND OIL SEALS

Figure 112 shows the crankshaft and related parts. Refer to it as needed for the following procedures.

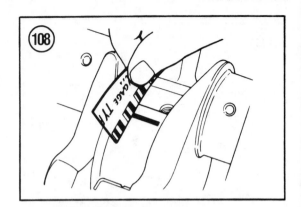

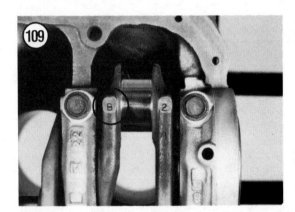

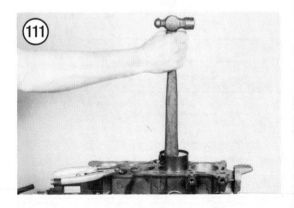

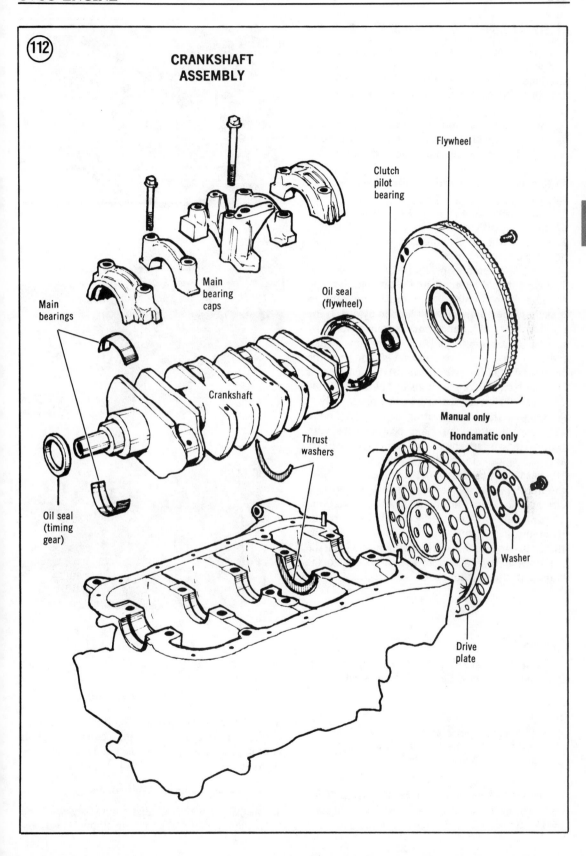

(112)

CRANKSHAFT ASSEMBLY

Flywheel

Clutch pilot bearing

Oil seal (flywheel)

Main bearing caps

Main bearings

Crankshaft

Oil seal (timing gear)

Thrust washers

Manual only

Hondamatic only

Washer

Drive plate

Crankshaft/Main Bearing Removal

1. Remove the engine from the car as described in this chapter.

2. Remove the timing belt cover and timing belt as described in this chapter. When removing the timing belt, be careful not to nick or twist it.

3. Disconnect the return spring at the belt tensioner. Then unscrew the lock and pivot bolts from the belt tensioner and remove it. See **Figure 113**.

4. Remove the flywheel as described in this chapter.

5. Remove the oil pan and oil pump assembly as described in this chapter.

6. Remove the connecting rod bearing caps as described in this chapter.

7. Check for numbers on the main bearing caps. The caps should be numbered 1 through 5. If the numbers aren't visible, wire brush the caps to make sure the numbers aren't hidden by dirt. If the numbers still don't appear, make your own.

8. Check crankshaft end play. Set up a dial indicator as shown in **Figure 114** and pry the crankshaft back and forth against the pointer. If end play exceeds specifications in **Table 1** or **Table 2**, replace the thrust bearings during reassembly.

9. Remove the main bearing cap bolts (**Figure 115**), then remove the main bearing caps with bearing inserts attached. Lay the main bearings and bearing caps in order on a clean surface.

10. Push the piston/connecting rod assemblies toward the tops of their cylinders to provide clearance for crankshaft removal and installation.

11. Carefully remove the crankshaft from the main bearing journals in the block so that the thrust bearing surfaces are not damaged. Handle the crankshaft with care to avoid damage to the crankshaft finished surfaces.

Inspection

1. Clean the crankshaft thoroughly in solvent. Blow out the oil passages with compressed air.

NOTE
If you don't have precision measuring equipment, have a machine shop perform Step 2 and Step 3.

2. Check crankpins and main bearing journals for wear, scoring and cracks. Check all journals against specifications (end of chapter) for wear, taper and out-of-roundness. If necessary, have the crankshaft reground.

3. Check the crankshaft for bending. Mount the crankshaft between accurate centers (such as V-blocks or a lathe) and rotate it one full turn with a dial indicator contacting the center journal. If bent beyond specifications, the crankshaft must be reground or replaced.

Main Bearing Clearance Measurement

1. Install the main bearings previously removed from the cylinder block in their original positions,

3. Remove the main bearing cap and bearing insert. Compare the width of the flattened Plastigage to the markings on the envelope to determine bearing clearance. See **Figure 108**. Compare the narrowest point on the Plastigage with the widest point to determine journal taper. Compare with **Table 1** or **Table 2**.

4. If bearing clearance is greater than specified, use the following steps to select new bearings.

5. The crankshaft main journals are marked with numbers (1, 2, 3 or 4; see **Figure 116**) which indicate journal diameter. The engine block (flywheel side) is marked with a series of Roman numerals (I, II, III or IV) which indicate the block bore dimension. Any combination of numbers and Roman numerals may be used in any engine.

NOTE
With the crankshaft side of the block facing upward (block upside down), the top Roman numeral marking indicates the block bore dimension starting at the crankshaft pulley end of the block and then continues working across to the flywheel end.

6. Referring to **Table 7**, select new bearings by cross-referencing the main journal number (**Figure 116**) with the block bore Roman numeral. Where the 2 columns intersect, the new bearing insert color is indicated.

7. After new bearings have been installed, use Plastigage to recheck clearance with specifications. If the clearance is not within specifications, either the crankshaft or the block main bearing bores are worn beyond tolerance. Take the parts to a Honda dealer or qualified specialist for further service.

8. Repeat Steps 1-7 for each main bearing.

Crankshaft/Main Bearing Installation

1. Make sure bearings, main caps and cylinder block bearing saddles are clean.

2. Position bearing halves in the block and caps. Be sure the bearing locating tangs are correctly positioned in the cylinder block and bearing cap notches. Be sure the oil holes in the bearings align with the oil holes in the block. See **Figure 117**.

3. Position the thrust bearings on the fourth main bearing bore. See **Figure 118**. The thrust bearing oil grooves face outward, away from the journal.

4. Coat the bearings freely with clean engine oil. Lay the crankshaft in the block. Coat the crankshaft journals with clean engine oil.

5. Install the bearing caps and tighten the bolts slightly. Be sure the caps are in numerical order, with No. 1 at the front of the engine.

then install the crankshaft on these bearings. Be careful not to damage the sides of the thrust bearings.

2. Cut a piece of Plastigage the width of each main bearing journal. Lay the Plastigage on the journals. Install the main bearing caps (complete with bearing inserts) and tighten to specifications at the end of the chapter.

NOTE
Do not place Plastigage across the crankpin oil holes. Do not rotate the crankshaft while the Plastigage is in place.

6. Tighten the cap bolts to specifications. Tighten in 2 or 3 stages, starting with the center cap and working outward. Rotate the crankshaft during tightening to make sure it isn't binding. If the crankshaft is difficult to turn, stop and find out why before tightening further. Check for foreign material on bearings and journals. Make absolutely certain bearings are the correct size, especially if the crankshaft has been reground. Never use undersize bearings if the crankshaft has not been reground.

7. Recheck crankshaft end play (**Figure 114**).

Main Bearing Oil Seals

To remove the timing belt seal, remove the front cover, timing belt and crankshaft sprocket as described in this chapter. To remove the flywheel side seal, remove the transaxle and clutch housing as described in Chapter Nine and the oil pan as described in this chapter. Then remove the flywheel as described in this chapter.

1. Thread a small sheet metal screw into the seal and, using a pair of pliers, remove the seal by twisting the screw outward.

2. Using a suitable drift, drive in the seal until it seats against the block. On both seals, make sure the seal lip faces toward the inside of the engine.

3. Apply gasket sealer at the seal-to-block mating surface before installing the oil pan gasket.

4. Assemble the engine as described in this chapter. If the transaxle was removed, install it as described in Chapter Nine.

CYLINDER BLOCK INSPECTION

1. Clean the block thoroughly with solvent and check all core plugs for leaks. Replace any core plugs that are suspect. It is a good idea to replace all of them. While cleaning, check oil and water passages for dirt, sludge and corrosion. If the passages are very dirty, the block should be boiled out by a dealer or machine shop.

NOTE
Block boiling necessitates replacement of all core plugs. However, a block dirty enough to need boiling almost certainly needs these parts replaced anyway.

2. Check the block for cracks. It is a good idea to have the block Magnafluxed by a machine shop for hairline cracks that may not be visible.

3. Check flatness of the cylinder block's top surface. Use an accurate straightedge as shown in **Figure 119**. Measure diagonally, along the block and at right angles to the block centerline. Have the block resurfaced if warped beyond specifications.

4. Measure cylinder bore with a bore gauge. Measure in the thrust direction (side to side) and the axial direction (front to rear). Take these measurements at the top, center and bottom of the cylinder. See **Figure 120**. Compare the measurements to specifications at the end of the chapter. If the cylinders exceed maximum tolerances, they must be rebored. Reboring is also necessary if the cylinder walls are badly scuffed or scored.

FLYWHEEL/TORQUE CONVERTER DRIVE PLATE

Removal/Installation

1. Remove the engine as described in this chapter.
2. On manual transaxle models, remove the clutch from the flywheel. See Chapter Nine.
3. Unbolt the flywheel or drive plate from the crankshaft. See **Figure 112**.
4. Install by reversing Steps 1-3. Tighten bolts to specifications (**Table 3**). Tighten gradually in a diagonal pattern.

Flywheel Runout

With the flywheel bolted to the crankshaft, flywheel runout can be checked with a dial indicator.

1. Mount a dial indicator with its plunger touching the machined clutch contact surface.
2. Rotate the flywheel by hand and read the amount of runout on the dial indicator. If runout exceeds specifications at the end of the chapter, refer the flywheel to a Honda dealer for further service.

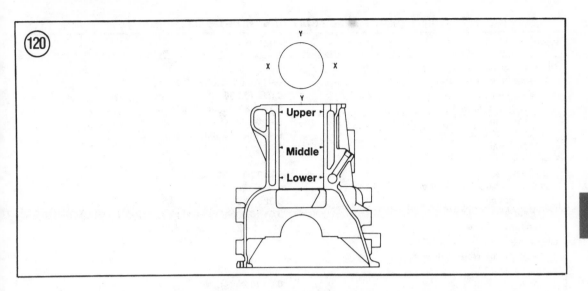

Table 1 ENGINE SPECIFICATIONS (1976-1978)

Item	mm (in.)
Cylinder head	
Transverse warpage	Not specified
Wear limit	0.05 (0.0020)
Cylinder block	
Transverse warpage	0.08 (0.0032)
Wear limit	0.10 (0.004)
Piston bore inside diameter	74.00-74.020 (2.9134-2.9142)
Wear limit	74.05 (2.9154)
Bore taper	0.007-0.012 (0.00028-0.00047)
Wear limit	0.05 (0.0020)
Inner diameter difference	
among cylinders (maximum)	0.02 (0.0008)
Inner diameter finishing limit	0.25 (0.0098)
Piston	
Skirt outer diameter	73.950-73.970 (2.9114-2.9120)
Maximum clearance in cylinder	0.070 (0.00275)
Wear limit	
1976-1977	0.100 (0.0040)
1978	0.15 (0.0059)
Minimum clearance in cylinder	0.030 (0.00120)
Wear limit	0.030 (0.00120)
Top/second ring groove width	1.510-1.520 (0.0594-0.0598)
Wear limit	1.55 (0.0610)
Oil ring groove width	4.005-4.020 (0.1577-0.1583)
Wear limit	4.05 (0.1594)
Piston rings	
Top/second ring-to-piston	
clearance	0.020-0.045 (0.0008-0.0018)
Wear limit	0.13 (0.051)
Top/second ring groove width	0.2-0.4 (0.0079-0.0158)
Wear limit	0.6 (0.0236)
Oil ring end gap	0.3-0.9 (0.0118-0.0354)
Wear limit	1.1 (0.0433)

(continued)

Table 1 ENGINE SPECIFICATIONS (1976-1978) (continued)

Item	mm (in.)
Connecting rods	
Interference, pin-to-rod	0.014-0.04 (0.0006-0.0016)
Wear limit	0.016 (0.00063)
Crankpin, axial play	0.15-0.30 (0.0059-0.0118)
Wear limit	0.4 (0.0158)
Runout, maximum	0.12 per 100 (0.0047 per 3.94)
Wear limit	0.15 per 100 (0.0059 per 3.94)
Crankshaft	
Journal diameter	50.006-50.030 (1.9687-1.96971)
Journal taper/out-of-round,	
maximum	0.005 (0.0002)
Wear limit	0.01 (0.0004)
Crankpin diameter	41.975-42.00 (1.6526-1.6535)
Crankshaft	
Crankpin taper/out-of-round,	
maximum	0.005 (0.0002)
Wear limit	0.01 (0.0004)
Crankshaft axial play	0.10-0.35 (0.0040-0.0138)
Wear limit	0.45 (0.0177)
Runout, maximum	0.3 (0.0012)
Wear limit	0.05 (0.0020)
Bearings	
Bearing-to-journal clearance	0.026-0.044 (0.0010-0.0017)
Wear limit	0.07 (0.0028)
Bearing-to-crankpin clearance	0.020-0.038 (0.0008-0.0015)
Wear limit	0.07 (0.0028)
Camshaft	
Axial play	0.05-0.15 (0.0020-0.0059)
Wear limit	0.5 (0.0197)
Oil clearance	0.05-0.098 (0.0020-0.0039)
Wear limit	0.15 (0.0059)
Runout	0.03 (0.0012)
Lobe height	
Auxiliary intake	43.982-44.222 (1.7316-1.7410)
Main intake	
1976-1977	37.735-37.975 (1.4856-1.4951)
1978	37.923-38.163 (1.4930-1.5025)
Main exhaust	
1976-1977	37.735-37.975 (1.4856-1.4951)
1978	37.954-38.194 (1.4943-1.5037)
Valves	
Tappet clearance	See Chapter Three
Valve stem outside diameter	
Auxiliary intake	5.48-5.49 (0.2157-0.2161)
Wear limit	5.45 (0.2146)
Main intake	6.58-6.59 (0.2591-0.2594)
Wear limit	6.55 (0.2579)
Main exhust	6.55-6.56 (0.2579-0.2583)
Wear limit	6.52 (0.2567)
Stem-to-guide clearance	
Auxiliary intake	0.02-0.05 (0.0008-0.0020)
Wear limit	0.08 (0.0032)
Main intake	0.02-0.05 (0.0008-0.0020)
Wear limit	0.08 (0.0032)
Main exhaust	0.05-0.08 (0.0020-0.0032)
Wear limit	0.12 (0.0047)

(continued)

Table 1 ENGINE SPECIFICATIONS (1976-1978) (continued)

Item	mm (in.)
Valve seats	
Width, auxiliary intake	0.56 (0.0221)
Wear limit	1.0 (0.03941)
Width, main intake, exhaust	1.4 (0.0551)
Wear limit	2.0 (0.0787)
Recession main intake, exhaust	0 (0)
Wear limit	0.2 (0.0079)
Valve springs	
Length (free) 1976-1977	
Auxiliary intake	29.1 (1.1457)
Wear limit	28.0 (1.1024)
Main intake	
Inner	40.2 (1.5827)
Wear limit	39.0 (1.5354)
Outer	39.95 (1.5728)
Wear limit	38.9 (1.5315)
Exhaust	
Inner	52.0 (2.0472)
Wear limit	50.5 (1.9881)
Outer	53.8 (2.1181)
Wear limit	52.2 (2.0551)
Length (free) 1978	
Auxiliary intake	29.1 (1.1457)
Wear limit	28.0 (1.1024)
Main intake	
Inner and outer	42.3 (1.6654)
Wear limit	40.8 (1.6063)
Exhaust	
Inner	50.5 (1.9882)
Wear limit	49.0 (1.9291)
Outer	53.8 (2.1181)
Wear limit	52.3 (2.0591)
Valve springs	
Squareness	
Auxiliary valve wear limit	1.0 (0.0394)
Main intake and exhaust	
wear limit	1.75 (0.0689)
Valve guides	
Inside diameter	
Auxiliary valve	5.51-5.53 (0.2169-0.2177)
Wear limit	5.55 (0.2185)
Main intake and exhaust	6.61-6.63 (0.2602-0.2610)
Wear limit	6.65 (0.2618)
Oil pump	
Inner-to-outer rotor/radial	
clearance	0.15 (0.0059)
Wear limit	0.2 (0.0079)
Pump body-to-rotor/radial	
clearance	0.10-0.18 (0.0039-0.0071)
Wear limit	0.2 (0.0079)
Pump body-to-rotor side	
clearance	0.03-0.10 (0.0012-0.0039)
Wear limit	0.15 (0.0059)
Pump drive gear backlash	0.04-0.10 (0.0016-0.0039)
Pump drive gear side clearance	0.05-0.30 (0.0020-0.01181)
Rocker assembly	
Rocker arm-to-shaft clearance	0.08 (0.0032)

Table 2 ENGINE SPECIFICATIONS (1979-ON)

Item	mm	in.
Cylinder head		
Warp, maximum	0.05	0.002
Cylinder block		
Warp, standard	0.08	0.0032
Warp, maximum	0.10	0.004
Cylinder bore inside diameter		
Standard	77.00-77.02	3.0315-3.0323
Maximum	77.05	3.0335
Bore taper		
Standard	0.007-0.012	0.0003-0.0005
Maximum	0.05	0.002
Piston diameter		
Standard (1979-1981)	76.960-76.980	3.0229-3.0307
Standard (1982-on)	76.960-76.990	3.030-3.031
Minimum (1979-1981)	76.96	3.0229
Minimum (1982-on)	76.95	3.0295
Piston clearance to bore		
Standard	0.02-0.07	0.0008-0.0028
Maximum	0.15	0.006
Piston rings		
Compression ring side clearance		
Standard	0.020-0.045	0.0008-0.0018
Maximum	0.13	0.051
Compression ring end gap		
Standard	0.15-0.35	0.006-0.014
Maximum	0.6	0.024
Oil ring end gap		
Standard	0.3-0.9	0.012-0.035
Maximum	1.1	0.043
Connecting rods		
Piston pin diameter	17.994-18.0	0.7084-0.7087
Big-end play		
Standard	0.15-0.30	0.006-0.012
Maximum	0.4	0.016
Bend or twist		
Standard	0.12 per 100	0.0047 per 3.94
Maximum	0.15 per 100	0.0059 per 3.94
Crankshaft		
Journal diameter	50.006-50.030	1.9687-1.9671
Journal and crankpin taper/out of round		
Standard	0.005	0.0002
Maximum	0.010	0.0004
Crankpin diameter	41.976-42.0	1.6526-1.6535
Crankshaft end play		
Standard	0.10-0.35	0.004-0.014
Maximum	0.45	0.018
Crankshaft bend		
Standard	0.03	0.0012
Maximum	0.05	0.002
Bearings		
Bearing-to-main journal clearance		
Standard (1979-1981)	0.026-0.044	0.0010-0.0017
Standard (1982-on)	0.026-0.055	0.0010-0.0022
Maximum	0.07	0.0028
Bearing-to-crankpin clearance		
Standard	0.020-0.038	0.0008-0.0015
Maximum (continued)	0.07	0.0028

Table 2 ENGINE SPECIFICATIONS (1979-ON) (continued)

Item	mm	in.
Camshaft		
End play		
Standard	0.05-0.15	0.002-0.006
Maximum	0.5	0.020
Oil clearance		
Standard	0.05-0.098	0.002-0.004
Maximum	0.15	0.006
Bend	0.03	0.0012
Lobe height		
1979 manual		
Auxiliary	43.737-44.057	1.7219-1.7345
Main intake	37.923-38.163	1.4930-1.5025
Exhaust	38.004-38.244	1.4962-1.5057
1979 automatic		
Auxiliary intake	43.737-44.057	1.7219-1.7345
Main intake	37.546-37.786	1.4782-1.4786
Exhaust	37.628-37.868	1.4814-1.4909
1980 manual		
Auxiliary	43.737-44.057	1.7219-1.7345
Main intake	37.923-38.163	1.4930-1.5025
Exhaust	38.004-28.244	1.4962-1.5057
1980 automatic		
Auxiliary (non-California)	43.737-44.057	1.7219-1.7345
Auxiliary (California)	33.328-33.648	1.3121-1.3247
Main intake (non-California)	37.546-37.786	1.4782-1.4876
Main intake (California)	37.923-38.163	1.4930-1.5025
Exhaust (non-California)	37.628-37.868	1.4814-1.4909
Exhaust (California)	38.004-38.244	1.4962-1.5057
1981-on		
Auxiliary	33.328-33.648	1.3121-1.3247
Main intake	37.923-38.163	1.4930-1.5025
Exhaust	38.004-38.244	1.4962-1.5057
Valves		
Valve stem diameter		
Auxiliary intake		
Standard	6.572-6.587	0.2587-0.2593
Minimum	6.54	0.2575
Main intake		
Standard	6.98-6.99	0.2748-0.2752
Minimum	6.95	0.2736
Main exhaust		
Standard	6.94-6.95	0.2732-0.2736
Minimum	6.91	0.272
Stem-to-guide clearance		
Auxiliary intake		
Sandard	0.023-0.058	0.0009-0.0023
Maximum (1979-1981)	0.09	0.0035
Maximum (1982-on)	0.08	0.0031
Main intake		
Standard	0.02-0.05	0.0008-0.0020
Maximum (1979-1981)	0.10	0.0039
Maximum (1982-on)	0.08	0.0031
Main exhaust		
Standard	0.06-0.09	0.0024-0.0035
Maximum (1979-1981)	0.14	0.0055
Maximum (1982-on)	0.12	0.0047

(continued)

4

Table 2 ENGINE SPECIFICATIONS (1979-ON) (continued)

Item	mm	in.
Valve seats		
Width, auxiliary intake (1979-1981)		
Standard	0.20-0.50	0.008-0.020
Maximum	0.7	0.030
Width, auxiliary intake (1982-on)		
Standard	0.35-0.49	0.014-0.015
Maximum	1.0	0.04
Width, main intake and exhaust		
Standard	1.25-1.50	0.049-0.061
Maximum	2.0	0.08
Valve springs		
Free length, 1979		
Auxiliary intake	34	1 11/32
Main intake (inner and outer)	42	1 21/32
Exhaust		
Inner	50.5	2
Outer	54	1 7/64
Free length, 1980		
Auxiliary intake	28.5	1.12
Main intake/exhaust (all)	42.3	1.67
Free length, 1981-on		
Auxiliary intake	29.7	1.17
Main intake/exhaust (all)	29.7	1.17
Maximum bend		
Auxiliary valves	1.0	0.039
Main intake/exhaust (all)	1.75	0.069
Valve guide diameter		
Auxiliary valves		
1979-1980 standard	5.535-5.555	0.2179-0.2187
1979-1980 maximum	5.58	0.2197
1981-on standard	6.61-6.63	0.260-0.261
1981-on maximum	6.55	0.258
Main intake/exhaust valves		
Standard	7.01-7.03	0.276-0.277
Maximum	7.05	0.278
Oil pump		
Inner-to-outer rotor clearance		
1979 standard	0.15	0.006
1979 maximum	0.2	0.008
1980-1981 standard	0.04-0.14	0.002-0.006
1980-1981 maximum	0.2	0.008
Pump body-to-rotor radial clearance		
Standard	0.10-0.18	0.004-0.007
Maximum	0.2	0.008
Pump body-to-rotor side clearance		
Standard	0.03-0.10	0.001-0.004
Maximum	0.15	0.006
Pump drive gear backlash	0.04-0.10	0.0016-0.0039
Pump drive gear side clearance	0.05-0.30	0.002-0.012

Table 3 TIGHTENING TORQUES

Part	N•m	ft.-lb.
Timing belt adjustment and pivot bolts		
1976-1978, 1980-1981	43	31
1979	32	23
1982-on	30	22
Upper timing belt cover	10	7
Lower timing belt cover	10	7
Cylinder head bolts*	60	43
Oil pump gear cover		
1976-1982	10	7
1983-on	12	9
Valve cover crown nuts	10	7
Camshaft pulley bolt	30	22
Rocker arm bolts		
Small bolts	12	9
Large bolts	22	16
Auxiliary valve locknut	80	58
Crankshaft pulley bolt		
1976-1980	85	61
1981	115	83
Water pump pulley bolts		
(1979-1981)	10	7
(1982-on)	12	9
Connecting rod bearing caps		
1976-1978	28	20
1979-1981	32	23
1982-on	29	21
Main bearing caps		
1976-1978	48	35
1979-on	66	48
Flywheel		
Accord (1976-1978)	53	38
Accord (1979-1980)	68-74	49-54
Accord (1981-on)	105	76
Prelude (1979-1980)	71	51
Prelude (1981-1982)	105	76
Torque converter drive plate		
Accord (1976-1980)	53	38
Accord (1981-on)	75	54
Prelude (1979-1980)	49	35
Prelude (1981-1982)	75	54
Oil pump		
1976-1981 Accord	12	9
1979-1981 Prelude	10	7
1982-on	12	9
Oil pan		
1976-1981	8-12	6-9
1982-on (bolts)	12	9
1982 (nuts)	12	9
1983 (nuts)	10	7
Oil pan drain bolt		
1976-1980	40-45	29-33
1981	40-50	29-36
1982-on	45	33

* See text for tightening sequence.

Table 4 CONNECTING ROD BEARING SELECTION

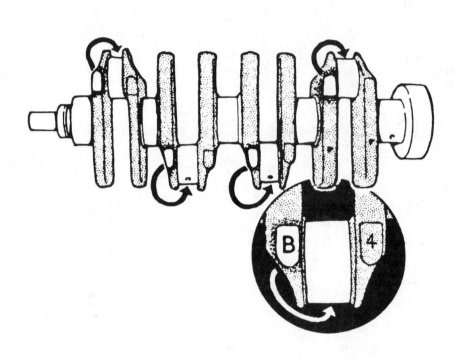

Crankshaft Rod Journal Identification Letters	Connecting Rod Identification Numbers			
	1	2	3	4
A	Red	Pink	Yellow	Green
B	Pink	Yellow	Green	Brown
C	Yellow	Green	Brown	Black
D	Green	Brown	Black	Blue

Crankpin Journal Tolerance:

Journal Identification Letters	Tolerance
A	0 to −0.006mm (0 to −0.0002 in.)
B	−0.006 to −0.012mm (−0.0002 to −0.0005 in.)
C	−0.012 to −0.018mm (−0.0005 to −0.0007 in.)
D	−0.018 to −0.024mm (−0.0007 to −0.0009 in.)

Connecting Rod Bore Tolerance:

Bore Identification Numbers	Tolerance
1	0 to +0.006mm (0 to +0.0002 in.)
2	+0.006 to +0.012mm (+0.0002 to +0.0005 in.)
3	+0.012 to +0.018mm (+0.0005 to +0.0007 in.)
4	+0.018 to +0.024mm (+0.0007 to +0.0009 in.)

Bearing Tolerance:

Bearing Color	Tolerance
Red	−0.005 to −0.008mm (−0.0002 to −0.0003 in.)
Pink	−0.002 to −0.005mm (−0.0001 to −0.0002 in.)
Yellow	+0.001 to −0.002mm (+0.00004 to −0.0001 in.)
Green	+0.004 to +0.001mm (+0.0002 to +0.00004 in.)
Brown	+0.007 to +0.004mm (+0.0003 to +0.0002 in.)
Black	+0.010 to +0.007mm (+0.0004 to +0.0003 in.)
Blue	+0.013 to +0.010mm (+0.0005 to +0.0004 in.)

Table 5 CRANKSHAFT MAIN BEARING SELECTION

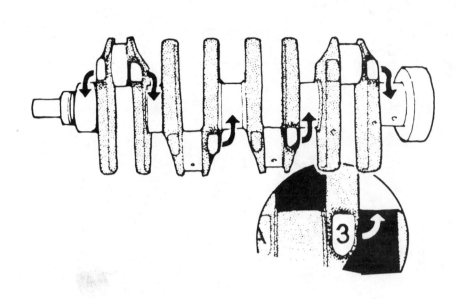

Crankshaft Main Journal Identification Numbers	Crankshaft Bore Identification Numerals			
	I	II	III	IIII
1	Red	Pink	Yellow	Green
2	Pink	Yellow	Green	Brown
3	Yellow	Green	Brown	Black
4	Green	Brown	Black	Blue

Main Journal Tolerance:

Journal Identification Number	Tolerance
1	+0.030 to +0.024mm (+0.0012 to +0.0009 in.)
2	+0.024 to +0.018mm (+0.0009 to +0.0007 in.)
3	+0.018 to +0.012mm (+0.0007 to +0.0005 in.)
4	+0.012 to +0.006mm (+0.0005 to +0.0002 in.)

Cylinder Counterbore Tolerance:

Bore Identification	Tolerance
I	+0.040 to +0.046mm (+0.0016 to +0.0018 in.)
II	+0.046 to +0.052mm (+0.0018 to +0.0020 in.)
III	+0.052 to +0.058mm (+0.0020 to +0.0023 in.)
IIII	+0.058 to +0.064mm (+0.0023 to +0.0025 in.)

Bearing Tolerance:

Bearing Color	Tolerance
Red	−0.002 to −0.005mm (−0.0001 to −0.0002 in.)
Pink	+0.001 to −0.002mm (+0.00004 to −0.0001 in.)
Yellow	+0.004 to +0.001mm (+0.0002 to +0.00004 in.)
Green	+0.007 to +0.004mm (+0.0003 to +0.0002 in.)
Brown	+0.010 to +0.007mm (+0.00004 to +0.0003 in.)
Black	+0.013 to +0.010mm (+0.0005 to +0.0004 in.)
Blue	+0.016 to +0.013mm (+0.0006 to +0.0005 in.)

NOTE: If you own a 1985 model, first check the Supplement at the back of the book for any new service information.

CHAPTER FIVE

12-VALVE ENGINE

The 1983-on Prelude and 1984 Accord are powered by a single overhead cam engine.

The version of this engine used in the 1983 Prelude and 1984 Accord is similar in principle to the CVCC engine used in earlier models. As with earlier models, each engine cylinder uses 2 combustion chambers—a main combustion chamber and an auxiliary combustion chamber. The main and auxiliary chambers are connected by openings. The auxiliary combustion chambers admit a rich fuel-air mixture. The main combustion chambers admit a lean fuel-air mixture from 2 main carburetors. The rich mixture is ignited and in turn ignites the lean mixture. This provides efficient combustion and reduced exhaust emissions.

The version used in 1984 Preludes does not have auxiliary intake valves or auxiliary combustion chambers. Except for this, it is basically the same as the 1983 Prelude engine.

Both versions of the engine use 2 main intake valves and one exhaust valve per cylinder. For this reason, the engine is designated "12-valve" by the manufacturer.

The engine is transversely mounted and uses a cast titanium-aluminum cylinder head. The engine block is made of cast iron. The camshaft is driven by the crankshaft through a toothed belt. The same toothed belt drives the oil pump, which is mounted on the front of the engine. The distributor is driven directly by the camshaft.

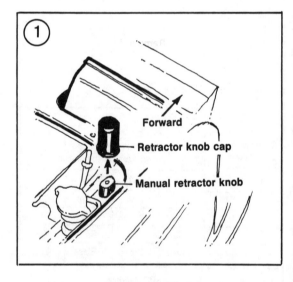

Engine displacement is 1829 cc (111 cu. in.). Engine specifications and tightening torques are listed in **Table 1-Table 4** at the end of the chapter.

ENGINE REMOVAL

WARNING
At all times during this procedure, keep the rear wheels securely blocked so the car will not roll in either direction.

1. Disconnect the negative cable from the battery, then disconnect the positive cable.

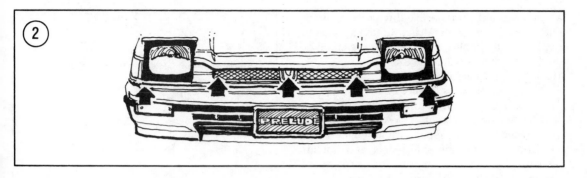

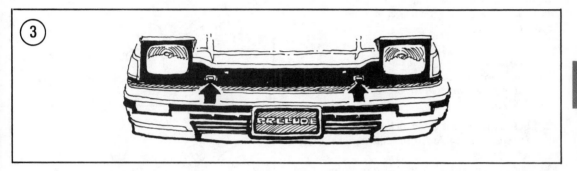

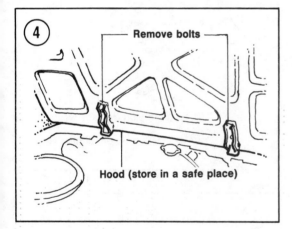

Remove bolts

Hood (store in a safe place)

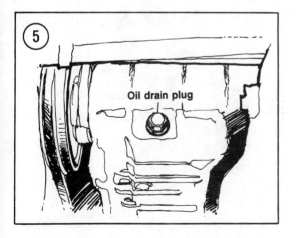

Oil drain plug

NOTE
Steps 2-4 apply to Preludes only.

2. Remove the headlight retracting knob caps (**Figure 1**). Turn the knobs to open the headlights.
3. Remove the grille securing screws (**Figure 2**) and take the grille off.
4. Unbolt the hood brackets (**Figure 3**). Have an assistant support one side of the hood and lift the hood off.

NOTE
Step 5 and Step 6 apply to Accords only.

5. Unbolt the hood hinges and remove the hood. See **Figure 4**.
6. Remove the splash shield from under the car.
7. Remove the oil filler cap. Place a pan beneath the oil drain plug (**Figure 5**) and drain the oil. Once the oil has drained, reinstall the drain plug, using a new gasket.
8. Remove the radiator cap. Place a pan beneath the radiator drain valve (**Figure 6**) and drain the radiator.

WARNING
Ethylene glycol is poisonous and may attract animals. Do not store the drained antifreeze where it is accessible to children or pets.

9. Remove the transaxle filler plug (manual) or filler plug/dipstick (automatic). See **Figure 7**. Place

a pan beneath the transaxle and remove the drain plug. Use a 3/8 in. drive ratchet without a socket to remove the drain plug. Let the transmission oil or fluid drain, then reinstall the drain plug.

10. Disconnect the following:
   a. Ignition coil wires (**Figure 8**).
   b. Brake booster vacuum hose. **Figure 9** shows the Prelude installation. The Accord is similar.
   c. Engine secondary ground cable (**Figure 10**).

11. Disconnect the air intake duct and hot air intake duct, then remove the air cleaner cover. See **Figure 11** (Prelude) or **Figure 12** (Accord). On Accords, remove the air cleaner as described in Chapter Six.

> *CAUTION*
> *During the next step, do not use pliers to detach the cable. Do not kink the cable. The cable must be replaced if kinked.*

12. Loosen the throttle cable locknut and adjusting nut. Detach the cable from the bracket and carburetor linkage.

13. Unplug the No. 1 control box connector. **Figure 13** shows the Prelude installation. The Accord is similar. Detach the control box from its bracket and let it hang next to the engine.

14. On Preludes, locate the evaporative emission system charcoal canister. See **Figure 14**. Disconnect the purge control solenoid vacuum hose, then disconnect the fuel line from the filter. Plug the fuel line so it won't drip gasoline.

15. On all Accords, disconnect the purge control solenoid vacuum hose from the charcoal canister. On California and high altitude Accords, remove the air jet controller as well. See **Figure 15**.

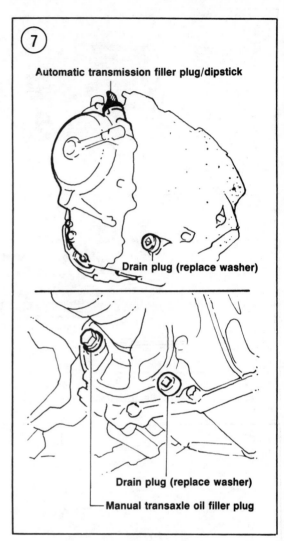

Automatic transmission filler plug/dipstick

Drain plug (replace washer)

Drain plug (replace washer)

Manual transaxle oil filler plug

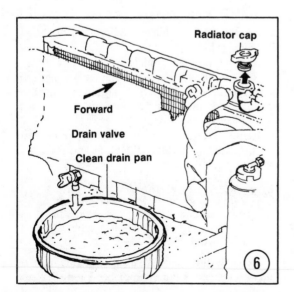

Radiator cap

Forward

Drain valve

Clean drain pan

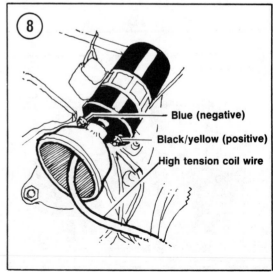

Blue (negative)

Black/yellow (positive)

High tension coil wire

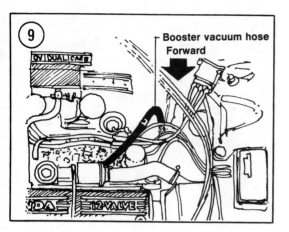

⑨ Booster vacuum hose
Forward

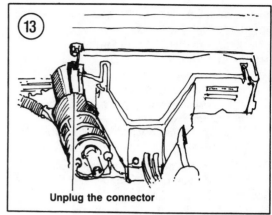

⑬ Unplug the connector

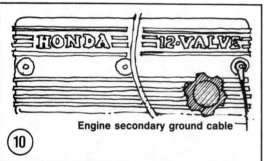

Engine secondary ground cable

⑩

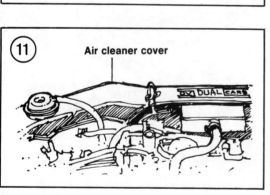

⑪ Air cleaner cover

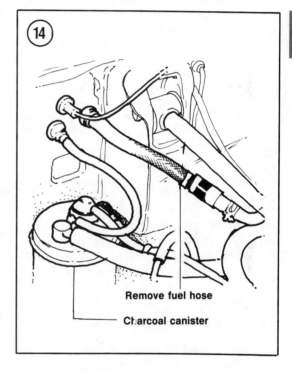

⑭ Remove fuel hose

Charcoal canister

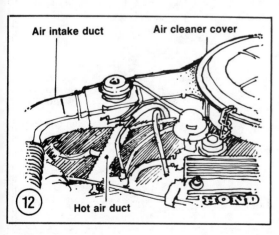

Air intake duct   Air cleaner cover

⑫ Hot air duct

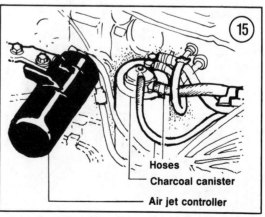

⑮ Hoses

Charcoal canister

Air jet controller

5

16. On the following Prelude models, remove the air jet controller (**Figure 16**):
   a. 1983 California and high altitude.
   b. All 1984.

> *NOTE*
> *During the next step, label the heater hoses so they can be reconnected properly. Do not disconnect the heater valve cable.*

17. Disconnect the radiator and heater hoses from the engine. See **Figure 17** (Prelude) and **Figure 18** (Accord).

18. If equipped with a manual transaxle, disconnect the clutch cable from the release fork. See Chapter Nine for details.

19. If equipped with automatic transaxle, disconnect the fluid cooler hoses (**Figure 19**). Cap or plug the hoses and their fittings to keep out dirt, then hang the hoses out of the way.

20. Disconnect the battery negative cable from its attaching point on the transaxle.

21. Disconnect the starter cable from the starter.

22. Unplug the engine harness connectors (**Figure 20**).

> *CAUTION*
> *During the next step, do not remove the speedometer cable holder or the speedometer gear may fall into the transaxle.*

23. On cars without power steering, remove the speedometer cable clip. Pull the speedometer cable out of the holder. See **Figure 21**.

> *CAUTION*
> *During the next step, do not disconnect the hoses from the speed sensor.*

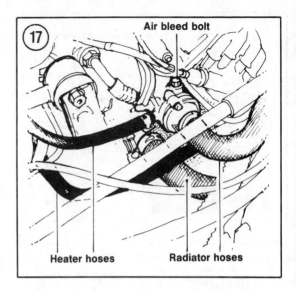

Air bleed bolt
Heater hoses
Radiator hoses

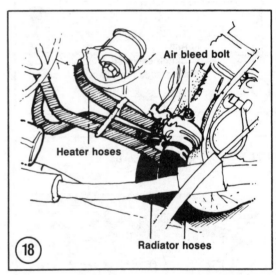

Air bleed bolt
Heater hoses
Radiator hoses

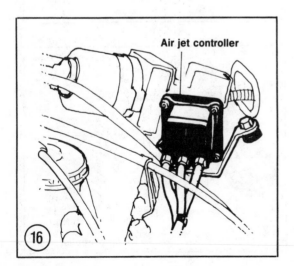

Air jet controller

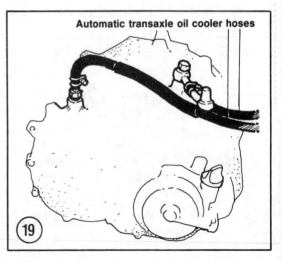

Automatic transaxle oil cooler hoses

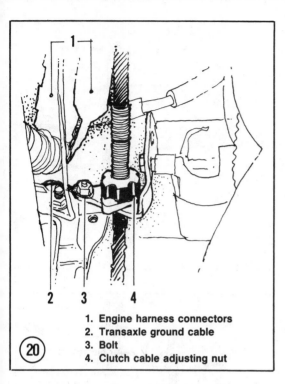

1. **Engine harness connectors**
2. **Transaxle ground cable**
3. **Bolt**
4. **Clutch cable adjusting nut**

⑳

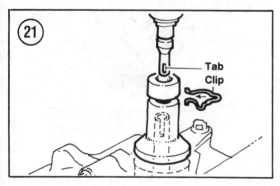

Tab
Clip

㉑

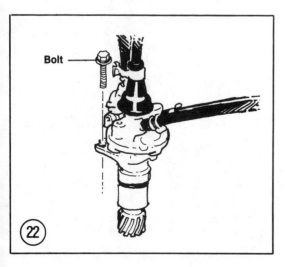

Bolt

㉒

NOTE
Steps 24-27 apply to cars with power steering.

24. Detach the speed sensor (**Figure 22**). Lay the speed sensor and its hoses out of the way.
25. Remove the power steering belt adjusting bolt and take the belt off.
26. Detach the power steering pump from its bracket. Lay the pump and hoses out of the way.
27. Detach the power steering hose bracket from the cylinder head. See **Figure 23**.

NOTE
Steps 28-30 apply to Accords only.

28. Remove the center beam from beneath the car. See **Figure 24**.
29. Loosen the radius rod nut (**Figure 24**).
30. Spray penetrating oil such as WD-40 on the exhaust pipe-to-manifold nuts and exhaust pipe bracket bolts. See **Figure 25**. Remove the nuts and bolts, then remove the exhaust pipe.

WARNING
During the next steps, do not disconnect the air conditioning hoses. They contain refrigerant under high pressure which can cause frostbite if it touches skin and blindness if it touches the eyes.

31. Disconnect the compressor clutch wire (**Figure 26**).

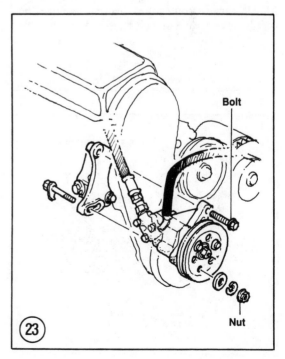

Bolt

Nut

㉓

32. Loosen the compressor drive belt adjusting bolt. **Figure 27** shows the Prelude arrangement. The Accord is similar. Take the drive belt off.

33. Remove the compressor mounting bolts. Lift the compressor off the engine with hoses attached, then tie it to the center beam (Prelude) or front bulkhead (Accord).

> *NOTE*
> *Step 34 and Step 35 apply to cars with manual transaxles.*

34. Remove the shift yoke rod attaching bolt (**Figure 28**).

35. Detach the shift lever torque rod from the clutch housing. See **Figure 29**.

> *NOTE*
> *Steps 36-38 apply to cars with automatic transaxles.*

36. Remove the center console.

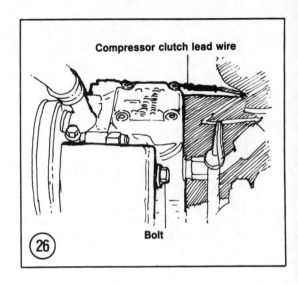

Compressor clutch lead wire

Bolt

26

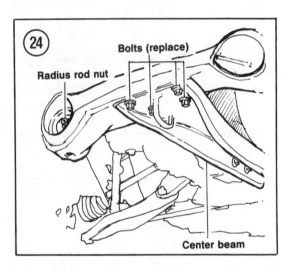

24

Radius rod nut

Bolts (replace)

Center beam

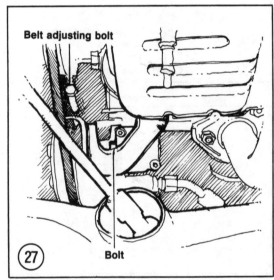

Belt adjusting bolt

Bolt

27

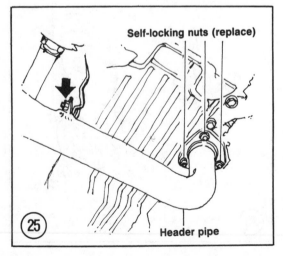

Self-locking nuts (replace)

25

Header pipe

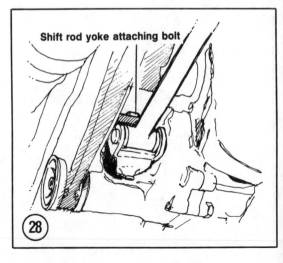

Shift rod yoke attaching bolt

28

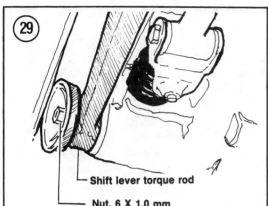

Shift lever torque rod

Nut, 6 X 1.0 mm

37. Place the shift lever in REVERSE. Remove the lockpin assembly from the end of the shift cable. See **Figure 30**.

38. Remove the shift cable mounting bolts (**Figure 31**). Remove the cable holder.

CAUTION
During the next step, do not loosen the upper locknut or the transaxle shift points will be changed.

39. Disconnect the end of the throttle control cable from the transaxle throttle lever. See **Figure 32**. Loosen the lower locknut, but not the upper

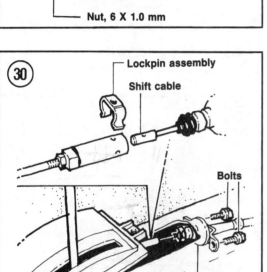

Lockpin assembly

Shift cable

Bolts

Shift cable

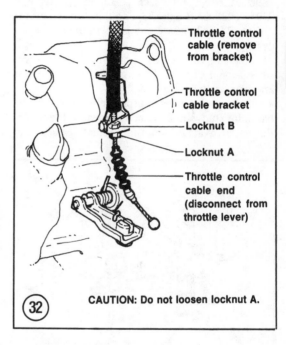

Throttle control cable (remove from bracket)

Throttle control cable bracket

Locknut B

Locknut A

Throttle control cable end (disconnect from throttle lever)

CAUTION: Do not loosen locknut A.

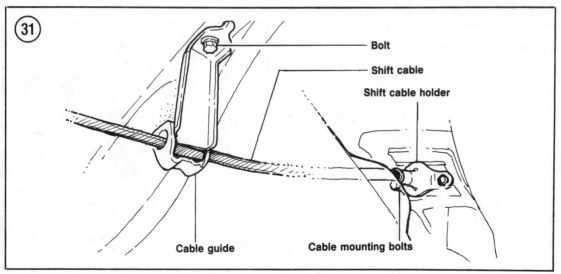

Bolt

Shift cable

Shift cable holder

Cable guide

Cable mounting bolts

locknut, then detach the throttle control cable from the bracket.

NOTE
Steps 40-44 apply to Preludes only.

40. Remove the cotter pin and castle nut from each tie rod end.

CAUTION
If you use a fork-type separator during the next step, do not apply enough force to damage the tie rod end dust boots.

41. Detach the tie rod ends from the steering knuckles. Use a puller such as Honda tool part No. 07941-6920001 (**Figure 33**) or a fork-type separator (**Figure 34**). These are available from tool rental dealers.

42. Remove the cotter pin from each lower suspension ball-joint. Unscrew the ball-joint nut approximately halfway.

43. Pull each lower suspension arm off its ball-joint stud with a puller as shown in **Figure 35**. Pullers are available from tool rental dealers.

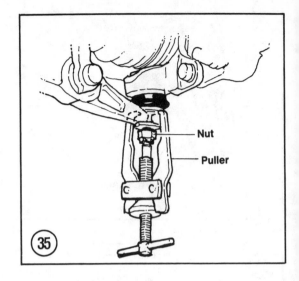

Nut

Puller

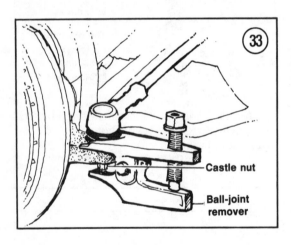

Castle nut

Ball-joint remover

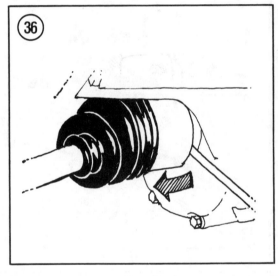

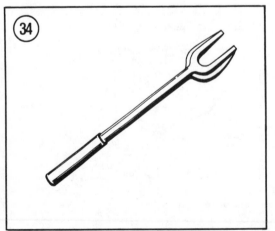

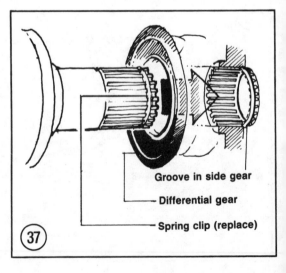

Groove in side gear

Differential gear

Spring clip (replace)

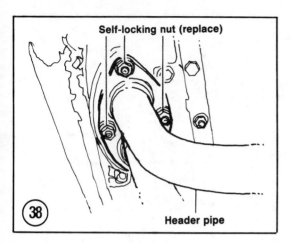

Self-locking nut (replace)

(38) Header pipe

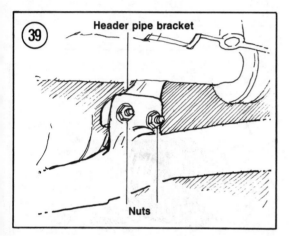

(39) Header pipe bracket

Nuts

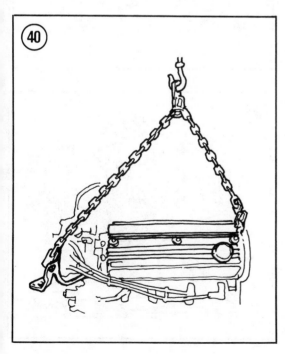

(40)

CAUTION
During the next step, take care not to damage the differential oil seals.

44. Turn each steering knuckle as far outboard as it will go. Gently pry the inner end of each axle shaft out of the transaxle as shown in **Figure 36**, then pull each axle shaft out of the transaxle. Discard the axle shaft spring clips (**Figure 37**). They must not be reused.

45. Remove the nuts that secure the exhaust pipe to the manifold. See **Figure 38**.

46. Detach the exhaust pipe bracket from the transaxle (**Figure 39**), then pull the exhaust pipe out of the way. Discard the exhaust pipe gasket and self-locking nuts. They must not be reused.

NOTE
Step 47 and Step 48 apply to Accords only.

47. Remove the drive shafts as described in Chapter Ten.

48. If equipped with cruise control, label and disconnect the cruise control vacuum lines at the intake manifold.

NOTE
For the next step, a portable hydraulic crane type hoist is the easiest to use. These are available from tool rental dealers.

49. Attach a hoist to the engine lifting brackets. See **Figure 40**. Raise the hoist just enough to take slack out of the chain.

NOTE
Steps 50-52 apply to Preludes only.

50. Unplug the No. 2 control box connector (**Figure 41**). Detach the control box from its bracket and let it hang next to the engine.

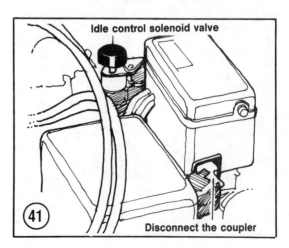

Idle control solenoid valve

(41) Disconnect the coupler

5

51. If equipped with air conditioning, unplug the idle control solenoid valve wire. See **Figure 41**. Detach the solenoid from the body and lay it out of the way with tubes attached.

52. Remove the air chamber (**Figure 42**).

53. Remove the engine mounting bolts shown in **Figure 43**. Push the engine mount into the bracket as shown in **Figure 44**.

54. Remove the front and rear engine mounting nuts. See **Figure 45** and **Figure 46**.

55. Remove the alternator as described in Chapter Eight.

56. Unbolt the rear torque rod from the engine. See **Figure 47**. Loosen the bolt that secures the torque rod to the frame and pivot the torque rod up out of the way.

> *CAUTION*
> *At this point, all linkages, wires and hoses should be disconnected. Recheck this to make sure nothing can hamper engine removal.*

57. Slowly raise the engine and transaxle approximately 6 inches. See **Figure 48**. Stop raising at this point and make sure the engine and transaxle are completely disconnected from the car.

58. Pull the engine and transaxle up and out of the engine compartment, then move them away from the car. Remove the transaxle from the engine and transfer the engine to a suitable stand or work surface.

> *CAUTION*
> *To prevent damage or deterioration, tie plastic bags over the ends of the drive shafts. Coat all precision-finished surfaces with clean engine oil or grease.*

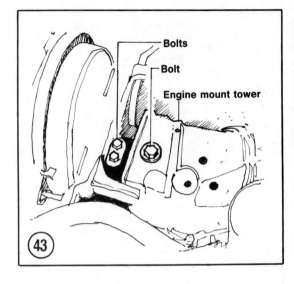

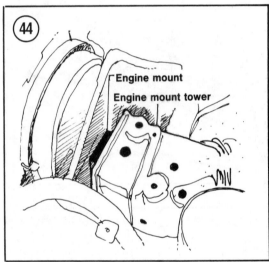

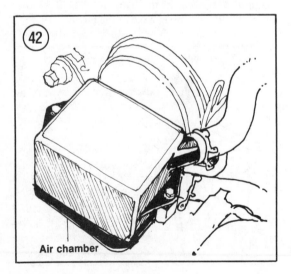

46

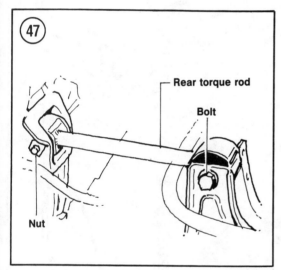

47

Rear torque rod

Bolt

Nut

48

ENGINE INSTALLATION

Installation is the reverse of removal, plus the following.

1. Tighten the engine mountings in the order shown in **Figure 49** (Prelude) or **Figure 50** (Accord). Tightening torques are listed in **Table 2**.
2. Fill the engine and transaxle with oils recommended in Chapter Three.
3. Fill and bleed the cooling system as described in Chapter Seven.
4. On Preludes, use new spring clips on the inner ends of the axle shafts. Make sure the spring clips fit securely into the differential.
5. On Accords, install the drive shafts as described in Chapter Ten.
6. Adjust the throttle cable as described in Chapter Six.
7. If equipped with a manual transaxle, check clutch pedal free play as described in Chapter Nine.
8. If equipped with automatic transaxle, have throttle control cable adjustment checked by a Honda dealer or other qualified specialist.

DISASSEMBLY SEQUENCES

The following sequences are checklists that tell how much of the engine to remove and disassemble to do a specific type of service.

To use these sequences, remove and inspect each part mentioned. Then reverse the sequences to install the parts. Each part is covered in detail in this chapter, unless otherwise noted.

Decarbonizing or Valve Service

1. Remove the exhaust and intake manifolds (Chapter Six).
2. Remove the cylinder head.
3. Remove the rocker arms and camshaft.
4. Have a professional mechanic remove and inspect valves (this includes auxiliary valves on 1983 Preludes and 1984 Accords). Inspect valve guides and seats, repairing or replacing as necessary.
5. Assemble by reversing Steps 1-4.

Valve and Ring Service

1. Perform Steps 1-4 of *Decarbonizing or Valve Service*.
2. Remove the oil pan.
3. Remove the pistons together with the connecting rods.
4. Remove the piston rings. It is not necessary to separate the pistons from the connecting rods

5

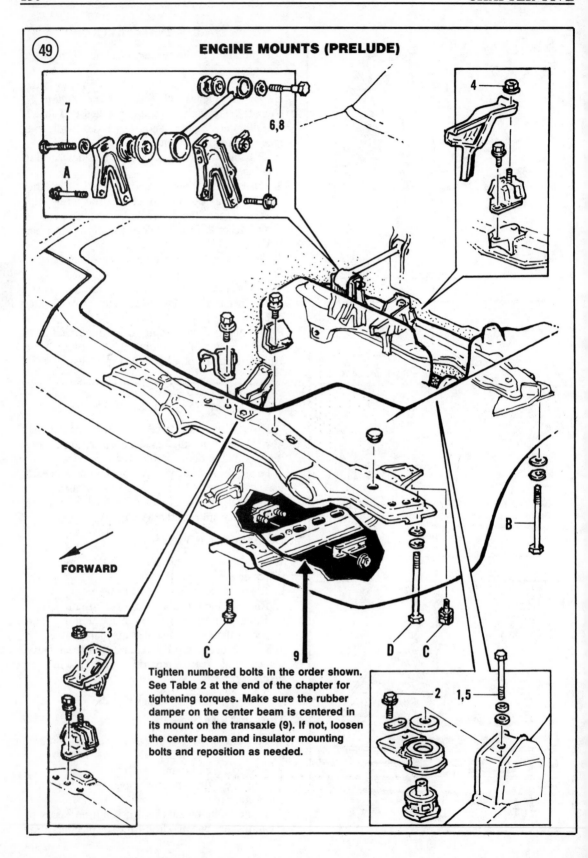

ENGINE MOUNTS (PRELUDE)

FORWARD

Tighten numbered bolts in the order shown. See Table 2 at the end of the chapter for tightening torques. Make sure the rubber damper on the center beam is centered in its mount on the transaxle (9). If not, loosen the center beam and insulator mounting bolts and reposition as needed.

ENGINE MOUNTS (ACCORD)

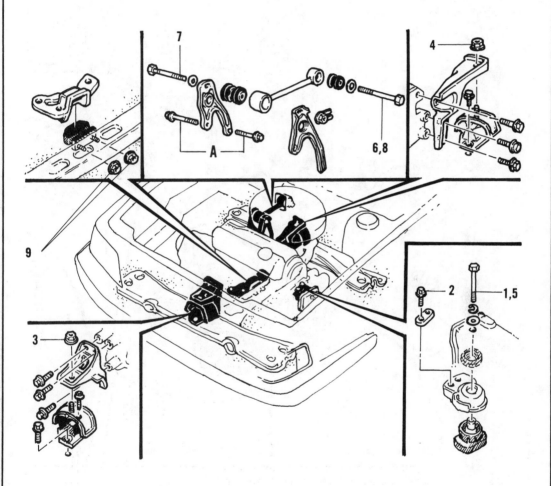

Tighten numbered bolts in the order shown.
See Table 2 at the end of the chapter for
tightening torques. Make sure the rubber
damper on the center beam is centered in
its mount on the transaxle. If not, loosen
the damper and center beam fasteners (9),
center the damper and retighten the fasteners.

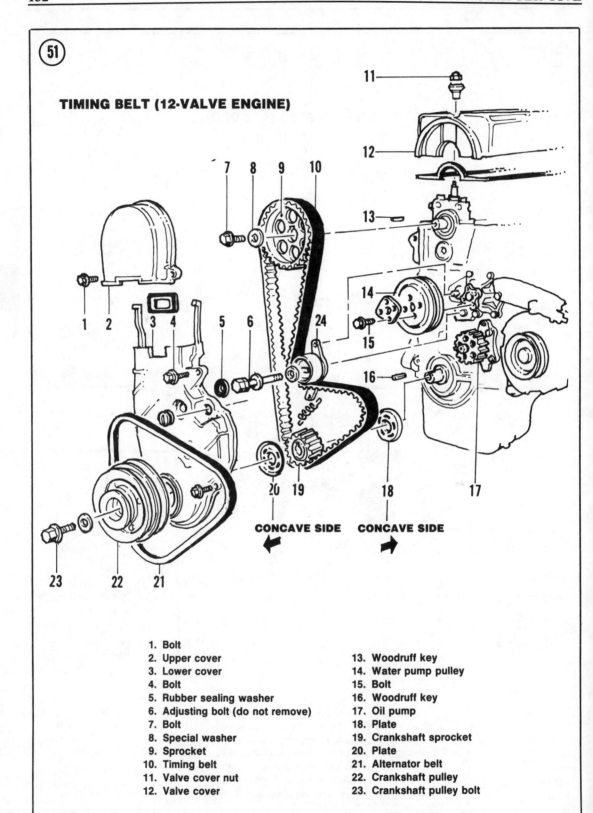

51

TIMING BELT (12-VALVE ENGINE)

CONCAVE SIDE ◄   CONCAVE SIDE ►

1. Bolt
2. Upper cover
3. Lower cover
4. Bolt
5. Rubber sealing washer
6. Adjusting bolt (do not remove)
7. Bolt
8. Special washer
9. Sprocket
10. Timing belt
11. Valve cover nut
12. Valve cover
13. Woodruff key
14. Water pump pulley
15. Bolt
16. Woodruff key
17. Oil pump
18. Plate
19. Crankshaft sprocket
20. Plate
21. Alternator belt
22. Crankshaft pulley
23. Crankshaft pulley bolt

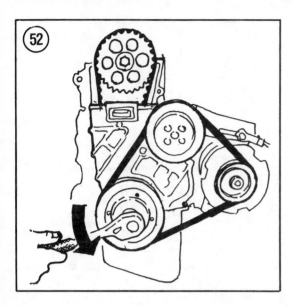

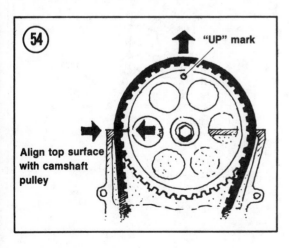

"UP" mark

Align top surface
with camshaft
pulley

unless a piston, connecting rod or piston pin needs repair or replacement.

5. Assemble by reversing Steps 1-4.

General Overhaul

1. Remove the engine.

2. Remove the alternator and distributor (Chapter Eight).

3. Remove the fuel pump, carburetor and manifolds.

4. Remove the water pump and thermostat (Chapter Seven).

5. Remove the timing belt.

6. Remove the cylinder head.

7. Remove the rocker arms and camshaft.

8. Remove the flywheel or torque converter drive plate.

9. Remove the oil pan and oil pump.

10. Remove the piston/connecting rod assemblies.

11. Remove the crankshaft.

12. Inspect the cylinder block.

13. Assemble by reversing Steps 1-11.

TIMING BELT

Refer to **Figure 51** for the following procedures.

Removal

1. Remove the timing belt upper cover.

> *NOTE*
> *During the next step, turn the engine with a socket on the crankshaft pulley as shown in Figure 52. If the engine is in the car, the crankshaft pulley bolt can be reached through the left wheel well as shown in Figure 53.*

2. Turn the engine so No. 1 piston is at top dead center on its compression stroke. When this occurs, the camshaft "UP" mark will be at the top and its timing mark will be aligned with the valve cover surface as shown in **Figure 54**. In addition, the crankcase pointer will point to the top dead center mark. See **Figure 55** (manual) or **Figure 56** (automatic).

3. If equipped with power steering, loosen the power steering pump mounting bolts. Remove the drive belt, detach the power steering pump from the engine and tie it out of the way. It is not necessary to disconnect the pump hoses.

4. If equipped with air conditioning, remove the compressor drive belt as described under *Drive Belts* in Chapter Three.

5. Remove the alternator drive belt as described under *Drive Belts* in Chapter Three.

6. Remove the air chamber (**Figure 42**). Remove the air chamber support bracket.

7. Support the engine with a hoist.

8. Remove 3 bolts securing the engine mount at the drive belt end of the engine. See **Figure 43**. Push the mount into the bracket as shown in **Figure 44**.

9. Remove the water pump pulley.

10. Remove the crankshaft pulley bolt and take off the crankshaft pulley. Use a puller if pulley removal is difficult. Pullers are available from tool rental dealers.

11. Remove the timing belt lower cover.

12. Loosen the timing belt adjusting bolt. Pry the belt tensioner away from the belt to release tension, then tighten the adjusting bolt.

13. Slide the outer guide off the crankshaft.

14. Draw an arrow on the timing belt with chalk to indicate its direction of rotation (counterclockwise, viewed from the timing belt end of the engine).

15. Slide the timing belt off the pulleys.

Inspection

> *CAUTION*
> *Do not crimp the timing belt. Do not fold it lengthwise. Do not bend it at more than a 90 degree angle. Do not bend it into an arc smaller than 25 mm (1 in.) in diameter.*

1. Replace the timing belt if it is soaked with oil.

2. Check the belt teeth for wear at the points shown in **Figure 57**. Replace the belt if wear can be seen.

3. Check the belt pulleys on crankshaft and camshaft for wear or damage.

   a. If the crankshaft pulley is worn or damaged, slip it off the crankshaft. Use a puller if the pulley is difficult to remove.

   b. If the camshaft pulley is worn or damaged, remove the retaining bolt and special washer (**Figure 58**). Take the pulley off.

4. If the timing belt pulleys are removed, inspect their keys in crankshaft and camshaft for wear or damage. Replace as needed.

Installation

Installation is the reverse of removal, plus the following.

1. Make sure the belt is completely clean and dry before installation. Clean off any oil, grease or solvent.

2. Make sure the camshaft and crankshaft timing marks are positioned as shown in **Figures 54-56**.

3. Adjust belt tension. To do this, loosen the adjusting bolt. Turn the crankshaft

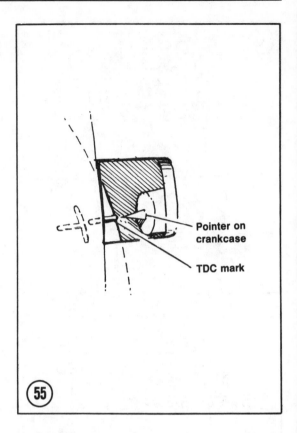

Pointer on crankcase

TDC mark

(55)

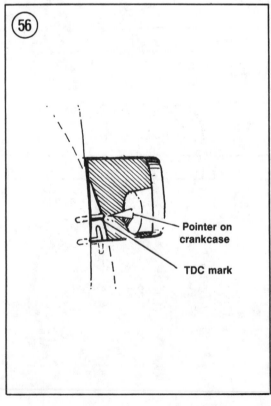

(56)

Pointer on crankcase

TDC mark

Inspect for wear

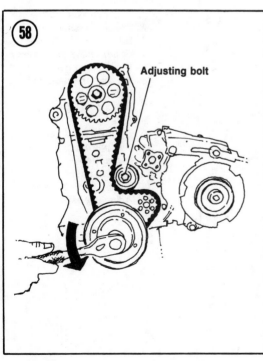

Adjusting bolt

counterclockwise (**Figure 58**). Turn the crankshaft just enough so the belt travels 3 teeth. The tensioner will automatically place the correct tension on the belt.

4. Once belt tension is adjusted, tighten the adjusting bolt to specifications (end of chapter).

CYLINDER HEAD

Figure 59 shows the Prelude cylinder head installation. The Accord cylinder head is the same, except for the carburetor and intake manifold.

Removal

1. Make sure coolant temperature is below 38° C (100° F) before removing the cylinder head.
2. Disconnect the negative cable from the battery.
3. Place a pan beneath the radiator drain valve and drain the cooling system. If the coolant is clean, save it for reuse.

> *WARNING*
> *Ethylene glycol is poisonous and may attract animals. Do not leave the drained coolant where it is accessible to children or pets.*

4. Turn the engine so No. 1 piston is at top dead center on its compression stroke. Also, the crankcase pointer will align with the TDC mark. When this occurs, the camshaft "UP" mark will be at the top and its timing mark will be aligned with the valve cover surface as shown in **Figure 54**. In addition, the crankcase pointer will point to the top dead center mark. See **Figure 55** (manual) or **Figure 56** (automatic).
5. Disconnect the brake booster vacuum hose (**Figure 60**).
6. Disconnect the air intake duct and hot air duct from the air cleaner. **Figure 61** shows the Prelude installation. The Accord is similar.
7. Disconnect the engine secondary ground cable from the valve cover. See **Figure 62**.
8. Remove the air cleaner and carburetor(s) as described in Chapter Six.
9. Remove the distributor as described in Chapter Eight.
10. Label all hoses running from No. 1 control box to the tubing manifold. Disconnect the hoses. **Figure 63** shows the Prelude installation. The No. 1 control box on Accords is similar.
11. On 1983 California and high altitude models, label and disconnect the air jet controller hoses. See **Figure 64**:
   a. 1983 California and high altitude Preludes.
   b. All 1984 Preludes.
   c. 1984 California and high altitude Accords.

5

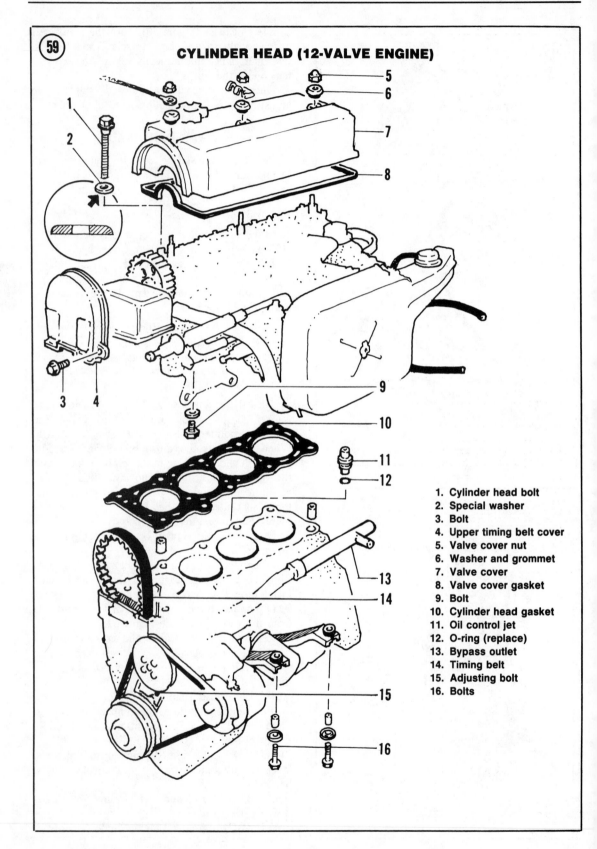

CYLINDER HEAD (12-VALVE ENGINE)

1. Cylinder head bolt
2. Special washer
3. Bolt
4. Upper timing belt cover
5. Valve cover nut
6. Washer and grommet
7. Valve cover
8. Valve cover gasket
9. Bolt
10. Cylinder head gasket
11. Oil control jet
12. O-ring (replace)
13. Bypass outlet
14. Timing belt
15. Adjusting bolt
16. Bolts

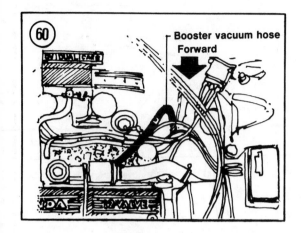

Booster vacuum hose Forward

Air cleaner cover

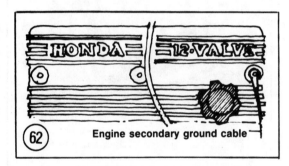

Engine secondary ground cable

12. Label the heater hoses so they can be reconnected properly. See **Figure 65**. Disconnect the upper radiator hose and heater hoses from the cylinder head.

13. Remove the hose running from the thermostat housing to intake manifold.

14. Unplug the wiring connector from the temperature gauge sending unit on the intake manifold.

15. If equipped with power steering, detach the pump from the engine and lay it aside. It is not necessary to disconnect the pump hoses.

16. On Preludes, unplug the No. 2 control box connector (**Figure 66**). Lift the control box off its bracket and let it hang next to the engine.

17. If equipped with air conditioning, label and disconnect the idle control solenoid hoses. **Figure 66** shows the Prelude installation. The Accord version is similar.

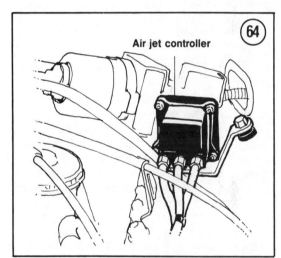

Air jet controller

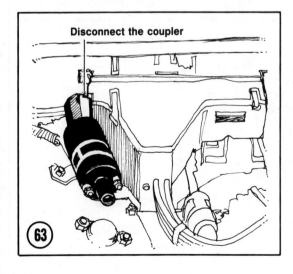

Disconnect the coupler

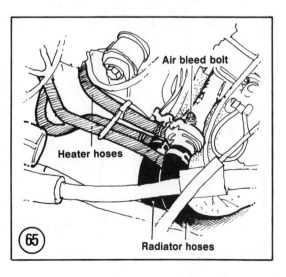

Air bleed bolt

Heater hoses

Radiator hoses

18. Remove the air chamber (**Figure 67**).

19. Remove the nuts and washers securing the valve cover and remove the cover and gasket.

20. Working beneath the car, detach the exhaust pipe from the manifold and transaxle. Pull the exhaust pipe clear of the manifold.

21. Remove the air cleaner base mounting bolts.

22. Disconnect the hose running from intake manifold to breather chamber.

23. Remove the timing belt and its camshaft pulley as described in this chapter.

24. Loosen the cylinder gead bolts in the order shown in **Figure 68**. Loosen the bolts in several stages, 1/3 turn at a time, until all bolts are loose. This is necessary to prevent warping the cylinder head.

25. Once the head bolts are loose, remove them and lift the cylinder head off the block. If this is difficult, tap gently with a rubber mallet.

CAUTION
Do not pry the head off. This will damage the gasket surface.

Rocker Assembly and Camshaft Inspection

Refer to **Figure 69** for this procedure.

1. Set up a dial indicator as shown in **Figure 70**. Pry the camshaft back and forth against the pointer and note the reading (camshaft end play). If it exceeds specifications at the end of the chapter, inspect the thrust surfaces on cylinder head and camshaft. Replace the cylinder head or camshaft, whichever is worn.

2. Loosen the rocker assembly mounting bolts in stages, 2 turns at a time, in a crisscross pattern. This is necessary to prevent damaging the valves or cylinder head.

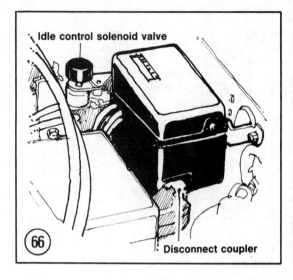

Idle control solenoid valve

66

Disconnect coupler

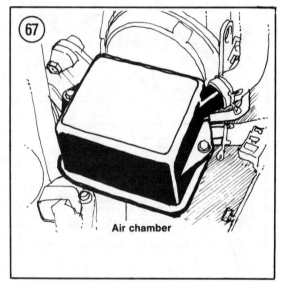

67

Air chamber

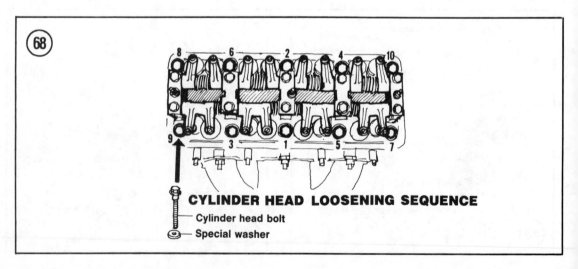

68

CYLINDER HEAD LOOSENING SEQUENCE

Cylinder head bolt

Special washer

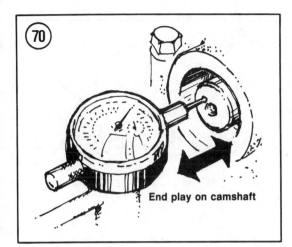

End play on camshaft

3. Lift the rocker assembly off the cylinder head.

4. Lift the camshaft out of the bearing saddles in the cylinder head.

5. Wipe the camshaft and its bearing surfaces clean with a lint-free cloth. Check the camshaft lobes and journals for obvious wear or damage. Replace the camshaft if these can be seen. Replace the cylinder head if camshaft bearing surfaces in the head are damaged.

6. Check cam bearing clearance with Plastigage. Lay the camshaft in its bearing saddles. See **Figure 71**. Lay a strip of Plastigage wire (**Figure 72**) across each camshaft journal.

7. Install the rocker assembly (**Figure 73**). Tighten to specifications (end of chapter). Tighten each bolt 2 turns at a time in the order shown in **Figure 73**.

5

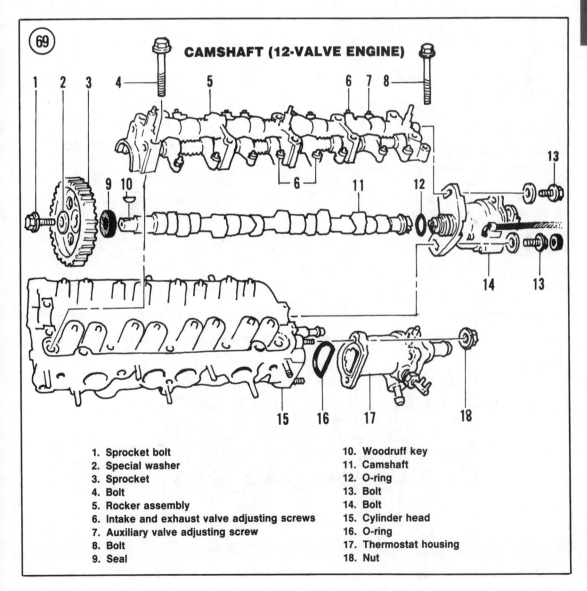

CAMSHAFT (12-VALVE ENGINE)

1. Sprocket bolt
2. Special washer
3. Sprocket
4. Bolt
5. Rocker assembly
6. Intake and exhaust valve adjusting screws
7. Auxiliary valve adjusting screw
8. Bolt
9. Seal
10. Woodruff key
11. Camshaft
12. O-ring
13. Bolt
14. Bolt
15. Cylinder head
16. O-ring
17. Thermostat housing
18. Nut

8. Loosen the rocker assembly bolts 2 turns at a time in a crisscross pattern. Lift the rocker assembly off the head.

9. Lay the Plastigage envelope next to the flattened Plastigage to determine clearance. See **Figure 71**. If clearance is excessive, have the camshaft and bearings checked for wear by a machine shop. If the camshaft is worn, replace it. If the bearings are worn, replace the cylinder head.

10. Have the camshaft checked for lobe wear and runout by a machine shop.

11. Take the rocker assembly apart. Lay the parts in order on a clean workbench. See **Figure 74** (1983 Prelude and 1984 Accord) or **Figure 75** (1984 Prelude).

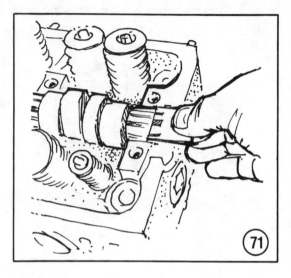

> *NOTE*
> *Rocker arms and stands are not interchangeable. They must be returned to their original positions if they are reused.*

12. Thoroughly clean the rocker assembly and camshaft in solvent.

13. Check all parts for obvious wear or damage. Replace as needed.

14. Slide the rocker arms onto their original positions on the shafts. Grasp each end of the rocker arm between thumb and finger and try to twist it back and forth. There should be little or no twisting movement (sliding movement is okay). If any rocker arm is loose, have the rocker arms and shaft checked for wear by a machine shop.

Cylinder Head Inspection

1. Check the cylinder head for water leaks before cleaning.

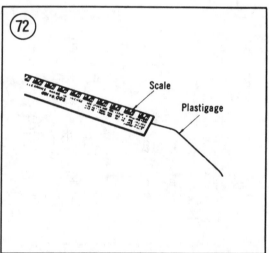

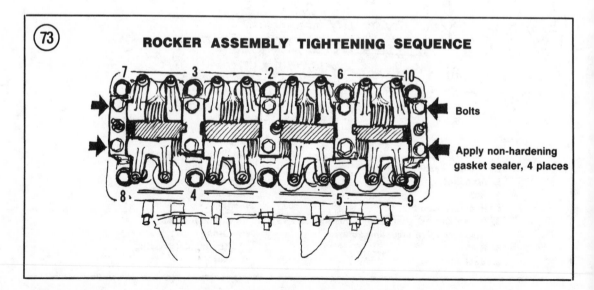

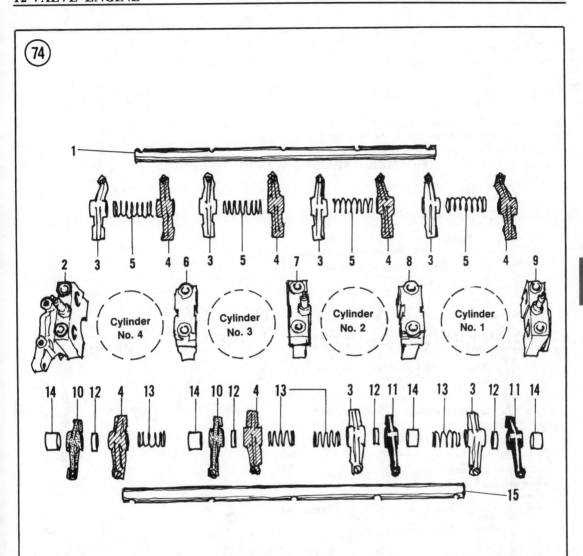

1. Rocker shaft A
2. Right end bearing cap
3. B
4. A
5. Rocker arm spring A (4 places)
6. Right bearing cap
7. Center bearing cap
8. Left bearing cap
9. Left end bearing cap
10. Rocker arm D (2 places)
11. C
12. Collar B (4 places)
13. Rocker arm spring B (4 places)
14. Collar A (4 places)
15. Rocker shaft B

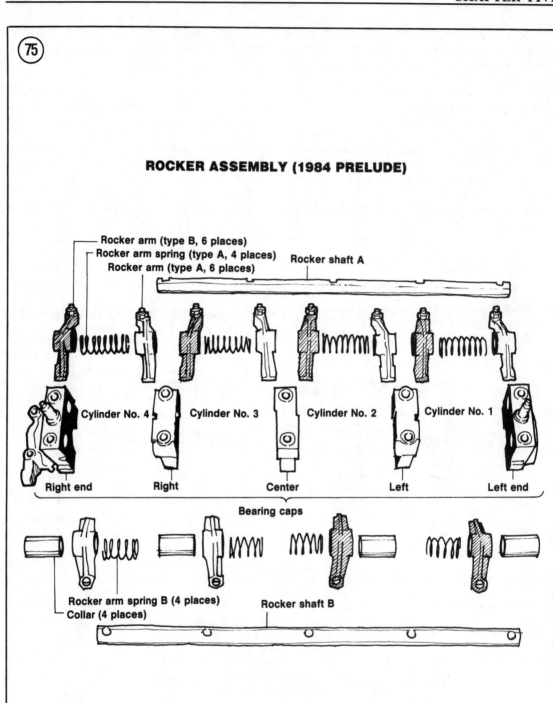

ROCKER ASSEMBLY (1984 PRELUDE)

2. Clean the cylinder head thoroughly with solvent. While cleaning, check for cracks or other visible damage. Look for corrosion or foreign material in oil or water passages. Clean the passages with a stiff spiral wire brush, then blow them out with compressed air.

3. Check the cylinder head bottom surface for flatness. Place an accurate straightedge along the surface (**Figure 76**). If there is any gap between cylinder head and straightedge, measure it with a feeler gauge as shown. Measure in the directions shown in **Figure 77**. Have the cylinder head resurfaced by a machine shop if the gap exceeds 0.05 mm (0.002 in.).

NOTE
If camshaft bearing clearances are not within specifications, do not resurface the head, since it must be replaced.

4. Check the manifold mating surfaces on the cylinder head for flatness in the same manner as the bottom surface.

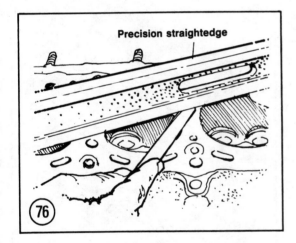

Precision straightedge

76

5. Check studs in the cylinder head for condition. Replace damaged studs.

Cylinder Head Decarbonizing

1. Without removing valves, remove all deposits from combustion chambers, intake ports and exhaust ports. Use a scraper made of hardwood. Be careful not to scratch or gouge the cylinder head.

2. After all carbon is removed from combustion chambers and ports, clean the entire head in solvent.

3. Clean away all carbon on the piston tops. Do not remove the carbon ridge at the top of the cylinder bore.

Cylinder Head Assembly

1. Liberally coat the rocker shafts with clean engine oil. Assemble the rocker assembly, referring to **Figure 74** or **Figure 75**.

2. Liberally coat the camshaft journals with engine oil. Lay the camshaft in the head.

3. Install the rocker assembly (**Figure 73**). Tighten the rocker assembly bolts in stages, 2 turns at a time, in the order shown in **Figure 73**.

4. Install a new oil seal at the front end of the camshaft. Coat the seal lip and the sealing surface on the camshaft with clean engine oil. Tap the seal in with a tool such as Honda seal driver part No. 07947-SB00100 (**Figure 78**).

Cylinder Head Installation

Installation is the reverse of removal, plus the following.

1. Be sure the cylinder head, block and cylinder bores are clean. Check all visible oil passages for cleanliness.

2. Install a new cylinder head gasket. Never reuse an old head gasket. Make sure the cylinder block

5

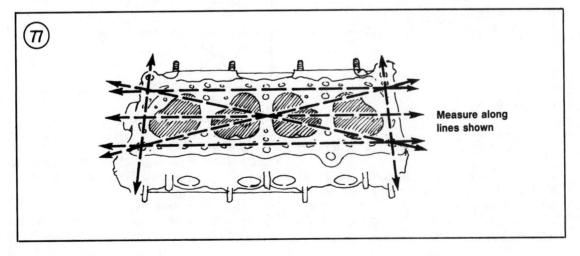

77

Measure along lines shown

dowels and oil control jet are in their proper positions. See **Figure 79**.

CAUTION
During the next step, do not let the block dowels scratch the cylinder head surface.

3. Position the cylinder head on the block.
4. Install the cylinder head bolts and special washers. See **Figure 80**. Tighten the cylinder head bolts in 2 stages. Follow the sequence in **Figure 80**. Tighten the bolts to 30 N•m (22 ft.-lb.) in the first stage. Tighten them to 68 N•m (49 ft.-lb.) in the second stage.
5. Change the oil. This is necessary to remove any water that may have leaked into oil passages when the cylinder head was removed.
6. Fill the cooling system with a 50/50 mixture of ethylene glycol-based antifreeze and water.

VALVES AND VALVE SEATS

General practice among those who do their own service is to remove the cylinder head and take it to a machine shop for inspection and service. Valve service requires special knowledge and expensive machine tools. Since the cost of a professional valve job is low in relation to the required effort and equipment, this is usually the best approach, even for experienced mechanics. Valve specifications are given in **Table 1**.

OIL PAN, OIL PUMP AND PRESSURE RELIEF VALVE

Oil Pan Removal/Installation

1. Remove the dipstick.
2. Drain the oil from the pan.

WARNING
Be sure engine and transaxle are securely supported before performing the next step. Otherwise, they may shift or drop and cause serious injury.

3. Remove the front exhaust pipe and center beam.
4. Unbolt the oil pan from the engine. See **Figure 81**. Tap the pan with a rubber mallet to break the gasket seal, then lower it clear.
5. Unbolt the oil pickup tube from the engine, then take it out. See **Figure 81**.

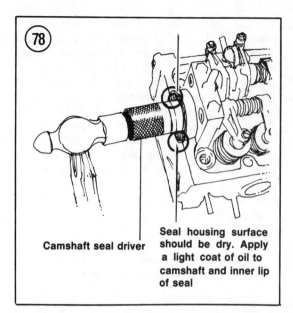

Camshaft seal driver — Seal housing surface should be dry. Apply a light coat of oil to camshaft and inner lip of seal

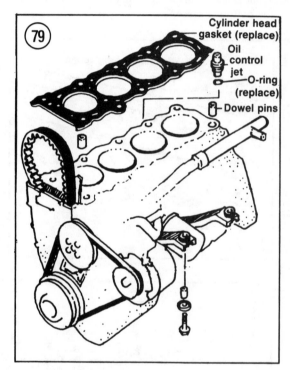

Cylinder head gasket (replace)
Oil control jet
O-ring (replace)
Dowel pins

6. Remove all traces of old gasket and sealer from engine and oil pan.
7. Thoroughly clean the pickup tube and the inside of the oil pan with solvent. If the parts are hard to clean, a machine shop can boil them out for a small fee.
8. Install by reversing Steps 1-5. Use a new pan gasket. Apply sealer to the 4 corners of the pan (**Figure 81**).

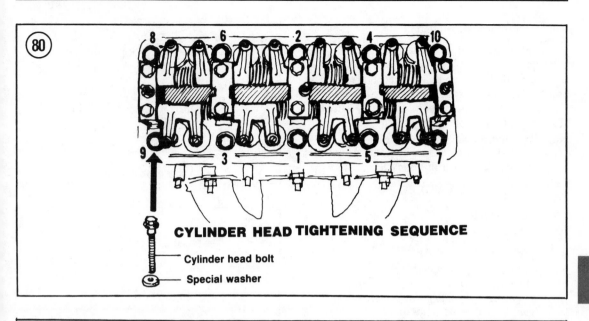

CYLINDER HEAD TIGHTENING SEQUENCE

— Cylinder head bolt

— Special washer

5

OIL PAN AND OIL PUMP PRESSURE (12-VALVE ENGINE)

1. Oil pressure switch
2. Oil filter base
3. Oil filter
4. Bolt
5. Pickup tube and screen
6. Nut
7. Bolt
8. Oil pan
9. Washer (replace)
10. Oil pan drain plug
11. Gasket
12. Bolt
13. Oil pump
14. Nut

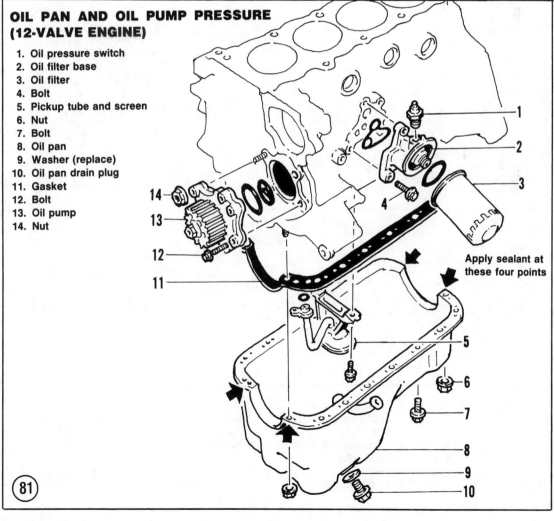

Apply sealant at these four points

Oil Pump Removal/Installation

1. Remove the timing belt as described in this chapter.
2. Loosen the oil pump pulley nut (**Figure 82**). The nut has left-hand threads (unscrews clockwise).
3. Remove the oil pump bolts and nut (**Figure 82**). Take the oil pump off the engine.
4. Installation is the reverse of removal. Use a new gasket and O-ring. Apply gasket sealer around the O-ring groove as shown in **Figure 83**.

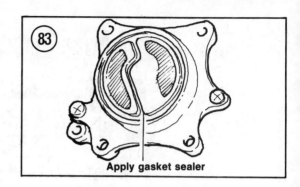
Apply gasket sealer

FLYWHEEL

Removal/Installation

1. Either remove the transaxle or remove the engine and transaxle and separate them.

> *WARNING*
> *Removing the transaxle without removing the engine requires a commercial hoist. Jackstands do not provide sufficient safety. Read the transaxle removal procedure in Chapter Nine. If you don't have access to a commercial hoist, remove the engine and transaxle and separate them.*

2. Remove the clutch from the flywheel. See Chapter Nine.
3. Unbolt the flywheel from the crankshaft (**Figure 84**).
4. Installation is the reverse of removal. Tighten the flywheel bolts evenly to specifications (**Table 2**).

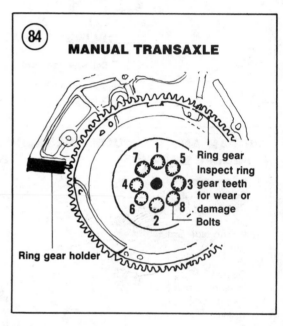
MANUAL TRANSAXLE
Ring gear
Inspect ring gear teeth for wear or damage
Bolts
Ring gear holder

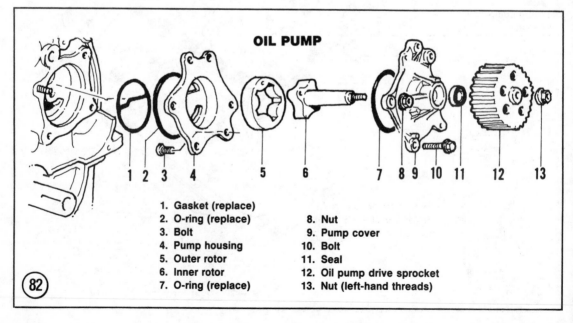
OIL PUMP

1. Gasket (replace)
2. O-ring (replace)
3. Bolt
4. Pump housing
5. Outer rotor
6. Inner rotor
7. O-ring (replace)
8. Nut
9. Pump cover
10. Bolt
11. Seal
12. Oil pump drive sprocket
13. Nut (left-hand threads)

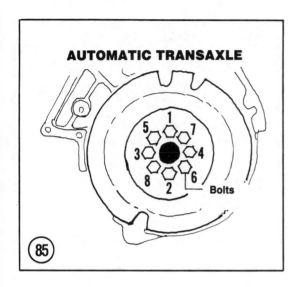

AUTOMATIC TRANSAXLE

Bolts

(85)

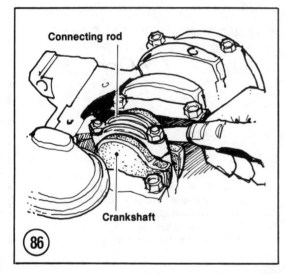

Connecting rod

Crankshaft

(86)

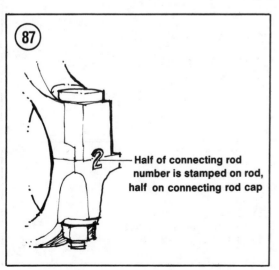

(87)

Half of connecting rod
number is stamped on rod,
half on connecting rod cap

Inspection

1. Check the flywheel for scoring or wear. If the surface is glazed or slightly scratched, have it resurfaced by a machine shop. Replace the flywheel if damage is severe.

2. Inspect the flywheel ring gear teeth. If broken, chipped or excessively worn, replace the flywheel.

TORQUE CONVERTER DRIVE PLATE

The torque converter drive plate, used with automatic transaxles, is inspected, removed and installed in the same manner as the manual transaxle flywheel. See **Figure 85**. The drive plate must be replaced if the ring gear is damaged.

PISTONS AND CONNECTING RODS

CAUTION
When performing the following procedures, handle the piston assemblies with care. Do not clamp the piston in a vise or allow it to hit against another piston or object. Conditions such as these can ruin the piston.

Piston/Connecting Rod Removal

1. Remove the cylinder head and oil pan as described in this chapter.

2. Remove the carbon ridge from the top of each cylinder bore with a ridge reamer. These are available from tool rental dealers.

CAUTION
Do not cut more than 1/32 in. into the ring travel area when using the ridge reamer.

3. Rotate the crankshaft so the connecting rod is centered in the bore at the bottom of its travel.

4. Measure the clearance between connecting rod and crankshaft with a feeler gauge (**Figure 86**). This is connecting rod big-end play. Replace the connecting rod if big-end play exceeds specifications (end of chapter).

5. Measure connecting rod bearing clearance as described in this chapter.

NOTE
*Numbers are stamped on connecting rods and caps. See **Figure 87**. These are reference numbers for bearing selection. They do not indicate the position of the connecting rod in the block. Make your own labels for connecting rod position. Number the connecting rods 1 through 4, with No. 1 at the timing belt end of the engine.*

5

6. Remove the nuts securing the connecting rod cap. Lift off the cap, together with the lower bearing half. See **Figure 88**.

7. Push the connecting rod and piston out the top of the bore with a wooden hammer handle (**Figure 89**).

8. Remove rings with a ring remover (**Figure 90**).

Piston Cleaning and Inspection

1. Clean the pistons thoroughly in solvent. Scrape carbon deposits from the piston's top with a flat blunt-edge scraper made of plastic or hardwood. Brush the pistons as needed with a plastic or natural bristle brush (not metal).

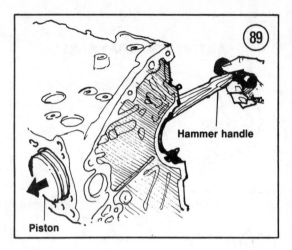

Hammer handle

Piston

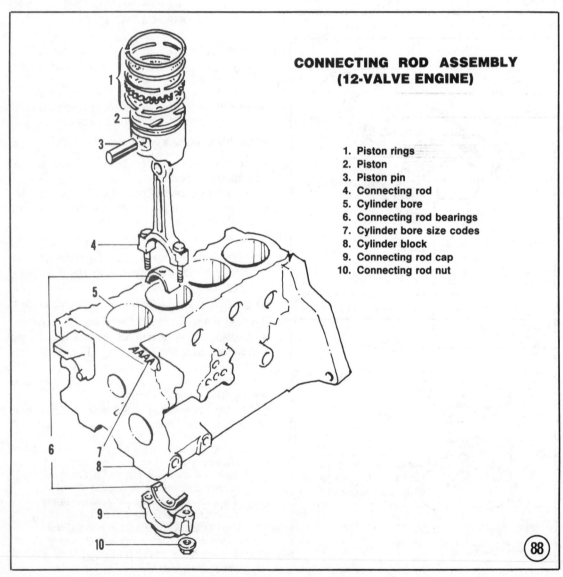

CONNECTING ROD ASSEMBLY
(12-VALVE ENGINE)

1. Piston rings
2. Piston
3. Piston pin
4. Connecting rod
5. Cylinder bore
6. Connecting rod bearings
7. Cylinder bore size codes
8. Cylinder block
9. Connecting rod cap
10. Connecting rod nut

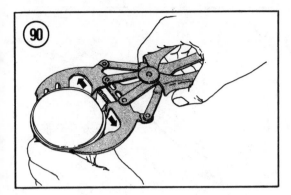

2. Clean piston ring grooves with a ring groove cleaner or squared-off piece of piston ring.

CAUTION
If you use a piece of piston ring to clean the grooves, be careful not to scratch the grooves.

3. Check the piston for cracks at the skirts, ring grooves, pin bosses and top. Any noticeable fault requires that the piston be replaced.

4. Measure piston diameter at a point 2 mm (0.08 in.) from the bottom of the skirt. See **Figure 91**. If diameter is not within specifications at the end of the chapter, replace the piston.

NOTE
Before selecting replacement pistons, inspect the cylinder block as described in this chapter. If inspection indicates a need to rebore the cylinders, the pistons must be replaced with oversized pistons.

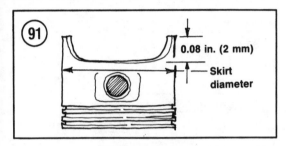

5. Repeat this procedure for all cylinders and pistons.

Piston Pin Clearance Check

Place the connecting rod assembly in a vise. Rock the piston as shown in **Figure 92**. Any rocking motion (not sliding) indicates wear in the piston, piston pin, connecting rod or all 3. Take the connecting rod and piston assembly to a machine shop for further inspection and service.

Connecting Rod Bearing Clearance Measurement

1. Place connecting rods and upper bearing halves on the proper crankpins (connecting rod journals).

2. Cut a piece of Plastigage the width of the bearing. Place the Plastigage on the bearing, then install the lower bearing half and cap.

NOTE
Do not place Plastigage over the crankpin oil hole.

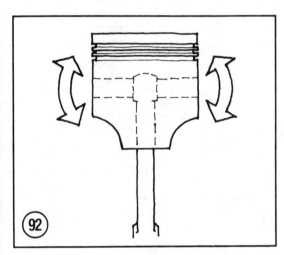

3. Tighten the connecting rod cap to specifications (end of chapter). Do not rotate the crankshaft while the Plastigage is in place.

4. Remove the connecting rod cap. Compare the width of the flattened Plastigage to the scale on the envelope (**Figure 93**). If clearance is excessive, install the next thicker bearing, referring to **Table 3** at the end of the chapter.

5. Recheck clearance with the thicker bearing. Keep trying thicker bearings until clearance is within specifications. If the thickest bearing available does not bring clearance within specifications, install a new crankshaft.

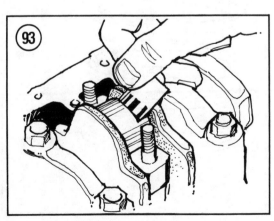

Connecting Rod Inspection

Have connecting rod straightness checked by a dealer or machine shop. If bend or twist exceeds specifications (end of chapter), straighten or replace the connecting rod.

Piston Ring Fit/Installation

1. Check the ring gap of each piston ring. To do this, position the ring 15-20 mm (0.6-0.8 in.) from the bottom of the bore and square it by tapping gently with an inverted piston.

2. Measure ring gap with a feeler gauge as shown in **Figure 94**. Compare with specifications at the end of the chapter.

3. Check side clearance of the rings as shown in **Figure 95**. Place the feeler gauge beneath the ring, all the way into the groove. The feeler gauge should slide all the way around the piston without binding. Any wear that occurs will form a step at the inner portion of the ring groove's lower edge. If large steps are detected (**Figure 96**), the piston should be replaced. Compare the inserted feeler gauge size with the specifications at the end of this chapter.

4. Using a ring expander tool, carefully install the oil ring assembly. See **Figure 97**. Stagger the oil ring gaps as shown in **Figure 98**. Do not position any of the gaps in line with the front-to-rear or side-to-side directions of an installed engine.

5. Install the compression rings with the ring expander. Identify second compression and top compression rings by their chamfers. See **Figure 99** (1983) or **Figure 100** (1984). The manufacturer's marks must be up as shown in **Figure 97**. Position the ring gaps as shown in **Figure 98**.

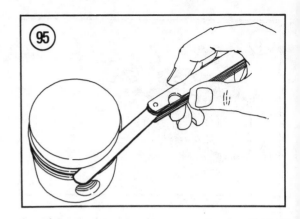

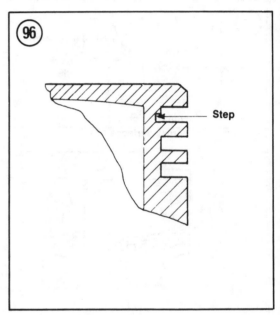

Step

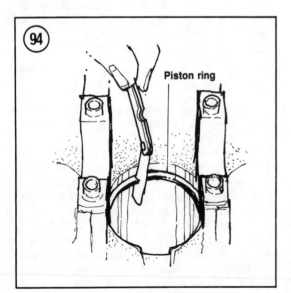

Piston ring

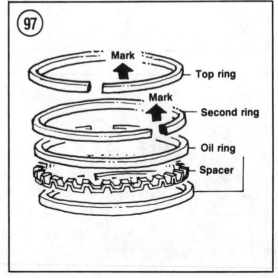

Mark — Top ring

Mark — Second ring

Oil ring

Spacer

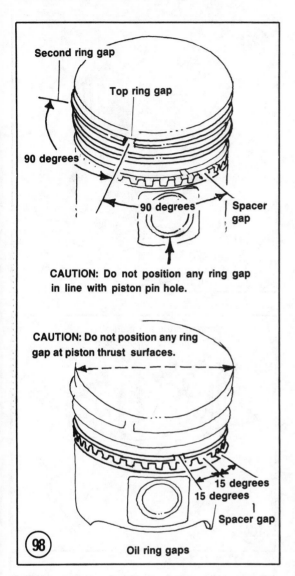

CAUTION: Do not position any ring gap in line with piston pin hole.

CAUTION: Do not position any ring gap at piston thrust surfaces.

98 Oil ring gaps

Installing Piston/ Connecting Rod Assembly

1. Make sure the pistons are correctly installed on the connecting rods. The side of the piston that goes nearest the intake manifold is marked (**Figure 101**). The connecting rod oil hole also goes nearest the manifold.

2. Be sure the ring gaps are positioned correctly (**Figure 98**).

3. Immerse the entire piston in clean engine oil. Coat the cylinder wall with oil.

4. Slide a ring compressor over the rings. Compress the rings into the grooves. See **Figure 102**.

5. Place pieces of hose over the connecting rod studs. This will prevent the studs from scratching the crankshaft during installation.

NOTE
If you don't have the right size hose, wrap the studs with tape.

5

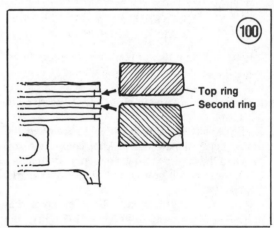

100 Top ring / Second ring

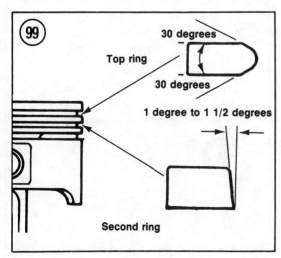

99 30 degrees / Top ring / 30 degrees / 1 degree to 1 1/2 degrees / Second ring

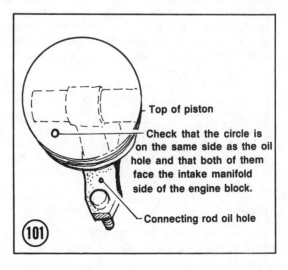

101 Top of piston / Check that the circle is on the same side as the oil hole and that both of them face the intake manifold side of the engine block. / Connecting rod oil hole

6. Install the piston/connecting rod assembly in the cylinder as shown in **Figure 102**. Tap lightly with a wooden hammer handle to insert the piston. Be sure the piston mark and connecting rod oil hole are on the same side of the engine as the intake manifold.

CAUTION
Use extreme care not to let the connecting rod nick the crankpin.

7. Coat the connecting rod bearings and their crankpins with clean engine oil. Place the bearings in connecting rod and cap. Be sure the alignment tangs fit in the notches in connecting rod and cap.
8. Install the connecting rod cap. Make sure the rod and cap number marks are on the same side. Tighten the cap nuts to specifications (end of chapter).
9. Recheck connecting rod big-end play (**Figure 86**).

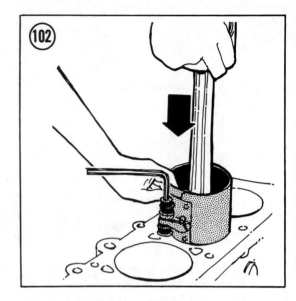

CRANKSHAFT AND MAIN BEARINGS

Refer to **Figure 103** for the following procedures.

Removal

1. Remove the engine from the car as described in this chapter.
2. If you haven't already done so, remove the timing belt, oil pan and pickup, connecting rod caps and flywheel or torque converter drive plate.
3. Check the main bearing caps for number marks (**Figure 104**).
4. Measure crankshaft end play. Set up a dial indicator as shown in **Figure 105**. Pry the crankshaft back and forth against the dial gauge pointer and note the reading. Compare with specifications at the end of the chapter. If clearance exceeds specifications, replace the crankshaft thrust washers and recheck. If clearance is still excessive, replace the crankshaft.
5. Unbolt the main bearing caps. Loosen the caps in 2 or 3 stages, working outward from the center.
6. Check main bearing clearance with Plastigage as described in this chapter.
7. Lift the crankshaft out of the block. Remove the oil seal from each end of the crankshaft. Lay the crankshaft, bearings and caps in order on a clean workbench.

Inspection

1. Clean the crankshaft thoroughly in solvent. Blow out the oil passages with compressed air.

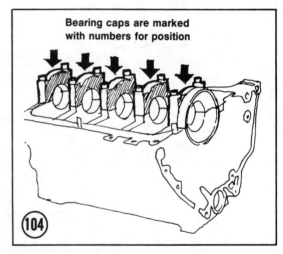

Bearing caps are marked with numbers for position

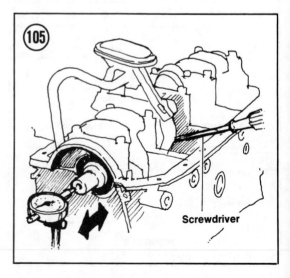

Screwdriver

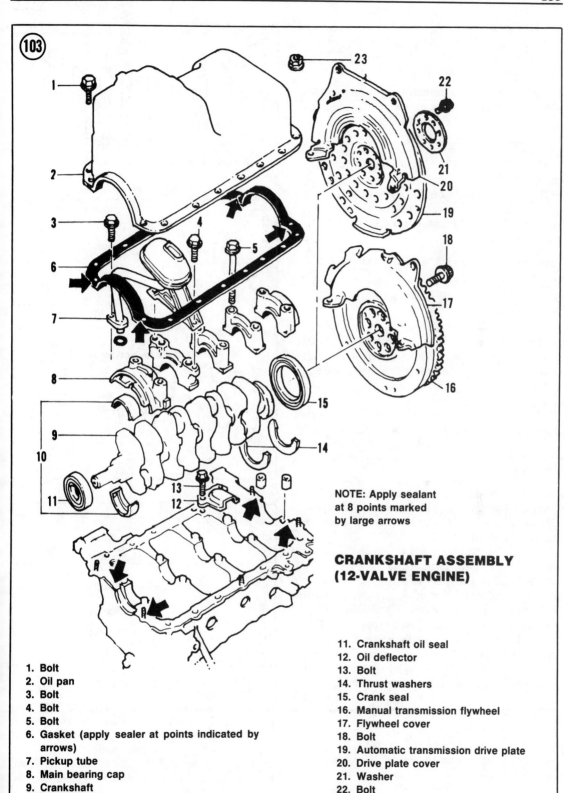

NOTE: Apply sealant
at 8 points marked
by large arrows

CRANKSHAFT ASSEMBLY (12-VALVE ENGINE)

1. Bolt
2. Oil pan
3. Bolt
4. Bolt
5. Bolt
6. Gasket (apply sealer at points indicated by arrows)
7. Pickup tube
8. Main bearing cap
9. Crankshaft
10. Main bearing inserts

11. Crankshaft oil seal
12. Oil deflector
13. Bolt
14. Thrust washers
15. Crank seal
16. Manual transmission flywheel
17. Flywheel cover
18. Bolt
19. Automatic transmission drive plate
20. Drive plate cover
21. Washer
22. Bolt
23. Nut

NOTE
If you don't have precision measuring equipment, have a machine shop perform Step 2 and Step 3.

2. Check crankpins and main bearing journals for wear, scoring and cracks. Check all journals against specifications (end of chapter) for wear, taper and out-of-roundess. If the crankshaft is worn beyond specifications, replace it.

3. Check the crankshaft for bending. Mount the crankshaft between accurate centers (such as V-blocks or a lathe) and rotate it one full turn with a dial indicator contacting the center journal. If bent beyond specifications, the crankshaft must be reground or replaced.

Main Bearing Clearance Measurement

1. If the crankshaft has been removed from the block, install it together with its original upper bearing halves.

2. Cut a piece of Plastigage the width of the bearing to be measured and lay it on the crankshaft journal. Install the main bearing cap with lower bearing half and tighten to specifications at the end of the chapter.

NOTE
Do not place Plastigage across crankshaft oil holes. Do not rotate the crankshaft while the Plastigage is in place.

3. Remove the main bearing cap and bearing half. Compare the width of the flattened Plastigage to the markings on the envelope to determine bearing clearance. See **Figure 93**.

4. If bearing clearance is not within specifications at the end of the chapter, select bearings as described in the following steps.

5. The crankshaft journals are marked with numbers (1, 2, 3 or 4; see **Figure 106**). These indicate journal diameter. The flywheel end of the engine block is marked with, letters or Roman numerals (**Figure 107**) which indicate the bore of the main bearing caps and saddles when the caps are installed on the engine. Any combination of numbers (crankshaft) or Roman numerals (cylinder block) can be used with any engine.

NOTE
With the crankshaft side of the block facing upward, the top mark indicates the crankshaft bearing bore nearest the flywheel end of the engine. The next mark down indicates the next bearing bore, etc.

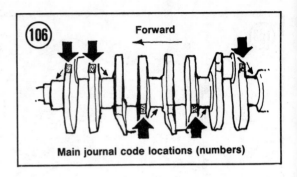
Main journal code locations (numbers)

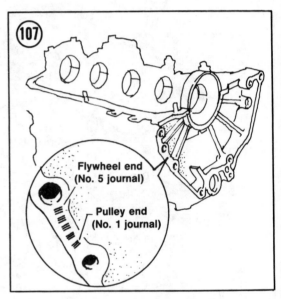
Flywheel end (No. 5 journal)
Pulley end (No. 1 journal)

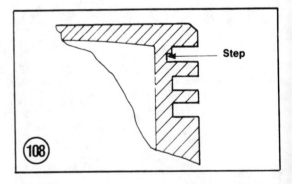
Step

6. Referring to **Table 4** at the end of the chapter, select new bearings by cross-referencing the main journal OD number with the bearing bore's Roman numeral. Where the 2 columns intersect, the new bearing color is indicated.

7. Recheck bearing clearance with the new bearings. Keep trying until bearing clearance is within specifications. If bearing clearance cannot be brought into specifications by changing bearings, replace the crankshaft.

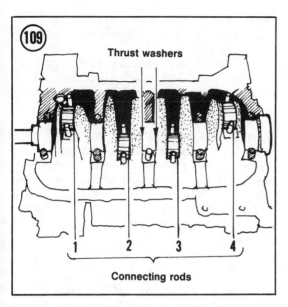

Thrust washers

1   2   3   4

Connecting rods

(109)

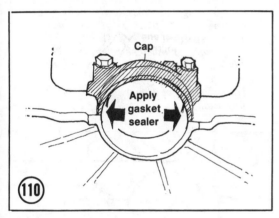

Cap

Apply gasket sealer

(110)

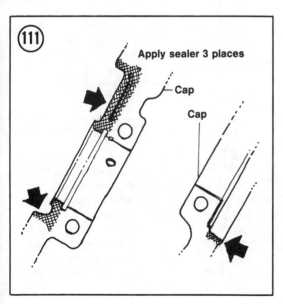

Apply sealer 3 places

Cap

Cap

(111)

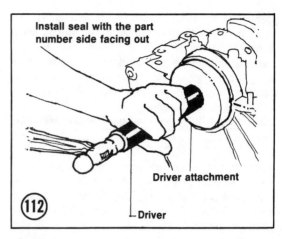

Install seal with the part number side facing out

Driver attachment

Driver

(112)

Crankshaft/Main Bearing Installation

1. Make sure bearings, main caps and cylinder block bearing saddles are clean.

2. Position bearing halves in the block and caps. Be sure the bearing locating tangs are correctly positioned in the cylinder block and bearing cap notches. See **Figure 108**. Be sure the oil holes in the bearings align with the oil holes in the block.

3. Position the thrust washers next to the center bearing saddle and cap.

NOTE
The thrust washer oil grooves face outward, away from the center bearing saddle and cap.

4. Coat the bearings freely with clean engine oil. Lay the crankshaft in the block. Coat the crankshaft journals with clean engine oil.

5. If the connecting rods are already in the block, fit the crankpins into No. 2 and No. 3 connecting rods. See **Figure 109**. Install the connecting rod caps and tighten the nuts finger-tight. Fit the No. 1 and No. 4 crankpins into their connecting rods, then install the caps and tighten the nuts finger-tight.

6. Install the bearing caps and tighten the bolts slightly.

7. Apply a light coat of non-hardening gasket sealer to the seams where No. 1 bearing cap and No. 5 bearing cap meet the block. See **Figure 110** and **Figure 111**.

8. Tap new oil seals into both ends of the crankshaft with a suitable drift. See **Figure 112**. The part number on each seal faces outward (away from the engine).

9. Tighten the cap bolts to specifications. Tighten in 2 or 3 stages, starting with the center cap and working outward. Rotate the crankshaft during

5

tightening to make sure it isn't binding. If the crankshaft is difficult to turn, stop and find out why before tightening further. Check for foreign material on bearings and journals. Make absolutely certain bearings are the correct size. If in doubt, recheck bearing clearances with Plastigage as described in this chapter.

10. Recheck crankshaft end play (**Figure 105**).

CYLINDER BLOCK INSPECTION

1. Clean the block thoroughly with solvent and check all core plugs for leaks. Replace any core plugs that are suspect. It is a good idea to replace all of them. While cleaning, check oil and water passages for dirt, sludge and corrosion. If the passages are very dirty, the block should be boiled out by a dealer or machine shop.

> *NOTE*
> *Block boiling necessitates replacement of all core plugs. However, a block dirty enough to need boiling almost certainly needs these parts replaced anyway.*

2. Check the block for cracks. It is a good idea to have the block Magnafluxed by a machine shop to check for hairline cracks that may not be visible.

3. Check flatness of the cylinder block's top surface. Use an accurate straightedge as shown in

Figure 113. Measure in the directions shown in **Figure 114**. Have the block resurfaced if warped beyond specifications.

4. Measure cylinder bores for wear, taper and out-of-roundness with a bore gauge. A machine shop can do this inexpensively if you don't have a bore gauge. Measure the bores at top, center and bottom, in front-to-rear and side-to-side directions. See **Figure 115**. Bore sizes are stamped on the block as shown. Reading from left to right, the bore grades apply to cylinders 1 through 4. Compare the measurements to specifications at the end of the chapter. If the cylinders exceed maximum tolerances, they must be rebored. Reboring is also necessary if the cylinder walls are badly scuffed or scored.

> *NOTE*
> *If the block is lightly scuffed or scored, it can be honed with a 220-grit hone in a 60 degree crosshatch pattern. However, if the block must be honed beyond specified diameter to clean up the surface, it must be rebored. Light vertical scratches are okay, as long as they do not run the full length of the bore and are not deep enough to snag a fingernail.*

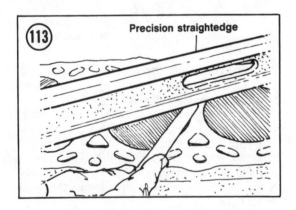

Precision straightedge

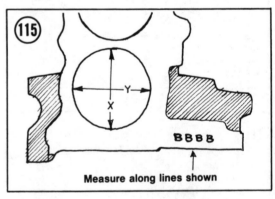

Measure along lines shown

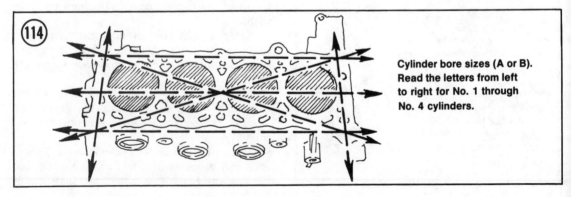

Cylinder bore sizes (A or B).
Read the letters from left
to right for No. 1 through
No. 4 cylinders.

Table 1 SPECIFICATIONS (12-VALVE ENGINE)

Item	mm	in.
Cylinder head		
Maximum warp	0.05	0.002
Height	90.0	3.54
Camshaft		
End play (standard)	0.05-0.15	0.002-0.006
End play (maximum)	0.5	0.002
Bearing clearance (standard)		
Journals 1, 3, 5	0.05-0.09	0.002-0.004
Journals 2, 4	0.13-0.17	0.005-0.007
Bearing clearance (maximum)		
Journals 1, 3, 5	0.15	0.006
Journals 2, 4	0.23	0.009
Bend		
Standard	0.03	0.001
Maximum	0.06	0.02
Lobe height (1983 Prelude)		
Manual		
Auxiliary intake	36.74	1.446
Main intake A	38.86	1.530
Main intake B	38.41	1.512
Main exhaust	38.99	1.535
Automatic		
Auxiliary intake	36.74	1.446
Main intake A	38.67	1.522
Main intake B	38.22	1.505
Main exhaust	38.61	1.520
Lobe height (1984 Prelude)		
Manual		
Intake A	38.86	1.530
Intake B	38.41	1.512
Exhaust	38.92	1.532
Automatic		
Intake A	38.67	1.522
Intake B	38.22	1.505
Exhaust	38.42	1.513
Lobe height (1984 Accord)		
Manual		
Auxiliary intake	36.74	1.446
Main intake A	37.899	1.492
Main intake B	38.028	1.497
Exhaust	37.776	1.487
Automatic		
Auxiliary intake	36.74	1.446
Main intake A	37.705	1.484
Main intake B	38.157	1.502
Exhaust	37.776	1.487
Valves (1983 Prelude)		
Stem outside diameter, standard		
Auxiliary intake	6.572-6.587	0.2587-0.2593
Main intake	6.58-6.59	0.2591-0.2594
Main exhaust	6.94-6.95	0.2732-0.2736
Stem outside diameter, maximum		
Auxiliary intake	6.54	0.257
Main intake	6.55	0.258
Main exhaust	6.91	0.272

(continued)

5

Table 1 SPECIFICATIONS (12-VALVE ENGINE) (continued)

Item	mm	in.
Valves (1983 Prelude)		
Stem-to-guide clearance, standard		
Auxiliary intake	0.02-0.05	0.001-0.002
Main intake	0.02-0.05	0.001-0.002
Main exhaust	0.06-0.09	0.002-0.004
Stem-to-guide clearance, maximum		
Auxiliary intake	0.08	0.003
Main intake	0.08	0.003
Main exhaust	0.12	0.005
Stem installed height, standard		
Auxiliary intake	36.78	1.448
Main intake	48.59	1.913
Main exhaust	47.66	1.876
Stem installed height, maximum		
Auxiliary intake	37.68	1.483
Main intake	49.34	1.943
Main exhaust	48.41	1.906
Valves (1984 Prelude)		
Stem outside diameter, standard		
Intake	6.58-6.59	0.2591-0.2594
Exhaust	6.94-6.95	0.2732-0.2736
Stem outside diameter, maximum		
Intake	6.55	0.258
Exhaust	6.91	0.272
Stem-to-guide clearance, standard		
Intake	0.02-0.05	0.001-0.002
Exhaust	0.06-0.09	0.002-0.004
Stem-to-guide clearance, maximum		
Intake	0.08	0.003
Exhaust	0.12	0.005
Stem installed height, standard		
Intake	48.59	1.913
Exhaust	47.66	1.876
Stem installed height, maximum		
Intake	49.34	1.943
Exhaust	48.41	1.906
Valves (1984 Accord)		
Stem outside diameter, standard		
Auxiliary intake	6.572-6.587	0.2587-0.2593
Main intake	6.58-6.59	0.2591-0.2594
Main exhaust	6.94-6.95	0.2732-0.2736
Stem outside diameter, maximum		
Auxiliary intake	6.54	0.257
Main intake	6.55	0.258
Main exhaust	6.91	0.272
Stem-to-guide clearance, standard		
Auxiliary intake	0.02-0.05	0.001-0.002
Main intake	0.02-0.05	0.001-0.002
Main exhaust	0.06-0.09	0.002-0.004

(continued)

Table 1 SPECIFICATIONS (12-VALVE ENGINE) (continued)

Item	mm	in.
Valves (1984 Accord)		
Stem-to-guide clearance, maximum		
Auxiliary intake	0.08	0.003
Main intake	0.08	0.003
Main exhaust	0.12	0.005
Stem installed height, standard		
Auxiliary intake	36.78	1.448
Main intake	48.59	1.913
Main exhaust	47.66	1.876
Stem installed height, maximum		
Auxiliary intake	37.68	1.483
Main intake	49.34	1.943
Main exhaust	48.41	1.906
Valve seat width, standard		
Auxiliary (if so equipped)	0.353-0.494	0.014-0.019
Main (intake and exhaust)	1.25-1.55	0.049-0.061
Valve seat width, maximum		
Auxiliary (if so equipped)	1.0	0.04
Main (intake and exhaust)	2.0	0.08
Valve springs (1983 Prelude)		
Free length, standard		
Auxiliary intake	31.7	1.25
Main intake	48.3	1.90
Main exhaust (inner)	39.8	1.57
Main exhaust (outer)	47.8	1.88
Free length, minimum		
Auxiliary intake	31.0	1.22
Main intake	47.2	1.85
Main exhaust (inner)	38.8	1.53
Main exhaust (outer)	46.8	1.84
Maximum bend	1.75	0.068
Valve springs (1984 Prelude)		
Free length, standard		
Intake	49.2	1.94
Exhaust (inner)	39.8	1.57
Exhaust (outer)	49.8	1.96
Free length, minimum		
Intake	47.2	1.85
Exhaust (inner)	38.8	1.53
Exhaust (outer)	46.8	1.84
Maximum bend	1.75	0.068
Valve springs (1984 Accord)		
Free length, standard		
Auxiliary intake	31.7	1.25
Main intake (inner)	39.8	1.57
Main intake (outer)	46.88	1.846
Main exhaust (inner)	39.8	1.57
Main exhaust (outer)	47.8	1.88
Free length, minimum		
Auxiliary intake	31.0	1.22
Main intake (inner)	38.8	1.53
Main intake (outer)	46.13	1.816
Main exhaust (inner)	38.8	1.53
Main exhaust (outer)	46.8	1.84
Maximum bend	1.75	0.068

(continued)

5

Table 1 SPECIFICATIONS (12-VALVE ENGINE) (continued)

Item	mm	in.
Valve guides		
Inside diameter (standard)		
Auxiliary intake	6.61-6.63	0.260-0.261
Main intake	6.61-6.63	0.260-0.261
Main exhaust	7.01-7.03	0.276-0.277
Inside diameter (maximum)		
Auxiliary intake	6.65	0.262
Main intake	6.65	0.262
Main exhaust	7.05	0.278
Rocker arm-to-shaft clearance, maximum	0.08	0.003
Cylinder block		
Surface warp, standard	0.08	0.003
Surface warp, maximum	0.10	0.004
Bore diameter, standard		
Grade A	80.01-80.02	3.1500-3.1504
Grade B	80.00-80.01	3.1496-3.1500
Bore diameter, maximum		
Grade A	80.05	3.1516
Grade B	80.04	3.1512
Taper, standard	0.07-0.012	0.0003-0.0005
Taper, maximum	0.05	0.002
Reboring limit	0.5	0.02
Pistons, 1983		
Skirt diameter, standard		
A piston	79.975-79.998	3.1486-3.1495
B piston	79.965-79.988	3.1482-3.1491
Skirt diameter, minimum		
A piston	79.965	3.1482
B piston	79.955	3.1478
Piston-to-bore clearance		
Standard	0.012-0.045	0.0005-0.0018
Maximum	0.075	0.003
Compression ring gap		
Standard	0.20-0.35	0.008-0.014
Maximum	0.6	0.024
Oil ring gap		
Standard	0.20-0.70	0.008-0.030
Maximum	1.1	0.043
Ring side clearance (compression rings only)		
Standard	0.020-0.045	0.0008-0.0018
Maximum	0.13	0.005
Pistons, 1984		
Skirt diameter, standard		
A pisto	79.98-79.99	3.1488-3.1492
B piston	79.97-79.98	3.1484-3.1488
Skirt diameter, minimum		
A piston	79.97	3.1484
B piston	76.96	3.1480
Piston-to-bore clearance		
Standard	0.02-0.04	0.0008-0.0016
Maximum	0.08	0.003
Compression ring gap		
Standard	0.20-0.35	0.008-0.014
Maximum	0.6	0.024

(continued)

Table 1 SPECIFICATIONS (12-VALVE ENGINE) (continued)

Item	mm	in.
Pistons, 1984		
Oil ring gap		
Standard (Prelude)	0.20-0.70	0.008-0.030
Standard (Accord)	0.20-0.90	0.008-0.035
Maximum	1.1	0.043
Ring side clearance (compression rings only)		
Standard	0.020-0.045	0.0008-0.0018
Maximum	0.13	0.005
Connecting rods		
Big-end play, standard	0.15-0.30	0.006-0.012
Big-end play, maximum	0.40	0.016
Crankshaft		
Main journal diameter		
1983 Prelude	50-006-50.030	1.9687-1.9697
1984 Prelude	49.970-49.994	1.9673-1.9683
1984 Accord	50.000-50.024	1.9685-1.9694
Rod journal diameter	44.976-45.000	1.7707-1.7717
Journal taper and out-of-round, maximum	0.005	0.0002
End play (standard)	0.10-0.35	0.004-0.014
End play (maximum)	0.45	0.18
Bend (standard)	0.03	0.0012
Bend (maximum)	0.06	0.0024
Main bearing clearance		
Standard (1983)	0.020-0.049	0.0008-0.0019
Standard (1984)	0.026-0.055	0.0010-0.0022
Maximum	0.07	0.003
Connecting rod bearing clearance		
Standard	0.020-0.038	0.0008-0.0015
Maximum	0.07	0.003
Oil pump		
Inner to outer rotor clearance		
Standard	0.15	0.006
Maximum	0.2	0.008
Outer rotor to body clearance		
Standard	0.0-0.18	0.004-0.007
Maximum	0.2	0.008
Rotor to body clearance		
Standard	0.03-0.108	0.001-0.004
Maximum	0.15	0.006

5

Table 2 TIGHTENING TORQUES

Fastener	Thread size	N•m	ft.-lb.
Prelude engine installation*			
No. 1	10×1.25 mm	Snug	—
No. 2	8×1.25 mm	29	21
No. 3	10×1.25	20	14
No. 4	10×1.25	20	14
No. 5	10×1.25	39	28
No. 6	12×1.25	Snug	—
No. 7	12×1.25	75	54
No. 8	12×1.25	75	54
No. 9	10×1.25	20	14
A (2 bolts)	10×1.25	65	47
B	12×1.25	75	54
C (2 bolts)	10×1.25	45	33
D	—	(continued) 49	35

Table 2 TIGHTENING TORQUES (continued)

Fastener	Thread size	N•m	ft.-lb.
Accord engine installation*			
No. 1	10×1.25	Snug	—
No. 2	10×1.25	55	40
No. 3	10×1.25	20	14
No. 4	10×1.25	20	14
No. 5	10×1.25	39	28
No. 6	12×1.25	Snug	—
No. 7	12×1.25	75	54
No. 8	12×1.25	75	54
No. 9	10×1.25	20	14
A	10×1.25	65	47
Valve cover nut	6	10	
Cylinder head bolts	10×1.25	68	49
Timing belt upper cover bolts			
1983-1984	6×1.0	10	7
Timing belt adjustment bolt	—	43	31
Rocker assembly bolts	8×1.25	22	16
	6×1.0	12	9
Distributor mounting bolts	6×1.0	12	9
Thermostat housing nuts	8×1.25	22	16
Camshaft sprocket bolt	8×1.25	38	27
Auxiliary valve holder nut	—	80	58
Timing belt lower cover bolts			
1983	6×1.0	12	9
1984	6×1.0	10	7
Water pump pulley bolts			
1983	6×1.0	10	7
1984	6×1.0	12	9
Crankshaft pulley bolt	12×1.25	115	83
Oil pan bolts			
1983	6×1.0	12	9
1984	6×1.0	14	10
Oil pan nuts	6×1.0	10	7
Flywheel bolts	12×1.0	105	76
Drive plate bolts	12×1.0	75	54
Connecting rod nuts	8×0.75	32	23
Oil filter base bolts	6×1.0	12	9
Oil pump bolts	6×1.0	12	9
Oil pump nuts			
1983	6×1.0	10	7
1984	6×1.0	12	9
Oil pump cover screws	6×1.0	7	5
Manifolds (Prelude)			
Intake manifold nuts	8×1.25	22	16
Exhaust manifold nuts	8×1.25	28	20
Exhaust header pipe nuts	10×1.25	55	40
Manifolds (Accord)			
Intake manifold nuts	8×1.25	22	16
Exhaust manifold nuts	10×1.25	32	22

* Tighten numbered bolts in order shown in text.

Table 3 CONNECTING ROD BEARING SELECTION

Connecting rod code number	1	2	3	4
Rod journal letter				
A	Red	Pink	Yellow	Green
B	Pink	Yellow	Green	Brown
C	Yellow	Green	Brown	Black
D	Green	Brown	Black	Blue

Table 4 MAIN BEARING SELECTION

Crankshaft code number	I or A	II or B	III or C	IV or 4
Crankshaft bore code letter or number				
1	Red	Pink	Yellow	Green
2	Pink	Yellow	Green	Brown
3	Yellow	Green	Brown	Black
4	Green	Brown	Black	Blue

5

NOTE: If you own a 1985 model, first check the Supplement at the back of the book for any new service information.

CHAPTER SIX

FUEL, EXHAUST AND EMISSION CONTROL SYSTEMS

This chapter includes service procedures for the air cleaner, carburetor, fuel pump and fuel system-related emission controls. **Table 1** is at the end of the chapter.

AIR CLEANER

The air cleaner uses a paper element, which should be replaced at the intervals specified in Chapter Three. The air cleaner also incorporates several emission control devices.

Element Replacement

Refer to **Figure 1** (all Accord and 1979-1982 Prelude) or **Figure 2** (1983-on Prelude).

1. Remove the center wing nut and washer.
2. Unlatch the wire hooks and remove the cover. Remove and discard the air cleaner element. If the inside of the housing is dirty, wipe it clean with a damp cloth (do not let debris fall into the carburetor).
3. Install a new filter element. Then place the cover in position and secure it with the wire hooks and wing nut.

NOTE
*On some models, arrows have been stamped on the air cleaner cover and on the intake tunnel (**Figure 3**). These arrows should be aligned after installing the cover.*

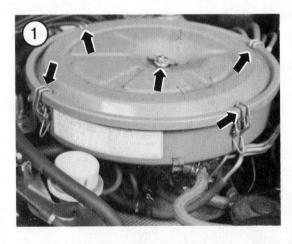

Air cleaner back
Air cleaner element
Air cleaner case

AIR CLEANER (1983-ON PRELUDE)

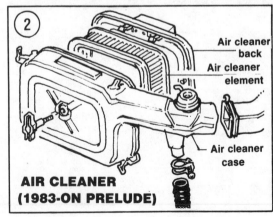

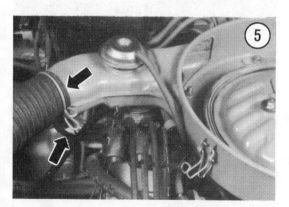

Housing Removal/Installation

All Accord, 1979-1982 Prelude

Several vacuum lines and hoses are attached to the air cleaner. These differ according to model year and the area in which the car was first sold. Each plays an important part in the operation and efficiency of the engine. Use the following removal and installation procedures as a general guide. For specific information for your particular Honda, refer to the vehicle emission control information and vacuum hose routing diagram decals on the engine hood. See **Figure 4**.

> *NOTE*
> *In addition to using the emission decals on your car's hood, tag all lines and hoses before removal to help with reinstallation.*

1. Remove the center wing nut and washer. Then detach the wire clips securing the air cleaner cover. See **Figure 1**. Remove the air cleaner cover and air filter.
2. Remove the clamps from the fresh air duct and hot air duct at the air cleaner. See **Figure 5**.
3. Disconnect the vacuum line at the air control diaphragm (**Figure 6**).
4. If equipped with power steering, remove the power steering hose clamp at the air cleaner housing (do not disconnect any hose fittings). Set the hose aside.
5. Loosen and remove the air cleaner housing inside and outside attaching screws (**Figure 7** and **Figure 8**).
6. Lift up the air cleaner housing (**Figure 9**). Label and disconnect the hoses that attach to the bottom of the air cleaner.

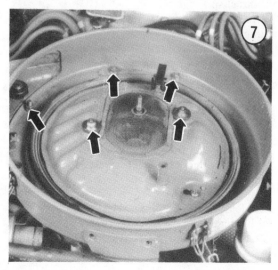

7. Check the air cleaner housing carefully to make sure all hoses and tubes are disconnected or removed, then remove the air cleaner assembly.

8. Install in the reverse order.

1983-on Prelude

Refer to **Figure 2** for this procedure.

1. Disconnect the intake hose and hot air hose from the air cleaner intake duct.

2. Remove the wing nut and release the wire clips. Take off the air cleaner cover and remove the element.

3. Label and disconnect the hoses that attach to the air cleaner base.

4. Remove the base mounting nuts and take the base off. See **Figure 10**.

5. Installation is the reverse of removal.

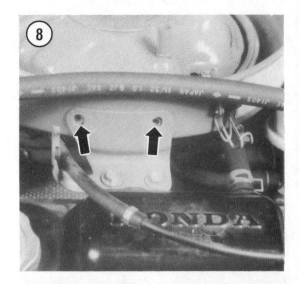

CARBURETOR
(ACCORD; 1979-1982 PRELUDE)

The engine is equipped with a 3-barrel, 2-stage carburetor. A manual choke is used on 1976-1977 models. Beginning on 1978 models, an automatic choke is used. The operation of the carburetor is much like a 2-barrel type, with the addition of a third venturi and throttle which supply fuel and air to the auxiliary intake valves.

The only carburetor service practical for home mechanics is removal, installation, choke cable adjustment (manual-choke models) and the periodic adjustments described under *Tune-up* in Chapter Three. Major servicing should be entrusted to a Honda dealer or mechanic familiar with Honda emission controls.

Removal/Installation

1. Remove the air cleaner assembly as described in this chapter.

2. Label and disconnect all vacuum hoses at the carburetor.

3. Disconnect the throttle cable at the carburetor. See *Throttle Cable* in this chapter for details.

4. Disconnect the fuel line at the 3-way joint (**Figure 11**).

5. On manual choke models, loosen the screw in the choke cable sheath clamp far enough to remove the sheath from beneath the clamp. Disconnect the choke cable end from the choke arm.

6. Unscrew the carburetor mounting nuts and remove the carburetor from the manifold. Do not remove the insulator. Cover the openings in the manifold with a clean rag.

7. Installation is the reverse of these steps. Make certain all vacuum hoses and emission control hoses are correctly connected. Replace any hoses

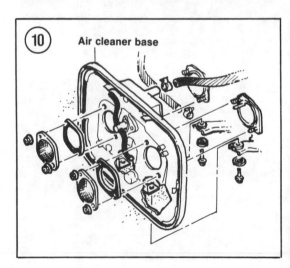

Air cleaner base

that are cracked, chafed or show signs of deterioration. When the installation is complete, adjust the throttle cable (and manual choke cable, if so equipped) as described in this chapter.

Manual Choke Inspection

This procedure applies to 1976-1977 models only.
1. Remove the air cleaner cover to provide visual access to the carburetor butterfly valve.
2. Have an assistant operate the choke knob in and out while you check to see that the butterfly valve and choke mechanism operate smoothly without any noticeable sticking or binding.
3. Push the choke knob all the way in. The butterfly valve should be all the way open.
4. Pull the choke knob to the second detent position. The butterfly valve should just close. Then pull the choke knob all the way out. The butterfly valve should be completely closed.
5. If the choke butterfly valve failed to operate correctly when performing Steps 1-4, clean or have it repaired as necessary. Then adjust the choke cable as described in this chapter.

Choke Cable Adjustment

This procedure applies to 1976-1977 models only.
1. *Butterfly valve fails to open properly:* Loosen locknut. Turn the choke cable adjusting nut in until the butterfly valve moves off the positioning stop tab. Then turn the adjusting nut out so the valve just touches the stop tab. Tighten locknut and recheck adjustment. See **Figure 12**.
2. *Butterfly valve fails to close properly:* Inspect the butterfly valve and shaft for binding and excessive amounts of dirt. Also check the return spring operation. Clean or replace as needed.

CARBURETORS
(1983-ON PRELUDE)

The 1983 and later Prelude uses two slide-valve carburetors similar to those used on motorcycles. On 1983 models, a small auxiliary carburetor supplies fuel to the engine's auxiliary intake valves. The auxiliary intake valves and auxiliary carburetor are not used on 1984 Preludes.

The carburetors are extremely complicated and tampering with them may void your emission control warranty. The only procedures recommended for home mechanics are removal and installation. Periodic adjustments require special equipment. Carburetor adjustment and service should be done by a Honda dealer or a mechanic familiar with Honda emission controls.

Removal/Installation

Refer to **Figure 13** for this procedure.
1. Remove the air cleaner and air cleaner base as described in this chapter.
2. Label and disconnect all carburetor vacuum lines. On 1984 models, label and disconnect the air jet controller vacuum lines at the vacuum tube manifold.
3. Disconnect the throttle cable. See *Throttle Cable* in this chapter for details.
4. Drain the cooling system as described under *Cooling System Flushing* in Chapter Seven. If the coolant is clean, save it for reuse.

> *WARNING*
> *Antifreeze is poisonous and may attract animals. Do not store the drained coolant where it is accessible to children or pets.*

5. Disconnect the coolant hoses from the thermowax valve and intake manifold.
6. Unplug the carburetor electrical connectors.
7. Disconnect the evaporative emission canister hoses that connect to the carburetor assembly.

6

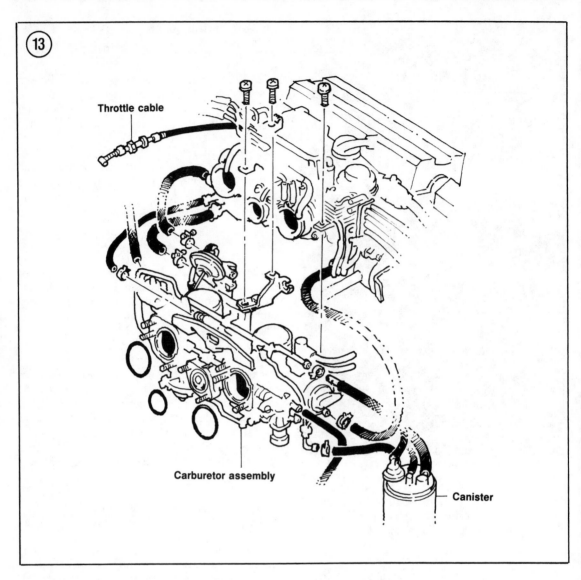

⑬

Throttle cable

Carburetor assembly

Canister

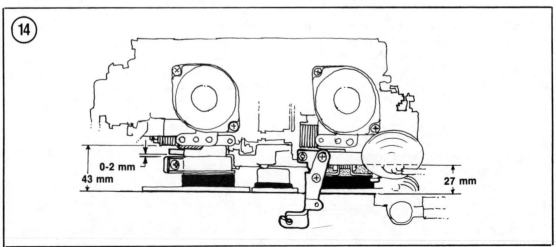

⑭

0-2 mm
43 mm

27 mm

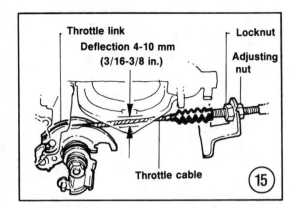

Throttle link

Deflection 4-10 mm
(3/16-3/8 in.)

Locknut

Adjusting nut

Throttle cable

(15)

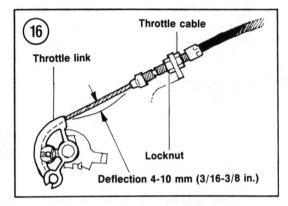

(16)

Throttle cable

Throttle link

Locknut

Deflection 4-10 mm (3/16-3/8 in.)

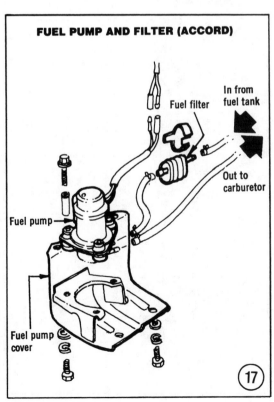

FUEL PUMP AND FILTER (ACCORD)

Fuel filter

In from fuel tank

Out to carburetor

Fuel pump

Fuel pump cover

(17)

8. Disconnect the main fuel hose. Plug or cap the end of the hose so it won't drip gasoline and create a fire hazard.

9. Loosen the insulator bands, then remove the carburetor assembly together with the vacuum tube manifold.

10. If necessary, remove the vacuum tube manifold attaching screws and take the vacuum tube manifold off the carburetor assembly.

11. Installation is the reverse of removal, plus the following:

  a. Check the dimensions shown in **Figure 14** and make sure the carburetor spigots are inserted fully into the insulators.

  b. Fill and bleed the cooling system as described in Chapter Seven.

  c. Have carburetor synchronization, idle speed and idle mixture adjusted by a Honda dealer or other qualified specialist.

THROTTLE CABLE

Adjustment

See **Figure 15** (all Accord, 1979-1982 Prelude) or **Figure 16** (1983-on Prelude).

1. Remove the air cleaner as described in this chapter.

2. Check the throttle cable for signs of fraying and chafing and replace it if its condition is in doubt; a faulty cable can stick, resulting in an extremely hazardous condition.

3. With your hand, check the free play in the throttle linkage. It should be 4-10 mm (0.16-0.40 in.). If the free play is less or more than this, loosen the locknut and turn the adjuster sleeve clockwise to increase the free play or counterclockwise to decrease it. When the free play is correct, hold the adjuster sleeve to prevent it from turning further and tighten the locknut.

4. When the throttle linkage free play has been adjusted, have an assistant depress the throttle pedal all the way to the floor and hold it there. Check the position of the throttle valves. Both the primary and secondary valves should be fully open. Readjust the throttle cable adjusting nut, if necessary, to obtain fully open valves.

FUEL PUMP

The Honda is equipped with an electric fuel pump located, along with the fuel filter, on the tank rear mounting bracket. Refer to the following illustrations:

  a. **Figure 17**—1976-1981 Accord.

  b. **Figure 18**—1982 and later Accord.

6

c. **Figure 19**—1979-1982 Prelude.

d. **Figure 20**—1983 and later Prelude.

If the fuel pump is suspected of being faulty (see *Troubleshooting*, Chapter Two), check the line connections to make sure they are tight. Also make certain the mounting bolts and the fuel pump body screws are tight.

1. Before testing the fuel pump on 1976-1977 models, disconnect the yellow/red wire from the oil pressure switch located above the oil filter.

2. Before testing the fuel pump on 1978 and later models, do the following:

a. Locate the fuse panel underneath the dashboard. Remove the screws securing the fuse box to the dashboard and allow it to hang down.

b. Pull down the junction box which contains the fuel pump cutoff relay.

c. Disconnect the cutoff relay connector from the junction box and connect a jumper wire between the 2 black/yellow wire pins in the junction box. See **Figure 21** (1976-1981 Accord and 1979-1982 Prelude), **Figure 22**

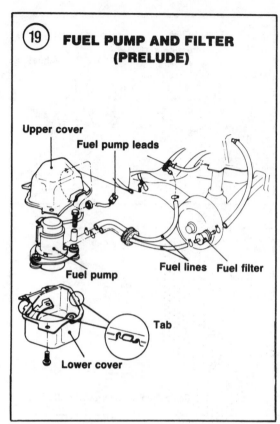

(19) **FUEL PUMP AND FILTER (PRELUDE)**

Upper cover

Fuel pump leads

Fuel pump

Fuel lines   Fuel filter

Tab

Lower cover

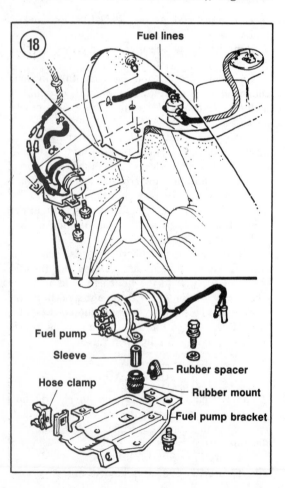

(18) Fuel lines

Fuel pump

Sleeve

Hose clamp

Rubber spacer

Rubber mount

Fuel pump bracket

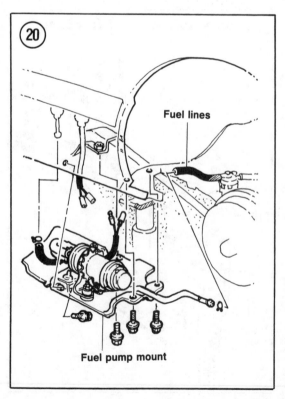

(20)

Fuel lines

Fuel pump mount

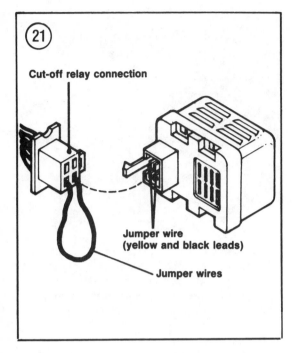

㉑

Cut-off relay connection

**Jumper wire
(yellow and black leads)**

Jumper wires

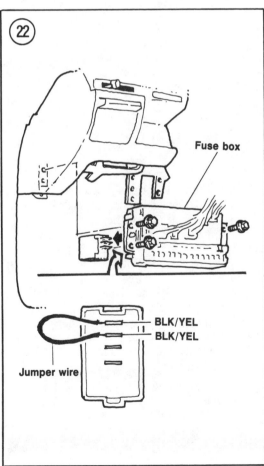

㉒

Fuse box

BLK/YEL
BLK/YEL

Jumper wire

(1982 and later Accord) or **Figure 23** (1983 and later Prelude).

3. Perform the fuel pump testing procedures in Chapter Two. Fuel pump specifications are in **Table 1**. After completing tests, reconnect the oil pressure white lead (1976-1977 models) or reconnect the cutoff relay connector and reinstall the fuse panel on 1978 and later models.

Removal/Installation

Fuel pumps on all models are nonrebuildable. If the fuel pump is bad, it must be replaced. Refer to **Figures 17-20**.

1. Securely block both front wheels so the car will not roll in either direction.

2. Jack up the rear end of the car and place it on jackstands.

3. Disconnect the negative cable from the battery. Remove the fuel pump cover retaining bolts.

4. Unplug the electrical leads from the pump. Unscrew the bolts that hold the pump in place and lower the pump to provide access to the fuel lines.

5. Disconnect the lines from the pump and remove it. Disconnect the lines from the filter and remove it. Plug the ends of the fuel lines to prevent fuel leakage.

6. Reverse Steps 1-5 to install the pump and filter. Make certain the filter is installed correctly with

6

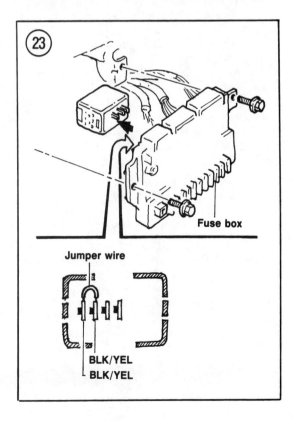

㉓

Fuse box

Jumper wire

BLK/YEL
BLK/YEL

regard to fuel flow and the lines are correctly installed.

7. Reconnect the electrical leads and the battery ground cable. Check for and correct any leaks in the lines and connections before reinstalling the cover on the fuel pump.

FUEL TANK

Repairs to the fuel tank should be entrusted to an expert. Even under the best of conditions, the fuel tank is a potentially dangerous item with the destructive effectiveness of a carefully designed bomb. Even during such routine operations as removal and installation, extreme care should be exercised with regard to heat, flames and potential electrical sparks. It is a good idea, when dealing with procedures involving the fuel tank, to keep a good fire extinguisher close by.

Removal/Installation

1. Disconnect the negative cable from the battery.
2. Remove the fuel tank drain bolt (**Figure 24**) and catch the fuel in a safe, sealable container large enough to hold all of the fuel remaining in the tank.
3. Expand the fuel lines clips with needlenose pliers and slide them up each of the lines several inches. **Figure 25** shows typical connecting and mounting joints. Carefully pull each of the lines loose from its connection, taking care not to damage the lines.
4. Loosen the lower clamp on the filler hose (**Figure 25**) and pull it off the tank connection.
5. Disconnect the electrical leads from the fuel level sender unit.
6. With an assistant helping to support the tank, remove all fasteners and straps securing the tank to the car. Then lower the tank and remove it.

> *WARNING*
> *Always store or place fuel tank away from any source of flame or sparks which could cause the tank to explode.*

7. Install the tank by reversing these steps. Make certain all of the connections are clean and tight. Pour about one gallon of gasoline into the tank and check for leaks. Then start the engine and check again. Immediately repair any leaks that are found.

FUEL LINE REPAIRS

With the exception of replacing short lengths of rubber fuel hose that are easily accessible, fuel line repairs should be entrusted to a Honda dealer. Not

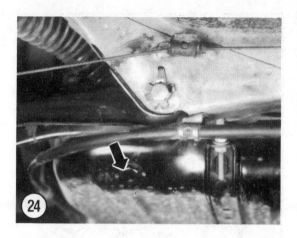

only does removal and replacement of the fuel feed lines require removal of access panels, but the lines must also be sealed where they pass through the body panels to prevent moisture from entering the car.

EXHAUST AND INTAKE MANIFOLDS

The intake and exhaust manifolds on 1976-1983 Accords and 1979-1982 Preludes must be removed as an assembly. On 1984 Accords and 1983 and later Preludes, the manifolds are on opposite sides of the cylinder head and can be removed separately.

Removal/Installation
(1976-1980, Except 1980
California Automatic)

Refer to **Figure 26** for this procedure.
1. Set the handbrake. Place the transaxle in FIRST (manual) or PARK (automatic).
2. Jack up the front end of the car and place it on jackstands.
3. Disconnect the exhaust pipe at the exhaust manifold.
4. Remove the jackstands from under the car and lower the car to the ground.
5. Drain the cooling system as described in Chapter Seven. If the coolant is clean, drain it into a clean container and save it for reuse.

> *WARNING*
> *Antifreeze is poisonous and may attract animals. Do not store the drained coolant where it is accessible to children or pets.*

6. Disconnect the coolant hoses at the intake manifold.

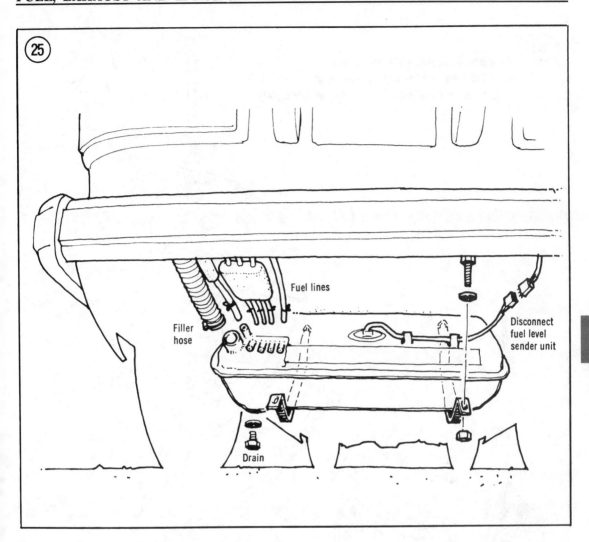

6

7. Remove the air cleaner assembly and carburetor as described in this chapter. Discard the carburetor base gasket.

8. Remove the heat shield from the top of the intake manifold.

9. Loosen, but do not remove, the 4 intake manifold-to-exhaust manifold attaching bolts.

CAUTION
The manifolds should come off easily during the next step. If not, recheck to make sure all fasteners have been removed. Do not force the manifolds off.

10. Remove the nuts attaching the intake and exhaust manifolds to the cylinder heads. Then remove both manifolds as a unit.

11. Remove the 4 intake manifold-to-exhaust manifold through bolts and separate the manifold. Discard the riser gaskets.

12. Remove all traces of the manifold gasket from the cylinder head.

13. Assemble the intake and exhaust manifolds together, using a new riser gasket between the manifolds. Install the 4 intake manifold-to exhaust manifold through-bolts and tighten finger-tight only. Do not torque these bolts at this time. Install the exhaust manifold cover to the bottom of the exhaust manifold if removed.

NOTE
*When installing the 4 through bolts and washers, make sure to install the washers with the concave side facing down (**Figure 26**).*

14. Install a new manifold gasket to the cylinder head.

15. Install the intake and exhaust manifold unit into position against the cylinder head. Install the

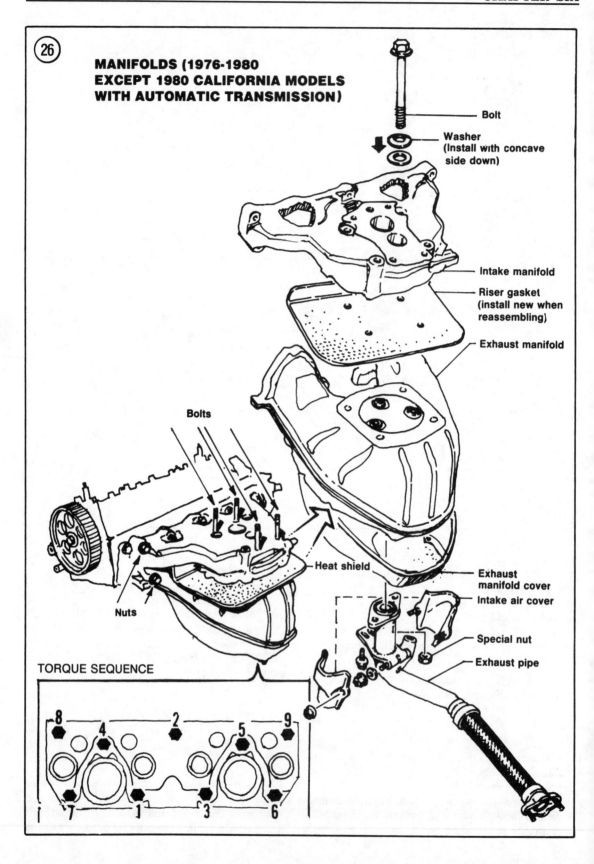

㉖

**MANIFOLDS (1976-1980
EXCEPT 1980 CALIFORNIA MODELS
WITH AUTOMATIC TRANSMISSION)**

Bolt

Washer
(Install with concave
side down)

Intake manifold

Riser gasket
(install new when
reassembling)

Exhaust manifold

Bolts

Heat shield

Exhaust
manifold cover

Intake air cover

Special nut

Exhaust pipe

Nuts

TORQUE SEQUENCE

8 2 9
4 5
7 1 3 6

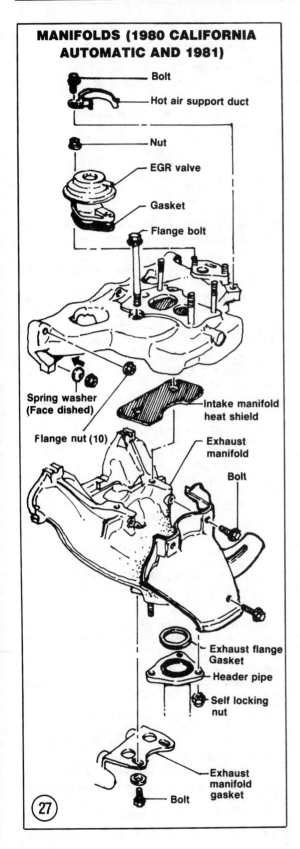

MANIFOLDS (1980 CALIFORNIA AUTOMATIC AND 1981)

- Bolt
- Hot air support duct
- Nut
- EGR valve
- Gasket
- Flange bolt
- Spring washer (Face dished)
- Intake manifold heat shield
- Flange nut (10)
- Exhaust manifold
- Bolt
- Exhaust flange Gasket
- Header pipe
- Self locking nut
- Exhaust manifold gasket
- Bolt

㉗

manifold and secure with new concave washers and nuts.

NOTE
When installing the manifold assembly nuts and washers, make sure to install the washers with the concave side facing toward the cylinder head.

16. Tighten the 9 manifold assembly bolts in 2 stages in the sequence shown in **Figure 26**. First tighten to 10 N•m (7 ft.-lb), then to 20-24 N•m (14-17 ft.-lb.).

17. Now tighten the 4 intake manifold-to-exhaust manifold through bolts in a crisscross pattern to the following torques:
    a. 1976-1979—22-28 N•m (16-20 ft.-lb.).
    b. 1980—25 N•m (18 ft.-lb.).

18. Installation is completed by reversing Steps 1-8. Be sure to install a new carburetor base gasket. When attaching exhaust pipe to manifold, install a new flange gasket. Tighten exhaust pipe-to-manifold nuts to 45 N•m (33 ft-lb.).

6

Removal/Installation
(1980 California Automatic
and All 1981)

Refer to **Figure 27** for this procedure. Special tool Honda part No. H/C 83023 is required to remove the middle manifold attaching bolts. If this tool is not available, the cylinder head must be removed together with the intake/exhaust manifold assembly to provide access to the middle bolts. Cylinder head removal is described in Chapter Four.

1. Set the handbrake. Place the transaxle in FIRST (manual) or PARK (automatic).

2. Jack up the front end of the car and place it on jackstands.

3. Disconnect the exhaust pipe at the exhaust manifold.

4. Remove the jackstands from under the car and lower the car to the ground.

5. Drain the cooling system as described in Chapter Seven. If the coolant is clean, drain it into a clean container and save it for reuse.

WARNING
Antifreeze is poisonous and may attract animals. Do not store the drained coolant where it is accessible to children or pets.

6. Disconnect the coolant hoses at the intake manifold.

7. Remove the air cleaner assembly and carburetor as described in this chapter. Discard the carburetor base gasket.

8. Remove the intake manifold heat shield from the top of the intake manifold.

9. Disconnect the EGR hose at the EGR valve.

10. Remove the middle manifold attaching nuts using Honda special tool part No. H/C 83023. Then remove the remaining manifold attaching nuts. Remove both manifolds as a unit.

11. Remove the 2 intake manifold-to-exhaust manifold through bolts and separate the manifolds. Discard the center heat shield.

12. Remove all traces of the manifold gasket from the cylinder head.

13. Assemble the intake and exhaust manifolds together, making sure to install a new heat shield between both manifolds. Install the 2 intake manifold-to-exhaust manifold through bolts and tighten finger-tight only. Do not torque these bolts at this time. Install the exhaust manifold cover to the bottom of the exhaust manifold if removed.

14. Install a new manifold gasket onto the cylinder head.

15. Install the intake and exhaust manifold unit into position against the cylinder head. Install the manifold and secure with new concave washers and nuts.

NOTE
When installing the manifold unit nuts and washers, make sure to install the washers with the concave side facing toward the cylinder head.

NOTE
To install the middle washers and nuts, first bend a piece of wire to form a hook on one end. Place one washer onto the hook and position the wire and washer next to one cylinder head-to-manifold stud. Push the washer onto the stud with a screwdriver. Repeat for opposite washer and both nuts.

16. Tighten the manifold assembly bolts in 2 stages in a crisscross pattern (**Figure 27**). First tighten to 10 N•m (7 ft.-lb.), then to 22 N•m (16 ft.-lb.).

17. Now tighten the 2 intake manifold-to-exhaust manifold through bolts to 22 N•m (16 ft.-lb.).

18. Installation is completed by reversing Steps 1-9. Make sure to install a new carburetor base gasket. When attaching exhaust pipe to manifold, install a new flange gasket. Tighten exhaust pipe-to-manifold nuts to 45 N•m (33 ft.-lb.).

Removal/Installation
(1982-1983 Accord)

Refer to **Figure 28** for this procedure.

1. Set the handbrake. Place the transaxle in FIRST (manual) or PARK (automatic).

2. Jack up the front end of the car and place it on jackstands.

CAUTION
During the following step, use a 6-point socket to prevent rounding off the nuts. Do not use an impact wrench.

3. Apply penetrating oil such as WD-40 to the exhaust pipe-to-manifold nuts, then take the nuts off. Pull the exhaust pipe downward away from the manifold.

4. Unbolt the exhaust manifold bracket from the exhaust manifold.

5. Remove the air cleaner as described in this chapter.

6. Detach the air suction tube from the air chamber.

7. Remove the carburetor as described in this chapter. Remove the carburetor heat shield and discard the gaskets.

8. Drain the cooling system as described in Chapter Seven. If the coolant is clean, store it in a clean container for reuse.

WARNING
Antifreeze is poisonous and may attract animals. Do not store the drained coolant where it is accessible to children or pets.

CAUTION
The manifolds should come off easily during the next step. If they do not, recheck to make sure all fasteners have been removed. Do not pry the manifolds off.

9. Remove the manifold assembly nuts and washers, then take the assembly off.

10. Remove the flange bolts to separate the intake manifold from the exhaust manifold.

11. Remove the jackstands and lower the front end of the car to the ground.

12. Clean all traces of old gasket from the manifolds and cylinder head.

13. Check all threads for damage. Repair or replace damaged fasteners as needed.

14. Place a new heat shield between the intake and exhaust manifolds. Tighten the flange bolts (**Figure 29**) finger-tight.

15. Place a new manifold gasket over the cylinder head studs.

INTAKE AND EXHAUST MANIFOLDS
(1983 ACCORD)

1. Bolt
2. Air suction valve
3. Gasket
4. Carburetor heat shield
5. EGR valve
6. Nut
7. Bolt
8. Gasket
9. Hot air duct support
10. Gasket
11. Bolt
12. Intake manifold
13. Flare connection
14. Flare nuts
15. Air suction tube
16. Bolt
17. Exhaust manifold shroud
18. Bolt
19. Header pipe
20. Nut
21. Exhaust manifold bracket
22. Bolt
23. Gasket
24. Exhaust manifold
25. Bolt
26. Anti-afterburn valve bracket
27. Engine hanger
28. Nut
29. Spring washer
    (dished side toward engine)
30. Gasket

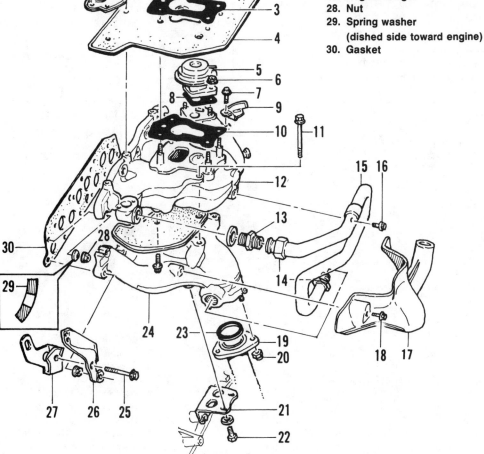

6

16. Tighten the manifold nuts in the order shown in **Figure 30**. Tighten in 2 stages, first to 10 N•m (7 ft.-lb.), then to 22 N•m (16 ft.-lb.).

17. Tighten the flange bolts (**Figure 29**) to 22 N•m (16 ft.-lb.).

18. Reconnect the coolant hoses.

19. Reinstall the carburetor and heat shield, using new gaskets.

20. Reconnect the suction tube to the air chamber.

21. Install the air cleaner.

22. Make sure the transaxle is still in FIRST (manual) or PARK (automatic). Make sure the handbrake is still set.

23. Jack up the front end of the car and place it on jackstands.

24. Install a new flange gasket between the exhaust pipe and manifold. Install the exhaust pipe-to-manifold nuts and tighten to 50 N•m (36 ft.-lb.).

Intake Manifold Removal/Installation (1984 Accord, 1983-on Prelude)

Refer to **Figure 31** (1984 Accord) or **Figure 32** (1983 and later Prelude).

1. Remove the carburetor(s) as described in this chapter.

2. Label and disconnect the hoses and tubes that connect the intake manifold to the engine.

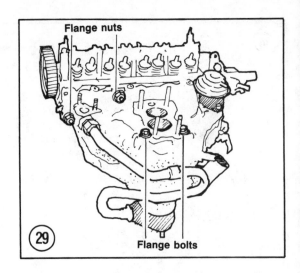

Flange nuts

Flange bolts

(29)

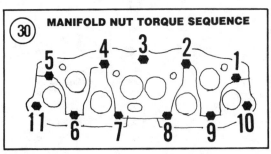

(30) **MANIFOLD NUT TORQUE SEQUENCE**

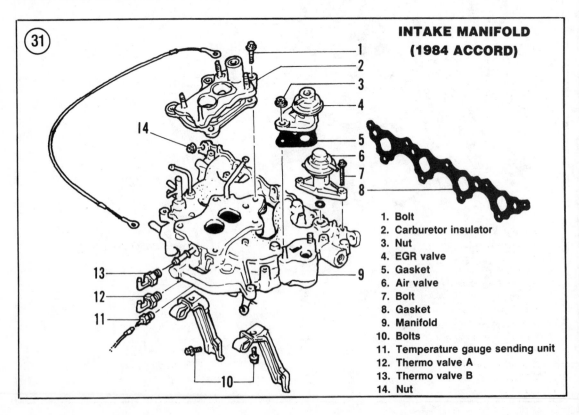

(31) **INTAKE MANIFOLD (1984 ACCORD)**

1. Bolt
2. Carburetor insulator
3. Nut
4. EGR valve
5. Gasket
6. Air valve
7. Bolt
8. Gasket
9. Manifold
10. Bolts
11. Temperature gauge sending unit
12. Thermo valve A
13. Thermo valve B
14. Nut

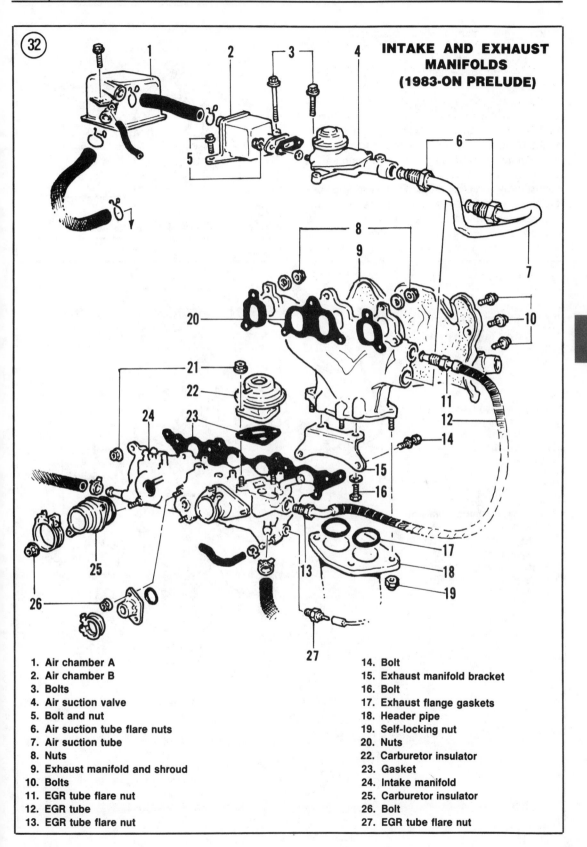

INTAKE AND EXHAUST MANIFOLDS (1983-ON PRELUDE)

1. Air chamber A
2. Air chamber B
3. Bolts
4. Air suction valve
5. Bolt and nut
6. Air suction tube flare nuts
7. Air suction tube
8. Nuts
9. Exhaust manifold and shroud
10. Bolts
11. EGR tube flare nut
12. EGR tube
13. EGR tube flare nut
14. Bolt
15. Exhaust manifold bracket
16. Bolt
17. Exhaust flange gaskets
18. Header pipe
19. Self-locking nut
20. Nuts
21. Nut
22. Carburetor insulator
23. Gasket
24. Intake manifold
25. Carburetor insulator
26. Bolt
27. EGR tube flare nut

3. Remove the manifold brace brackets.

> *CAUTION*
> *The manifold should come off easily during the next step. If not, check to be sure all fasteners have been removed. Do not pry the manifold off.*

4. Remove the manifold fasteners and take the manifold off.

5. Clean all traces of old gasket from the manifold and cylinder head.

6. Install by reversing Steps 1-3. Use new gaskets. Tighten the manifold-to-head fasteners evenly, in a crisscross pattern, to 22 N•m (16 ft.-lb.). Tighten the brace bracket fasteners to 22 N•m (16 ft.-lb.).

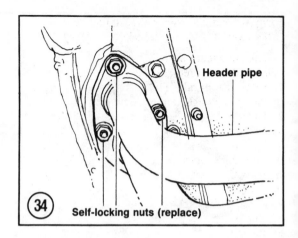

Header pipe

③④ Self-locking nuts (replace)

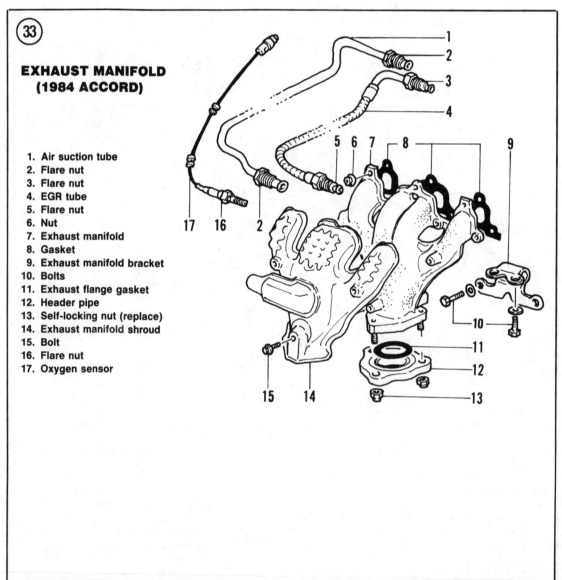

③③

EXHAUST MANIFOLD (1984 ACCORD)

1. Air suction tube
2. Flare nut
3. Flare nut
4. EGR tube
5. Flare nut
6. Nut
7. Exhaust manifold
8. Gasket
9. Exhaust manifold bracket
10. Bolts
11. Exhaust flange gasket
12. Header pipe
13. Self-locking nut (replace)
14. Exhaust manifold shroud
15. Bolt
16. Flare nut
17. Oxygen sensor

**Exhaust Manifold Removal/Installation
(1984 Accord, 1983-on Prelude)**

Refer to **Figure 33** (1984 Accord) or **Figure 32** (1983 and later Prelude).

1. Set the handbrake. Place the transaxle in FIRST (manual) or PARK (automatic).

2. Jack up the front end of the car and place it on jackstands.

3. Disconnect the exhaust pipe from the manifold (**Figure 34**). Detach the exhaust pipe bracket (**Figure 35**), then pull the pipe downward away from the manifold.

4. Remove the exhaust manifold bracket.

5. Unplug the oxygen sensor wire and remove the EGR tube.

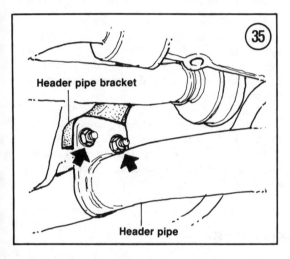

Header pipe bracket

Header pipe

6. Remove the exhaust manifold shroud.

CAUTION
The manifold should come off easily during the next step. If it doesn't, check to be sure all fasteners have been removed. Do not pry the manifold off.

7. Remove the manifold fasteners and take the manifold off.

8. Remove all traces of old gasket from the engine and manifold.

9. Installation is the reverse of removal. Tighten the manifold fasteners evenly, in a crisscross pattern, to specifications in **Figure 33** or **Figure 32**.

EXHAUST SYSTEM

The exhaust system consists of the exhaust manifold, hot air cover, exhaust pipe and silencer. A catalytic converter is used on 1980 automatic transaxle models and on all 1981 and later models. A typical exhaust system is shown in **Figure 36**. The catalytic converter system is shown in **Figure 37**.

WARNING
The exhaust system operates at very high temperatures. Be sure the system is cool enough to touch before performing any of the following procedures.

Exhaust Pipe Removal/Installation

1. Set the handbrake. Securely block both rear wheels so the car will not roll in either direction.

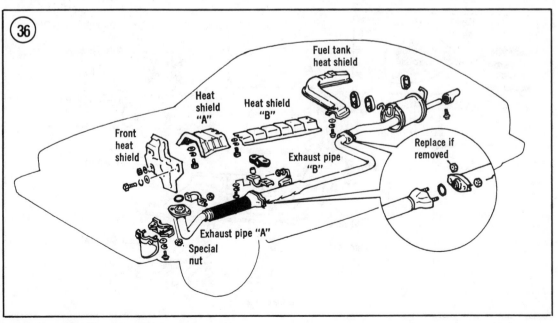

Fuel tank heat shield

Heat shield "A"

Heat shield "B"

Front heat shield

Exhaust pipe "B"

Replace if removed

Exhaust pipe "A"

Special nut

2. Jack up the front of the car and place it on jackstands.

3. Spray penetrating oil on all of the exhaust pipe fasteners which will be loosened or removed.

4. Unscrew the bolts from the front exhaust pipe bracket and remove them from the pipe (**Figure 36**).

5. Unscrew the nuts from the exhaust pipe/manifold flange joint and lower the pipe. Lower the front of the car, jack up the rear and support it with jackstands.

6. Unscrew the muffler mounting bolt (**Figure 36**). Disconnect the muffler and the exhaust pipe from the 2 rubber mounts and lower the complete system. On those vehicles equipped with catalytic converter, refer to *Catalytic Converter Removal/Installation* in this chapter and remove the unit.

7. Unscrew the muffler/exhaust pipe flange nuts (**Figure 36**) and separate the 2 assemblies.

8. Installation is the reverse of these steps. Always use new gaskets when installing the exhaust pipe and muffler. Replace the rubber mounts if they show signs of deterioration.

Catalytic Converter Removal/Installation

Refer to **Figure 37** for this procedure.

1. Set the handbrake. Securely block both rear wheels so the car will not roll in either direction.

2. Raise the vehicle front end and secure with jackstands.

3. Remove the bottom support bar from the rubber mounts.

4. Unscrew the catalytic converter to exhaust pipe attaching bolts and remove the catalytic converter.

5. If the heat shield is damaged, remove it from its bottom position on the converter.

6. Installation is the reverse of these steps. Replace the heat shield lock plates if the shield was removed from the converter. Tighten the converter to exhaust pipe attaching nuts to 34 N•m (25 ft.-lb.) in the sequence shown in **Figure 37**.

Muffler Replacement

Refer to **Figure 36** for this procedure.

1. Place the transaxle in FIRST (manual) or PARK (automatic). Securely block both front wheels so the car will not roll in either direction.

2. Jack up the rear end of the car and support it on jackstands.

3. Unscrew the muffler to exhaust pipe flange nuts.

4. Unscrew the muffler mounting bolts, disconnect the muffler from the rubber mount and remove it.

5. Reverse the removal steps to install the muffler. Use a new gasket and replace the rubber mount if it shows signs of deterioration.

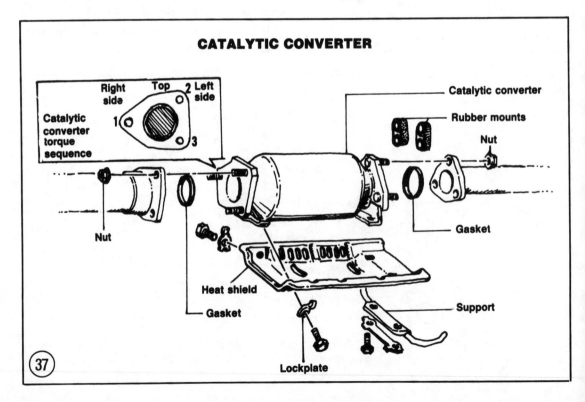

CATALYTIC CONVERTER

Right side — Top — 2 Left side

Catalytic converter torque sequence

Catalytic converter

Rubber mounts

Nut

Nut

Gasket

Heat shield

Gasket

Support

Lockplate

(37)

EMISSION CONTROL SYSTEMS

By-products of the combustion process that takes place in a gasoline-fueled automobile engine include carbon monoxide (CO), oxides of nitrogen (NOx) and hydrocarbons. In addition, evaporation of gasoline in the fuel tank and carburetor produce additional hydrocarbons. All three types of emissions are considered air pollutants.

Federal and, in some areas, state and local laws have been passed which limit the amounts of these pollutants which can be released into the atmosphere by automobiles. Automobile manufacturers have been required to modify their engines to meet the standards established by these laws.

Honda Motor Company uses a number of systems to restrict harmful and illegal emissions. These systems include:

    a. Crankcase emission control system.
    b. Evaporative emission control system.
    c. Exhaust emission control system.

Emission Control Maintenance

Emission control maintenance should be limited to the tasks described in Chapter Three. If your car is still under warranty, Honda requires this maintenance to be performed by an authorized Honda dealership or qualified service facility. Detailed receipts must be kept showing the required maintenance was performed. If these conditions are not met, your warranty could be affected.

While the majority of all emission control tasks should be left to a Honda dealer, it is important system maintenance to routinely inspect all system hoses for deterioration and check the tubes for cracks. Replace any that are not satisfactory. Check the connections to make sure they are tight and leak-free. If a hose or tube is to be replaced, pay careful attention to the routing of the piece being removed and route the new piece in the same manner. Tighten all connections securely.

CRANKCASE EMISSION CONTROL SYSTEM

Most, but not all, of the exhaust gases are discharged through the exhaust system. Some of the gases, as well as some of the raw air-fuel mixture, are "blown by" the piston rings and collect in the crankcase. If the blowby is allowed to remain in the crankcase and combine with the oil, it forms sludge, varnish or acids. The latter sometimes attacks bearings and other metal parts.

When the mixture of blowby and oil fumes cools, it condenses and dilutes the oil which eventually destroys its lubricating effectiveness.

The 1976-1983 Accord models and 1979-1982 Preludes use a dual return system to control the emission of crankcase gases. See **Figure 38**. Intake manifold vacuum is used to return the gases to the combustion chamber. When the car is operating at low speed, the gases are routed through the return passage below the throttle plate. At higher speeds, some of the gases are routed through the air cleaner and carburetor and some are routed through the return passage. The gases are replaced with fresh air drawn in through the air cleaner as shown in **Figure 38**.

The engine used in 1984 Accords and 1983 and later Preludes is equipped with a positive crankcase ventilation (PCV) valve. See **Figure 39** (Accord) or **Figure 40** (Prelude). The valve regulates the flow of blowby gases into the intake manifold according to engine conditions.

Required maintenance intervals and procedures for the crankcase emission control system are described in Chapter Three.

EVAPORATIVE EMISSION CONTROL SYSTEM

This system controls the emission of gasoline vapors from the carburetor and fuel tank. The system consists of the fuel filler cap, fuel tank, a liquid/vapor separator, charcoal canister and a number of different inline components, depending upon the vehicle's model year and whether it is a 49-state, California or high-altitude model. Also included in the system are connecting hoses and pipes.

EXHAUST EMISSION CONTROL SYSTEMS

The exhaust emission control system actually is a group of subsystems designed to control emissions when the engine is idling, accelerating, cruising and decelerating. Subsystems used are:

    a. Stratified charge system (except 1984 Prelude).
    b. Intake air temperature control.
    c. Carburetor-related systems.
    d. Anti-afterburn valve.
    e. Air jet controller.
    f. Exhaust gas recirculation.
    g. Catalytic converter.

The actual subsystems used on your vehicle depend upon the model year and whether it is a 49-state, California or high-altitude model.

6

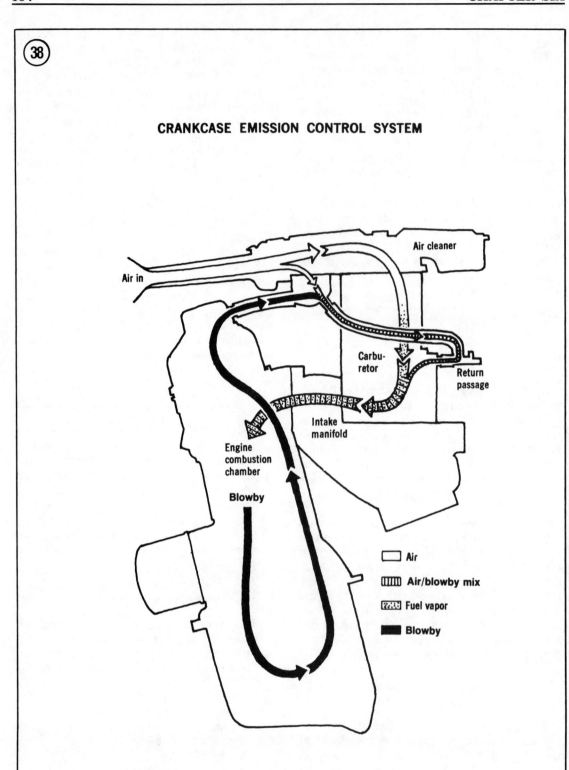

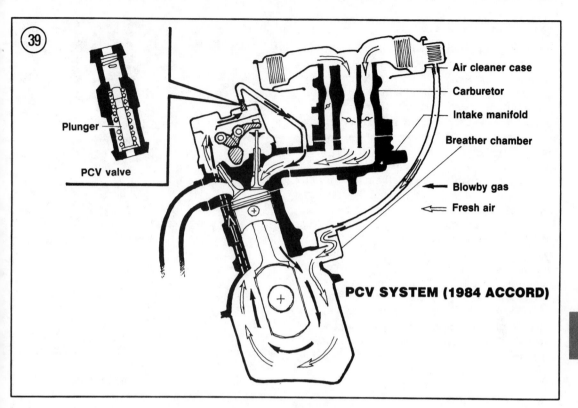

PCV SYSTEM (1984 ACCORD)

Plunger

PCV valve

Air cleaner case

Carburetor

Intake manifold

Breather chamber

Blowby gas

Fresh air

6

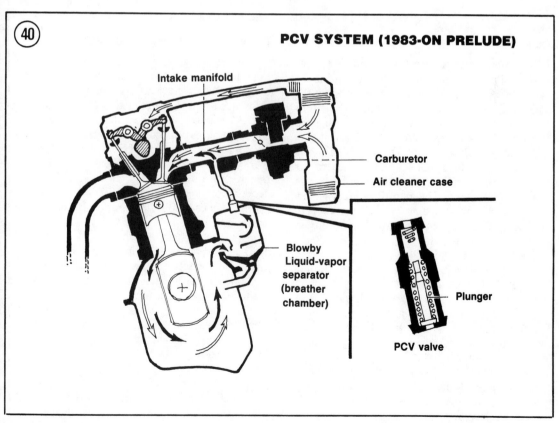

PCV SYSTEM (1983-ON PRELUDE)

Intake manifold

Carburetor

Air cleaner case

Blowby
Liquid-vapor
separator
(breather
chamber)

Plunger

PCV valve

Stratified Charge Engine

This engine modification system uses 2 combustion chambers in each cylinder; the main chamber and the auxiliary chamber. An extremely lean air-fuel mixture is introduced into the main chamber, while a rich mixture is introduced into the auxiliary chamber. Each cylinder has a main intake valve, an auxiliary intake valve and a single exhaust valve (except the 1983 Prelude and 1984 Accord, which have 2 main intake valves).

The spark plug ignites the small amount of rich mixture in the auxiliary chamber and the resulting combustion ignites the lean mixture in the main chamber. Since the main chamber is much larger than the auxiliary chamber, the overall air-fuel mixture is very lean. This tends to hold the formation of carbon monoxide during the combustion process to a minimum. The slow, stable combustion in the main chamber tends to keep peak temperature low and this reduces the formation of oxides of nitrogen. The temperature is kept high enough, however, to keep hydrocarbon emissions low.

Intake Air Temperature Control System

The intake air temperature control system consists of an air control valve located in the air cleaner intake duct. The valve is controlled by the temperature of the intake air and it in turn maintains the temperature of the air entering the carburetor at approximately 100° F. The valve is connected to a door in the intake duct which allows the selection of fresh outside air, preheated air from an oven near the exhaust manifold or a combination of both. This permits a very narrow range of intake air temperature to be maintained, regardless of outside temperature. This results in lower exhaust emissions.

Inspect the system as follows.

1. Start the engine and bring to normal operating temperature. Cooling fan must be on.

2. Remove the air cleaner cover and element as described under *Air Cleaner* in this chapter.

3. Immediately check the position of the air control door. **Figure 41** shows the air cleaner door on all Accords and 1979-1982 Preludes. The door on 1983 and later Preludes is basically the same. It should be closed. If not, check the door for possible binding. If door operation is good, refer further service to a Honda dealer.

Ignition Timing Control System

The ignition timing control system controls the ignition spark according to the engine's load, temperature of the coolant and speed. In general, at low temperatures the system allows the distributor advance to be controlled by direct manifold vacuum. After the coolant warms up (typically above 149° F for cars with manual transmissions; above 158° for automatics), the control systems vary the amount of advance according to varying load and speed conditions.

Exhaust Gas Recirculation System

The exhaust gas recirculation (EGR) system is used to reduce the emission of oxides nitrogen (NOx). Relatively inert exhaust gases are introduced into the combustion chamber through the EGR valve and the intake manifold. This slightly reduces peak combustion temperatures and so reduces the formation of NOx. The EGR system recirculates exhaust gas when the engine is operating at normal temperatures during acceleration and cruising. EGR flow is stopped during periods of idle, deceleration and cold engine operation.

Inspect the system as follows.

1. Disconnect the vacuum hose from the EGR valve and connect a vacuum gauge in its place.

2. Attach a tachometer to the engine following manufacturer's instructions.

3. Start the engine and accelerate to 4,500-5,000 rpm. No vacuum should be indicated on the vacuum gauge. If there is, refer further testing to a Honda dealer.

Catalytic Converter

Catalytic converters reduce air pollutants by promoting further burning of the exhaust gases.

The converter is located in the exhaust line ahead of the muffler and contains a material coated with platinum or palladium. Both of these materials are catalysts. As the exhaust gases pass over them, they cause further oxidation (burning) and thereby lower the level of carbon monoxide and unburned hydrocarbons. The catalytic converter should be checked for general condition at the same time the remainder of the exhaust system is checked. See Chapter Three. To prevent premature failure of the catalytic converter, use only unleaded fuel.

FUEL REQUIREMENTS

To maintain your Honda's warranty, it is important to use an unleaded gasoline with 91 Research octane number or higher (86 octane number or higher measured by the Cost of Living Council formula). This is to prevent engine knock (spontaneous and premature combustion of the gasoline-air mixture in the cylinders). Besides decreasing fuel economy and engine power, engine knock can damage engine parts (if allowed to continue).

When operating your car, you should remember that changing conditions can also change the octane requirements for your engine. For example, as your car ages, it will have a tendency to knock more. In addition, heavy loads or operating in low-humidity areas for extended periods of time can have the same effect. To be safe, you should carefully select the correct octane rating for your car by performing the following test.

1. Tune your car as described in Chapter Three. Make sure that it is operating in good mechanical condition.

2. Run your car until it is nearly empty. Then fill it up with the brand of gasoline you usually buy (at least 91 octane rating as specified by Honda).

3. Drive the car to bring to normal operating temperature. Come to a complete stop, then accelerate hard.

4. Light pinging under heavy load is normal. If the engine knocks or pings excessively, use up the gasoline and refill with the next higher grade. Repeat Step 3.

5. If the engine does not knock, this is the gasoline you should be using. If the engine does knock with the higher octane, there is some type of mechanical trouble which is causing the engine to knock. Other than a gasoline with an octane rating too low, consider the following conditions as the possible cause of engine knock:

   a. Incorrect ignition timing.

   b. Incorrectly adjusted carburetor.

   c. Carbon deposits collected in the cylinder head or on top of the pistons.

6

Table 1 FUEL PUMP SPECIFICATIONS

Year	Pressure (psi)	Displacement*
1976-1977	2-2 1/2 psi	500 cc @ 12 volts
1978	2-3	500 cc @ 12 volts
1979-1983 Accord	2-3	680 cc @ 12 volts
1984 Accord	2 1/2-3	550 cc @ 12 volts
1979-1984 Prelude	2-3	680 cc @ 12 volts

* Volume per minute.

NOTE: If you own a 1985 model, first check the Supplement at the back of the book for any new service information.

CHAPTER SEVEN

COOLING, HEATING
AND AIR CONDITIONING

The cooling system consists of a pressurized radiator, thermostat, thermoswitch, centrifugal water pump, electric fan and appropriate plumbing. Refer to the following illustrations:

   a. **Figure 1**—1976-1983 Accord, 1979-1982 Prelude.

   b. **Figure 2**—1984 Accord, 1983-on Prelude.

The heater is a hot water type which circulates engine coolant through a small radiator (heater core) located behind the instrument panel. Air is drawn in through a cowl vent by a fan and blown over the radiator to heat the interior of the car.

This chapter includes service procedures for the cooling system, heater and air conditioner.

COOLANT

Use only ethylene glycol-based antifreeze compatible with aluminum engines.

The coolant should be mixed with water in accordance with the coolant manufacturer's instructions to provide freeze protection to -34° F. Even if your climate does not require this degree of protection, the coolant is an excellent corrosion inhibitor.

> *CAUTION*
> *Do not use a solution of less than 50% or more than 60% coolant. Too little antifreeze will not provide enough protection against freezing or corrosion. Too much will lower cooling efficiency.*

COOLING SYSTEM

The cooling system should be inspected and the coolant changed at intervals recommended in Chapter Three. If the coolant appears dirty or rusty, the system should be cleaned with a chemical cleaner and flushed with clean water. Severe corrosion may require pressure flushing, a job for a dealer or radiator shop.

Inspection

1. Check coolant level by observing the liquid in the recovery system reservoir (**Figure 3**). The radiator cap (**Figure 4**) should not be removed. If additional coolant is required, it should be added to the recovery reservoir. Level should be at the "COLD FULL" mark when the engine is cold and at the "HOT FULL" mark when the engine is hot.

2. Check water pump operation by squeezing the upper radiator hose when the engine is operating at normal temperature. If pressure surges are felt, the water pump is functioning. If not, check for a plugged vent hole in the pump.

> *WARNING*
> *The engine must be cool before performing the next step.*

> *NOTE*
> *The next step should not be done periodically. Perform this check only if there is repeated coolant loss and no visible leak. An alternative method is to*

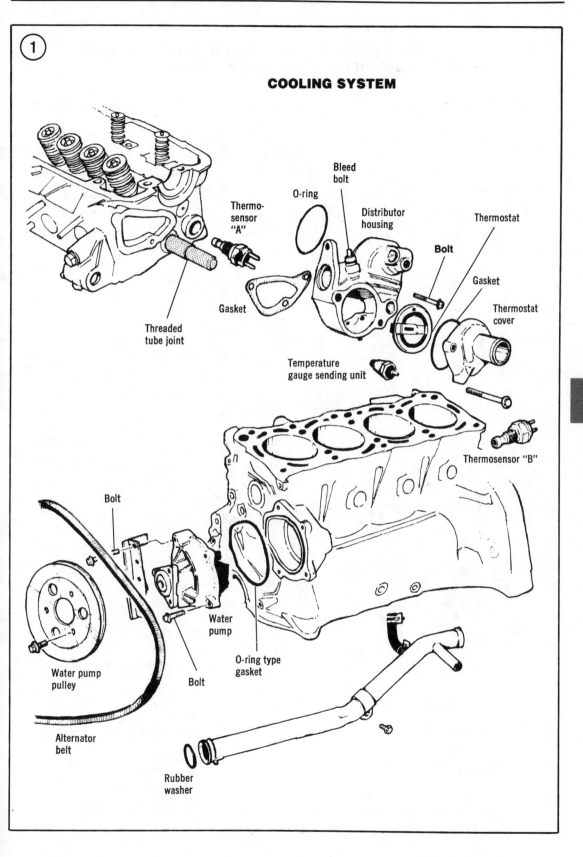

① COOLING SYSTEM

Bleed bolt

O-ring

Thermo-sensor "A"

Distributor housing

Thermostat

Bolt

Gasket

Thermostat cover

Gasket

Threaded tube joint

Temperature gauge sending unit

Thermosensor "B"

Bolt

7

Water pump

Water pump pulley

Bolt

O-ring type gasket

Alternator belt

Rubber washer

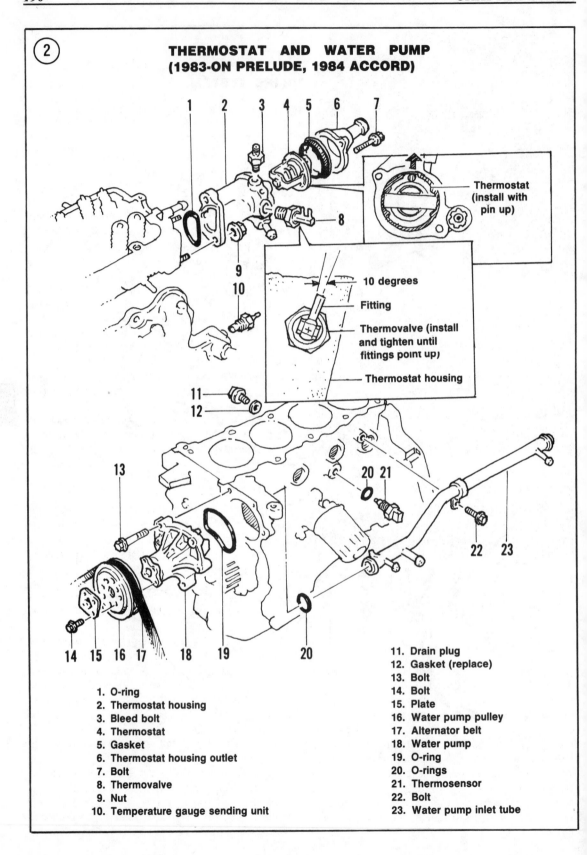

② **THERMOSTAT AND WATER PUMP
(1983-ON PRELUDE, 1984 ACCORD)**

Thermostat
(install with
pin up)

10 degrees

Fitting

Thermovalve (install
and tighten until
fittings point up)

Thermostat housing

1. O-ring
2. Thermostat housing
3. Bleed bolt
4. Thermostat
5. Gasket
6. Thermostat housing outlet
7. Bolt
8. Thermovalve
9. Nut
10. Temperature gauge sending unit
11. Drain plug
12. Gasket (replace)
13. Bolt
14. Bolt
15. Plate
16. Water pump pulley
17. Alternator belt
18. Water pump
19. O-ring
20. O-rings
21. Thermosensor
22. Bolt
23. Water pump inlet tube

have the cooling system pressure tested by a Honda dealer, radiator shop or service station. Check the price of a pressure test before performing the next step.

3. Check for exhaust leaks into the cooling system by draining coolant until level is just above the top of the cylinder head. Remove the thermostat as described in this chapter, then reinstall the thermostat housing. Remove the water pump drive belt. Start the engine and accelerate it several times while observing coolant in the radiator. If the level rises or bubbles appear, chances are that exhaust gases are leaking into the cooling system. A common cause of this problem is a defective head gasket.

Flushing

> *WARNING*
> *The engine must be cool for this procedure. If the radiator cap is removed while the engine is hot, a fountain of scalding coolant may shoot out of the radiator, bounce off the hood and spray all over you.*

1. Remove the radiator cap (**Figure 4**).
2. Drain the cooling system as follows:
  a. On all models, open the radiator drain tap.
  b. On 1981-1983 Accord and 1981-1982 Preludes, remove the block drain plug from the right side of the block near the oil filter.
  c. On 1984 Accords and 1983-on Preludes, remove the drain plug from the block on the side opposite the oil filter.
3. Remove the coolant recovery tank from its bracket (**Figure 3**) and pour out the coolant. Reinstall the tank in its bracket.
4. Once the system is drained, close the reservoir drain tap and reinstall the block drain plug (if removed).
5. Add a sufficient amount of water through the radiator hole to fill the system and run the engine to circulate the water.
6. Repeat Steps 1-5 as needed until drained water is clear of rust and other debris. When the drained water appears clean, close the radiator drain tap and install the block drain plug (if removed).

Refilling

Before refilling the cooling system, check the coolant hoses for damage. Replace damaged hoses as described in this chapter.

1. Be sure all hoses are connected and the radiator and recovery tank caps are removed.
2. Loosen the cooling system bleed valve. See **Figure 5** (1976-1983 Prelude and 1979-1982 Accord) or **Figure 6** (1984 Prelude and 1983-on Accord).
3. Fill the cooling system with a 50/50 mixture of ethylene glycol-based antifreeze and water to the base of the radiator filler neck. Add sufficient coolant to the recovery tank to raise fluid level to the "COLD FULL" mark. Continue to add coolant and water until the coolant running out of the bleed valve is free of air bubbles. Then close the bleed valve and install the recovery tank cap. Don't install the radiator cap yet.
4. Set the heater temperature control on HIGH and start the engine. Allow it to run until it is thoroughly warmed up (the fan goes on at least twice). Then close the valve and fill the radiator to the bottom of the filler neck. Install the radiator

7

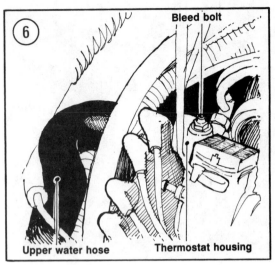

Bleed bolt

Upper water hose   Thermostat housing

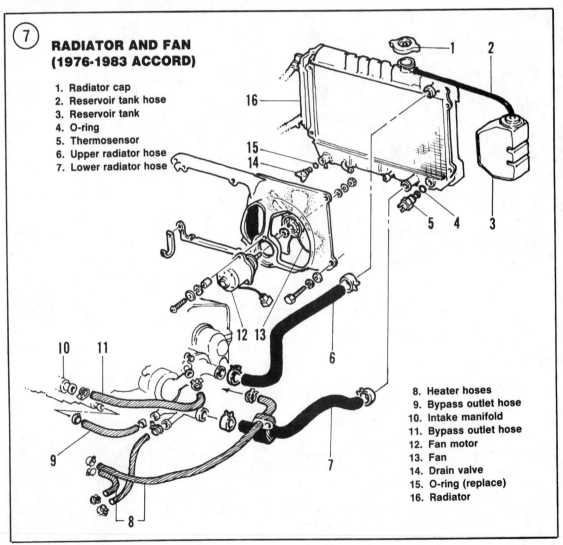

RADIATOR AND FAN
(1976-1983 ACCORD)

1. Radiator cap
2. Reservoir tank hose
3. Reservoir tank
4. O-ring
5. Thermosensor
6. Upper radiator hose
7. Lower radiator hose

8. Heater hoses
9. Bypass outlet hose
10. Intake manifold
11. Bypass outlet hose
12. Fan motor
13. Fan
14. Drain valve
15. O-ring (replace)
16. Radiator

cap and check all cooling system connections for leaks.

5. Drive the car several miles, then recheck coolant level in the recovery tank. It takes some time for all the air to be removed from the system. Maintain fluid level between the "COLD FULL" and "HOT FULL" marks.

Pressure Check

A cooling system pressure check should be done if the system requires repeated topping up and there is no visible leak. The test can be done by a Honda dealer or radiator shop. Some service stations can also perform the pressure check.

RADIATOR

Removal/Installation

1. Drain the radiator as described under *Cooling System Flushing*.

2. Disconnect the upper radiator hose and recovery tank hose from the radiator. Refer to the following illustrations:

    a. **Figure 7**—1976-1983 Accord.
    b. **Figure 8**—1984 Accord.
    c. **Figure 9**—1979-1982 Prelude.
    d. **Figure 10**—1983-on Prelude.

3. Disconnect the lower hose from the radiator.

4. On models equipped with an engine oil cooler, detach the oil cooler from the side of the radiator.

5. On models equipped with an automatic transaxle, disconnect the transaxle oil cooler hoses from the radiator. Cap or plug the ends of the hoses and their fittings on the radiator to keep out dirt. Tie the hoses up out of the way.

6. Disconnect the electrical connectors at the fan motor and the thermoswitch leads at the radiator.

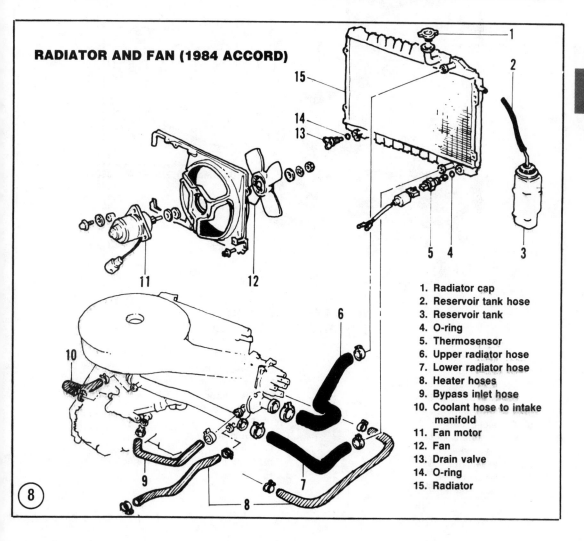

RADIATOR AND FAN (1984 ACCORD)

1. Radiator cap
2. Reservoir tank hose
3. Reservoir tank
4. O-ring
5. Thermosensor
6. Upper radiator hose
7. Lower radiator hose
8. Heater hoses
9. Bypass inlet hose
10. Coolant hose to intake manifold
11. Fan motor
12. Fan
13. Drain valve
14. O-ring
15. Radiator

7

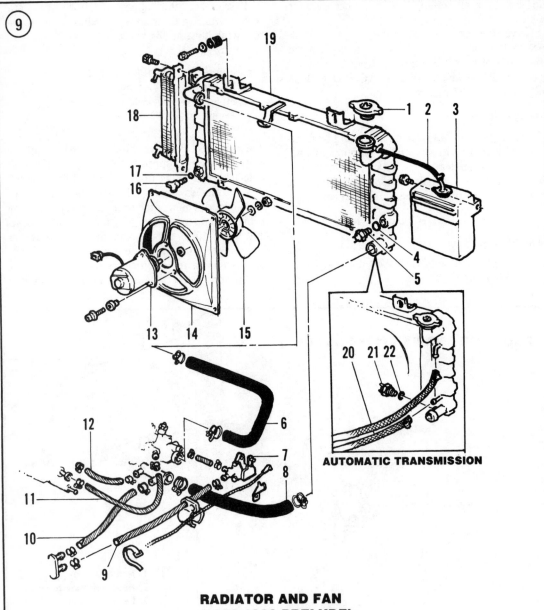

**RADIATOR AND FAN
(1979-1982 PRELUDE)**

1. Radiator cap
2. Coolant reservoir tank hose
3. Coolant reservoir tank
4. O-ring
5. Thermosensor
6. Upper radiator hose
7. Heater valve
8. Lower radiator hose
9. Heater inlet hose
10. Heater outlet hose

11. Bypass inlet hose
12. Bypass outlet hose
13. Fan motor
14. Fan shroud
15. Fan
16. Drain valve
17. O-ring
18. Engine oil cooler (with automatic transaxle)
19. Radiator

AUTOMATIC TRANSMISSION

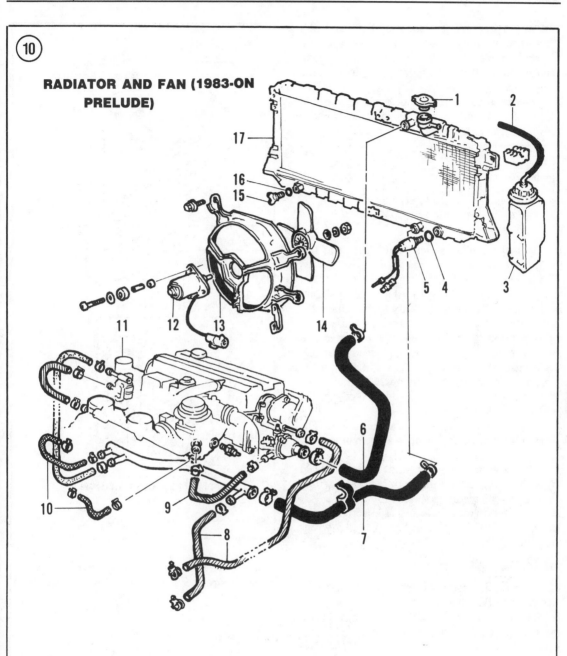

RADIATOR AND FAN (1983-ON PRELUDE)

1. Radiator cap
2. Coolant reservoir tank hose
3. Coolant reservoir tank
4. O-ring
5. Thermosensor
6. Upper radiator hose
7. Lower radiator hose
8. Heater hoses
9. Bypass inlet hose
10. To carburetor
11. Wax case
12. Fan motor
13. Fan shroud
14. Fan
15. Drain valve
16. O-ring
17. Radiator

7. Remove the radiator mounting bolts and pull the radiator up and out of the engine compartment. On some models the bolts are accessible through the front grille. It may be necessary to remove the grille to gain access to the bolts on other models.

8. Installation is the reverse of removal. Fill and bleed the cooling system as described under *Cooling System Flushing.*

THERMOSTAT

Removal/Testing

> *WARNING*
> *The engine must be cool for this procedure.*

1. Drain the cooling system as described in this chapter.

2. Remove the bolts that attach the thermostat cover, then remove the thermostat. Refer to **Figure 1** or **Figure 2**. It is not necessary to disconnect the hose from the cover. If the thermostat is in the open position when removed, it is defective and must be replaced. If it is closed, proceed to Step 3.

3. Immerse the thermostat in a pan of water along with a thermometer. See **Figure 11**. Suspend the thermostat with wire so it doesn't touch the bottom or sides of the pan.

4. Heat the water and watch the thermostat. The thermostat should begin to open at the temperature specified in **Table 1**.

5. Keep heating the water until the thermostat opens fully, the recheck the thermometer. It should indicate the temperature specified in **Table 1**.

6. If the thermostat performs as described, it is okay. If it fails to open or opens at the wrong temperature, replace it.

Installation

If a new thermostat is being installed, test it as described in this chapter.

1. Set the thermostat in the housing with the spring facing into the engine. Make sure the thermostat pin is upward as shown in **Figure 1** or **Figure 2**.

2. Set a new gasket in place and install the cover. Tighten the cover bolts securely.

3. Fill and bleed the cooling system as described in this chapter.

THERMOSWITCH

The thermoswitch controls the operation of the electric fan motor by sensing the coolant temperature. The thermoswitch can be removed without draining the cooling system, provided the radiator cap is installed. A small amount of coolant

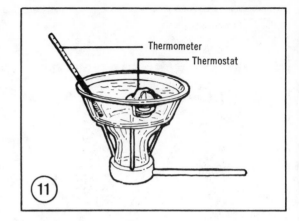

Thermometer

Thermostat

⑪

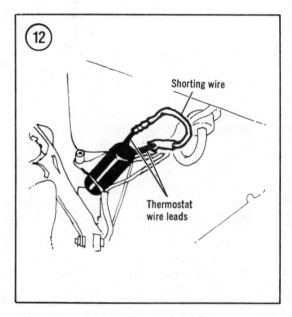

⑫

Shorting wire

Thermostat wire leads

will be lost when the switch is removed and this must be replaced after the switch has been installed.

Testing

1. Warm the engine until coolant temperature reaches "fan operating temperature" in **Table 1**. The fan motor should start.

> *WARNING*
> *The fan may come on suddenly during the next step. Keep your hands and hair out of the way.*

2. If the fan does not start, shut the engine off. Disconnect the wiring from the fan thermoswitch and short the disconnected wires together as shown in **Figure 12**. Turn the ignition switch ON (but don't start the engine):

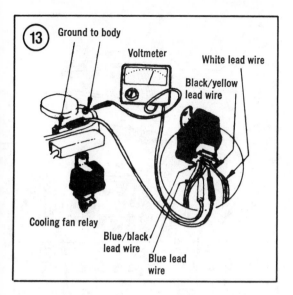

(13) Ground to body

Voltmeter

White lead wire

Black/yellow lead wire

Cooling fan relay

Blue/black lead wire

Blue lead wire

a. If the fan runs, replace the thermoswitch as described in this chapter.

b. If the fan doesn't run, go to Step 3.

3. Check for voltage between the blue and black wires in the cooling fan connector with a voltmeter:

a. If no voltage is present, check for a blown fuse or loose terminals or connectors.

b. If voltage is present, test the fan motor as described in this chapter.

4. On 1977 and later models, check the cooling fan relay by shorting the blue lead to ground and connecting a voltmeter positive lead to the blue-black lead wire. Connect the voltmeter negative probe to ground. See **Figure 13**. Turn the ignition switch to ON, but don't start the engine. If the circuit is okay, battery voltage will be indicated on the voltmeter. If no voltage is shown, check for a blown fuse and check the white and black/yellow wires for continuity. If all test okay, replace the relay and repeat the test.

Removal/Installation

> *WARNING*
> *Let the engine cool before performing this test.*

1. Place a pan beneath the radiator to catch dripping coolant.

2. Disconnect the thermoswitch wires, unscrew the thermoswitch and remove the O-ring.

3. Screw in the new thermoswitch, using a new O-ring. Connect the electrical wires.

4. Fill and bleed the cooling system as described in this chapter.

COOLING FAN

The electric cooling fan is controlled by the thermoswitch. See **Figures 7-10**.

Testing

The fan should turn on and off at the temperatures indicated in **Table 1**. If not, test the thermoswitch as described in this chapter. If the thermoswitch is good, unplug the fan wiring connector. Connect the fan motor terminals directly to the car's battery with lengths of wire. The motor should run. If not, replace it.

Removal/Installation

1. Remove the radiator as described in this chapter.

2. Remove the fan shroud mounting screws and take the shroud off the radiator.

3. Unscrew the fan hub nut and remove the fan and washers.

4. Remove the fan motor mounting screws and take the fan motor off the shroud.

5. Installation is the reverse of removal, plus the following:

a. Test the fan motor before installation by connecting it directly to the car's battery with lengths of wire. Make sure the fan runs before installing it.

b. Fill and bleed the cooling system as described under *Cooling System Flushing*.

WATER PUMP

A water pump will often warn of impending failure by making noise or leaking.

Removal/Installation

The water pump is positioned on the front of the engine block. See **Figure 1** or **Figure 2**. When replacing the water pump, be sure to have a replacement O-ring available.

1. Drain the cooling system as described in this chapter.

2. Loosen the alternator adjusting bolt and push the alternator toward the engine to loosen the belt. Take the belt off the alternator and water pump pulleys.

3. Unbolt the pulley from the water pump and take it off.

4. Unbolt the water pump from the engine. Take off the water pump and its O-ring. On 1976-1983 Accords and 1979-1982 Preludes, remove the water pump-to-timing cover seal as well.

7

5. Installation is the reverse of removal, plus the following:

    a. Use a new O-ring between the water pump and engine.

    b. On 1976-1983 Accords and 1979-1982 Preludes, use a new seal between the timing cover and water pump if the old one was damaged.

    c. Tighten the water pump bolts to specifications in **Table 2**.

    d. Adjust the alternator drive belt as described in Chapter Three.

    e. Fill and bleed the cooling system as described under *Cooling System Flushing*.

HEATER

The following sections provide removal and installation procedures for the heater blower unit. Removal of the heater assembly on all except early Preludes requires removal of the entire dashboard, including the safety pad, radio and instrument cluster. This is a complicated procedure which should be done by a Honda dealer or automotive electrical shop.

Blower Motor Removal/Installation (1976-1981 Accord)

Refer to **Figure 14** for this procedure.

1. Disconnect the negative cable from the battery.

2. Remove the glove compartment attaching screws (**Figure 15**). Tilt the glove compartment so its right-hand stop comes out through the opening, then take the glove compartment out.

3. Remove the blower unit mounting bolts (**Figure 14**).

4. Disconnect the blower unit vacuum hose and wiring connector, then take the unit out.

5. Installation is the reverse of removal.

Blower Unit Removal/Installation (1982-on Accord)

1. Disconnect the negative cable from the battery.

2. Remove 3 screws and take out the lower right side dash panel.

3. Remove the screws from the glove compartment hinges.

4. Reach under the dash. With a short Phillips screwdriver, remove the 2 horizontal screws securing the upper edge of the glove compartment catch cloth. See **Figure 16**.

5. Remove the vertical screw from the front side of the catch cloth.

6. Tilt the glove compartment to the right and take it out.

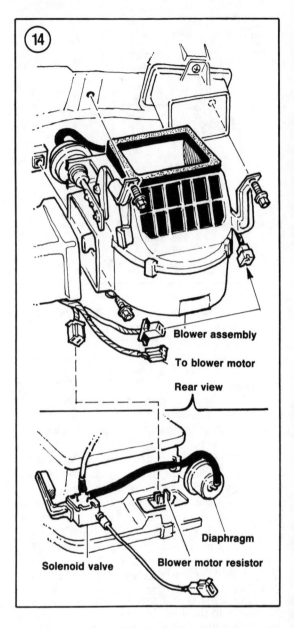

Blower assembly

To blower motor

Rear view

Solenoid valve

Diaphragm

Blower motor resistor

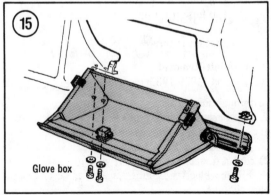

Glove box

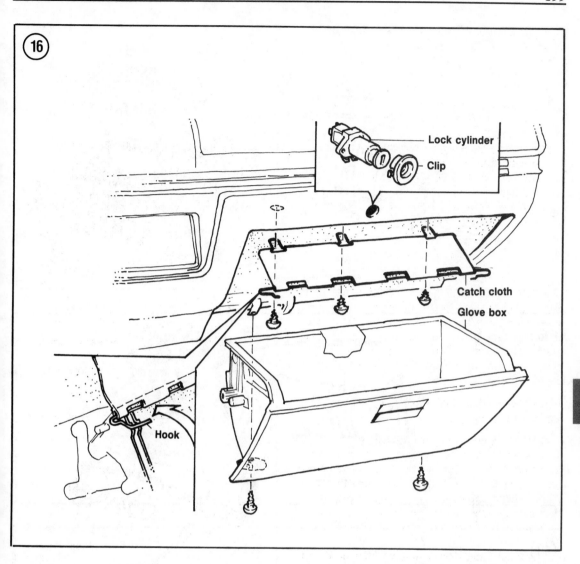

(16)

Lock cylinder

Clip

Catch cloth

Glove box

Hook

7

7. Remove the floor duct and molded insulator.

8. Remove the blower duct (**Figure 17**).

9. Remove the blower mounting bolts and lower the blower to the floor.

10. Unplug the wiring connector and disconnect the vacuum hose from the blower. Take the blower out.

11. Installation is the reverse of removal.

**Blower Unit Removal/
Installation (1979-1982 Prelude)**

Refer to **Figure 18** for this procedure.

1. Disconnect the negative cable from the battery.

2. Remove the glove compartment hinge screws and take out the glove compartment.

3. Pry the retainer clips out of the heater duct ends. Compress the duct to shorten it, then take it out.

4. Remove the blower mounting bolts. Turn the blower onto its right side and lay it on the floor.

5. Unplug the wiring connectors and disconnect the control cable, then take the blower out.

6. Installation is the reverse of removal.

**Heater Removal/Installation
(1979-1982 Prelude)**

Refer to **Figure 19** for this procedure.

1. Disconnect the negative cable from the battery.

2. Drain the radiator as described under *Cooling System Flushing* in this chapter.

3. Remove the lower dash panel.

4. Label the heater hoses. Place a container beneath them to catch dripping coolant, then detach them from the firewall fittings.

5. Remove the clip and disconnect the cable from the heater valve.

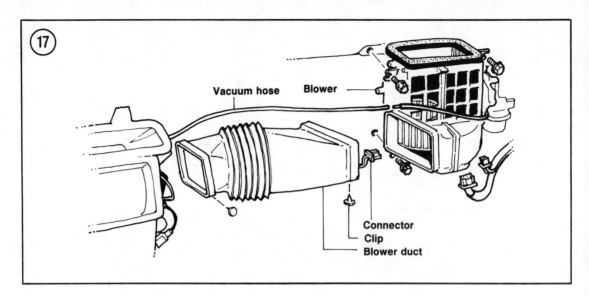

(17)

Vacuum hose   Blower

Connector
Clip
Blower duct

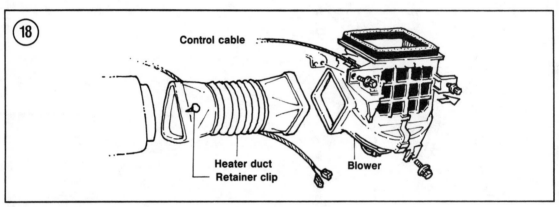

(18)

Control cable

Heater duct
Retainer clip

Blower

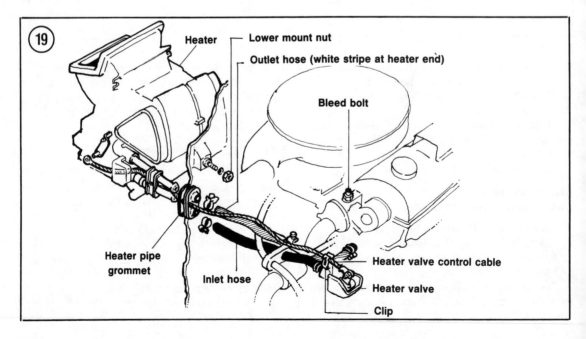

(19)

Heater   Lower mount nut

Outlet hose (white stripe at heater end)

Bleed bolt

Heater pipe
grommet

Inlet hose

Heater valve control cable

Heater valve

Clip

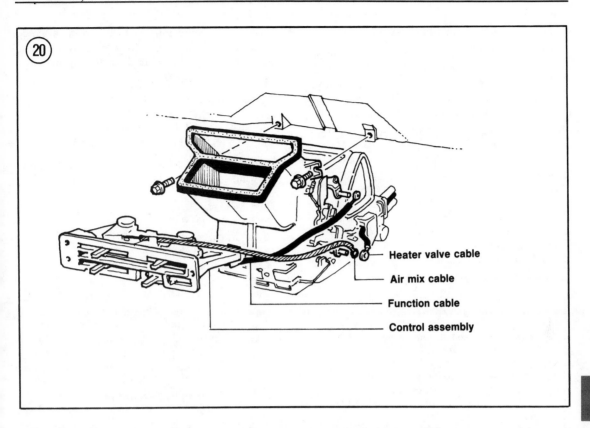

⑳

Heater valve cable

Air mix cable

Function cable

Control assembly

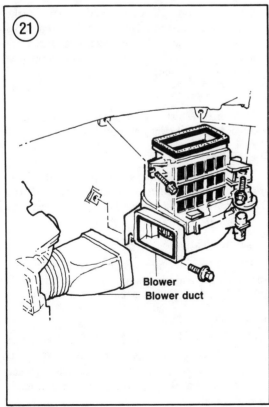

㉑

Blower
Blower duct

7

6. Remove the heater duct.

WARNING
Do not disconnect the refrigerant hoses during the next step. They contain refrigerant under pressure, which can cause frostbite if it touches skin and blindness if it touches the eyes.

7. If equipped with air conditioning, remove the evaporator mounting bolt and duct bands. Push the evaporator to the right to detach it from the heater.

8. Label the control cables and detach them from the heater. See **Figure 20**.

9. Remove the heater mounting bolts and take the heater out.

10. Installation is the reverse of removal.

**Blower Removal/Installation
(1983-on Prelude)**

1. Disconnect the negative cable from the battery.

2. Remove the glove compartment.

3. Remove the blower duct (**Figure 21**).

4. Unplug the blower wiring connector and disconnect the vacuum line.

5. Remove the blower mounting bolts and take the blower out.

6. Installation is the reverse of removal.

AIR CONDITIONING

This section covers the maintenance and minor repairs that can prevent or correct most air conditioning problems. Major repairs require special training and tools and should be left to a Honda dealer or air conditioning shop.

SYSTEM OPERATION

Figure 22 shows a typical Honda air conditioning system. The 6 basic components are common to all air conditioning systems:

a. Compressor.
b. Condenser.
c. Receiver/drier.
d. Sight glass.
e. Expansion valve.
f. Evaporator.

> *WARNING*
> *The components, connected with high-pressure hoses and tubes, form a closed loop. The refrigerant in the system is under very high pressure. It can cause frostbite if it touches skin and blindness if it touches the eyes. If discharged near a flame, the refrigerant forms poisonous gas. If the refrigerant can is hooked up wrong, it can explode. For these reasons, read this **entire** section before working on the system.*

For practical purposes, the cycle begins at the compressor. The refrigerant, in a warm, low-pressure vapor state, enters the low-pressure side of the compressor. It is compressed to a high-pressure hot vapor and pumped out of the high-pressure side to the condenser.

Air flow through the condenser removes heat from the refrigerant and transfers the heat to the outside air. As the heat is removed, the refrigerant condenses to a warm, high-pressure liquid.

The refrigerant then flows to the receiver/drier where moisture is removed and impurities are filtered out. The refrigerant is stored in the receiver/drier until it is needed. The receiver/drier incorporates a sight glass that permits visual monitoring of the condition of the refrigerant as it flows. From the receiver/drier, the refrigerant then flows to the expansion valve. The expansion valve is thermostatically controlled and meters refrigerant to the evaporator. As the refrigerant leaves the expansion valve it changes from a warm, high-pressure liquid to a cold, low-pressure liquid.

In the evaporator, the refrigerant removes heat from the passenger compartment air that is blown across the evaporator's fins and tubes. In the process, the refrigerant changes from a cold, low-pressure liquid to a warm, high-pressure vapor. The vapor flows back to the compressor, where the cycle begins again.

GET TO KNOW YOUR VEHICLE'S SYSTEM

With **Figure 22** as a guide, locate each of the following components in turn:

a. Compressor.
b. Condenser.
c. Receiver/drier.
d. Sight glass.
e. Expansion valve.
f. Evaporator.

Compressor

The compressor is located on the same end of the engine as the alternator and is driven by a V-belt. The large pulley on the front of the compressor contains an electromagnetic clutch. This activates and operates the compressor when the air conditioning is switched on.

Condenser

The condenser is mounted in front of the radiator. Air passing through the fins and tubes removes heat from the refrigerant in the same manner it removes heat from the engine coolant as it passes through the radiator.

Receiver/Drier

The receiver/drier is a small tank-like unit, mounted in the engine compartment.

Sight Glass

The sight glass allows the refrigerant to be inspected visually when the system is in operation. The refrigerant's appearance is used to troubleshoot the system.

Expansion Valve

The expansion valve is located between the receiver/drier and the evaporator. It is mounted on the cooling unit in the passenger compartment.

Evaporator

The evaporator is located in the passenger compartment, inside the cooling unit. Warm air is blown across the fins and tubes, where it is cooled and dried and then ducted into the passenger compartment.

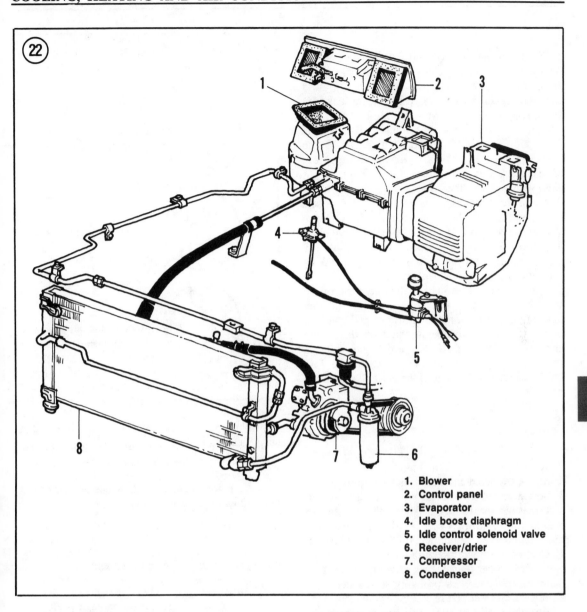

1. Blower
2. Control panel
3. Evaporator
4. Idle boost diaphragm
5. Idle control solenoid valve
6. Receiver/drier
7. Compressor
8. Condenser

ROUTINE MAINTENANCE

Preventive maintenance of the air conditioning system is easy; at least once a month, even in cold weather, start your engine, turn on the air conditioner and operate·it at each of the control settings. Operate the air conditioner for about 5 minutes. This will ensure that the compressor seal will not deform from sitting in the same position for a long period of time. If this occurs, the seal is likely to leak.

The efficiency of the air conditioning system also depends in great part on the efficiency of the cooling system. This is because the heat from the condenser passes through the radiator. If the cooling system is dirty or low on coolant, it may be impossible to operate the air conditioner without overheating. Inspect the coolant. If necessary, flush and refill the cooling system as described in this chapter.

With an air hose and a soft brush, clean the radiator and condenser fins and tubes to remove bugs, leaves and other imbedded debris.

Check drive belt tension as described in Chapter Three.

If the condition of the cooling system thermostat is in doubt, test it as described in this chapter.

Once you are sure the cooling system is in good condition, the air conditioning system can be inspected.

Inspection

1. Clean all lines, fittings and system components with solvent and a clean rag. Pay particular attention to the fittings; oily dirt around connections almost certainly indicates a leak. Oil from the compressor will migrate through the system to the leak. Carefully tighten the connection, but don't overtighten and strip the threads. If the leak persists, it will soon be apparent once again as oily dirt accumulates. Clean the sight glass with a clean, dry cloth.

2. Clean the condenser fins and tubes with a soft brush and an air hose or with a high-pressure stream of water from a garden hose. Remove bugs, leaves and other imbedded debris. Carefully straighten any bent fins with a screwdriver, taking care not to puncture or dent the tubes.

3. Start the engine and check the operation of the blower motor and the compressor clutch by turning the controls on and off. If either the blower or the clutch fails to operate, shut off the engine and check the fuses. If they are blown, replace them. If not, remove them and clean the fuse holder contacts. Then check the clutch and blower operation again.

Testing

1. Place the transaxle in NEUTRAL (manual) or PARK (automatic). Set the handbrake.
2. Start the engine and run it at a fast idle.
3. Set the temperature control to its coldest setting and the blower to high. Allow the system to operate for 10 minutes with the doors open. Then shut them and set the blower on its lowest setting.
4. Check air temperature at the outlet. It should be noticeably colder than the surrounding air. If not, the refrigerant level is probably low. Check the sight glass as described in the following step.
5. Run the engine at a fast idle and switch on the air conditioning. Look at the sight glass (**Figure 23**) and check for the following:
   a. Bubbles—the refrigerant level is low.
   b. Oily or cloudy—the system is contaminated. Have it serviced by a dealer or air conditioning shop.
   c. Clear glass—either there is enough refrigerant, too much or the system is so close to empty it can't make bubbles. If there is no difference between the inlet and outlet air temperatures, the system is probably near empty.
6. If the system does blow cold air, it either has the right amount of refrigerant or too much. To tell which, turn off the air conditioner while watching the sight glass. If the refrigerant foams, then clears

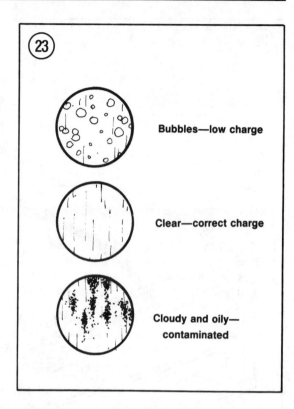

up, the amount is correct. If it doesn't foam, but stays clear, there is too much.

REFRIGERANT

The air conditioning system uses a refrigerant called dichlorodifluoromethane or R-12.

> *WARNING*
> *R-12 creates freezing temperatures when it evaporates. This can cause frostbite if it touches skin and blindness if it touches the eyes. If discharged near an open flame, R-12 creates poisonous gas. If the refrigerant can is hooked up to the pressure side of the compressor, it may explode. Always wear safety goggles when working with R-12.*

Charging

Recharging of partially discharged or empty air conditioning systems can be done by home mechanics, using commercially available recharge kits.

If a hose has been disconnected or any internal part of the system exposed to air, the system should be evacuated and recharged by a dealer or air conditioning shop.

Recharge kits are available from auto parts stores. Be sure the kit includes a gauge set. Kits are available which do not include gauge sets, but these do not provide warning of an overcharged system. Overcharging the system can damage components.

NOTE
Gauge sets are expensive, but so is having the system professionally recharged. Compare the price of a gauge set to the cost of a recharging job before proceeding.

Carefully read and understand the gauge manufacturer's instructions before charging the system.

Troubleshooting

If the air conditioner fails to blow cold air, the following steps will help locate the problem.

1. First, stop the car and look at the control settings. One of the most common air conditioning problems occurs when the temperature is set for maximum cold and the blower is set on low. This promotes ice build-up on the evaporator fins and tubes, particularly in humid weather. Eventually, the evaporator will ice over completely and restrict air flow. Turn the blower on high and place a hand over an air outlet. If the blower is running but there is little or no air flowing through the outlet, the evaporator is probably iced up. Leave the blower on high and turn the temperature control off or to its warmest setting, then wait. It will take 10-15 minutes for the ice to start melting.

2. If the blower is not running, the fuse may be blown, there may be a loose wiring connection or the motor may be burned out. First, check the fuse block for a blown or incorrectly seated fuse. Then check the wiring for loose connections.

3. Shut off the engine and inspect the compressor drive belt. If loose or worn, tighten or replace. See Chapter Three.

4. Start the engine. Check the compressor clutch by turning the air conditioning on and off. If the clutch does not activate, its fuse may be blown or the evaporator temperature-limiting switches may be defective. If the fuse is defective, replace it. If the fuse is not the problem, have the system checked by a Honda dealer or air conditioning shop.

5. If the system checks out okay to this point, start the engine, turn on the air conditioner and watch the refrigerant through the sight glass. If it fills with bubbles after a few seconds, the refrigerant level is low. If the sight glass is oily or cloudy, the system is contaminated and should be serviced by a shop as soon as possible. Corrosion and deterioration occur very quickly and if not taken care of at once will result in a very expensive repair job.

6. If the system still appears to be operating as it should but air flow into the passenger compartment is not cold, check the condenser and cooling system radiator for debris that could block air flow. Recheck the cooling system as described under *Inspection*.

7. If the preceding steps have not solved the problem, take the car to a dealer or air conditioning shop for service.

Table 1 COOLING SYSTEM SPECIFICATIONS

Item	° C	° F
Thermostat starts to open	80-84	176-183
Thermostat fully open	95	203
Fan "on" temperature		
1976-1983 Accord, 1979-1982		
Prelude	88.5-91.5	191-197
1983-on Prelude, 1984 Accord	87-93	188-199
Fan "off" temperature		
1976-1983 Accord, 1979-1982		
Prelude	5 ±1.5*	23 ±3*
1983-on Prelude, 1984 Accord	83-85	181-185
* Degrees less than "on" temperature.		

Table 2 TIGHTENING TORQUES

Fastener	N•m	ft.-lb.
Water pump bolts		
1976-1981 Accord	10-14	7-10
1979-on Prelude, 1982-on Accord	12	9

NOTE: If you own a 1985 model, first check the Supplement at the back of the book for any new service information.

ELECTRICAL SYSTEMS

The Honda is equipped with a 12-volt, negative-ground electrical system. Included in this chapter are service and repair proceedures for the battery, starter, charging system and lighting system. Repairs to electrical components such as the alternator or starter motor are usually beyond the ability of inexperienced mechanics. Such repairs are best left to the professional mechanic who is equipped with specialized tools.

By using the troubleshooting procedures given in Chapter Two it is possible to isolate problems to a specific component, thus saving money in costly troubleshooting bills.

In most cases, it will be faster and more economical to obtain new or rebuilt components instead of making repairs. Make certain, however, that the new or rebuilt part is an exact replacement. Also, make sure the cause of the failure has been isolated and corrected before installing a replacement. For instance, an uncorrected short in a regulator will in all probability burn out a new alternator as quickly as it damaged the old one. If in doubt, always consult an expert.

Table 1 and **Table 2** are at the end of the chapter.

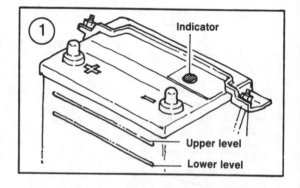

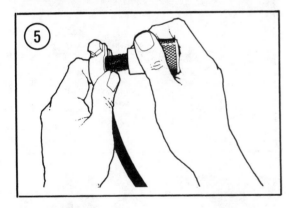

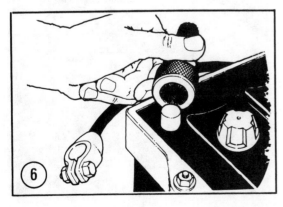

BATTERY

Care and Inspection

> *NOTE*
> *Original equipment sealed batteries on 1983 and later models are equipped with a condition indicator (**Figure 1** and **Figure 2**). If the indicator is red, battery electrolyte level is low. Since electrolyte cannot be added, the battery must be replaced. If the indicator is white, recharge the battery.*

1. Loosen the bolts in the terminal clamps far enough so the clamps can be spread slightly (**Figure 3**). Lift straight up on the clamps (negative first) to remove them from the posts.

> *CAUTION*
> *Twisting and prying on the clamps or the posts can result in serious damage to a battery that may otherwise be in good condition.*

> *NOTE*
> *The negative terminal is usually identified by a – sign or the letters "NEG." The positive terminal is usually identified by a + sign or the letters "POS." The color of the battery cables is not a reliable means of identifying terminals.*

> *NOTE*
> *Inexpensive terminal pullers are available from auto parts stores. Use one of these tools if the clamps are difficult to remove.*

2. Loosen the nuts on the battery hold-down bolts (**Figure 4**) and disconnect the lower ends of the bolts from the battery mount. Remove the hold-down bar and bolts and lift the battery out of the engine compartment.

3. Clean the top of the battery with a solution of baking soda and water, using a stiff bristle brush. Wipe clean with a cloth moistened in the solution.

> *CAUTION*
> *Take care not to allow the soda solution to enter any of the battery cells as this could seriously weaken the electrolyte. A small piece of tape can be placed over the ventilating hole in each cell cap to help keep out the solution.*

4. Clean both battery terminals and the battery cable terminals with a stiff brush or with one of the many tools made for this purpose. See **Figure 5** and **Figure 6**.

5. Examine the entire battery case for cracks.

8

6. Install battery in vehicle and connect the cables (positive first). Securely tighten the attaching bolts. Tighten the battery clamp bolts securely (**Figure 4**).

7. Coat the battery cables with a light grease or with Vaseline.

8. Check the electrolyte level and top up with distilled water if necessary.

Common Causes of Battery Failure

All batteries eventually fail. Their life can be prolonged, however, with a good maintenance program. Some of the reasons for premature failure are listed below.

1. Vehicle accessories left on overnight or longer causing an undercharged condition.

2. Slow driving speeds on short trips, causing an undercharged condition.

3. Vehicle electrical load exceeding the alternator capacity due particularly to aftermarket accessory equipment.

4. Charging system defects, such as a slipping alternator belt or faulty alternator or regulator.

5. Abuse of the battery, including failure to keep the battery terminals clean and allowing the battery to become too loose in the battery hold-down box.

Testing

This procedure applies to batteries with removable filler caps. Testing sealed maintenance-free batteries requires special equipment, but a service station can make the test for a nominal fee.

> *NOTE*
> *Original equipment sealed batteries on 1983 and later models are equipped with a condition indicator (**Figure 1** and **Figure 2**). If the indicator is red, battery electrolyte level is low. Since electrolyte cannot be added, the battery must be replaced. If the indicator is white, recharge the battery.*

Hydrometer testing is the best way to check battery condition. Use a hydrometer with numbered graduations from 1.100-1.300 rather than one with just color-coded bands. To use the hydrometer, squeeze the rubber ball, insert the tip in the cell and release the ball (**Figure 7**).

Draw enough electrolyte to float the weighted float inside the hydrometer. Note the number in line with the surface of the electrolyte. This is the specific gravity for the cell. Return the electrolyte to the cell from which it came.

The specific gravity of the electrolyte in each battery cell is an excellent indicator of that cell's condition. A fully charged cell will read 1.260 or

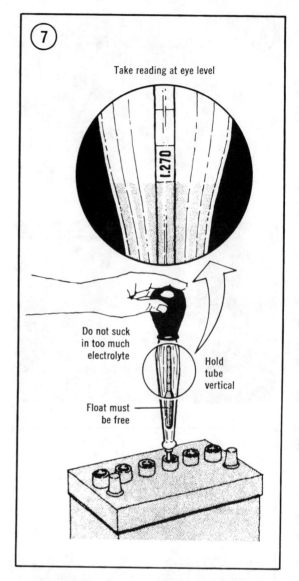

Take reading at eye level

1.270

Do not suck in too much electrolyte

Hold tube vertical

Float must be free

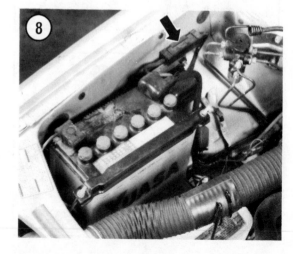

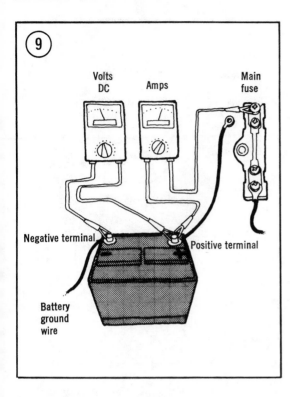

more at 20° C (68° F). If the cells test below 1.200, the battery must be recharged. Charging is also necessary if the specific gravity of the cell varies more than 0.025 from cell to cell.

NOTE
For every 10° F above 80° (25° C) electrolyte temperature, add 0.004 to specific gravity reading. For every 10° below 80° F (25° C), subtract 0.004.

Charging

The battery need not be removed from the car for charging. Just make certain that the area is well ventilated and that there is no chance of sparks or flames occurring near the battery.

WARNING
Charging batteries give off highly explosive hydrogen gas. If this explodes, it may spray battery acid over a wide area.

Disconnect the cables from the battery. On fillable batteries, make sure the electrolyte is fully topped up.

WARNING
Connect the charger to the battery before plugging it in.

Connect the charger to the battery—negative to negative, positive to positive. If the charger output

is variable, select a low setting (5-10 amps), set the voltage selector to 12 volts and plug the charger in. If the battery is severely discharged, allow it to charge for at least 8 hours. Batteries that aren't as badly discharged require less charging time. **Table 1** gives approximate charge rates. On fillable batteries, check charging progress with the hydrometer.

CHARGING SYSTEM

The charging system test procedures in this chapter require some test equipment (an ammeter and in some cases a voltmeter). If you have the equipment, it will be relatively easy to test the charging system yourself. If you don't have the equipment, it may be more practical to have the system tested by a shop. Many garages have charging system testing equipment which can isolate a problem to the alternator, regulator or battery. Tests using this type of professional equipment are relatively inexpensive. Before buying the necessary equipment for the following procedures, compare the price of the equipment with the cost of having the charging system professionally tested. Consider whether you will have any further use for equipment that you buy.

Alternator Test
(1976-1981 Accord,
1979-1982 Prelude)

This procedure applies to 1976-1981 Accords and 1979-1982 Preludes.

To test the alternator output, an ammeter that reads 60 amps or higher and a voltmeter are required. The battery must be fully charged and the drive belt properly tensioned.

1. Disconnect the battery negative cable. Disconnect the cable leading from the battery positive terminal to the main fuse (**Figure 8**). Connect the ammeter between the battery positive cable and the main fuse. See **Figure 9**. Reconnect the negative cable.

NOTE
On Prelude models, disconnect the white/blue choke heater wire at the firewall.

2. Turn the ignition switch ON and verify that the discharge warning light comes on. If the warning light does not come on, disconnect the white/blue wire connector at the voltage regulator and short the connector to ground:
   a. If the light goes on, the voltage regulator is probably faulty. Replace it and repeat the test.

8

b. If the warning light still does not come on, check fuse F9 and 10 (Accord) or fuse 4 (Prelude). If the fuse(s) are okay, check all related and connecting wires for open circuits. If circuits are okay, check for a burned out warning light bulb.

3. Disconnect the white/red wire connector from the voltage regulator. Connect a jumper wire between the battery positive post and the white/red wire pin in the connector. Start the engine and check the alternator output while operating the engine at 2,000 rpm:

a. If the maximum output is 47 amps, proceed to Step 3.

b. If there is no output or less output than specified is recorded, reconnect the white/red wire connector and disconnect the white/red wire connector at the back of the alternator. Connect a jumper from the white/red wire terminal at rear of alternator to the positive battery terminal and repeat the output test. If output is okay, check for an open circuit between the white/red wire connecting the regulator and alternator. If there is no output, check the white wire between the alternator and the main fuse for continuity. If there is continuity, have a Honda dealer disassemble the alternator for further internal checks.

4. Start the engine and observe the discharge warning light. The light should go out. If the alternator output is within specifications (47 amps) and the warning light stays on at idle speed but goes out as engine speed is increased or stays on all the time, check the alternator neutral wire circuit. This can be done by leaving the white/red voltage regulator wire connected and inserting voltmeter probes into the backs of pins (black wire and white/black wire) and checking the voltage while the engine is idling. Voltage should be half of the specified alternator output voltage (13.5 to 14.5) or approximately 7 volts:

a. If the voltage is approximately half, the alternator is operating properly. Replace the regulator.

b. If the voltage is less than 6.5 volts or more than 8.5 volts, have a Honda dealer check the alternator diodes.

c. If no voltage is observed, check for voltage across pins white/black wire and black wire from wire harness leading to back of alternator. If no voltage is present, refer further troubleshooting to a Honda dealer or automotive electrical shop. If half the output voltage is present, check for an open circuit in

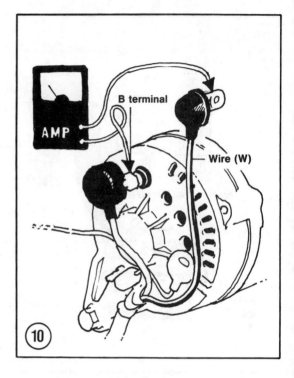

the white/black wire circuit between the alternator and the regulator.

Alternator Test
(1982-on Accord, 1983-on Prelude)

This procedure applies to 1982 and later Accords and 1983 and later Preludes.

The procedure requires an ammeter and a tune-up tachometer.

1. Connect a tune-up tachometer to the engine, following manufacturer's instructions.

2. With the engine off, disconnect the white wire from alternator terminal B. See **Figure 10**.

3. Connect an ammeter between the disconnected wire and its terminal as shown in **Figure 10**.

4. Start the engine. Turn on the following:

a. High beam headlights.

b. Rear window defogger.

c. Heater fan switch (high position).

5. Start the engine. Run it at different speeds and compare alternator output with **Figure 11A** (all except 1984 Accord) or **Figure 11B** (1984 Accord):

a. If alternator output is within specifications, the alternator is good.

b. If the alternator has no output or is not within specifications, check the charging system wiring for breaks or bad connections. If the wiring is good, replace the alternator or have it disassembled and tested by a Honda dealer or automotive electrical shop.

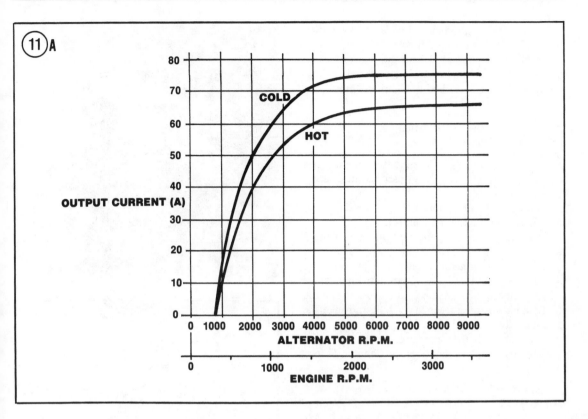

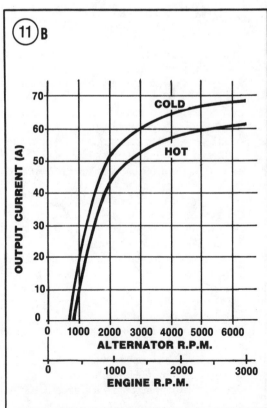

Alternator Removal/Installation
(1976-1981 Accord, 1979-1982 Prelude)

This procedure applies to 1976-1981 Accords and 1979-1982 Preludes.

1. Disconnect the negative cable from the battery (**Figure 1**).

2. Unplug the connector at the rear of the alternator and the oil pressure switch lead at the engine. See **Figure 12**.

3. Remove the alternator lockbolt and mounting bolt (**Figure 13**), remove the drive belt from the pulley and remove the alternator from the engine.

4. Install the alternator by reversing these steps. Make certain the alternator connector has been connected before connecting the negative battery cable. Refer to Chapter Three and adjust the drive belt tension.

Alternator Removal/Installation
(1982-on Accord)

1. Disconnect the negative cable from the battery.

2. Unplug the alternator wiring connector and remove the terminal nut. See **Figure 14** (1982-1983) or **Figure 15** (1984).

3. Remove the adjusting bolt. Loosen the pivot bolt and nut, push the alternator toward the engine and remove the drive belt.

8

4. Remove the alternator bracket bolts, then remove the alternator and bracket.

5. Separate the alternator from the bracket.

6. Installation is the reverse of removal. Adjust the drive belt as described in Chapter Three.

Alternator Removal/Installation (1983-on Prelude)

1. Disconnect the negative cable from the battery.

2. Remove the air cleaner as described in Chapter Six.

3. Pry up the connector locktabs as shown in **Figure 16** and unplug the connector.

4. Remove the terminal nut and disconnect the B terminal wire from the alternator.

5. Remove the adjusting bolt and pivot bolt nut. See **Figure 17**. Push the alternator toward the engine to loosen the drive belt and take the belt off.

6. Remove the alternator pivot bolt and take the alternator off.

7. Installation is the reverse of removal. Adjust the alternator belt as described in Chapter Three.

Voltage Regulator Test (1976-1981)

A functional test of the voltage regulator can be conducted very simply. However, if the regulator does not perform correctly, adjustment should be entrusted to a Honda dealer or an automotive electrical specialist. Before testing the regulator, refer to the performance test for the alternator to ensure it is operating correctly. The voltage regulator on the Accord is shown in **Figure 18**. On Prelude models, the voltage regulator is located behind the battery.

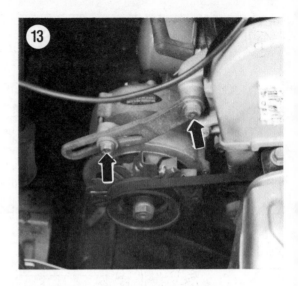

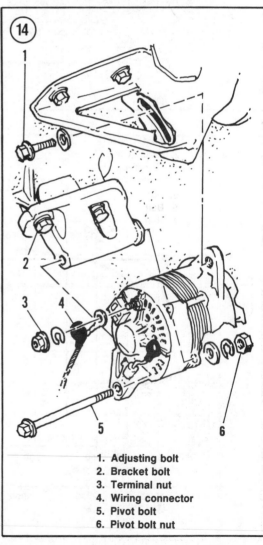

1. Adjusting bolt
2. Bracket bolt
3. Terminal nut
4. Wiring connector
5. Pivot bolt
6. Pivot bolt nut

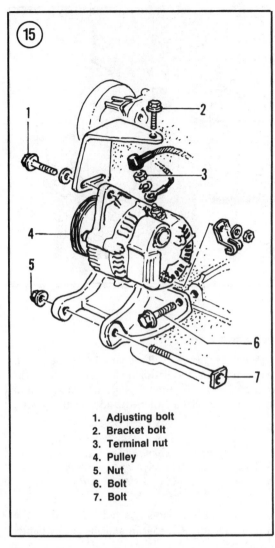

15

1. Adjusting bolt
2. Bracket bolt
3. Terminal nut
4. Pulley
5. Nut
6. Bolt
7. Bolt

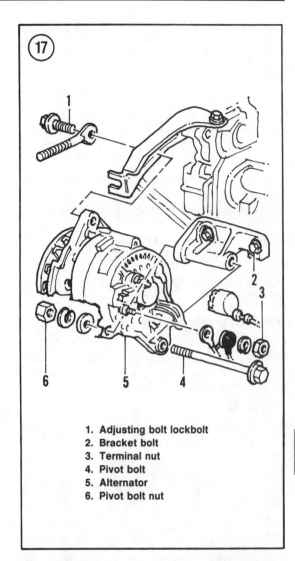

17

1. Adjusting bolt lockbolt
2. Bracket bolt
3. Terminal nut
4. Pivot bolt
5. Alternator
6. Pivot bolt nut

8

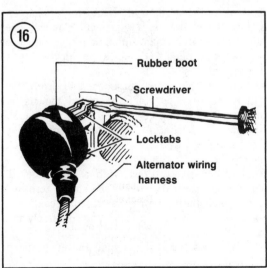

16

Rubber boot

Screwdriver

Locktabs

Alternator wiring
harness

18

A voltmeter will be required to perform this test.
1. Start the engine and allow it to idle. Disconnect the negative cable at the battery (**Figure 1**).

CAUTION
If the engine stops when the negative battery cable is removed, turn the ignition key to OFF, reinstall the negative battery cable and repeat Step 1. Do not attempt to start engine with negative battery cable disconnected.

2. Connect the positive lead of a voltmeter to the positive battery terminal. Connect the voltmeter negative lead to the disconnected battery negative cable.
3. Increase the engine speed to 2,000-2,500 rpm and read the voltage on the meter. It should be 13.5-14.5 volts. If the reading is incorrect, the regulator must be adjusted (by your Honda dealer) or replaced.

Voltage Regulator Test (1982-on)

Voltage regulator testing on 1982 and later models is complicated and in some cases requires special equipment. Refer testing to a Honda dealer or automotive electrical shop.

Voltage Regulator Replacement

This procedure applies to all models except the 1984 Accord. The 1984 Accord voltage regulator is mounted inside the alternator. Replacement requires partial disassembly of the alternator and should be done by a Honda dealer or automotive electrical shop.

The regulator is located as follows:
 a. 1976-1981 Accord—next to the battery (**Figure 18**).
 b. 1982-1983 Accord—next to the relay box (**Figure 19**).
 c. 1979-1982 Prelude—behind the battery.
 d. 1983-on Prelude—between the battery and the right-hand strut housing (**Figure 20**).
1. Disconnect the negative battery cable.
2. Disconnect the wiring harness connector at the voltage regulator.
3. Remove all attaching screws and remove the voltage regulator.
4. Installation is the reverse of these steps.

Charge Indicator Relay (1976-1981)

If the alternator and voltage regulator are operating satisfactorily and the charge indicator warning light remains on, the charge indicator relay, located in the voltage regulator, must be tested. This is a job for a Honda dealer or an automotive electrical specialist.

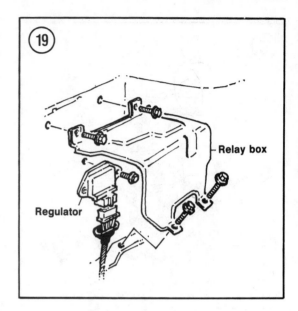

Relay box

Regulator

STARTER

Performance Test

The following test will tell you if a problem is in the starter or its wiring. The only equipment needed is a pair of jumper cables (the kind used to start cars with dead batteries) and a length of wire.

NOTE
This test is intended for starters that don't respond when the key is turned. If the starter fails to disengage when the key is released, replaced it with a new or rebuilt unit.

1. Make sure the battery is fully charged. Make sure the terminals are clean and the cables tightly connected.
2. Remove the starter as described in this chapter.
3. Lay the starter on the ground. Connect one jumper cable from the positive battery terminal to the starter terminal from which the thick wire was disconnected.
4. Connect the other jumper cable from the battery negative terminal to one of the starter mounting bolt flanges.
5. Connect a length of wire to the battery positive terminal. The wire must be long enough to reach the starter.
6. Hold the starter down with a heavy board. Touch the length of wire to the starter terminal from which the thin wire was disconnected. The starter should make a firm click and spin freely and rapidly:
 a. If it does, the starter is good and the problem is in the wiring.

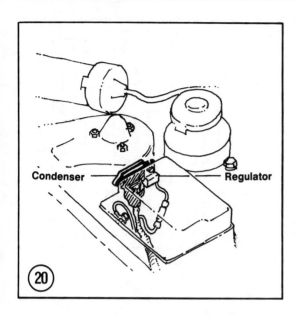

Condenser ———————— Regulator

(20)

b. If it doesn't click, the solenoid is probably bad. If it clicks, but spins sluggishly or not at all, the starter has an internal problem. Replace it with a new or rebuilt unit.

Removal/Installation

1. Disconnect the negative battery cable at the battery (**Figure 1**).
2. Disconnect the positive battery cable and the starter control cable at the starter. **Figure 13** shows a typical installation.
3. Unscrew the starter motor mounting bolts and pull the starter out of the engine.
4. Install the starter by reversing these steps. Make sure the connections are tight to ensure good electrical contact. Tighten the mounting bolts to 44 N•m (32 ft.-lb.).

IGNITION SYSTEM

The ignition system consists of the distributor, coil and primary and secondary circuit parts. The primary circuit parts are the battery, the contact breaker points or igniter and the ignition coil primary windings. The secondary circuit parts are the ignition coil secondary windings, rotor, distributor cap electrical contacts, spark plug cables and spark plugs.

On 1976-1983 Accords and 1979-1982 Preludes, the distributor is gear-driven through the camshaft. On 1984 Accords and 1983-on Preludes, the distributor is driven directly by the camshaft. Different distributor configurations have been used, depending upon year, state and altitude conditions.

All 1976-1978 distributors use a contact breaker point system. The contact points should be serviced and replaced periodically as specified in Chapter Three. Replace the rotor and condenser whenever contact points are replaced. Starting with 1979 models, a transistorized ignition system is used in which the breaker points and condenser are replaced by a pulse generator and reluctor. The transistorized distributor requires no periodic maintenance, other than checking the ignition timing as specified in Chapter Three.

Basic ignition system and spark plug troubleshooting information can be found in Chapter Two. These procedures, together with other troubleshooting procedures included in Chapter Two, can help you to determine the system or component which is operating incorrectly. If the ignition system is operating incorrectly, test procedures unique to the Honda ignition system are found in this section and can be used to troubleshoot and locate the problem source.

Test procedures for troubleshooting breaker point ignition systems (1976-1978) are found in **Figure 21**. For 1979 and later models, use the electronic ignition system test procedures in Chapter Two, together with test procedures for the ignition coil and spark plug wires in this chapter.

An ammeter and voltmeter, described in Chapter One, and jumper wires (**Figure 22**) are required to perform the test procedures.

8

BREAKER POINT IGNITION SYSTEM TESTING

Before starting actual troubleshooting on breaker point ignition systems, read the entire diagnostic chart (**Figure 21**). When required, the diagnostic chart will refer you back to procedures covered in this chapter for service and test information.

Primary Distributor Circuit Resistance

Excessive resistance in the distributor primary circuit will reduce available voltage to the ignition coil (which reduces coil output). This procedure uses a voltmeter to measure resistance in the circuit. High voltage indicates high resistance; voltage within specifications indicates acceptable resistance.

> *NOTE*
> *This procedure requires that the battery be fully charged. Test the battery as described in this chapter and charge or replace as required before beginning procedure.*

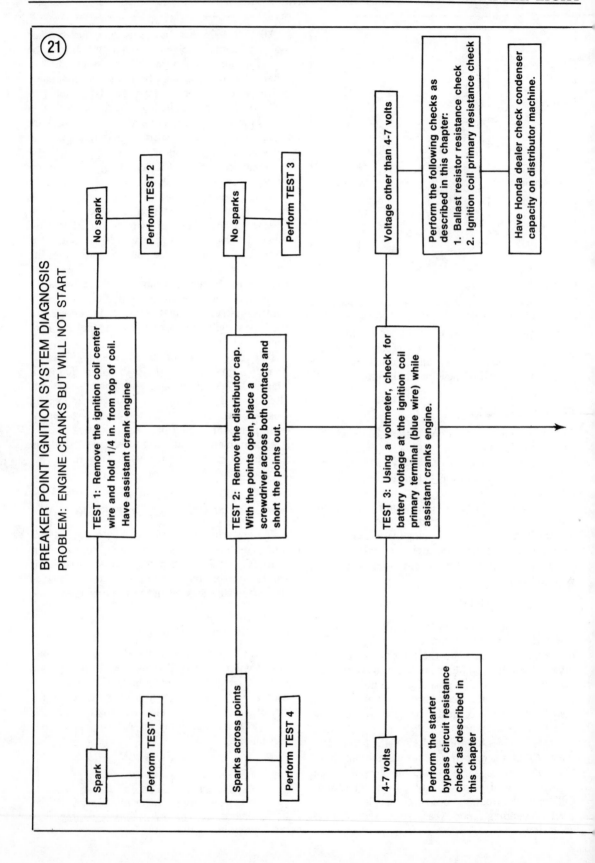

BREAKER POINT IGNITION SYSTEM DIAGNOSIS
PROBLEM: ENGINE CRANKS BUT WILL NOT START

(21)

TEST 1: Remove the ignition coil center wire and hold 1/4 in. from top of coil. Have assistant crank engine

No spark → Perform TEST 2

Spark → Perform TEST 7

TEST 2: Remove the distributor cap. With the points open, place a screwdriver across both contacts and short the points out.

No sparks → Perform TEST 3

Sparks across points → Perform TEST 4

TEST 3: Using a voltmeter, check for battery voltage at the ignition coil primary terminal (blue wire) while assistant cranks engine.

Voltage other than 4-7 volts → Perform the following checks as described in this chapter:
1. Ballast resistor resistance check
2. Ignition coil primary resistance check

Have Honda dealer check condenser capacity on distributor machine.

4-7 volts → Perform the starter bypass circuit resistance check as described in this chapter

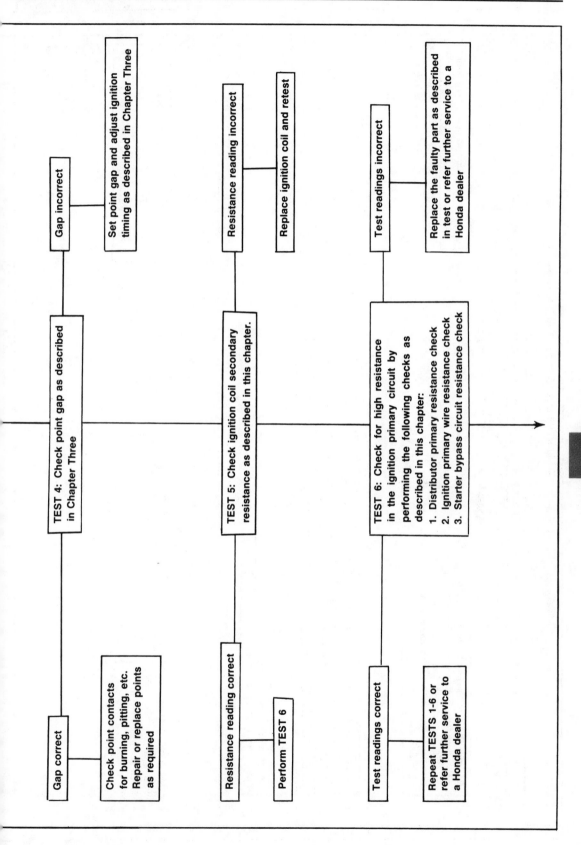

TEST 4: Check point gap as described in Chapter Three

Gap incorrect

Set point gap and adjust ignition timing as described in Chapter Three

Gap correct

Check point contacts for burning, pitting, etc. Repair or replace points as required

TEST 5: Check ignition coil secondary resistance as described in this chapter.

Resistance reading incorrect

Replace ignition coil and retest

Resistance reading correct

Perform TEST 6

TEST 6: Check for high resistance in the ignition primary circuit by performing the following checks as described in this chapter:

1. Distributor primary resistance check
2. Ignition primary wire resistance check
3. Starter bypass circuit resistance check

Test readings incorrect

Replace the faulty part as described in test or refer further service to a Honda dealer

Test readings correct

Repeat TESTS 1-6 or refer further service to a Honda dealer

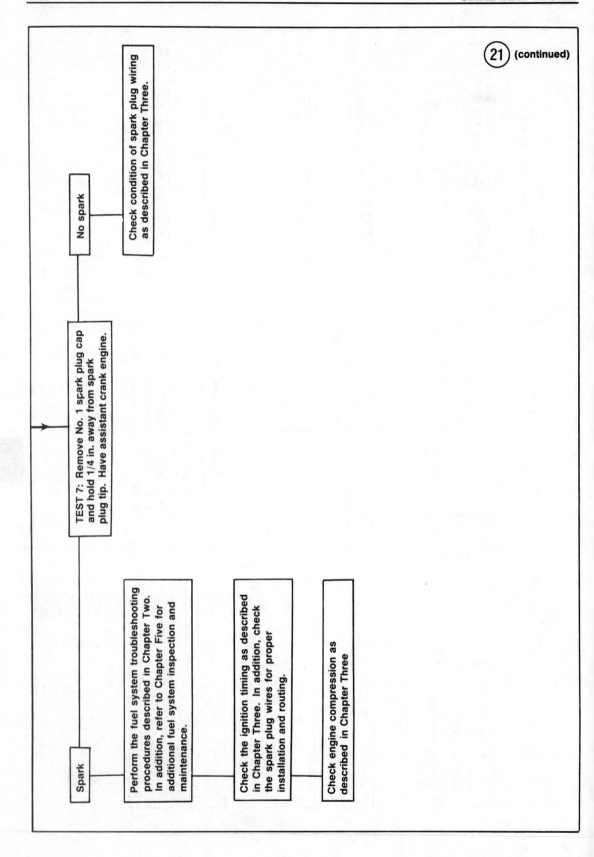

21 (continued)

No spark

Check condition of spark plug wiring as described in Chapter Three.

TEST 7: Remove No. 1 spark plug cap and hold 1/4 in. away from spark plug tip. Have assistant crank engine.

Spark

Perform the fuel system troubleshooting procedures described in Chapter Two. In addition, refer to Chapter Five for additional fuel system inspection and maintenance.

Check the ignition timing as described in Chapter Three. In addition, check the spark plug wires for proper installation and routing.

Check engine compression as described in Chapter Three

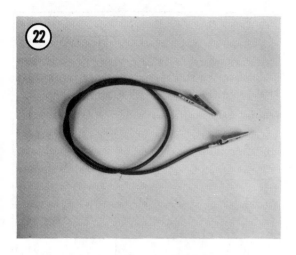

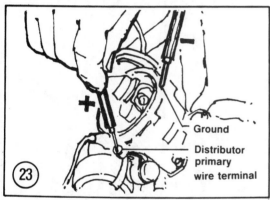

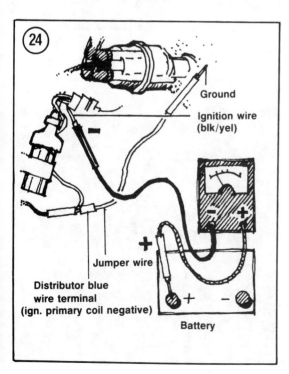

1. Remove the distributor cap. Contact points should be closed.

2. Set the voltmeter to the lowest voltage scale.

3. Referring to **Figure 23**, connect the voltmeter positive lead to the distributor primary terminal. Then connect the voltmeter negative lead to any good ground (bare metal in the engine compartment).

4. Have an assistant turn the key to ON and note the voltmeter reading. Normal resistance reading is 0-0.2 volts. If reading exceeds 0.2 volts, refer distributor to a Honda dealer for further testing.

Ignition Wire Circuit Resistance

Refer to **Figure 24** for this procedure.

1. Locate the distributor terminal blue wire (ignition primary coil negative terminal) and ground it using one jumper cable (**Figure 22**).

2. Attach voltmeter negative lead to the black/yellow wire coming from the emission control box. **Figure 25** shows the emission control box.

3. Attach voltmeter positive lead to the positive battery terminal.

4. Set the voltmeter to the lowest scale and turn the ignition switch to ON. The voltmeter reading should not exceed 0.4 volts. If it does, have a Honda dealer check the ignition switch.

Starter Bypass Circuit Resistance

1. Locate the distributor terminal blue wire (ignition coil negative terminal) and ground it using one jumper cable (**Figure 22**).

2. Attach voltmeter negative lead to the ignition coil positive terminal.

3. Attach voltmeter positive lead to the positive battery terminal.

8

4. Set the voltmeter to the lowest scale and turn the ignition switch to ON. The voltmeter should read approximately 6 volts or 1/2 of battery voltage. If voltage is correct, proced to Step 5. If not, perform the *Ballast Resistor Resistance Measurement* in this chapter.

5. Turn the ignition switch to START position and note reading on voltmeter. It should be 0.4 volts or less. If voltage reading is 0.5 volts or higher, check all wiring between the ignition primary coil terminal and the starter solenoid resistor bypass terminal. Repair if required. Then test ignition coil primary winding resistance as described under *Ignition Coil* in this chapter.

Ballast Resistor
Resistance Measurement

The ballast resistor is located under the windshield airscoop (**Figure 26**).

1. Remove the windshield airscoop at the base of the engine hood.

2. Disconnect the black/yellow and green wires from the ballast resistor.

3. Attach the positive and negative ohmmeter leads to the ballast resistor wire terminals (**Figure 26**).

4. Set the ohmmeter scale to its lowest resistance and note the reading. It should be 1.6 ohms ±10% at 70° F. If not, replace the ballast resistor.

BREAKERLESS IGNITION
SYSTEM TESTING

Breakerless ignition system test procedures practical for home mechanics are described in Chapter Two. If the procedures indicate a problem in the electronic module (also called an igniter or pulse generator), have the system tested by a Honda dealer or automotive electrical shop.

IGNITION COIL

A resistance check of the primary and secondary windings in the ignition coil can be made with an ohmmeter. A functional check requires a coil tester; this should be done by a Honda dealer or automotive electrical shop.

Resistance Check

1. Unplug the secondary lead from the coil. See **Figure 27**. Note the locations of the primary (thin) coil wires, then disconnect them from the coil.

2. Check the resistance of the primary winding by touching the ohmmeter probes to the primary positive and negative terminals on the coil. See **Figure 28**. Compare with specifications in **Table 2**.

3. Check the resistance of the secondary winding by touching the probes to the secondary terminal and the positive terminal (**Figure 29**). Specifications are in **Table 2**.

4. Replace the coil if the resistance readings in Step 2 or Step 3 are not within specifications.

Ignition Secondary Lead Test

The secondary lead running from distributor to ignition coil can be checked for resistance with an

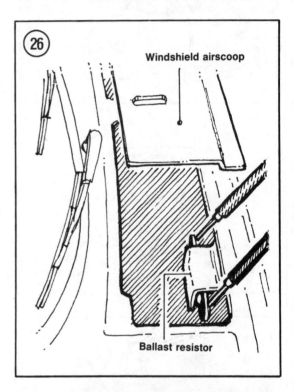

Windshield airscoop

Ballast resistor

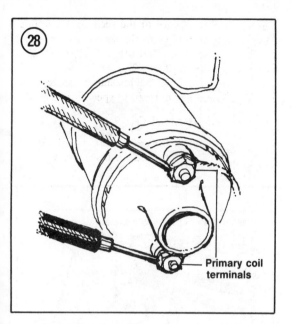

Primary coil terminals

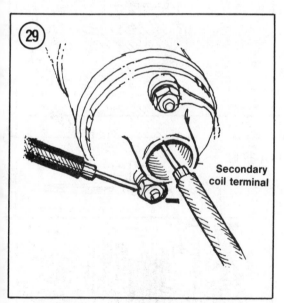

Secondary coil terminal

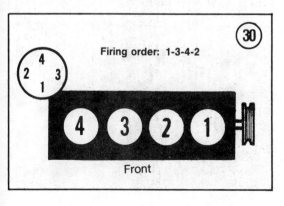

Firing order: 1-3-4-2

Front

ohmmeter. Disconnect the secondary lead from the distributor and ignition coil. Connect the probes from an ohmmeter to both ends of the secondary lead. Resistance should not exceed 25,000 ohms. If it does, replace the secondary lead.

CONDENSER

Condenser capacity testing requires a commercial condenser tester. This can be done by a properly equipped automotive electrical shop, but it may be faster and cheaper to buy a new one if you suspect the old one is defective. Compare the price of a new condenser with the cost of having the old condenser checked before choosing a course of action.

DISTRIBUTOR

All distributor repair except disassembly and parts replacement can be done with the distributor installed in the engine. Distributor disassembly should be done by a Honda dealer or automotive electrical shop.

Removal/Installation
(1976-1983 Accord, 1979-1982 Prelude)

1. Identify and label (with tape) each of the secondary leads (cylinder numbers 1, 2, 3, 4 and coil) and carefully pull them out of the distributor cap. Remove the cap from the distributor.
2. Remove the spark plugs as described in Chapter Three.

> *CAUTION*
> *Refer to **Spark Plug Removal** in Chapter Three for correct removal procedures.*

3. Rotate the crankshaft using a wrench on the pulley bolt to bring the No. 1 piston to top dead center on its compression stroke. This is indicated when the timing mark on the flywheel is lined up with the stationary TDC mark or pointer. See **Figure 30**. Note the position of the rotor in the distributor and make sure it points to the secondary terminal for No. 1 cylinder. This alignment represents basic timing and will make installation easier. To identify No. 1 terminal, refer to the following illustrations:
   a. 1976 manual—**Figure 31**.
   b. 1976 automatic—**Figure 32**.
   c. 1977-1978 manual and 49-state automatic—**Figure 31**.
   d. 1977-1978 California and high altitude automatic—**Figure 33**.
   e. 1979-1981—**Figure 34**.

8

f. All 1982, 1983 Accord—**Figure 34** (Hitachi type) or **Figure 35** (Toyo Denso type).

> *NOTE*
> *Be sure to check rotor position as well as the timing mark alignment. The timing marks also align when No. 4 cylinder is at TDC on its compression stroke.*

4. Disconnect the vacuum lines and unplug the distributor primary wiring.

5. Remove the distributor mounting bolt (**Figure 36**) and pull the distributor out of the engine.

> *NOTE*
> *If possible, avoid turning the engine with the distributor out. Installation will be easier if the engine is not turned.*

6. Installation is the reverse of removal, plus the following:

   a. On 1976-1978 models, line up the contact end of the rotor as shown in **Figure 37**.

   b. On 1979 and later models, line up the mark on the distributor drive gear with the mark on the housing. See **Figure 38**.

7. Carefully push the distributor into place. As the shaft is pushed all the way in, the helical drive gears will cause the rotor to turn about 30° (**Figure 39**).

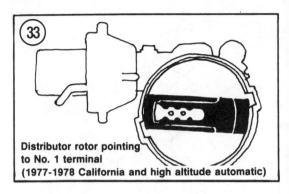

Distributor rotor pointing to No. 1 terminal
(1977-1978 California and high altitude automatic)

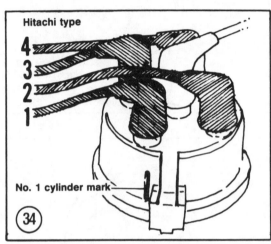

Hitachi type

No. 1 cylinder mark

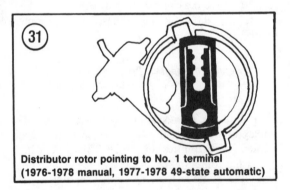

Distributor rotor pointing to No. 1 terminal
(1976-1978 manual, 1977-1978 49-state automatic)

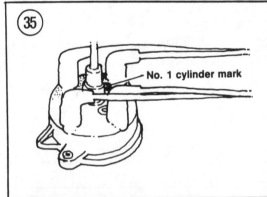

No. 1 cylinder mark

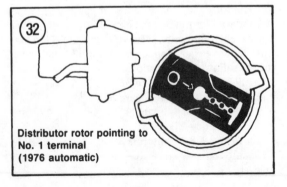

Distributor rotor pointing to No. 1 terminal
(1976 automatic)

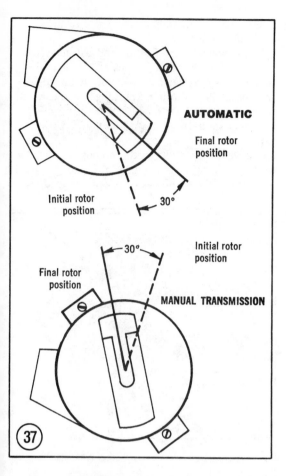

AUTOMATIC

Final rotor position

Initial rotor position

30°

30°

Initial rotor position

Final rotor position

MANUAL TRANSMISSION

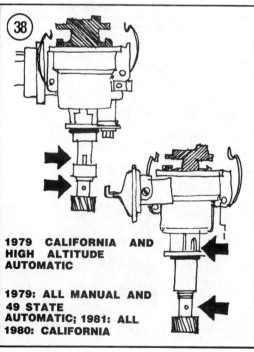

1979 CALIFORNIA AND HIGH ALTITUDE AUTOMATIC

1979: ALL MANUAL AND 49 STATE AUTOMATIC; 1981: ALL 1980: CALIFORNIA

8. When the distributor is seated, install and tighten the mounting bolt, install the cap and spark plugs and connect the secondary leads.

9. On 1976-1978 models, set the dwell as described under *Tune-up* in Chapter Three. On all models, set ignition timing as described in Chapter Three.

Removal/Installation
(1984 Accord, 1983-on Prelude)

1. Label the spark plug wires (Nos. 1 through 4; No. 1 farthest from distributor) and disconnect them from the spark plugs.

2. Disconnect the primary and secondary wires from the ignition coil. See **Figure 40**.

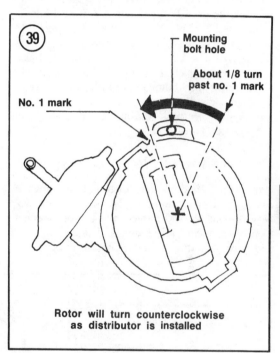

Mounting bolt hole

About 1/8 turn past no. 1 mark

No. 1 mark

Rotor will turn counterclockwise as distributor is installed

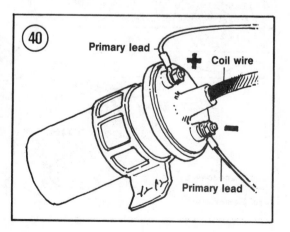

Primary lead

Coil wire

Primary lead

3. Disconnect the distributor vacuum line (**Figure 41**).

4. Remove the distributor hold-down bolts and take the distributor out of the cylinder head. **Figure 41** shows the Prelude distributor. The Accord distributor is basically the same, but the distributor cap differs slightly.

5. Installation is the reverse of removal, plus the following.

   a. Note that the distributor drive lug and the slot in the end of the camshaft are both offset so the distributor can be installed only one way. See **Figure 42**.

   b. Use a new O-ring on the distributor base.

   c. Connect the spark plug wires in the following order: 1-3-4-2 clockwise (viewed from the distributor end of the engine). No. 1 cylinder is farthest from the distributor. **Figure 43** identifies the cap terminals on Prelude engines. On Accords, the distributor cap has a mark for No. 1 cylinder. See **Figure 44** (Hitachi distributor cap) or **Figure 45** (Toyo Denso distributor cap).

   d. Adjust ignition timing as described in Chapter Three.

BODY ELECTRICAL SYSTEM

Instructions and pointers for troubleshooting the electrical wiring system are given in Chapter Two. Service which the owner/mechanic can be expected to perform includes isolation and repair of short and open circuits, wire connector and fuse replacement, switch replacement and sealed beam and other bulb replacement.

Maintenance of the lighting and wiring systems consists of an occasional check to see that wiring connections are clean and tight and that headlights are properly adjusted. Headlight adjustment should be done by a qualified specialist with the necessary special equipment.

Loose or corroded connectors can result in a discharged battery, dim lights and possible damage to the alternator or voltage regulator. Should insulation become burned, cracked, abraded, etc.,

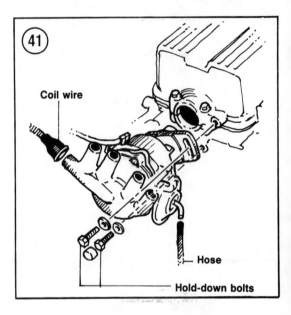

Coil wire

Hose

Hold-down bolts

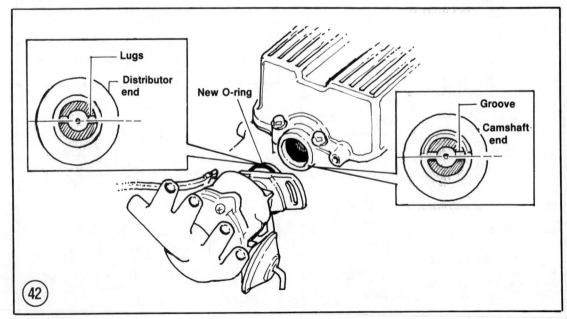

Lugs

Distributor end

New O-ring

Groove

Camshaft end

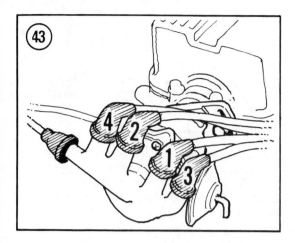

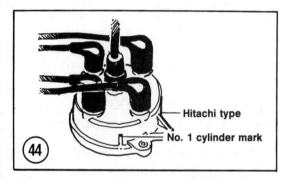

Hitachi type

No. 1 cylinder mark

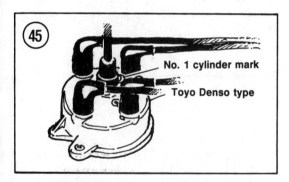

No. 1 cylinder mark

Toyo Denso type

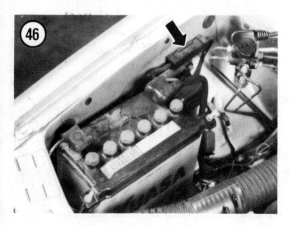

the affected wire or wiring harness should be replaced. Rosin core solder must always be used when splicing wires. Never use acid core solder on electrical connections. Splices should be covered with insulating tape.

Replacement wires must be of the same gauge as the replaced wire—never use a thinner wire. All harnesses and wires should be held in place with clips, cable ties or other holding devices to keep the wires from rubbing on other parts.

FUSES

Whenever a failure occurs in any part of the electrical system, always check to see if a fuse has blown. If one has, it will be indicated by blackening of the fuse or by a break in the metal link inside the fuse. Usually the trouble can be traced to a short circuit in the wiring connected to the blown fuse. This may be caused by worn-through insulation or by a wire that works its way loose and touches metal. Occasionally, the overload which causes a fuse to blow may occur in a switch or motor.

A blown fuse should be treated as more than a minor annoyance; it should serve also as a warning that something is wrong in the electrical system. Before replacing a fuse, determine what caused it to blow and then correct the trouble.

WARNING
Never replace a fuse with a fuse of higher amperage. Never replace a fuse with metal foil or other metallic material. Either of these could cause a fire and complete destruction of the car.

There are 2 fuse locations. The main fuse (fusible link) is located in the engine compartment near the battery (**Figure 46**). This fuse connects the starter motor relay to the rest of the electrical system. If no electrical power is available to any of the systems, check the link to see if it has burned through. Locate and correct the source of trouble before replacing the link.

The second fuse location is beneath the dashboard on the left side, inside the car. **Figure 47** is a typical fuse box diagram. To find the actual amperage rating for a particular fuse, pull down the fuse box in your car and read the fuse amperage number on the plastic sheet covering the fuses.

To inspect or replace fuses, pull down the fuse box and check the condition of the metal elements. Replace a defective fuse by carefully prying it out of its holder and snapping a new one in place.

8

LIGHTING SYSTEM

Headlight Replacement

1. Remove the screws from the outer headlight ring. Remove the ring and the sealed-beam unit.
2. Unplug the connector from the light. Plug a new light in and install it by lining up the lugs in the light with the recesses in the headlight inner mounting ring. Put the outer ring in place and install the screws.
3. If any of the headlight aiming screws were turned, have headlight aim checked by a Honda dealer or properly equipped lamp adjusting station.

Parking/Turn Indicator Lights

To change a bulb, remove the lens securing screws and take off the lens. Press in on the bulb, turn it counterclockwise and take it off. Install a new bulb by pushing in and turning it clockwise. Reinstall the lens and tighten the lens screws snugly, but not so tight that they crack the lens.

Side Marker Lights

Remove the screws and nuts which secure the lens and take the lens off. Press the bulb in and turn it counterclockwise to remove. Install in the reverse order.

Rear Combination Lights

All Accord, 1983-on Prelude

Lift the rear door or trunk lid and remove the access panel to gain access to the taillight housing. Pull out sockets to replace defective bulbs. Install in the reverse order.

1979-1982 Prelude

Remove the rear lens attaching screws and pull the lens and gasket away from the housing. Locate the defective bulb and remove it from its socket. Examine the lens gasket and replace if torn. Install in the reverse order.

License Plate Lights

1976-1980 Accord

Remove the nuts inside the trunk lid and pull the trunk assembly off. Separate the base and cover and replace the bulb. Install in the reverse order.

1981-on Accord, all Prelude

Remove the screws securing the license plate lens to the housing. Pull the bulb out. Install a new bulb by pushing it in and turning clockwise. Install the lens and secure it with the screws.

Interior Light

Pull or pry the lens off the light. Pull the bulb out of the spring contacts and install a new one. Push the lens back into position.

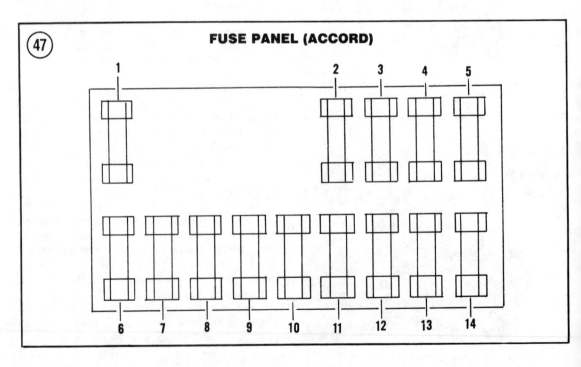

(47)   FUSE PANEL (ACCORD)

Table 1   BATTERY CHARGE PERCENTAGE

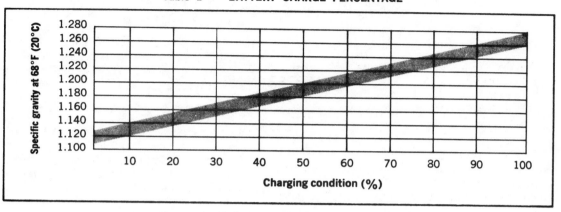

Table 2 IGNITION COIL SPECIFICATIONS

Coil primary resistance	
1976-1978	1.35-1.65 ohms
1979	1.78-2.08 ohms
1980 except California automatic transaxle	1.78-2.08 ohms
1980 California automatic transaxle	1.06-1.24 ohms
1981-on	1.06-1.24 ohms
Coil secondary resistance	
1976-1978	8,000-12,000 ohms
1979	8,800-13,200 ohms
1980 except California automatic transaxle	8,800-13,200 ohms
1980 California automatic transaxle	7,400-11,000 ohms
1981-on	7,400-11,000 ohms

8

CHAPTER NINE

CLUTCH AND TRANSAXLE

The clutch on all models is a single dry-disc type with diaphragm spring. The major components are the disc, pressure plate, release mechanism and linkage.

A hydraulic clutch linkage is used on 1976-1981 Accords and 1979-1982 Preludes. Pedal pressure is transmitted from the clutch master cylinder through the fluid line to the slave cylinder. The slave cylinder pushrod operates the release fork. The hydraulic linkage uses DOT 3 brake fluid (the same type used in the brake hydraulic system).

A cable clutch linkage is used on Accords from 1982-on and Preludes from 1983-on. Pedal pressure is transmitted to the release fork by a cable.

A 5-speed manual transaxle is standard. A 2-speed, 3-speed or 4-speed automatic is optional.

This chapter provides repair procedures for the clutch and replacement and adjustment procedures for the transmissions. Repair of the manual and automatic transaxles requires special tools and training and should be done by a dealer or other qualified specialist.

Table 1 and **Table 2** are at the end of the chapter.

CLUTCH

The clutch, linkage and release mechanism are shown in the following illustrations:

a. **Figure 1**—1976-1978 (hydraulic linkage).
b. **Figure 2**—1979-1981 Accord, 1979-1982 Prelude (hydraulic linkage).
c. **Figure 3**—1982-on Accord, 1983-on Prelude (cable linkage).

Clutch Adjustment
(Hydraulic Linkage)

Clutch adjustment is necessary to take up slack in the clutch linkage caused by release bearing and disc wear. The linkage should be adjusted whenever the clutch fails to disengage completely and whenever new parts are installed. Adjust as follows.

1. Measure play at the release fork and compare with **Table 1**. See **Figure 4**. If free play is incorrect, loosen the locknut (**Figure 5**), turn the adjusting nut to set free play and tighten the locknut.

2. Check clutch pedal height with the pedal fully released. Measure from the floor (without carpet) to the clutch pedal. See **Figure 5**. If pedal height is not within specifications (**Table 1**), loosen the stopper bolt locknut (**Figure 6**). Turn the clutch pedal stopper bolt to set pedal height, then tighten the locknut.

3. Check clutch pedal free play and compare with **Table 1**. If it is incorrect, loosen the locknut on the

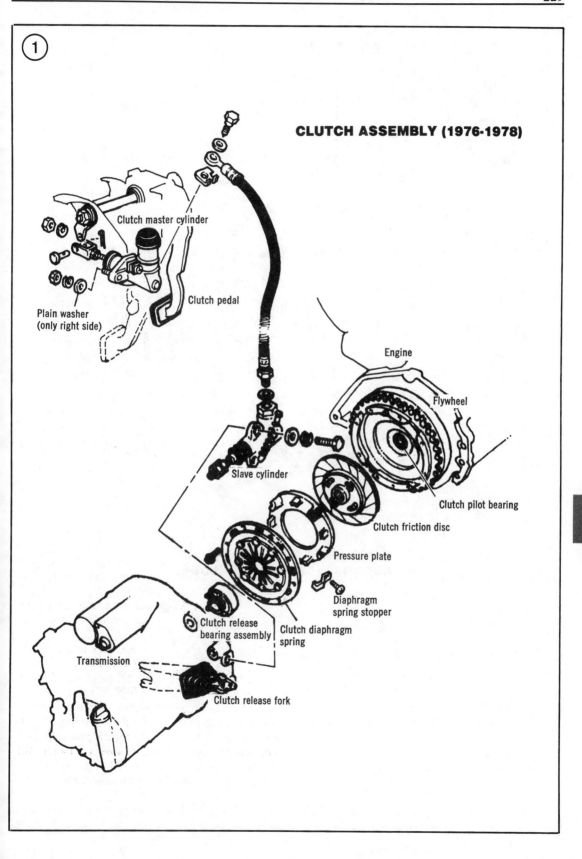

①

CLUTCH ASSEMBLY (1976-1978)

Clutch master cylinder

Plain washer
(only right side)

Clutch pedal

Engine

Flywheel

Slave cylinder

Clutch pilot bearing

Clutch friction disc

Pressure plate

Diaphragm
spring stopper

Clutch release
bearing assembly

Clutch diaphragm
spring

Transmission

Clutch release fork

9

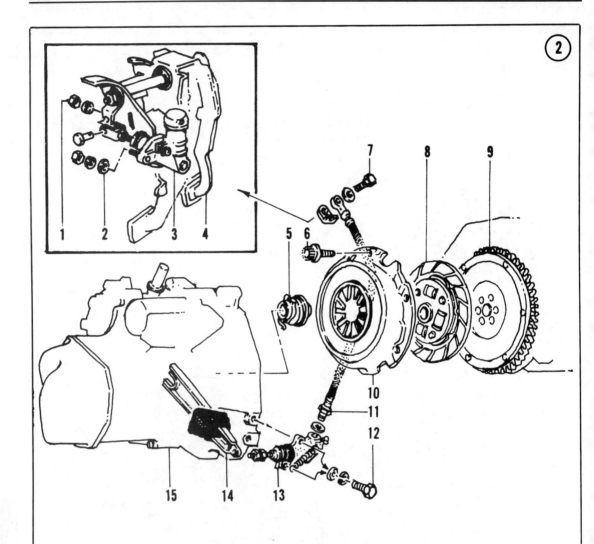

**CLUTCH ASSEMBLY (1979-1981
ACCORD, 1979-1982 PRELUDE)**

1. Nut
2. Washer (on right side only)
3. Clutch master cylinder
4. Clutch pedal
5. Clutch release bearing assembly
6. Bolt
7. Bolt
8. Clutch friction disc

9. Flywheel
10. Clutch cover
11. Nut
12. Bolt
13. Slave cylinder
14. Clutch release fork
15. Transmission

CLUTCH (1982-ON ACCORD, 1983-ON PRELUDE)

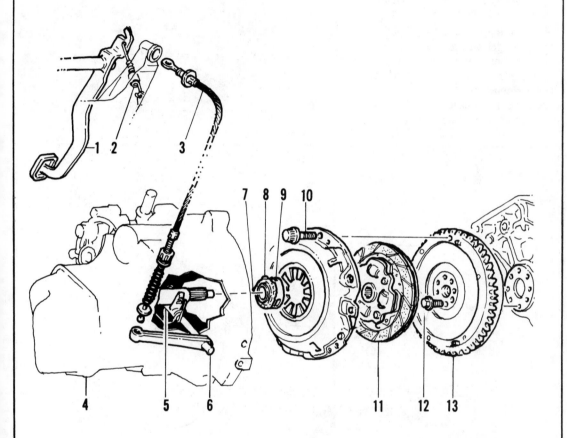

1. Pedal
2. Pedal return spring
3. Clutch cable
4. Transaxle
5. Release fork
6. Release shaft
7. Release bearing holder
8. Release bearing clips
9. Release bearing
10. Pressure plate bolt and pressure plate
11. Clutch disc
12. Flywheel bolt
13. Flywheel

pedal pushrod (**Figure 5**). Turn the pushrod as shown in **Figure 6** to change free play, then tighten the locknut.

Master Cylinder Removal/ Installation (Hydraulic Linkage)

> *CAUTION*
> *Brake fluid will damage paint. During this procedure, wipe up any spilled fluid immediately, then clean the spill area with soap and water.*

1. Remove the clip and clevis pin that attach the master cylinder pushrod to the clutch pedal.
2. With a container handy to catch dripping brake fluid, disconnect the hydraulic line from the master cylinder (**Figure 7**).
3. Remove the master cylinder mounting bolts and lift the master cylinder out.

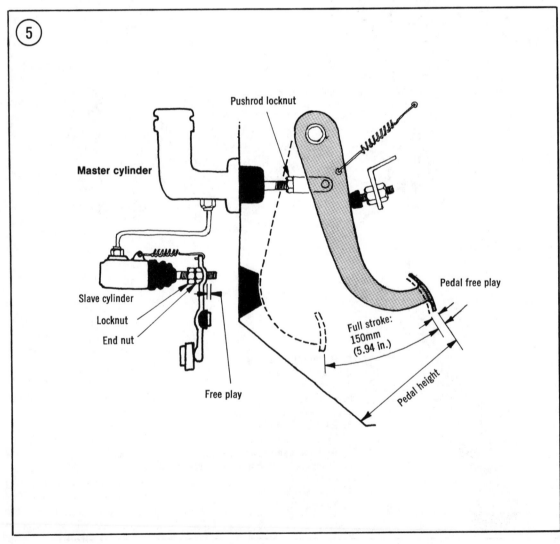

4. Installation is the reverse of removal. Bleed and adjust the clutch as described in this chapter.

Master Cylinder Overhaul
(Hydraulic Linkage)

Obtain a clutch master cylinder repair kit before starting overhaul. Refer to **Figure 8** for this procedure.

1. Remove the filler cap from the fluid reservoir. Pour the fluid from the cylinder.
2. Pull back the boot and remove the snap ring.

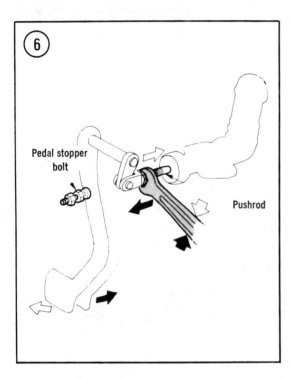

Pedal stopper bolt

Pushrod

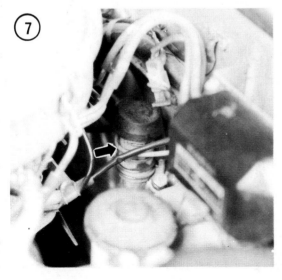

3. Pull the pushrod out of the master cylinder, together with the boot, snap ring and pushrod retainer.

NOTE
*The flange end of the pushrod retainer faces outward (**Figure 8**). It must be installed facing the same direction.*

WARNING
The piston may shoot out like a bullet during the next step. Point the open end of the master cylinder at a block of wood on the ground.

4. Blow air into the fluid line hole to force the piston out of the master cylinder. Use a service station air hose if you don't have a compressor.
5. If the reservoir is to be replaced with a new one, loosen its clamp screw and take the reservoir off. Do not remove the reservoir unless it is to be replaced.

NOTE
During the next 2 steps, note which way the piston cup and valve seal face. The new parts must be installed facing in the same direction.

6. Remove the piston cup from the piston. Replace the piston cup with a new one whenever the master cylinder is disassembled.
7. Disassemble the return spring assembly, referring to **Figure 8**.
8. Thoroughly clean all parts in clean brake fluid. Do not clean with gasoline, kerosene or solvent. These leave residues which will damage rubber parts.
9. Check the cylinder bore and piston for wear, scoring, pits, cracks or rust. Replace the master cylinder if these can be seen.
10. Assemble the return spring assembly, referring to **Figure 8**.
11. Be sure the sealing lips of the valve seal will face into the cylinder when the piston is installed.
12. Install a new piston cup on the piston. Position the cup so its lip (wide side) will face into the master cylinder when installed.
13. Coat the cylinder bore with clean brake fluid.
14. Dip the return spring assembly in clean brake fluid and install it in the cylinder.
15. Dip the piston in clean brake fluid and install it in the cylinder. Rotate the piston during installation.
16. Install the pushrod retainer on the pushrod. Be sure the retainer faces the direction shown in **Figure 8**. Slide the snap ring over the end of the pushrod and insert the pushrod assembly into the master cylinder. Position the snap ring so it secures

9

⑧

CLUTCH MASTER CYLINDER

1. Fluid reservoir
2. Master cylinder
3. Washer (on right side only)
4. Nut
5. Valve seal (note orientation)
6. Valve stem
7. Valve spring
8. Valve guide
9. Return spring
10. Spring retainer

11. Piston cup
12. Piston
13. Pushrod
14. Pushrod retainer (note orientation)
15. Snap ring
16. Boot
17. Nut
18. Yoke
19. Pedal pin

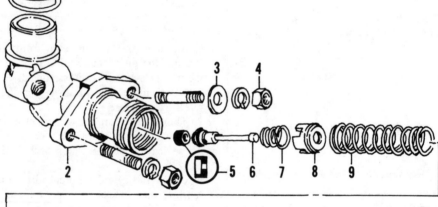

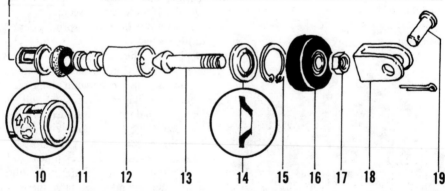

the pushrod retainer, then install the dust boot and pull its lip over the end of the master cylinder.

Slave Cylinder Removal/Installation (Hydraulic Linkage)

> *CAUTION*
> *Brake fluid will damage paint. If any fluid is spilled during this procedure, wipe it up immediately, then clean the spill area with soap and water.*

1. With a container handy to catch dripping brake fluid, disconnect the union bolt that secures the upper end of the slave cylinder fluid hose. See **Figure 1** or **Figure 2**.
2. Disconnect the return spring and pushrod at the slave cylinder.
3. Remove the mounting bolts and take the cylinder out.
4. Installation is the reverse of removal. Bleed and adjust the clutch as described in this chapter.

Slave Cylinder Overhaul (Hydraulic Linkage)

Refer to **Figure 9**.

1. Take the dust boot off the cylinder body.

2. Take out the piston. Remove and discard the piston cup.
3. Remove the bleed valve dust cap and unscrew the bleed valve.
4. Thoroughly clean all parts in clean brake fluid. Do not clean with solvent, kerosene or gasoline. These leave residues which can damage rubber parts.
5. Check the cylinder bore and piston for wear, scratches, rust, pits or cracks. Replace the slave cylinder if these can be seen.
6. Dip a new piston cup in brake fluid. Install the cup on the piston so the wide side will face into the cylinder body when the piston is installed.
7. Coat the cylinder bore and piston with brake fluid. Install the piston.
8. Position the dust boot on the cylinder body.
9. Install the bleed valve and its dust cap.

Clutch Bleeding (Hydraulic Linkage)

Bleeding the clutch hydraulic system is necessary whenever air enters it. This occurs when the clutch hydraulic line is disconnected. It can also result from a very low fluid level in the master cylinder

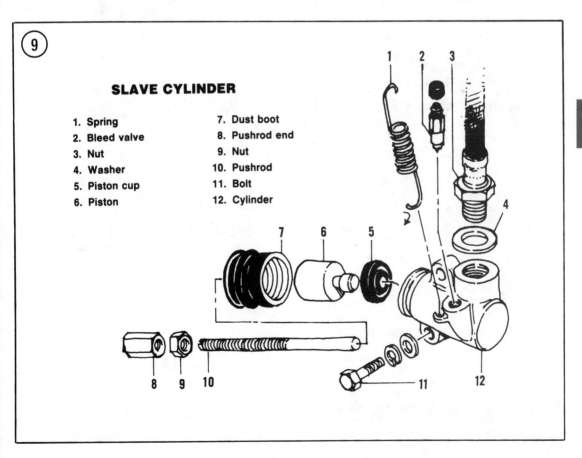

(9)

SLAVE CYLINDER

1. Spring
2. Bleed valve
3. Nut
4. Washer
5. Piston cup
6. Piston
7. Dust boot
8. Pushrod end
9. Nut
10. Pushrod
11. Bolt
12. Cylinder

9

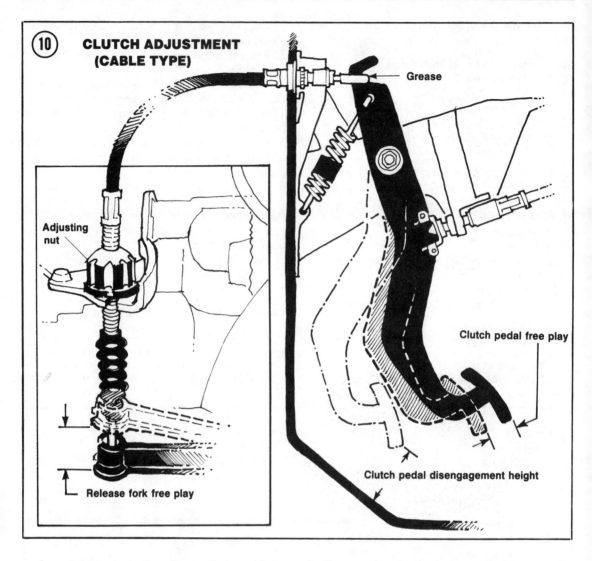

CLUTCH ADJUSTMENT (CABLE TYPE)

⑩

Grease

Adjusting nut

Clutch pedal free play

Release fork free play

Clutch pedal disengagement height

or from defective master or slave cylinders. Air in the system can make shifting gears very difficult.

> *NOTE*
> *This procedure requires 2 people, one to operate the clutch pedal and the other to open and close the bleed valve.*

1. Remove the dust cap from the bleed valve (**Figure 9**). Attach a plastic or rubber tube to the bleed valve. Place the other end of the tube in a clean glass jar containing several inches of clean brake fluid.

> *NOTE*
> *Do not allow the end of the tube to slip out of the brake fluid during bleeding. If this happens, air may enter the system and the bleeding procedure will have to be repeated.*

2. Top up the clutch master cylinder reservoir (**Figure 7**) with DOT 3 brake fluid.

> *NOTE*
> *Keep an eye on the master cylinder fluid level during the next steps. If the level is allowed to drop too low, air will be sucked into the system and the bleeding procedure will have to be repeated.*

3. Pump the pedal 2 or 3 times, then hold it to the floor.

4. While the pedal is down, open the bleed valve 1/3 to 1/2 turn. Let the mixed air and fluid escape. Close the bleed valve while the pedal is still down, then let the pedal up.

5. Repeat Step 3 and Step 4 until the fluid entering the jar is free of bubbles. Remove the tube, close the bleed valve and top up the master cylinder.

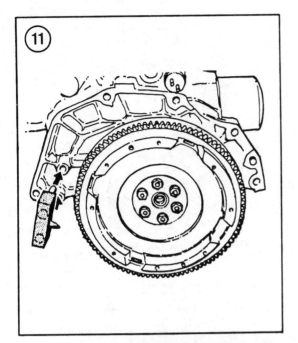

Clutch Adjustment (Cable Linkage)

The linkage should be adjusted to take up slack caused by clutch disc wear or cable stretching. The linkage should also be adjusted whenever new parts are installed.

1. Measure free play at the release fork (**Figure 10**). Compare with **Table 1**. Turn the adjusting nut to obtain specified free play.
2. Measure pedal free play and pedal height and compare with **Table 1**. If the measurements are not within specifications, check for a worn pedal or clutch disc. Clutch disc inspection requires removing the clutch as described in this chapter.

Cable Replacement (Cable Linkage)

1. Loosen the cable adjusting nut (**Figure 10**). Detach the cable end from the release fork, then detach the cable from the bracket.

2. Working in the passenger compartment, unhook the end of the cable from the top of the clutch pedal.
3. Installation is the reverse of removal. Adjust the clutch as described in this chapter.

Clutch Removal (All Models)

1. Either remove the transaxle as described in this chapter or remove the engine and transaxle as described in Chapter Four or Chapter Five and separate them.

> *WARNING*
> *Removing the transaxle without removing the engine requires supporting the car on a commercial hoist. Jackstands do not provide enough stability for safe transaxle removal. If you don't have access to a commercial hoist, remove the engine and transaxle as described in Chapter Four or Chapter Five, then separate them.*

2. Install a flywheel holding tool on the engine as shown in **Figure 11**. Honda flywheel holding tool part numbers for different models are:
   a. 1976-1977—No. 07924-6570000.
   b. 1978-1980—No. 07924-6340100.
   c. 1981-1983—07924-6890101.
   d. 1984—07924-PD20001.
3. Loosen the clutch mounting bolts 2 turns at a time, in a crisscross pattern, to prevent warping the pressure plate. When all bolts have been loosened enough to relax the diaphragm spring, unscrew them completely and remove the pressure plate and clutch disc.
4. On 1976-1978 models, separate the pressure plate and diaphram spring by removing the spring stoppers (**Figure 12**).

Clutch Inspection (All Models)

1. Clean the friction surface of the flywheel with a non-petroleum based cleaner such as alcohol or lacquer thinner. Check the surface for cracks or scoring. Light scoring and scratches can be removed with fine emery paper but if the damage is severe, the flywheel should be resurfaced by an automotive machine shop or replaced.

> *CAUTION*
> *If the facings are contaminated with grease, find and eliminate the cause before replacing the disc. Otherwise, the cleaned or new disc will become contaminated and could fail in a short time.*

2. Check the pilot bearing in the crankshaft for roughness and looseness. See **Figure 13**. The

9

bearing should turn easily and smoothly. If there is any doubt about its condition, replace it.

3. Check the diaphragm fingers (**Figure 14**) for wear, bending or damage. Check for cracks at the finger roots. Replace the diaphragm spring (1976-1978) or pressure plate assembly (1979-on) if these conditions are found.

4. Check the pressure plate surface for roughness or scratches. Minor scoring and scratches can be removed with No. 500 or 600 emery paper. Replace the pressure plate if scoring or scratches are serious.

5. Measure the pressure plate flatness with a straightedge and feeler gauge. Lay the straightedge across the pressure plate. If there is any gap between the straightedge and pressure plate, measure it with the feeler gauge as shown in **Figure 15**. Replace the pressure plate if the gap exceeds specifications in **Table 1**.

6. Measure disc thickness. Replace the disc if it is thinner than specified in **Table 1**.

7. Measure the depth of the holes in each friction surface. See **Figure 16**. Replace the disc if hole depth is less than specified in **Table 1**.

8. Check the pressure plate for cracks, scoring and the bluish tint that indicates overheating. Replace the pressure plate if these conditions are found.

9. Inspect the release bearing as described under *Release Mechanism* in this chapter. Never reuse a release bearing unless necessary. If it is necessary to reuse an old bearing, do not wash it in solvent; wipe it clean with a dry cloth.

Clutch Installation (All Models)

1. Be sure your hands are clean.

2. Inspect the disc facings, pressure plate and flywheel to be sure they are free of oil, grease or other foreign material.

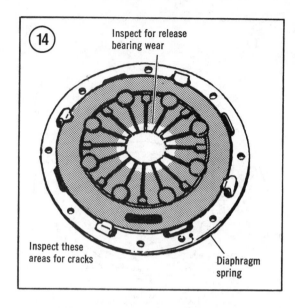

Inspect for release bearing wear

Inspect these areas for cracks

Diaphragm spring

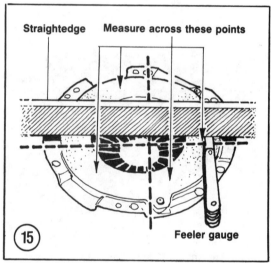

Straightedge Measure across these points

Feeler gauge

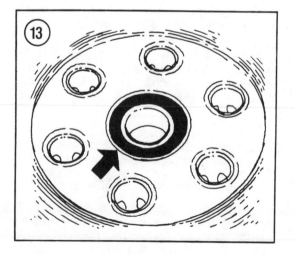

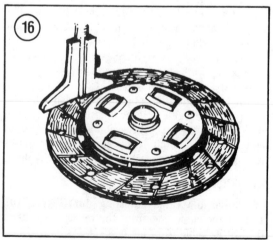

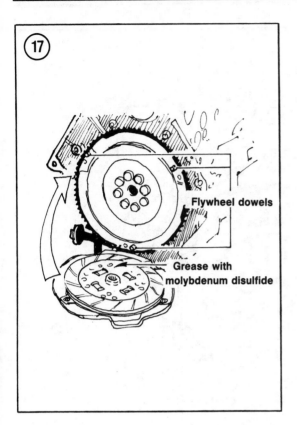

Flywheel dowels

Grease with molybdenum disulfide

3. On 1976-1978 models, position the diaphragm spring on the pressure plate and secure it with the spring stoppers (**Figure 12**).

4. On cable-linkage clutches, apply molybdenum disulfide grease to the center of the clutch disc. See **Figure 17**. Place the clutch disc on the pressure plate.

5A. On 1976-1978 models, line up the marks on the pressure plate with the mark on the flywheel and install the pressure plate (**Figure 18**).

5B. On 1979 and later models, align the dowel pins in the flywheel with the holes in the pressure plate and install the pressure plate. See **Figure 17**.

6. Center the clutch disc and pressure plate with a pilot shaft such as the one shown in **Figure 19**. Auto parts stores sell inexpensive pilot shafts. Tool rental dealers rent universal pilot shafts which can be adapted.

7. Install the clutch cover bolts. Tighten gradually in a crisscross pattern as shown in **Figure 20** (hydraulic clutch) or **Figure 21** (cable-operated clutch) to prevent warping the pressure plate. Once the bolts are tight, torque them to specifications in **Table 2**.

8. Remove the clutch pilot shaft and flywheel holding tool. Lubricate the pilot bearing with multipurpose grease.

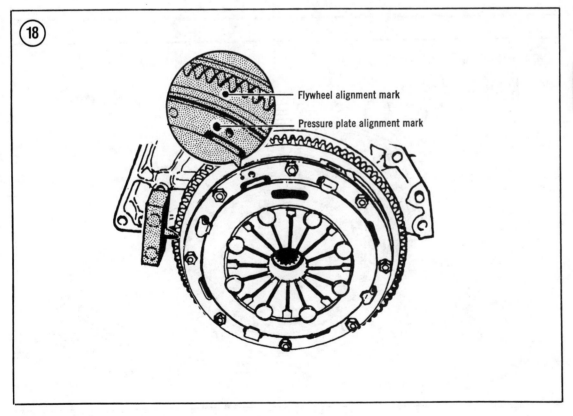

Flywheel alignment mark

Pressure plate alignment mark

9

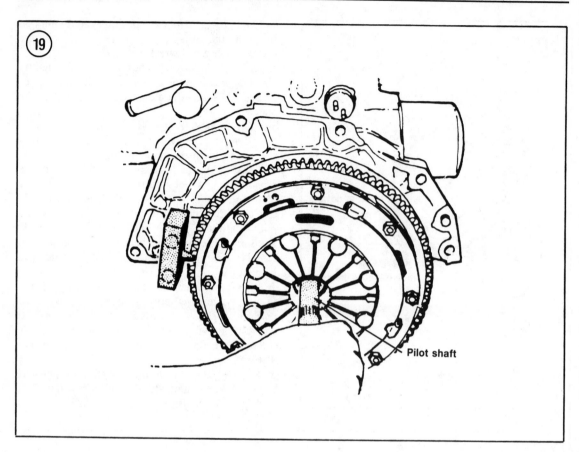

Pilot shaft

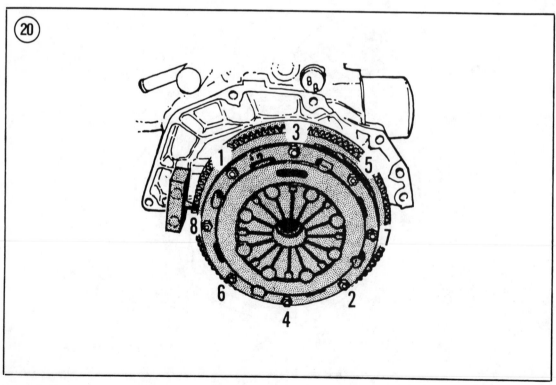

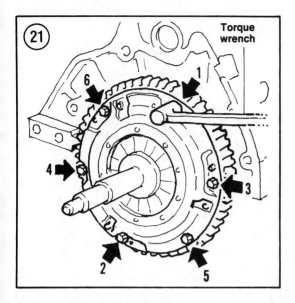

9. Reinstall the engine (if removed) and transaxle.

10. Adjust the clutch as described in this chapter. If equipped with a hydraulic linkage, bleed the clutch as described in this chapter.

Release Mechanism Removal

Either remove the transaxle as described in this chapter or remove the engine and transaxle as described in Chapter Four or Chapter Five and separate them.

> *WARNING*
> *Removing the transaxle without removing the engine requires supporting the car on a commercial hoist. Jackstands do not provide enough stability for safe transaxle removal. If you don't have access to a commercial hoist, remove the engine and transaxle as described in Chapter Four or Chapter Five, then separate them.*

Hydraulic clutch

1. Remove the boot and remove the set clip from the release fork. See **Figure 22**.

2. Remove the release fork from inside the clutch housing. See **Figure 23**.

Cable-operated clutch

1. Remove the 8 mm bolt and lockplate (**Figure 24**).

2. Slide the release shaft out of the clutch housing. Remove the release fork, together with the release bearing.

3. Pull the clip out of the holes in the release bearing, then take the release bearing off the release fork. See **Figure 25**.

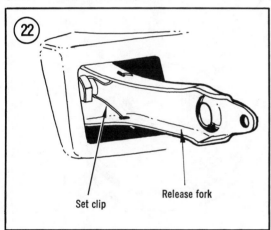

Set clip

Release fork

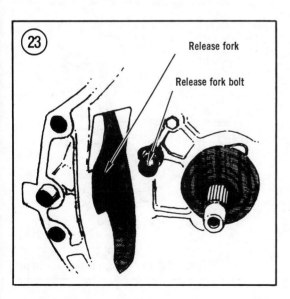

Release fork

Release fork bolt

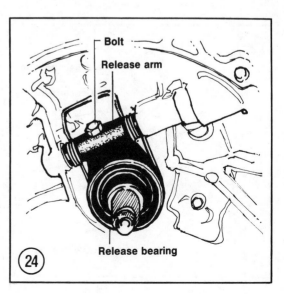

Bolt

Release arm

Release bearing

9

Release Mechanism Inspection (All Models)

1. Check the release fork (and release shaft on cable-operated clutches) for wear or damage. Replace worn or damaged parts.

2. Hold the release bearing outer race with one hand and spin the inner race with the other. See **Figure 26**. If the bearing is loose, rough or noisy, replace it.

3. Check the bearing for grease. The bearing is sealed, so grease on the outside means the bearing is leaking and must be replaced.

> *CAUTION*
> *Do not clean the release bearing in solvent or the grease inside will be dissolved and bearing will have to be replaced. Wipe the bearing with a dry cloth.*

4. If the release bearing is to be replaced on hydraulic clutches, have the old bearing pressed off the holder (**Figure 27**) and a new one pressed on by a machine shop. On cable-operated clutches, the hub and release bearing are replaced as a unit.

Release Mechanism Installation

Hydraulic clutch

1. Install the release bearing and hub on the release fork, then secure them with the set clips. Apply molybdenum disulfide grease to the bearing hub bore and to the release fork pivot point. See **Figure 28**.

2. Position the release fork in the clutch housing so the bearing is over the transaxle input shaft. Push the release fork onto its pivot as shown in **Figure 29**.

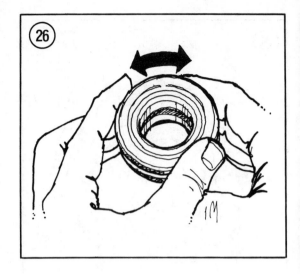

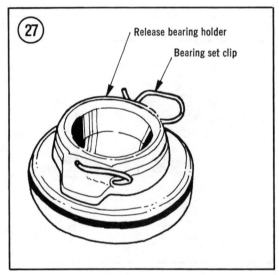

Release bearing holder

Bearing set clip

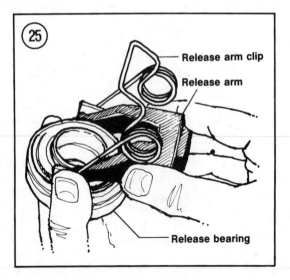

Release arm clip

Release arm

Release bearing

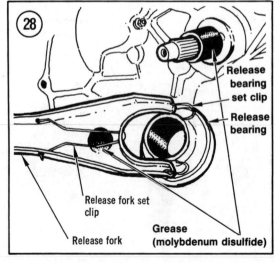

Release bearing set clip

Release bearing

Release fork set clip

Release fork

Grease (molybdenum disulfide)

Push

3. Install the transaxle on the engine. If the engine was removed, install the engine and transaxle in the car as described in Chapter Four or Chapter Five.

Cable-operated clutch

1. Align the release bearing clip holes with the release fork. See **Figure 30**. Apply molybdenum disulfide grease to the friction points as shown.

2. Install the clip in the locating holes to secure the release bearing to the fork. See **Figure 31**.

3. Position the release fork and bearing in the clutch housing. See **Figure 32**. Apply molybdenum disulfide grease to the release bearing contact surface and the input shaft sleeve as shown.

4. Install the release shaft in the clutch housing and release fork. Secure the shaft to the fork with the 8 mm bolt and a new lockplate. See **Figure 33**.

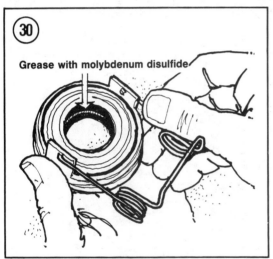

Grease with molybdenum disulfide

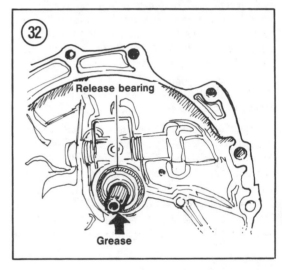

Release bearing

Grease

9

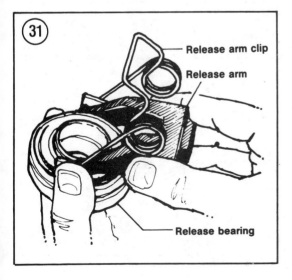

Release arm clip

Release arm

Release bearing

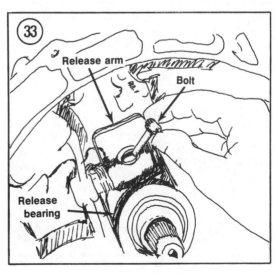

Release arm

Bolt

Release bearing

5. Move the release fork back and forth to make sure it moves smoothly. Make sure the fork is properly aligned with the bearing.

6. Install the transaxle on the engine. If the engine was removed from the car, install it together with the transaxle as described in Chapter Four or Chapter Five.

MANUAL TRANSAXLE

Manual transaxle repairs require special skills and tools and should be done by a Honda dealer or other qualified specialist. The following sections provide removal and installation procedures.

> *NOTE*
> *Check with the repair shop before removing the transaxle for repairs. They may want to road test the transaxle to diagnose problems. Although part of the labor charge could be saved by removing the transaxle yourself, it may be more practical to bring the car to the shop and have the whole job done there.*

Removal/Installation
(1976-1981 Accord, 1979-1982 Prelude)

> *WARNING*
> *Removing the transaxle without removing the engine requires supporting the car on a commercial hoist. Jackstands do not provide enough stability for safe transaxle removal. If you don't have access to a commercial hoist, remove the engine and transaxle as described in Chapter Four or Chapter Five, then separate them.*

1. Shift the transaxle to NEUTRAL.

2. Disconnect the battery ground cable at the battery (**Figure** 34) and at the transaxle housing (**Figure 35**).

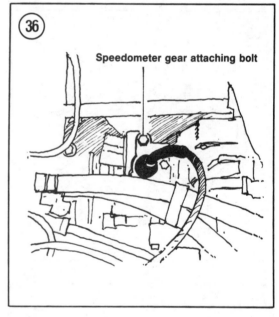

Speedometer gear attaching bolt

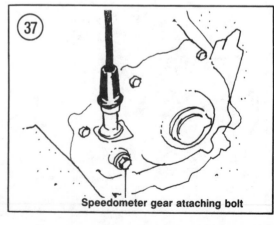

Speedometer gear attaching bolt

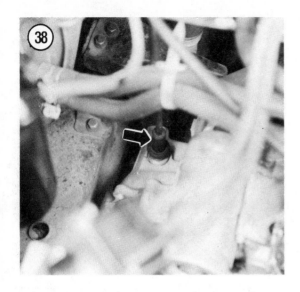

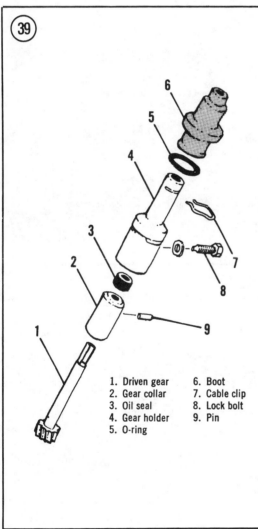

1. Driven gear
2. Gear collar
3. Oil seal
4. Gear holder
5. O-ring
6. Boot
7. Cable clip
8. Lock bolt
9. Pin

3. Disconnect the battery positive cable from the starter solenoid and disconnect the solenoid control wire. Unscrew the starter mounting bolts and remove the starter.

4. Label and disconnect wiring from the following components:

   a. Water temperature sending unit (yellow/green).

   b. Ignition timing thermoswitch.

   c. Backup light switch (green/black and yellow).

   d. 1979 and later models—distributor blue and red wires (Accord) or pink wires (Prelude).

5. Detach the clutch slave cylinder as described in this chapter. Place the slave cylinder out of the way.

6. Loosen the front wheel nuts. Raise the front end of the car on a commercial hoist and remove the front wheels.

7. Remove the transaxle drain plug and drain the oil into a container. Discard the oil.

8. Remove the splash shield from the right wheel well.

CAUTION
During the next step, do not remove the speedometer gear holder as the speedometer gear may fall into the transaxle housing. Figure 36 and Figure 37 show different methods of attaching the speedometer gear holder assembly to the clutch housing.

9A. *Non-power steering models:* Pull up the speedometer cable rubber boot (**Figure 38**) to provide access to the cable clip attachment. Then remove the clip (7, **Figure 39**) and pull the speedometer cable from the gear fitting on the transaxle.

NOTE
During the next step, do not remove the hose or attaching bolts from the speed sensor or power steering fluid will spill out.

9B. *Power steering models:* Remove the speed sensor securing bolt, then remove the sensor, hose and speedometer cable by pulling upward. Set the speed sensor assembly aside. See **Figure 40**.

10. Attach an engine lifting sling to the engine at the lifting points shown in **Figure 41**. Using a suitable engine hoist, remove all slack and place slight tension on the lifting sling. Make sure the tension on both legs of the sling is equal. Adjust the sling, if required.

11. Remove the cotter pin and locknut from the tie rod ball-joint (**Figure 42**) and the lower arm ball-joint (**Figure 43**). Then using Honda tool part

No. 07941-6710000, separate the joints as shown in **Figure 44**.

12A. *1976-1978 models:* Pry the circlip from the groove in the inboard end of each drive shaft. Then pull the shafts out of the transaxle.

12B. *1979-1981 Accord, 1979-1982 Prelude:* Using a screwdriver between the drive axle housing and transaxle housing (**Figure 45**), pry the inboard drive shaft ends out of the transaxle about 12.5 mm (1/2 in.). Then pull the shafts out of the transaxle.

13. *Accord models only:* Remove the center beam attaching bolts and remove the center beam (**Figure 46**).

14A. *1976-1978 modoels:* Use a punch to drive out the drift pin and remove the shift rod positioner (**Figure 47**).

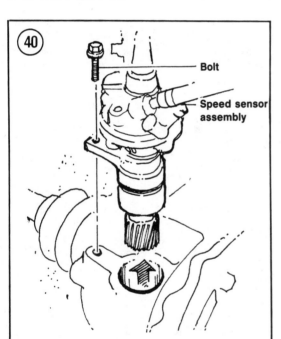

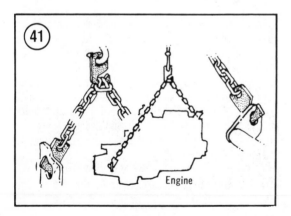

14B. *1979-1981 Accord, 1979-1982 Prelude:* Remove the shift rod yoke attaching bolt as shown in **Figure 48**.

15. Disconnect the shift rod positioner at the transaxle. See **Figure 49**.

16. Place a flat piece of wood on a jack lifting pad. Then position the jack underneath the engine oil pan and lift the engine to remove weight from the engine mounts.

17. *1981-1982 Prelude models:* From inside the engine compartment, remove the front and rear engine torque rods and the rear torque bracket. Remove the engine damper bracket at the transaxle. Then remove the rear engine mount and bracket.

> *NOTE*
> *Cut a piece of wood 1 in.×2 in.×4 in. before proceeding with Step 18.*

18. *1981-1982 Prelude models:* Place the wood block (see NOTE above) on the center beam directly below the oil pan. Then slowly lower the jack and allow the engine oil pan to rest on the wood block.

> *NOTE*
> *Step 19 completes transaxle removal for all models.*

19. Place a rolling jack underneath the transaxle and elevate the jack head until it contacts the transaxle. Unscrew the remaining transaxle mounting bolts. With the jack supporting the transaxle, pull the transaxle away from the engine until the main shaft is clear of the clutch. Lower the transaxle with the jack and remove it from the car.

20. Installation is the reverse of removal. Fill the transaxle with an oil recommended in Chapter Three.

9

Removal/Installation
(1982-on Accord, 1983-on Prelude)

WARNING
Removing the transaxle without removing the engine requires supporting the car on a commercial hoist. Jackstands do not provide enough stability for safe transaxle removal. If you don't have access to a commercial hoist, remove the engine and transaxle as described in Chapter Four or Chapter Five, then separate them.

1. Disconnect the negative cable from the battery, then from the transaxle.
2. Release the steering lock. Place the shift lever in NEUTRAL.
3. Disconnect the following wires in the engine compartment:
    a. Battery positive cable from starter motor.
    b. Black/white wire from starter solenoid.
    c. Green/black and yellow wires from backup light switch.
4. Separate the engine sub wire harness from the clip on the clutch housing.
5. Disconnect the clutch cable from the release lever. See *Clutch Cable Replacement* in this chapter.
6. *1982-1983 Accord:* Remove the starter mounting bolt (transmission side).
7. *1983-1984 Accord, 1984 Prelude:* Remove the 2 upper transmission mounting bolts.
8. Loosen the front wheel nuts. Raise the car on a commercial hoist and remove the front wheels.
9. Place a transmission jack beneath the transaxle. Transmission jacks, available from rental dealers, have cradles which prevent the transaxle from falling. They can also be adjusted for side-to-side tilt and approach angle.

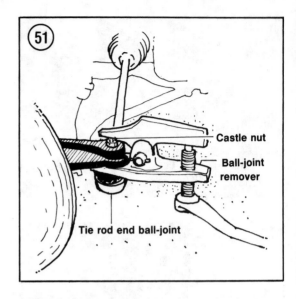

Castle nut

Ball-joint remover

Tie rod end ball-joint

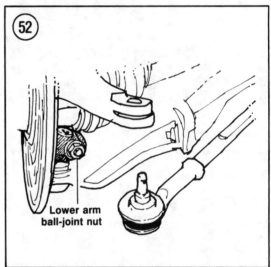

Lower arm ball-joint nut

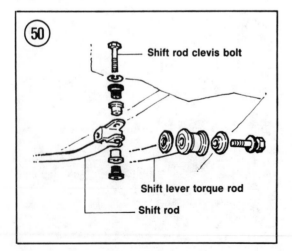

Shift rod clevis bolt

Shift lever torque rod

Shift rod

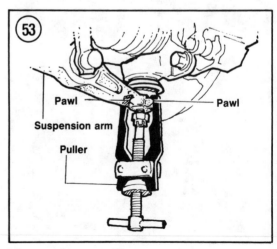

Pawl

Pawl

Suspension arm

Puller

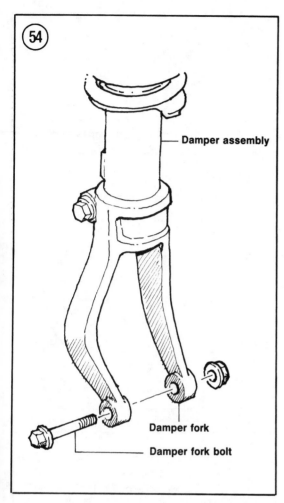

(54)

Damper assembly

Damper fork

Damper fork bolt

10. Remove the bolt that secures the speedometer drive holder to the transaxle. Pull the speedometer drive holder out and lay it aside.

11. Detach the shift lever torque rod from the clutch housing. Remove the shift rod clevis bolt. See **Figure 50**.

12. Remove the cotter pin and castle nut from each tie rod end. Separate the tie rod end from the knuckle arm with a puller such as Honda tool part No. 09741-6920001 (**Figure 51**).

13A. *Accord models:* Remove the pinch bolts from the lower arm ball-joints. Free the lower arms by tapping the ball-joints downward with a soft-faced mallet. See **Figure 52**.

13B. *Prelude models:* Remove the cotter pin from the lower ball-joint's castle nut. Loosen the nut halfway, then free the ball-joint from the knuckle arm with a puller as shown in **Figure 53**. Take the nut all the way off and separate the ball-joint from the knuckle arm.

14. *Prelude models:* Remove the nut from the damper fork bolt, then remove the damper fork bolt (**Figure 54**).

15. Turn each steering knuckle as far outboard as it will go. Pry the inboard end of each drive shaft about 12.5 mm (1/2 in.) out of the transaxle, then pull the drive shaft the rest of the way out.

16. Remove the radius rod from the right-hand side of the car. See *Front Suspension,* Chapter Ten.

17. Remove the bolts that secure the torque arm brackets to the clutch housing. See **Figure 55**.

18A. *1982-1983 Accord:* Remove the damper bracket from the center beam. See **Figure 56**.

18B. *1984 Accord, 1983-1984 Prelude:* Remove the damper bracket from the transmission. See **Figure 57**.

9

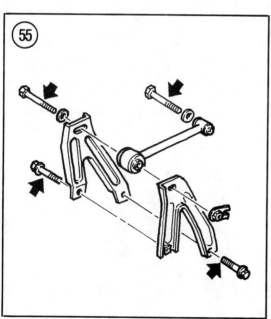

(55)

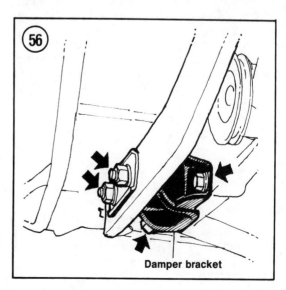

(56)

Damper bracket

19A. *1982-1983 Accord:* Remove the clutch housing bolts from both of the transmission mounting brackets. See **Figure 58**.

19B. *1984 Accord, 1983-1984 Prelude:* Remove the clutch housing bolts from the front transmission mount (**Figure 59**) and rear transmission mounting bracket (**Figure 60**).

20. Remove the clutch cover.

21. Remove the starter mounting bolt (Accord) or bolts (Prelude). Separate the starter from the transaxle and lower it away from the car. See **Figure 61**.

22. Pull the transmission away from the engine until it clears the dowels. Lower the transmission jack and roll the transaxle out from under the car.

23. Installation is the reverse of removal, plus the following:

   a. Clean and grease the release bearing friction surface.

   b. Make sure both dowel pins are installed in the clutch housing.

   c. Use a new spring clip on the end of each drive shaft. Work the left drive shaft into the transaxle as the transaxle is being installed.

   d. Make sure the drive shafts are pushed all the way into the transaxle. While pushing, feel for the engagement of the spring clips with the differential.

   e. Use a new O-ring, coated with oil, on the speedometer gear holder assembly.

   f. Fill the transaxle with an oil recommended in Chapter Three.

AUTOMATIC TRANSAXLE

A 2-speed automatic transaxle is optional on 1979 and earlier models. A 3-speed automatic was offered in 1980-on and a 4-speed automatic with lockup torque converter was offered for 1983-on.

This chapter provides simple checks and adjustments which can be done by home mechanics, as well as removal and installation procedures for the automatic transaxle. Major

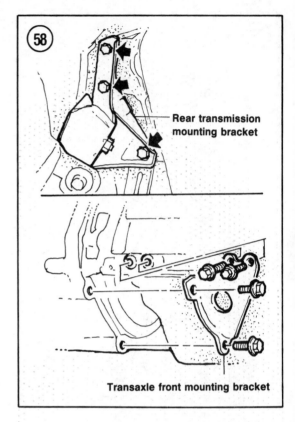

Rear transmission mounting bracket

Transaxle front mounting bracket

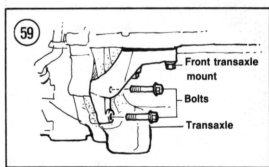

Front transaxle mount

Bolts

Transaxle

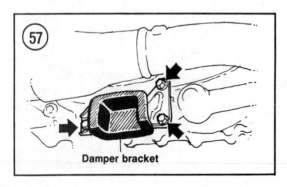

Damper bracket

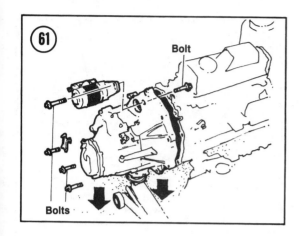

Bolt

Bolts

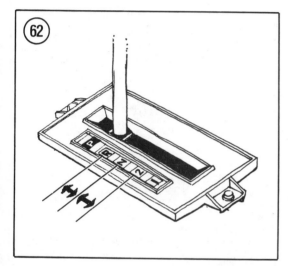

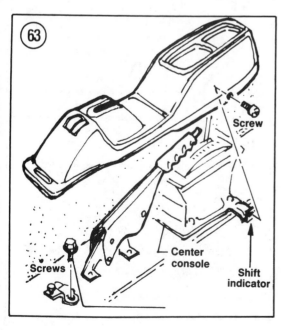

Screw

Screws

Center console

Shift indicator

repairs should be done by a Honda dealer or other qualified specialist.

Selector Lever Checking

1. Set the parking brake to lock the rear wheels. Start the engine, allow it to idle and press the footbrake.

2. Slowly move the lever back and forth from NEUTRAL to REVERSE and NEUTRAL to D2 (2-speed), D3 (3-speed) or D4 (4-speed). See **Figure 62**. The point at which the transmission can be felt to engage should be the same for both positions.

3. Make sure the lever cannot be moved from NEUTRAL to REVERSE without pressing the button on the selector lever handle. If it can, have a dealer repair the lever at once.

4. Shut off the engine and attempt to restart it with the lever in REVERSE and each of the DRIVE positions. The engine should not turn over when the key is turned to START. If it does, have the neutral safety switch tested by a Honda dealer or qualified specialist.

5. Make sure the backup lights come on only when the shift lever is in REVERSE. If they come on in any other position or don't come on at all, have the problem repaired by a Honda dealer or transmission shop.

6. With the car on a slope, move the lever to PARK and slowly release the brakes to see if the transaxle will prevent the car from rolling. If it doesn't, have the transaxle repaired by a Honda dealer or transmission shop.

Control Cable Adjustment (1976-1979)

1. Set the parking brake. Shift the gear selector into PARK and start the engine. Now shift the gear selector into REVERSE. Transmission engagement should be felt when shifting to REVERSE. If not, refer further service to a Honda dealer or transmission shop.

2. Turn the engine off. Working in the passenger compartment, remove the center console screws and take off the console (**Figure 63**).

3. Shift the gear selector to REVERSE. Referring to **Figure 64**, remove the retaining pin lock clip. Then remove the retaining pin from the end of the control cable. Do not disturb the cable position in the selector lever.

4. Compare the position of the pin hole in the end of the selector cable with that of the pin hole in the end of the selector arm. The pin hole in both the cable and selector lever arm should show exact alignment as indicated in **Figure 65**. If not, loosen the selector cable locknuts and adjust the cable as

9

required. When the cable and selector arm are in exact alignment, tighten the cable locknuts.

5. Secure the control cable with the retaining pin and lock clip.

> *NOTE*
> *If the retaining pin binds when inserted through the selector arm and cable, the cable is out of adjustment. Readjust as described in Step 4.*

6. Reinstall the center console (**Figure 63**).

7. Shift the gear selector to PARK. Start the engine and check the transaxle for proper alignment in all gears. If any gear does not engage properly, have the transaxle inspected by a Honda dealer or transmission shop.

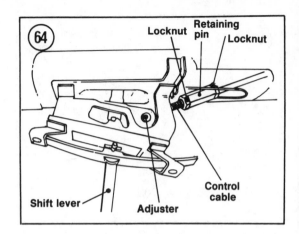

Control Cable Adjustment (1980-on)

1. Set the parking brake. Shift the gear selector into PARK and start the engine. Now shift the gear selector into REVERSE. Transmission engagement should be felt when shifting to REVERSE. If not, refer further service to a Honda dealer or transmission shop.

2. Turn the engine off. Working in the passenger compartment, remove the center console screws and take off the console (**Figure 63**).

3. Shift the gear selector to DRIVE. Referring to **Figure 66**, remove the shift cable lock pin through the opening in the transaxle shift linkage housing. Do not disturb the cable position in the cable adjuster.

4. Compare the position of the pin hole in the end of the selector cable with that of the pin hole in the end of the cable adjuster. The pin hole in both the cable and adjuster should show exact alignment as indicated in **Figure 67**. If not, loosen the selector cable locknut and adjust the cable as required. When the cable and cable adjuster are in exact alignment, tighten the cable locknuts.

5. Secure the control cable with the lockpin (**Figure 66**).

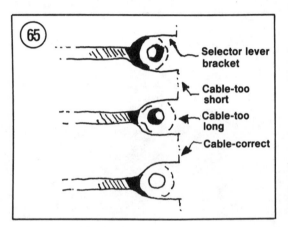

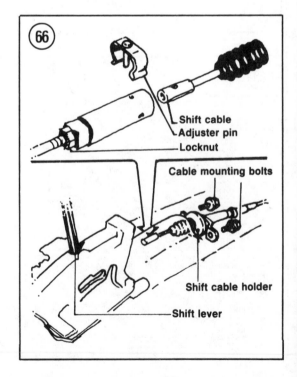

> *NOTE*
> *If the lockpin binds when inserted through the cable adjuster and cable, the cable is out of adjustment. Readjust as described in Step 4.*

6. Reinstall the center console (**Figure 63**).

7. Shift the gear selector to PARK. Start the engine and check the transaxle for proper alignment in all gears. If any gear does not engage properly, have the transaxle inspected by a Honda dealer or transmission shop.

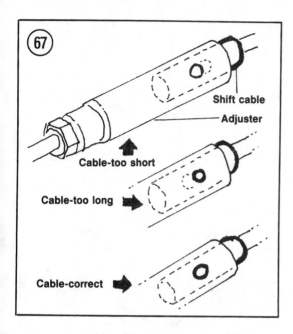

(67)

Shift cable

Adjuster

Cable-too short

Cable-too long

Cable-correct

Throttle Control Cable Adjustment (1980-on)

The throttle control cable controls automatic downshifting on 1980 and later models. Adjustment requires several special tools and should be done by a Honda dealer or transmission shop.

Removal/Installation

> *WARNING*
> *Removing the transaxle without removing the engine requires supporting the car on a commercial hoist. Jackstands do not provide enough stability for safe transaxle removal. If you don't have access to a commercial hoist, remove the engine and transaxle as described in Chapter Four or Chapter Five, then separate them.*

1. Release the steering lock and place the shift selector lever in NEUTRAL.
2. Disconnect the negative cable from the battery, then from the transaxle housing.
3. Unplug the following wiring connectors in the engine compartment:
   a. Positive battery cable and solenoid wire from starter motor.
   b. Backup light switch wires at transaxle case.
   c. *1976-1981 models:* Ignition timing thermosensor and coolant temperature sender wires at engine.
4. Disconnect the transaxle oil cooler inlet and outlet hoses at the transaxle. See **Figure 68**. Use wire to support the hoses in an upright position so fluid won't run out. Note the position of the sealing washers so they can be replaced during assembly.

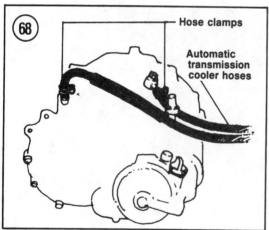

(68)

Hose clamps

Automatic transmission cooler hoses

> *CAUTION*
> *During the next step, do not remove the speedometer gear holder as the speedometer gear may fall into the transaxle housing. **Figure 69** and **Figure 70** show different methods of attaching the speedometer gear holder assembly to the clutch housing.*

5A. *Non-power steering models:* Pull up the speedometer cable rubber boot (**Figure 71**) to provide access to the cable clip attachment. Then remove the clip (7, **Figure 72**) and pull the speedometer cable from the gear fitting on the transaxle.
5B. *Power steering models:* Remove the speed sensor securing bolt, then remove the sensor hose

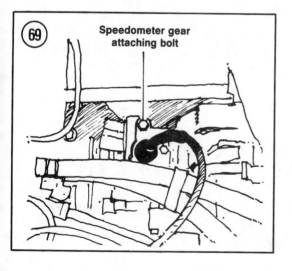

(69)

Speedometer gear attaching bolt

9

and speedometer cable by pulling upward. Set the assembly aside. See **Figure 73**.

> *NOTE*
> *Do not remove the hose or attaching bolts from the speed sensor assembly or power steering fluid will spill out.*

6A. *All Accord models, 1979-1982 Prelude:* Remove the starter mounting bolts on the transaxle side and the 2 upper transaxle mounting bolts.

6B. *1983-on Prelude:* Remove the starter mounting bolts and the 2 upper transaxle mounting bolts. Take the starter out.

7. *1980-on:* Referring to **Figure 74**, remove the throttle control cable as follows:
   a. Push the throttle control lever down and release the throttle cable.
   b. Loosen the throttle control cable locknut (A, **Figure 74**) and remove the cable from its mounting bracket. Do not turn locknut B. It will be needed as a marker to position the cable properly during installation.

8. Raise the car on a commercial hoist. See the introduction to this procedure.

> *WARNING*
> *Do not attempt to remove the transaxle when the car is supported by jackstands. They do not provide the stability for safe transaxle removal.*

9. Remove the front wheels.

10. Remove the transaxle drain plug and drain the transaxle oil into a pan. Install the drain plug, using a new washer.

11. Remove the access panel from the right fender well.

12. Attach an engine lifting sling to the engine at the points shown in **Figure 75**. Using a suitable engine hoist, remove all slack and place slight tension on the lifting sling. Make sure the tension on both legs of the chain is equal. Adjust the sling, if necessary.

13. Place a transmission jack beneath the transaxle. Transmission jacks, available from rental dealers, have cradles which will prevent the transaxle from falling. They can also be adjusted for side-to-side tilt and approach angle.

14. Remove the subframe center beam and splash shield.

15. *1976-1981 Accord:* Detach the front stabilizer bar from the radius rods. Remove the front self-locking nut from each radius rod. See Chapter Ten for details.

16. *1979-1982 Prelude:* Remove the front stabilizer bar.

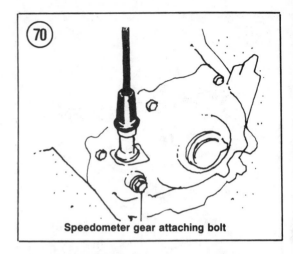

Speedometer gear attaching bolt

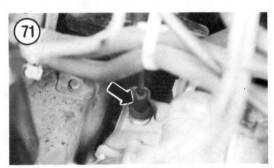

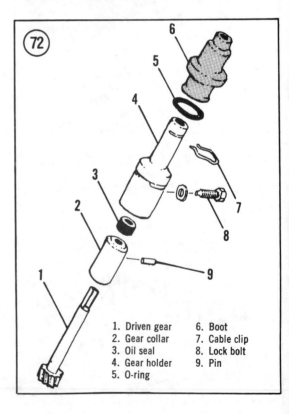

1. Driven gear
2. Gear collar
3. Oil seal
4. Gear holder
5. O-ring
6. Boot
7. Cable clip
8. Lock bolt
9. Pin

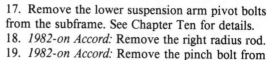

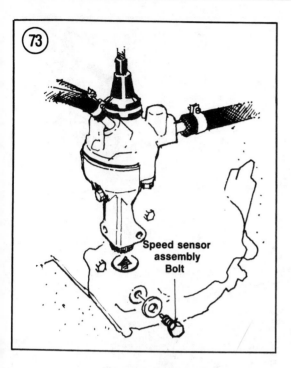

Speed sensor
assembly
Bolt

17. Remove the lower suspension arm pivot bolts from the subframe. See Chapter Ten for details.

18. *1982-on Accord:* Remove the right radius rod.

19. *1982-on Accord:* Remove the pinch bolt from the right ball-joint (**Figure 76**). Separate the ball-joint from the knuckle arm with a puller.

20. *1983-on Prelude:* Remove the cotter pin from the right ball-joint nut. Loosen the nut about halfway, then separate the ball-joint from the knuckle with a puller as shown in **Figure 77**.

21. Pivot each steering knuckle as far outboard as it will go.

22. Pry the inboard end of each drive shaft about 1/2 in. out of the transaxle, then pull the drive shaft ends all the way out of the transaxle.

23. *All Accord models, 1979-1982 Prelude:* Remove the remaining starter mounting bolt, lower the starter away from the car and take it out.

24. Remove the transaxle damper bracket at the front torque converter drive plate. Then remove the converter cover plate.

25. *1976-1979:* Refer to **Figure 78** and disconnect the control cable at the transaxle.

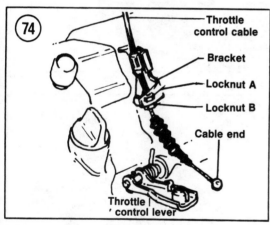

Throttle control cable

Bracket

Locknut A

Locknut B

Cable end

Throttle control lever

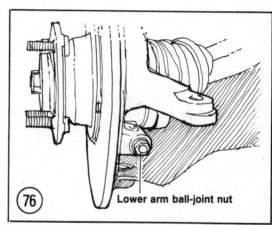

Lower arm ball-joint nut

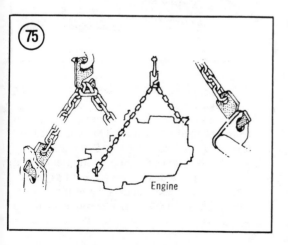

Engine

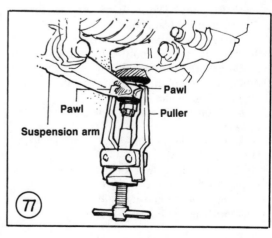

Pawl

Pawl

Puller

Suspension arm

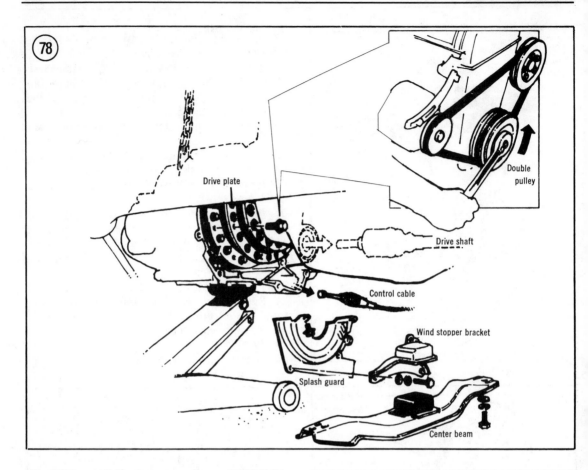

26. *1980-on:* Shift the transaxle to REVERSE. Then remove the center console as shown in **Figure 63** and separate the shift cable from the adjuster. See **Figure 64**. After loosening the cable inside the car, remove the shift cable holder bolts from underneath the car (**Figure 79**) and remove the cable together with the cable holder.

27. The torque converter is secured to the drive plate with bolts. To gain access to each bolt, turn the engine crankshaft using a socket placed on the crankshaft pulley bolt. Remove all torque converter-to-drive plate bolts.

28. Unscrew the remaining transaxle mounting bolts. With the jack supporting the transaxle, pull the transaxle away from the engine to clear the locating dowels. Lower the transaxle with the jack and pull it from under the car.

29. Installation is the reverse of removal, plus the following:

a. Make sure the locating dowels are installed in the transaxle housing.

b. When installing drive shafts, use new circlips and make sure each drive shaft is fully bottomed in the housing. Slide the drive shafts in until the circlips are felt to engage.

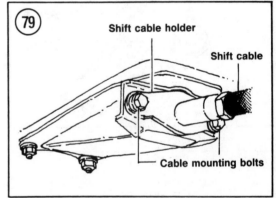

c. Use new aluminum washers when attaching oil cooler hoses.

d. After installation, fill the transaxle with an oil recommended in Chapter Three. Check fluid level and add or remove fluid as needed.

e. Check operation of the gearshift selector and adjust, if required, as described in this chapter.

f. On 1980 and later models, have the throttle cable adjusted by a dealer or other qualified specialist.

Table 1 CLUTCH SPECIFICATIONS

Item	mm	in.
Release fork play		
1976-1981 Accord	2.0-2.6	0.08-0.10
1982-on Accord	5.2-6.4	0.20-0.25
1979-1982 Prelude	2.0-2.6	0.08-0.10
1983-on Prelude	5.2-6.4	0.20-0.25
Pedal height (to bare floor)		
1976-1981 Accord	184	7.24
1982-1983 Accord	178	7.0
1984 Accord	180	7.1
1979-1982 Prelude	184	7.24
1983 Prelude	181	7.1
1984 Prelude	176	6.9
Pedal free play		
1976-1980 (all)	1-3	3/64-1/8
1981 Accord	20-30	3/4-1 3/16
1982-1983 Accord	10-30	3/8-1 3/16
1984 Accord	23-28	7/8-1 1/8
1981-1983 Prelude	10-30	3/8-1/3/16
1984 Prelude	23-28	7/8-1 1/8
Pressure plate warp, maximum	0.15	0.006
Disc thickness, minimum		
1976-1979	5.9-6.6	0.232-0.260
1980-on	5.7	0.22
Disc rivet hole depth, minimum	0.2	0.008

Table 2 CLUTCH TIGHTENING TORQUES

Fastener	N•m	ft.-lb.
Pressure plate bolts		
1976-1981 Accord	10-14	7-10
1982-on Accord	26	19
All Prelude	26	19

9

CHAPTER TEN

FRONT SUSPENSION, WHEEL BEARINGS AND STEERING

All models use a strut-type front suspension. The shock absorbers and springs are combined into single units. The struts are attached to the inner wheel wells at the top and to the lower suspension links at the bottom.

On all except the 1983 and later Prelude, the strut provides the upper locating point for the suspension, as well as spring and damping action. On 1983 and later Preludes, the strut provides spring and damping action, but the upper locating point is provided by an upper suspension arm. The lower locating point on all models is provided by a lower suspension arm.

A stabilizer bar is used on all models to control body lean.

All models use rack and pinion steering. Power steering is optional on all Accords and on 1979-1982 Preludes. Power steering is standard on 1983 and later Preludes.

This chapter provides all front suspension, wheel bearing and steering service procedures which are practical for home mechanics.

Specifications and tightening torques (**Tables 1-4**) are at the end of the chapter.

> *CAUTION*
> *All fasteners used in the front suspension and steering must be replaced with parts of the same type. **Do not** use replacement parts of lesser quality or substitute design, as this may affect the performance of vital components and systems or result in major repair expenses.*

Self-locking bolts and nuts are used at a number of points in the front suspension. In some cases, these should be replaced each time the nut or bolt is removed. These cases are noted during the procedures. In other cases, the fastener should be replaced if a nut or bolt can be threaded easily past its self-locking insert.

NOTE
Suspension parts tend to accumulate road dirt. Before beginning any suspension work, it is a good idea to clean the suspension. Coin-operated car washes work well for this.

WHEEL ALIGNMENT

Several front suspension angles affect the running and steering of the front wheels. These angles must be properly aligned to maintain

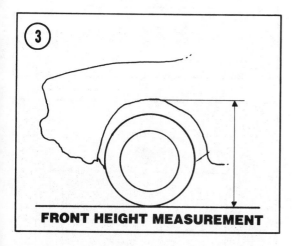

FRONT HEIGHT MEASUREMENT

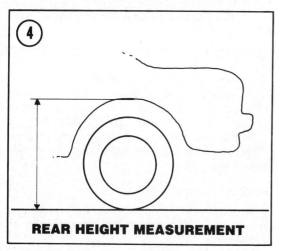

REAR HEIGHT MEASUREMENT

directional stability and ease of steering. The angles are:

    a. Caster.
    b. Camber.
    c. Steering axis inclination.
    d. Toe.

On all except the 1983 and later Prelude, toe is the only adjustable angle. If the other angles are found to be out of specifications, damage or wear is indicated.

On the 1983 and later Prelude, toe, caster and camber are adjustable.

Inspection

The steering and suspension angles are affected by several factors. Perform the following steps before checking adjustment.

1. Check tire pressure as described in Chapter Three.

2. Check tire wear as described in *Tire Wear Analysis,* Chapter Two.

3. Check play in ball-joints as described in this chapter.

4. Park the car on level ground. Make sure the car is empty:

    a. On 1976-1979 Accords, measure the distance from the bottom edges of the side marker lights, on both sides of the front and rear. See **Figure 1** and **Figure 2**.

    b. On 1980 and later Accords and all Preludes, measure from the top edges of the wheel wells as shown in **Figure 3** and **Figure 4**.

    c. Compare the measurements with **Table 2** at the end of the chapter. If they are not within specifications, check for broken or sagging springs.

5. Check shock absorbers for leaking or damage. Replace worn or damaged front shock absorbers as described in this chapter. Replace worn or damaged rear shock absorbers as described in Chapter Eleven.

6. Check the steering mechanism and tie rods for looseness.

7. Have wheel balance checked by a dealer or front-end shop.

8. Check rear suspension components for looseness.

9. Park the car on a level surface with the front wheels in the straight-ahead position. Grasp the steering wheel, move it alternately from left to right and note free play (the distance the steering wheel can be turned without moving the front wheels). Free play should be as specified at the end of the chapter. If it is more than this, check the

10

front suspension and steering linkage for wear or damage.

10. Try to move the steering wheel straight up and down. This should not be possible. If it is, the steering column bushings may be worn.

11. Check front wheel bearing end play as described under *Hubs and Knuckles* in this chapter.

Caster and Camber

Caster is the inclination from vertical of the line through the ball-joints. See **Figure 5**. Positive caster shifts the wheel forward; negative caster shifts the wheel rearward. Caster causes the wheels to return to the straight-ahead position after a turn. It also prevents the wheels from wandering due to uneven road surfaces.

Camber is the inclination of the wheel from vertical. With positive camber, the top of the tire leans outward; with negative camber, the top of the tire leans inward.

Caster and camber are not adjustable on any Accords or on 1979-1982 Preludes. While these angles can be adjusted on 1983 and later Preludes, adjustment requires special equipment and should be done by a Honda dealer or front-end shop.

Toe

This is the angle from straight ahead at which the wheels point when the car is at rest. See **Figure 6**. On some models, the wheels are set to toe slightly outward. The distance between the front edges (A, **Figure 6**) is slightly more than the distance between the rear edges (B). On other models, the wheels are set straight ahead, with a slight amount of toe-out or toe-in acceptable.

Although toe adjustment requires only a simple homemade tool, it usually isn't worth the trouble for home mechanics. Alignment shops include toe as part of the alignment procedure, so you probably won't save any money by doing it yourself. The procedure described here can be used for an initial toe setting after steering linkage repairs.

1. With the steering wheel centered, roll forward about 15 ft. onto a smooth, level surface.

2. Mark the center of the tread at the front and rear of each tire.

3. Measure the distance between forward chalk marks (A, **Figure 6**). Use 2 pieces of telescoping aluminum tubing. Telescope the tubing so each end contacts a chalk mark. Using a sharp scribe, mark the small diameter tubing where it enters the large diameter tubing.

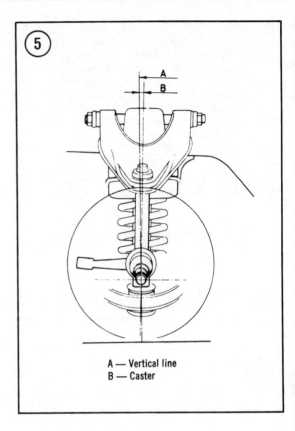

A — Vertical line
B — Caster

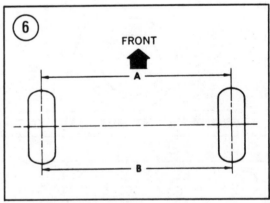

4. Measure between the rear chalk marks with the telescoping tubes. Make another mark on the small tube where it enters the large one. The distance between the 2 scribe marks is toe.

5. If toe is incorrect, loosen the tie rod locknuts (**Figure 7**). Rotate the tie rods to change toe, then tighten the clamps.

Steering Axis Inclination

Steering axis inclination is the inward or outward lean of the struts. It is not adjustable on the Honda.

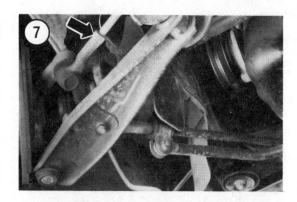

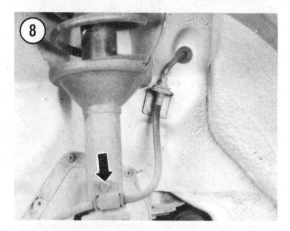

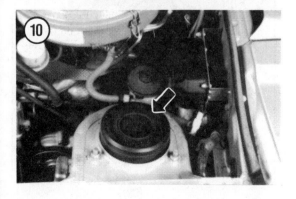

FRONT SUSPENSION
(1976-1981 ACCORD)

Strut Removal/Installation

1. Set the handbrake. Securely block both rear wheels so the car will not roll in either direction.

2. Loosen the front wheel nuts. Jack up the front end of the car, place it on jackstands and remove the front wheels.

3. Remove the securing bolt and detach the brake hose clamp from the strut. See **Figure 8**.

4. Remove the shock absorber pinch bolt at the steering knuckle. See **Figure 9**.

NOTE
The pinch bolt passes through a groove in the shock absorber, so it must be removed, not just loosened.

5. Push down on the knuckle and tap it with a hammer to free it. Then pull the knuckle down far enough to separate it from the bottom end of the strut.

WARNING
During the next step, do not remove the center nut (beneath the rubber cap in ***Figure 10***). *This could allow the coil spring to fly out and cause serious injury.*

6. Remove the nuts that secure the upper end of the strut.

7. Take the strut assembly to a Honda dealer or front-end shop for service, if necessary.

8. Install by reversing Steps 1-6. Tighten all fasteners to specifications in **Table 3**.

Shock Absorber Replacement

The front suspension strut must be disassembled to replace the shock absorber. Disassembly requires special tools and should be done by a Honda dealer or front-end shop. Part of the labor charge can be saved by removing the strut assemblies yourself and taking them to a shop for shock absorber replacement.

Coil Spring Replacement

The coil spring is part of the strut assembly. To remove a spring, remove the strut as described in this chapter. Take the strut assembly to a dealer for spring replacement, then install it using the same procedure.

Ball-joint Inspection

1. Set the handbrake. Securely block both rear wheels so the car will not roll in either direction.

10

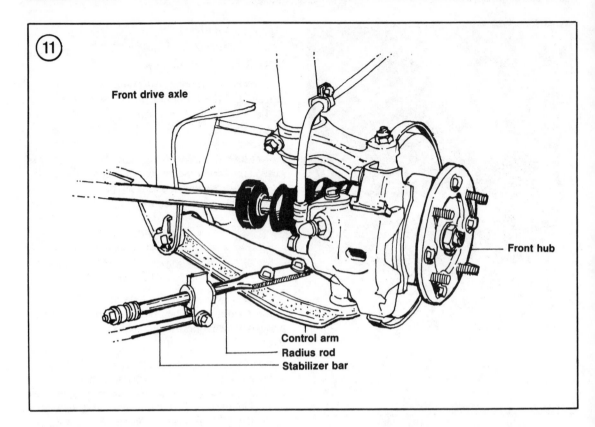

(11)

Front drive axle

Front hub

Control arm
Radius rod
Stabilizer bar

2. Jack up the front end of the car and place it on jackstands.

3. Attach a dial indicator to the lower control arm. Place the tip of the dial indicator on the knuckle near the ball-joint.

4. Place a pry bar between the knuckle and the lower control arm. Push and release the bar while observing the indicator movement. If the movement is 0.5 mm (0.020 in.) or more, replace the lower control arm as described in this chapter.

Lower Control Arm,
Ball-joints and
Stabilizer Bar Removal

Refer to **Figure 11** for this procedure.

1. Set the handbrake. Securely block both rear wheels so the car will not roll in either direction.

2. Loosen the front wheel nuts. Jack up the front end of the car, place it on jackstands and remove the front wheels.

3. Remove the cotter pin from the castle nut (**Figure 12**), then remove the nut.

4. Detach the steering knuckle from the control arm with a Honda ball-joint remover as shown in

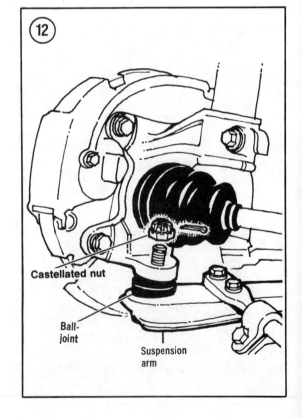

(12)

Castellated nut

Ball-joint

Suspension arm

Figure 13. To use the tool, drive the wedge into the holder to displace the ball-joint downward.

NOTE
See your Honda dealer for the correct ball-joint remover, as a number of different removers have been used for the different models and years.

5. Remove the nut from the front end of the radius rod (**Figure 11**). Remove the bolts from the stabilizer bar center mounts, then collect the clamps and bushings.

6. Bend back the locktab that secures the nut on the control arm's inboard pivot bolt. Remove the pivot bolt and nut, then remove the control arm.

7. Inspect all parts for wear or damage and replace as needed. If the ball-joint boot is worn or cracked, replace it using the special guide tool shown in **Figure 14**.

Lower Control Arm,
Ball-joints and Stabilizer
Bar Installation

Installation is the reverse of removal, plus the following.

1. Slide the end of the control arm into its position in the engine support beam and install the pivot bolt. Install the nut on the pivot bolt, but do not tighten it yet.

2. Lubricate the control arm ball-joint. Raise the outer end of the control arm so the ball-joint stud slides into the knuckle. Install the castle nut on the ball-joint stud, but don't tighten it yet.

3. Place a jack beneath the knuckle arm. Raise the knuckle arm just enough to lift the car off the jackstand on the side you are working on. Make sure the car is still supported by the jackstand on the opposite side.

4. Tighten the control arm pivot bolt and nut to specifications in **Table 3**. Then bend the pivot bolt locktab against the head of the bolt. Lower the car back onto the jackstand.

CAUTION
Do not use the same locktab that was used before removal.

5. Tighten the castle nut to specifications in **Table 3**. Install a new cotter pin through the nut and stud, then bend the cotter pin over to secure the nut.

FRONT SUSPENSION
(1982 AND LATER ACCORD)

Strut Removal/Installation

Refer to **Figure 15** for this procedure.

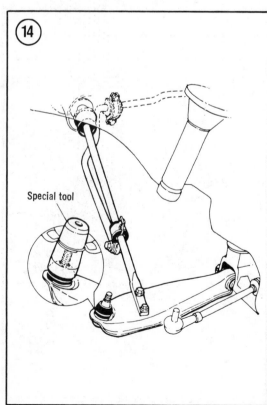

Special tool

10

1. Set the handbrake. Securely block both rear wheels so the car will not roll in either direction.
2. Loosen the front wheel nuts. Jack up the front end of the car, place it on jackstands and remove the front wheels.
3. Remove the securing bolt and detach the brake hose clamp from the strut. See **Figure 8**.

> *CAUTION*
> *Do not let the caliper hang by the brake hose during the next step.*

4. Unbolt the brake caliper as described in Chapter Twelve, then tie the caliper out of the way with wire. It is not necessary to disconnect the brake hose from the caliper.
5. Detach the stabilizer bar from the lower suspension arm as described in this chapter.
6. Remove the shock absorber pinch bolt at the steering knuckle. See **Figure 15**.

> *NOTE*
> *The pinch bolt passes through a groove in the shock absorber, so it must be removed, not just loosened.*

7. Push down on the knuckle and tap it with a hammer to free it. Then pull the knuckle down far enough to separate it from the bottom end of the strut.

> *WARNING*
> *During the next step, do not remove the center nut at the top of the strut. This could allow the coil spring to fly out and cause serious injury.*

8. Remove the nuts that secure the upper end of the strut. Lower the strut and take it out from under the car.
9. Take the strut assembly to a Honda dealer or front-end shop for service, if necessary.
10. Install by reversing Steps 1-8. Make sure the shock absorber aligning tab (**Figure 16**) aligns with the slot in the knuckle. Tighten all fasteners to specifications in **Table 3**.

> *CAUTION*
> *Replace the self-locking bolt at the bottom of the strut if it can be easily threaded past its self-locking insert.*

Shock Absorber Replacement

The front suspension strut must be disassembled to replace the shock absorber. Disassembly requires special tools and should be done by a Honda dealer or front-end shop. Part of the labor charge can be saved by removing the strut assemblies yourself and taking them to a shop for shock absorber replacement.

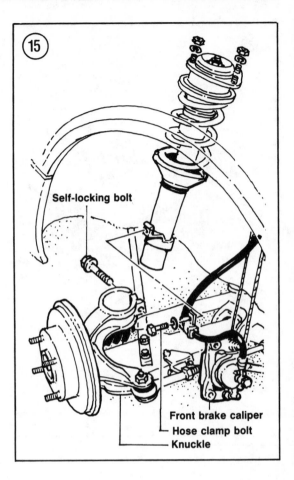

Self-locking bolt
Front brake caliper
Hose clamp bolt
Knuckle

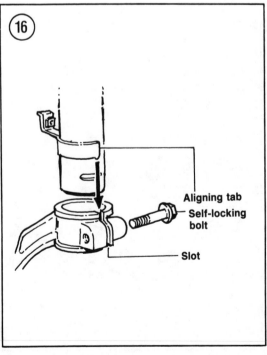

Aligning tab
Self-locking bolt
Slot

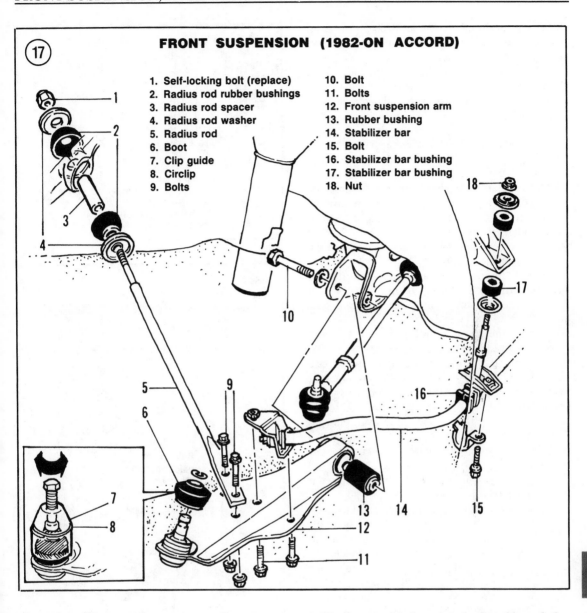

(17)

FRONT SUSPENSION (1982-ON ACCORD)

1. Self-locking bolt (replace)
2. Radius rod rubber bushings
3. Radius rod spacer
4. Radius rod washer
5. Radius rod
6. Boot
7. Clip guide
8. Circlip
9. Bolts
10. Bolt
11. Bolts
12. Front suspension arm
13. Rubber bushing
14. Stabilizer bar
15. Bolt
16. Stabilizer bar bushing
17. Stabilizer bar bushing
18. Nut

10

Coil Spring Replacement

The coil spring is part of the strut assembly. To remove a spring, remove the strut as described in this chapter. Take the strut assembly to a dealer for spring replacement, then install it using the same procedure.

Ball-joint Inspection

1. Set the handbrake. Securely block both rear wheels so the car will not roll in either direction.
2. Jack up the front end of the car and place it on jackstands.
3. Attach a dial indicator to the lower control arm. Place the tip of the dial indicator on the knuckle near the ball-joint.

4. Place a pry bar between the knuckle and the lower control arm. Push and release the bar while observing the indicator movement. If the movement is 0.5 mm (0.020 in.) or more, replace the lower control arm as described in this chapter.

Lower Control Arm, Stabilizer Bar and Radius Rod Removal/Installation

Refer to **Figure 17** for this procedure.
1. Set the handbrake. Securely block both rear wheels so the car will not roll in either direction.

2. Loosen the front wheel nuts. Jack up the front end of the car, place it on jackstands and remove the front wheels.

3. Place a jack beneath the outboard end of the lower control arm. Raise the jack enough to take tension off the radius rod and stabilizer bar, but not enough to raise the car off the jackstands.

4. Remove the stabilizer bar end bolts. Remove the nuts that secure the stabilizer bar center links to the brackets and take the stabilizer bar out.

5. Remove the self-locking nut from the front end of the radius rod. Discard this nut. It must be replaced with a new one whenever it is removed.

6. Unbolt the radius rod from the lower control arm and take it out.

7. Remove the pinch bolt and nut that secure the lower control arm ball-joint to the knuckle. See **Figure 18**. Remove the jack from beneath the lower control arm, then tap it downward with a brass or plastic hammer until the ball-joint stud separates from the knuckle.

8. Remove the lower control arm pivot bolt and washer. Take the lower control arm out.

9. Inspect all parts for wear or damage and replace as needed. If the ball-joint boot is worn or cracked, replace it using the special guide tool shown in **Figure 17**.

10. Installation is the reverse of removal, plus the following:

   a. Install the lower control arm pivot bolt loosely.

   b. Guide the ball-joint stud upward into the knuckle.

   c. Place a jack under the knuckle. Raise the jack just enough to lift the car off the jackstand on the side you are working on. Do not raise the car off the jackstand on the opposite side.

   d. Tighten the control arm pivot bolt and stabilizer bar bolts to specifications. Install a new radius rod nut and tighten to specifications. Lower the car back onto the jackstand.

   e. Tighten all other fasteners to specifications in **Table 3**.

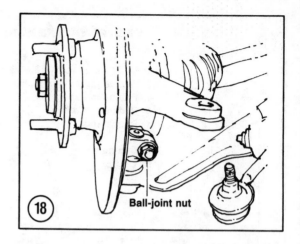

Ball-joint nut

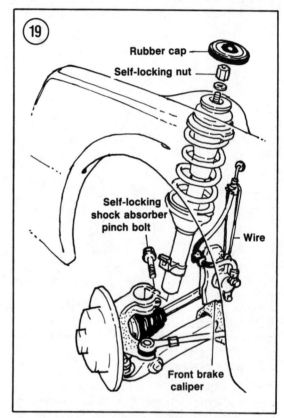

Rubber cap

Self-locking nut

Self-locking shock absorber pinch bolt

Wire

Front brake caliper

FRONT SUSPENSION
(1979-1982 PRELUDE)

Strut Removal/Installation

Refer to **Figure 19** for this procedure.

1. Set the handbrake. Securely block both rear wheels so the car will not roll in either direction.

2. Loosen the front wheel nuts. Jack up the front end of the car, place it on jackstands and remove the front wheels.

3. Remove the securing bolt and detach the brake hose clamp from the strut.

CAUTION
Do not let the caliper hang by the brake hose during the next step.

4. Unbolt the brake caliper as described in Chapter Twelve, then tie the caliper out of the way with wire. It is not necessary to disconnect the brake hose from the caliper.

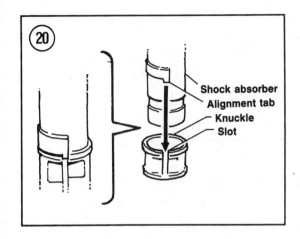

Shock absorber
Alignment tab
Knuckle
Slot

5. Remove the shock absorber pinch bolt at the steering knuckle.

NOTE
The pinch bolt passes through a groove in the shock absorber, so it must be removed, not just loosened.

6. Push down on the knuckle and tap it with a hammer to free it. Then pull the knuckle down far enough to separate it from the bottom end of the strut.

WARNING
During the next step, do not remove the spring seat nut (under the rubber cap and self-locking nut at the top of the strut). This could allow the coil spring to fly out and cause serious injury.

7. Remove the rubber cap, self-locking nut and washer from the upper end of the strut. Lower the strut and take it out from under the car.
8. Take the strut assembly to a Honda dealer or front-end shop for service, if necessary.
9. Install by reversing Steps 1-7. Make sure the shock absorber aligning tab (**Figure 20**) aligns with the slot in the knuckle. Tighten all fasteners to specifications in **Table 3**.

CAUTION
Replace the self-locking bolt at the bottom of the strut if it can be easily threaded past its self-locking insert.

Shock Absorber Replacement

The front suspension strut must be disassembled to replace the shock absorber. Disassembly requires special tools and should be done by a Honda dealer or front-end shop. Part of the labor charge can be saved by removing the strut assemblies yourself and taking them to a shop for shock absorber replacement.

Coil Spring Replacement

The coil spring is part of the strut assembly. To remove a spring, remove the strut as described in this chapter. Take the strut assembly to a dealer for spring replacement, then install it using the same procedure.

Ball-joint Inspection

1. Set the handbrake. Securely block both rear wheels so the car will not roll in either direction.
2. Jack up the front end of the car and place it on jackstands.
3. Attach a dial indicator to the lower control arm. Place the tip of the dial indicator on the knuckle near the ball-joint.
4. Place a pry bar between the knuckle and the lower control arm. Push and release the bar while observing the indicator movement. If the movement is 0.5 mm (0.020 in.) or more, replace the lower control arm as described in this chapter.

Lower Control Arm and Stabilizer Bar Removal

Refer to **Figure 21** for this procedure.
1. Set the handbrake. Securely block both rear wheels so the car will not roll in either direction.
2. Loosen the front wheel nuts. Jack up the front end of the car, place it on jackstands and remove the front wheels.
3. Remove the splash shield from under the car.
4. Place a jack beneath the outboard end of the lower control arm. Raise the jack enough to take tension off the stabilizer bar, but not enough to raise the car off the jackstands.
5. Remove the stabilizer bar end nuts. Remove the bolts that secure the stabilizer bar center links to the brackets and take the stabilizer bar out.
6. Inspect all parts for wear or damage and replace as needed. If the ball-joint boot is worn or cracked, replace it using the special guide tool shown in **Figure 21**.

Lower Control Arm and Stabilizer Bar Installation

Installation is the reverse of removal, plus the following.
1. Install the lower control arm in the frame. Install its pivot bolt loosely.
2. Install the stabilizer bar and its end bushings in the lower control arms. Position the stabilizer bar as follows:

a. On 1979-1981 models, position the side with a painted stripe on the passenger side of the car. Align the outer edges of the white paint

10

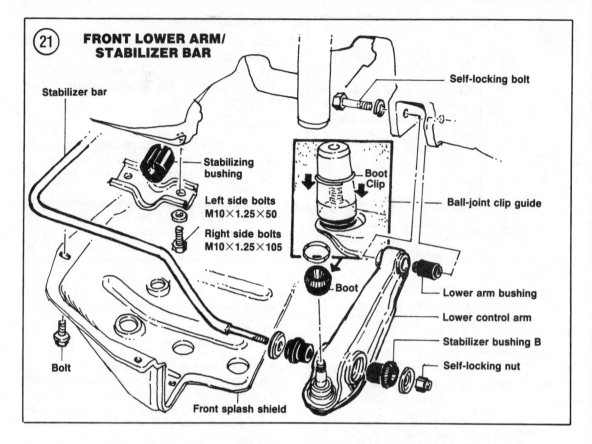

FRONT LOWER ARM/ STABILIZER BAR

(21)

- Stabilizer bar
- Self-locking bolt
- Stabilizing bushing
- Boot Clip
- Left side bolts M10×1.25×50
- Right side bolts M10×1.25×105
- Ball-joint clip guide
- Boot
- Lower arm bushing
- Lower control arm
- Stabilizer bushing B
- Self-locking nut
- Bolt
- Front splash shield

marks with the inner edges of the stabilizer bar bushings. See **Figure 22**.

b. On 1982 models, position the side with a yellow or green paint mark on the passenger side of the car. Align the outer edge of the mark with the inner edge of the stabilizer bar bushing. See **Figure 23**.

3. Install the stabilizer bracket bolts and tighten to specifications.

NOTE
The bolts for the left-hand bracket are 50 mm long; the bolts for the right-hand bracket are 105 mm long.

4. Place a jack under the knuckle. Raise it just enough to lift the car off the jackstand on the side you are working on. Do not raise the car off the opposite jackstand.

5. Tighten the lower control arm pivot bolt to specifications in **Table 4**. Lower the car back onto the jackstand.

6. Install new self-locking nuts on the ends of the stabilizer bar and tighten to specifications.

7. Install the front wheels.

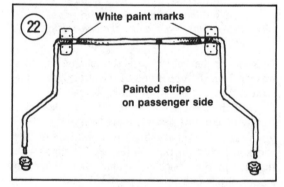

(22)

White paint marks

Painted stripe on passenger side

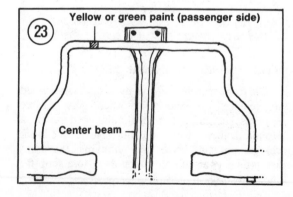

(23)

Yellow or green paint (passenger side)

Center beam

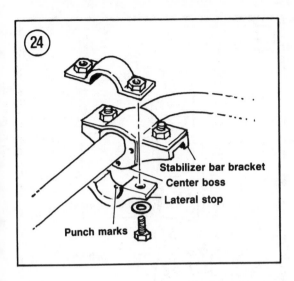

(24)

Stabilizer bar bracket
Center boss
Lateral stop
Punch marks

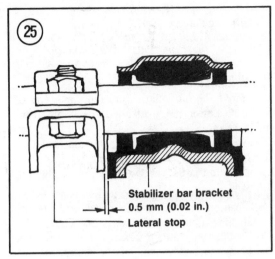

(25)

Stabilizer bar bracket
0.5 mm (0.02 in.)
Lateral stop

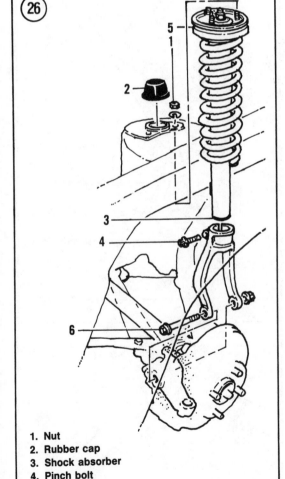

(26)

5
1
2
3
4
6

1. Nut
2. Rubber cap
3. Shock absorber
4. Pinch bolt
5. Damper fork
6. Damper fork bolt

NOTE
Steps 8-10 apply to 1982 models only.

8. Install the lateral stop against the stabilizer as shown in **Figure 24**. Make sure the rubber center boss on the bracket is directly in line with the punch marks on the stop. Do not tighten the stop bolts yet.

9. Measure the clearance between the lateral stop and the stabilizer bar bracket with a feeler gauge. See **Figure 25**. It should be 0.5 mm (0.020 in.). If not, reposition the lateral stop so the clearance is correct.

10. Once the lateral stop clearance is set correctly, tighten the lateral stop bolts to specifications in **Table 4**.

FRONT SUSPENSION (1983-ON PRELUDE)

Strut Removal/Installation

Refer to **Figure 26** for this procedure.
1. Set the handbrake. Securely block both rear wheels so the car will not roll in either direction.
2. Loosen the front wheel nuts. Jack up the front end of the car, place it on jackstands and remove the front wheels.
3. Remove the damper lockbolt (**Figure 26**).

NOTE
The damper lockbolt passes through a groove in the bottom of the damper, so it must be removed, not just loosened.

4. Remove the damper fork bolt (**Figure 26**) and take out the damper fork.

10

WARNING
During the next step, do not remove the center nut under the rubber cap at the top of the strut. This could allow the coil spring to fly out and cause serious injury.

5. Remove the nuts that secure the upper end of the strut. Lower the strut and take it out from under the car.

6. Take the strut assembly to a Honda dealer or front-end shop for service, if necessary.

7. Installation is the reverse of removal, plus the following:

   a. Position the strut in the wheel well with its alignment tab facing inboard. See **Figure 27**.

   b. Install the damper fork on the lower arm. Place the bottom end of the damper in the fork, making sure its aligning tab lines up with the slot in the damper fork. See **Figure 27**.

   c. Place a jack beneath the knuckle. Raise the jack just enough to lift the car off the jackstand on the side you are working on. Do not lift the car off the jackstand on the opposite side.

   d. Tighten the damper fork bolt and damper fork lockbolt to specifications in **Table 4**. Lower the car back onto the jackstand.

   e. Tighten the damper mounting nuts to specifications in **Table 4**.

Shock Absorber Replacement

The front suspension strut must be disassembled to replace the shock absorber. Disassembly requires special tools and should be done by a Honda dealer or front-end shop. Part of the labor charge can be saved by removing the strut assemblies yourself and taking them to a shop for shock absorber replacement.

Coil Spring Replacement

The coil spring is part of the strut assembly. To remove a spring, remove the strut as described in this chapter. Take the strut assembly to a dealer for spring replacement, then install it using the same procedure.

Upper Arm and Ball-joint Inspection

1. Set the handbrake. Securely block both rear wheels so the car will not roll in either direction.

2. Loosen the front wheel nuts. Jack up the front end of the car, place it on jackstands and remove the front wheels.

3. Rock the upper ball-joint back and forth with approximately 30 kg (65 lb.) force. Watch the

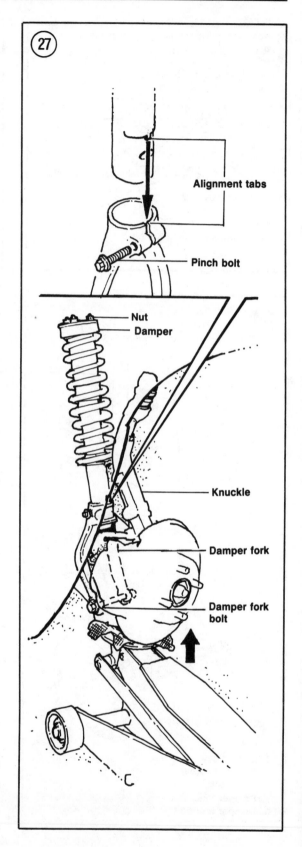

Alignment tabs

Pinch bolt

Nut
Damper

Knuckle

Damper fork

Damper fork bolt

upper arm bushings and ball-joint while rocking. If there is any play, replace the bushings or ball-joint as described in this chapter.

Upper Arm and Ball-joint
Removal/Installation

Refer to **Figure 28** for this procedure.

1. Set the handbrake. Securely block both rear wheels so the car will not roll in either direction.

2. Loosen the front wheel nuts. Jack up the front end of the car, place it on jackstands and remove the front wheels.

3. Remove the cotter pin and castle nut from the upper ball-joint stud. Separate the ball-joint stud from the knuckle with a separator such as Honda tool part No. 07941-6920001 (**Figure 29**).

4. Remove the self-locking nuts that secure the upper arm assembly. Take the assembly out.

5. Installation is the reverse of removal, plus the following:

   a. Tighten all fasteners to specifications in **Table 4**.

   b. Use a new cotter pin in the ball-joint stud and castle nut.

   c. Since the position of the ball-joint in the upper arm is used to set camber, have wheel alignment adjusted by a Honda dealer or front-end shop.

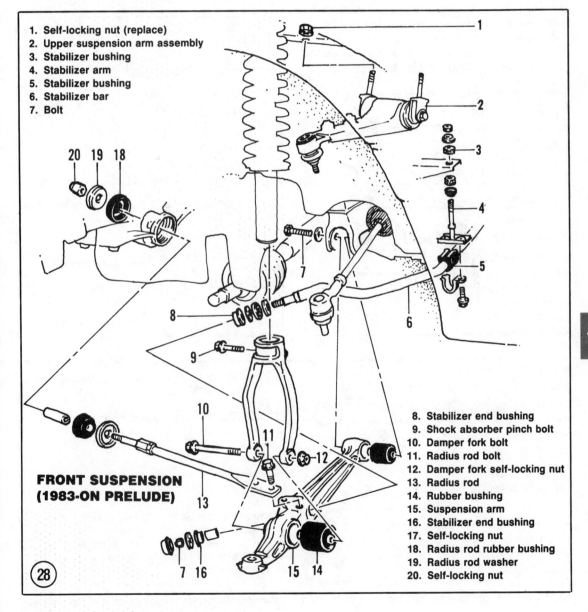

1. Self-locking nut (replace)
2. Upper suspension arm assembly
3. Stabilizer bushing
4. Stabilizer arm
5. Stabilizer bushing
6. Stabilizer bar
7. Bolt

8. Stabilizer end bushing
9. Shock absorber pinch bolt
10. Damper fork bolt
11. Radius rod bolt
12. Damper fork self-locking nut
13. Radius rod
14. Rubber bushing
15. Suspension arm
16. Stabilizer end bushing
17. Self-locking nut
18. Radius rod rubber bushing
19. Radius rod washer
20. Self-locking nut

**FRONT SUSPENSION
(1983-ON PRELUDE)**

28

10

Upper Arm and Ball-joint
Disassembly/Assembly

1. Place the anchor bolts in a vise and tighten it just enough to hold them in place. See **Figure 30**. Remove the upper arm bolt, anchor bolts and seals.

2. Position the upper arm in the vise as shown in **Figure 31**. Tap out the upper arm collar as shown, then tap out the upper arm bushings with a round-ended bar.

3. Thoroughly clean all parts in solvent.

4. Discard the upper arm bushings, upper arm bushing seals and upper arm collar. See **Figure 32**. Use new parts during assembly.

5. If the ball-joint boot is worn, cracked or deteriorated, remove it. Install a new boot as follows:

    a. *Clip type:* Pack the boot with grease as shown in **Figure 33**. Install the boot and squeeze out

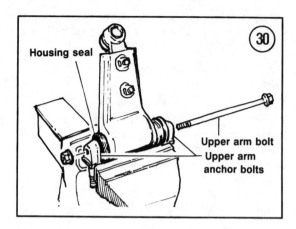

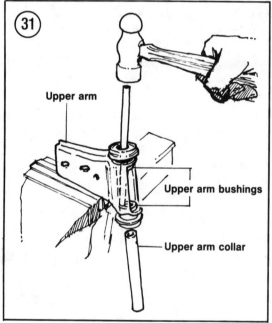

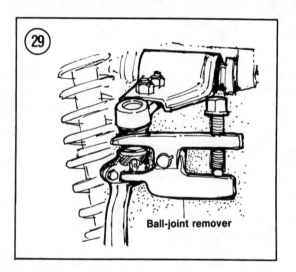

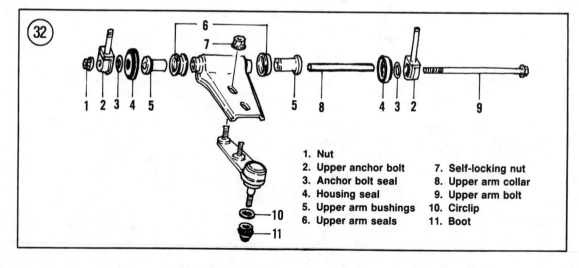

1. Nut
2. Upper anchor bolt
3. Anchor bolt seal
4. Housing seal
5. Upper arm bushings
6. Upper arm seals
7. Self-locking nut
8. Upper arm collar
9. Upper arm bolt
10. Circlip
11. Boot

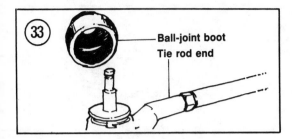

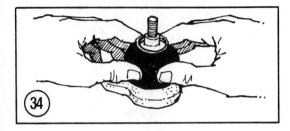

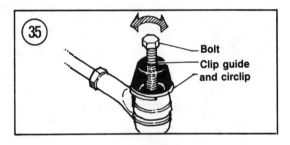

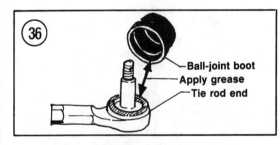

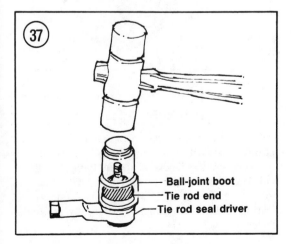

the air as shown in **Figure 34**. Install the boot clip on the clip guide (Honda tool part No. 07974-SA50800, **Figure 35**), then press the clip down onto the boot.

   b. *Press-on type:* Pack the boot and coat the ball-joint stud with grease as shown in **Figure 36**. Tap the boot onto the ball-joint with a seal driver such as Honda tool part No. 07974-6790000 (**Figure 37**), then apply gasket sealer to the mating points of boot and ball-joint.

6. If the ball-joint is loose or damaged, mark the position of the ball-joint self-locking nuts with a sharp scribe. Remove the self-locking nuts and take out the ball-joint. Install a new ball-joint as follows:

   a. Use the scribe marks as a guide so the ball-joint can be installed in the same position as the old one.

   b. Use new self-locking nuts if the old ones can be easily threaded past their self-locking inserts.

   c. Tighten the nuts to specifications in **Table 4**.

7. Apply multipurpose grease to the following points:

   a. Ends and insides of upper arm bushing.

   b. Sealing lips of upper arm bushing seals.

8. Apply gasket sealer to the following points (**Figure 38**):

   a. Threads of upper arm bolt.

   b. Underside of upper arm bolt head.

   c. Underside of self-locking nut.

CAUTION
Do not apply gasket sealer anywhere except to the specified areas.

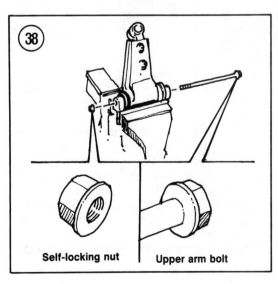

**Lower Arm, Stabilizer Bar and
Radius Rod Removal/Installation**

Refer to **Figure 28** for this procedure.

1. Set the handbrake. Securely block both rear wheels so the car will not roll in either direction.

2. Loosen the front wheel nuts. Jack up the front end of the car, place it on jackstands and remove the front wheels.

3. Place a jack beneath the lower arm. Raise the jack enough to relieve tension on the radius rod and stabilizer bar, but not enough to lift the car off the jackstands.

4. Loosen the self-locking nut at the front end of the radius rod. Tap around the washer with a hammer and drift until the washer comes loose, then remove the nut and washer.

5. Unbolt the radius rod from the lower control arm and take it out.

6. Remove the cap, self-locking nut, washer and bushing from each end of the stabilizer bar. Remove the stabilizer center brackets, then lower the stabilizer bar and take it out.

7. Remove the nut from the damper fork bolt. Lower the jack beneath the lower control arm and remove the damper fork bolt.

8. Remove the cotter pin from the lower control arm's ball-joint stud. Loosen the nut half the length of the ball-joint stud threads. Loosen the ball-joint stud with a puller like the one shown in **Figure 39**, then remove the nut and separate the ball-joint stud from the knuckle.

9. Remove the lower control arm pivot bolt and take out the lower control arm.

10. Check all parts for wear or damage, especially rubber bushings. Replace as needed. Have lower control arm bushings pressed out and new ones pressed in by a machine shop.

11. Installation is the reverse of removal, plus the following:

   a. Install the lower control arm and install its pivot bolt loosely.

   b. Install the damper fork bolt and install its nut loosely.

   c. Position the ends of the stabilizer bar in the control arms. Install the end nuts and center bracket bolts loosely.

   d. Place a jack beneath the lower arm. Raise the lower jack just enough to lift the car off the jackstand on the side you are working on. Do not lift the car off the jackstand on the opposite side.

   e. Tighten all fasteners to specifications in **Table 4**, then lower the jack.

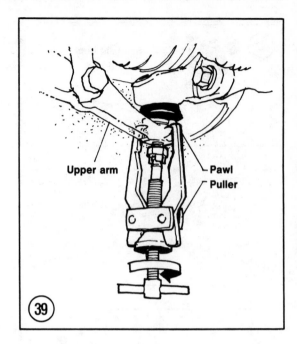

Upper arm — **Pawl** — **Puller**

㊴

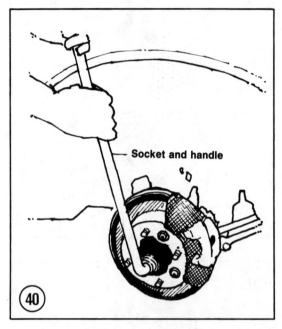

— **Socket and handle**

㊵

HUBS, KNUCKLES AND WHEEL BEARINGS

Wheel bearing replacement on all models requires disassembly of the hubs. This requires a hydraulic press and several special tools. The hubs and knuckles can be removed and installed by home mechanics, but disassembly and wheel bearing replacement should be done by a Honda dealer or machine shop.

(41)

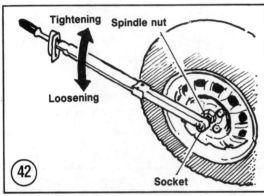

Tightening   Spindle nut

Loosening

(42)

Socket

Hub and Knuckle Removal/
Installation (1976-1981 Accord)

The hub and knuckle are removed as an assembly. The hub can be removed separately, but the wheel bearings must be replaced each time the hub is removed.

NOTE
The hub must be removed to remove the brake disc. Since hub removal requires replacement of the wheel bearings, have brake disc removal and installation done by a Honda dealer or machine shop.

1. Set the handbrake. Securely block both rear wheels so the car will not roll in either direction.

2. Loosen the front wheel nuts. Jack up the front end of the car, place it on jackstands and remove the front wheels.

WARNING
The nut mentioned in the next step is tightened to 150 N•m (108 ft.-lb.). Be sure the car is securely positioned on the jackstands. Do not pound on the breaker bar or the car may be knocked from the jackstands. At no time place any part of your body (including feet) under any part of the car.

3. Have an assistant press the brake pedal. Bend back the locktab on the spindle nut (**Figure 40**), then remove the nut with a breaker bar and 32 mm socket.

NOTE
A 1 1/4 in. socket will work if you don't have a 32 mm socket. Large sockets can sometimes be rented from tool rental dealers.

4. Remove the brake caliper as described in Chapter Twelve.
5. Remove the cotter pin and castle nut from the lower control arm ball-joint. Separate the ball-joint from the knuckle with a puller such as Honda tool part No. 07941-6710100 (**Figure 41**).
6. Remove the cotter pin and nut from the tie rod ball-joint, then separate the ball-joint from the steering knuckle with the tool shown in **Figure 41**.
7. Disconnect the strut from the knuckle as described under *Strut Removal/Installation* in this chapter.
8. With the shock absorber free of the knuckle, pull the hub/knuckle assembly outward and gently slide the drive shaft out of the end of the hub. Remove the hub/knuckle assembly.
9. Installation is the reverse of removal, plus the following:
    a. Use a new spindle nut.
    b. Tighten all fasteners to specifications in **Table 3**.
    c. Secure the new spindle nut with the locktab.
    d. Bleed the brakes as described in Chapter Twelve.

Hub and Knuckle
Removal/Installation
(1982-on Accord, All Prelude)

1. Set the handbrake. Securely block both rear wheels so the car will not roll in either direction.
2. Bend back the spindle nut locktab. Loosen the spindle nut with a breaker bar and 32 mm socket as shown in **Figure 42**.

10

3. Loosen the front wheel nuts. Jack up the front end of the car, place it on jackstands and remove the front wheels.

4. Remove the spindle nut.

5. Unbolt the brake caliper as described in Chapter Twelve. Tie the caliper out of the way. It is not necessary to disconnect the caliper brake hose.

6. Remove the brake disc retaining screws (**Figure 43**).

7. Thread 2 bolts (8×1.25 mm thread pattern, 12 mm minimum length) into the disc removal holes as shown in **Figure 43**. Tighten the bolts evenly to push the disc away from the hub, then take the disc off.

8. Remove the cotter pin and castle nut from the tie rod ball-joint. Separate the ball-joint stud from the tie rod with a puller such as the one shown in **Figure 44**.

9. Separate the lower ball-joint from the knuckle as follows:

  a. *1982-on Accord:* Remove the ball-joint pinch bolt and nut (**Figure 45**), then tap the knuckle downward with a brass or plastic hammer until the ball-joint stud separates from the knuckle.

  b. *1979-1982 Prelude:* Remove the cotter pin and castle nut from the ball-joint, then separate the ball-joint from the knuckle with a puller such as Honda tool part No. 07941-69200000 (**Figure 46**).

  c. *1983-on Prelude:* Remove the cotter pin from the ball-joint castle nut. Loosen the castle nut half the length of the ball-joint threads. Hook a puller to the lower arm as shown in **Figure 47**, pull the lower arm downward until it separates from the ball-joint stud, then remove the castle nut.

10. Remove the strut pinch bolt as described under *Strut Removal/Installation* in this chapter.

11. Tap the knuckle downward to free it from the shock absorber.

12. Gently pull the drive shaft out of the hub, then remove the hub and knuckle as an assembly.

13. Installation is the reverse of removal, plus the following:

  a. Install a new spindle nut and tighten it loosely.

  b. Tighten the strut pinch bolt as described under *Strut Removal/Installation* in this chapter.

  c. Tighten all fasteners except the spindle nut to specifications at the end of the chapter.

  d. Install the wheels and lower the car. Tighten the wheel nuts securely and tighten the spindle nut to specifications at the end of the chapter, with the car's weight resting on the wheels.

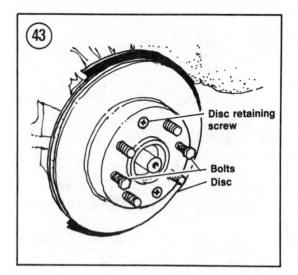

Disc retaining screw

Bolts

Disc

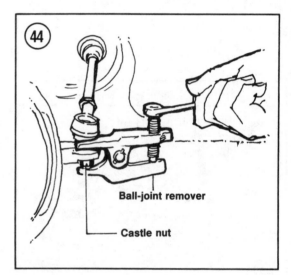

Ball-joint remover

Castle nut

Ball-joint nut

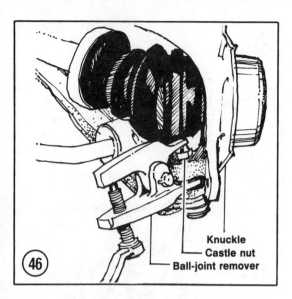

Knuckle
Castle nut
Ball-joint remover

(46)

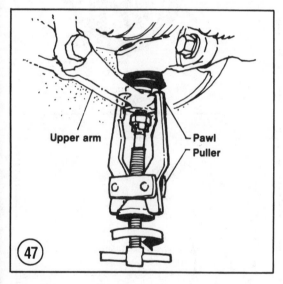

Upper arm
Pawl
Puller

(47)

(48)

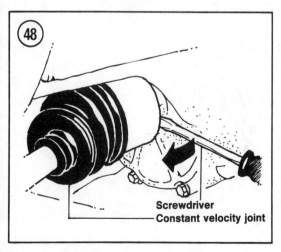

Screwdriver
Constant velocity joint

DRIVE AXLES

All models drive the front wheels with a pair of double-jointed drive axles. Constant velocity joints are used at each end of each drive axle. The following section provides removal and installation procedures for the axle shafts. Worn drive axles should be repaired by a Honda dealer or other qualified specialist.

Removal/Installation
(All Accord, 1979-1982 Prelude)

1A. *1976-1981 Accord:* Perform Steps 1-5 of *Hub and Knuckle Removal/Installation (1976-1981 Accord)* in this chapter.
1B. *1982-on Accord and all Prelude:* Perform Steps 1-9 of *Hub and Knuckle Removal/Installation (1982-on Accord and All Prelude)* in this chapter.

CAUTION
During the next step, do not pull on the shaft portion of the drive axle or you may pull the constant velocity joint apart.

2. Carefully pry the inboard end of the axle shaft out of the transaxle about 1/2 inch. See **Figure 48**. Grasp the metal part of the inboard constant velocity joint and pull it out of the transaxle.
3. Gently pull the knuckle away from the outboard end of the drive axle, then take the drive axle out.
4. Installation is the reverse of removal, plus the following:

   a. Use a new circlip on the inboard end of the drive axle.
   b. Push the drive axle in firmly so the circlip engages the differential (inside the transaxle).
   c. Use a new spindle nut on the outboard end of the drive axle.
   d. To tighten the spindle nut and front suspension fasteners, refer to the appropriate hub and knuckle installation procedure in this chapter.

Removal/Installation
(1983-on Prelude)

1. Set the handbrake. Securely block both rear wheels so the car will not roll in either direction.
2. Loosen the spindle nut with a 32 mm socket. See **Figure 49**.

NOTE
A 1 1/4 in. socket will work if you don't have a 32 mm socket. Large sockets can sometimes be rented from tool rental dealers.

10

3. Loosen the front wheel nuts. Jack up the front end of the car, place it on jackstands and remove the front wheels.

4. Drain the transaxle oil as described in Chapter Three.

5. Remove the damper fork bolt and damper fork lockbolt. See **Figure 50**.

6. Remove the cotter pin from the lower ball-joint's castle nut. Unscrew the nut half the length of the ball-joint stud's threads. Hook a puller to the lower arm as shown in **Figure 47** and pull the arm downward until it separates from the ball-joint stud. Remove the puller and castle nut, then pull the lower arm the rest of the way off the stud.

7. Pull the hub outward, off the outboard end of the drive axle.

8. Pry the inboard end of the drive axle approximately 1/2 in. out of the transaxle to free the retaining circlip. See **Figure 48**.

> *CAUTION*
> *Do not pull on the shaft of the drive axle during the next step or you may pull the constant velocity joint apart.*

9. Pull the drive axle out of the transaxle and take it out.

10. Installation is the reverse of removal, plus the following:

    a. Use a new spindle nut. Tighten the spindle nut to specifications after the front wheels have been installed and the car has been lowered to the ground.

    b. Fill the transaxle with an oil recommended in Chapter Three.

STEERING

The following sections provide removal and installation procedures for the steering wheel, non-power steering gear and power steering pump. Other procedures require special skills and tools and should be left to a Honda dealer or other qualified specialist.

Steering Wheel
Removal/Installation

Refer to the following illustrations:

    a. **Figure 51**—1976-1981 Accord.

    b. **Figure 52**—1982-on Accord, 1979-1982 Prelude (typical).

    c. **Figure 53**—1983-on Prelude.

1. Make sure the front wheels are in the straight-ahead position.

2. Disconnect the negative cable from the battery.

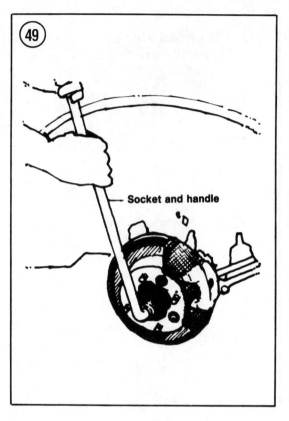

(49)

— Socket and handle

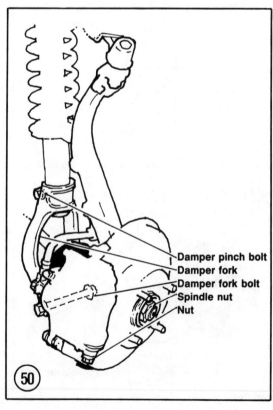

(50)

Damper pinch bolt
Damper fork
Damper fork bolt
Spindle nut
Nut

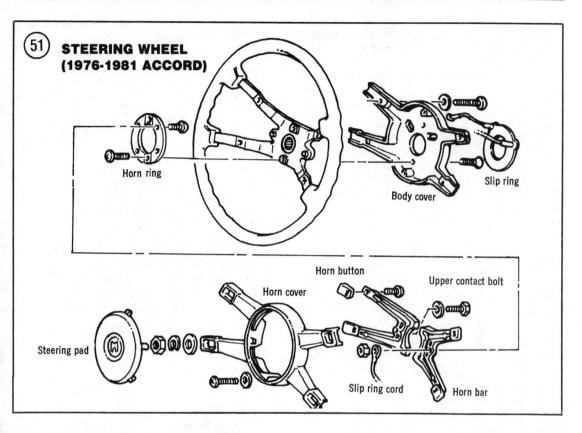

(51) **STEERING WHEEL (1976-1981 ACCORD)**

Horn ring

Body cover

Slip ring

Horn button

Horn cover

Upper contact bolt

Steering pad

Slip ring cord

Horn bar

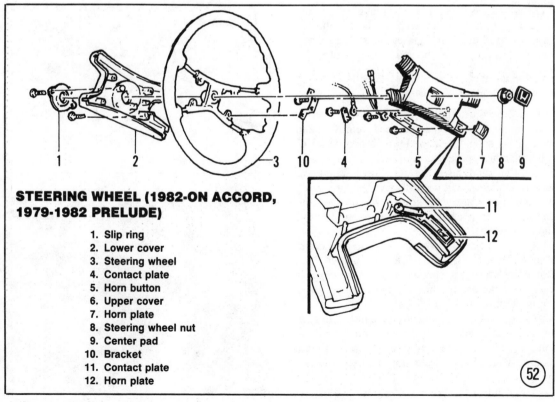

STEERING WHEEL (1982-ON ACCORD, 1979-1982 PRELUDE)

1. Slip ring
2. Lower cover
3. Steering wheel
4. Contact plate
5. Horn button
6. Upper cover
7. Horn plate
8. Steering wheel nut
9. Center pad
10. Bracket
11. Contact plate
12. Horn plate

10

(52)

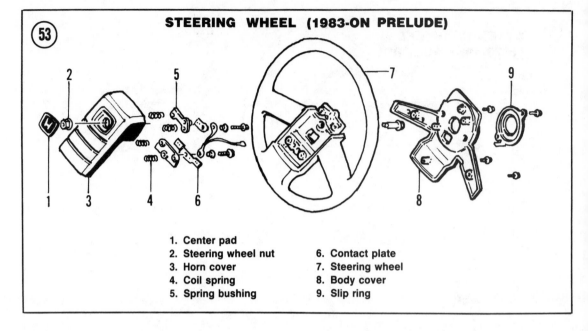

STEERING WHEEL (1983-ON PRELUDE)

1. Center pad
2. Steering wheel nut
3. Horn cover
4. Coil spring
5. Spring bushing
6. Contact plate
7. Steering wheel
8. Body cover
9. Slip ring

3. Remove the pad from the center of the steering wheel.

4. Remove the steering wheel nut.

5. Pull the steering wheel off. Rock it gently from side to side while pulling to free it from the column.

6. Installation is the reverse of removal. Make sure the front wheels and the steering wheel are in the straight-ahead position. Tighten the steering wheel nut to specifications at the end of the chapter.

Steering Gear
Removal/Installation (Accord)

This procedure applies to non-power steering gears only. Power steering gear removal and installation should be done by a Honda dealer or other qualified specialist.

1. Set the handbrake. Securely block both rear wheels so the car will not roll in either direction.

2. Loosen the front wheel nuts. Jack up the front end of the car, place it on jackstands and remove the front wheels.

3. Attach a hoist to the engine as described under *Engine Removal,* Chapter Four or Chapter Five. Raise the hoist just enough to take the engine's weight off the engine mounts, but not enough to strain the mounts or to lift the car.

4. Remove the cotter pin and castle nut from each tie rod end. Detach the tie rod ends from the knuckles with a tie rod puller as shown in **Figure 54**. See your Honda dealer for the exact tie rod puller for your car. A number of pullers have been used, depending on model year.

5. On all except 1981 models, disconnect the exhaust pipe from the manifold.

6. *Manual transaxle models:* On 1976-1978 models, drive the pin out of the gearshift rod (**Figure 55**). On 1979 and later models, shift the transaxle into low or third gear and remove the shift rod yoke bolt (**Figure 56**). On all models, disconnect the shift lever torque arm from the transaxle (**Figure 57**).

7. Unbolt the center beam (**Figure 58**) from the crossmembers. Take the center beam out.

8. *1976-1980 automatic transaxle models:* Remove the engine center mount. Unbolt the transaxle splash guard (**Figure 59**) from the transaxle and remove it. Then disconnect the shift cable (**Figure 60**).

NOTE
The bolt mentioned in the next step must be removed, not just loosened.

9. Remove the pinch bolt that secures the bottom universal joint to the pinion shaft, then disconnect the joint. See **Figure 61**.

10A. *1976-1980:* Remove the steering gear mounting bolts (**Figure 61**). Turn the steering wheel all the way to the left. Lower the rack until the pinion shaft is clear of the body. Rotate the rack until the pinion shaft is facing down. Move the rack to the right until the left tie rod is clear and remove the rack assembly through the left side.

10B. *1981-on:* Push the rack all the way to the right (the full left turn position). Remove the rack mounting bolts (**Figure 61**). Lower the rack until the pinion shaft clears the body. Rotate the rack forward until the pinion shaft comes around and points to the rear. Move the gearbox to the right until the left tie rod is clear of the body. Lower the gearbox and take it out through the left side of the car.

10

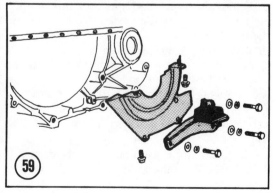

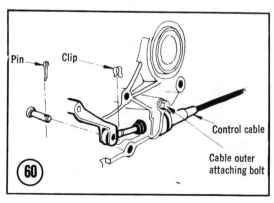

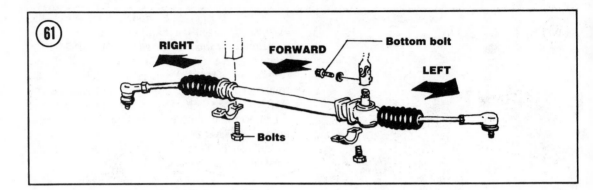

61

RIGHT

FORWARD

Bottom bolt

LEFT

Bolts

11. Installation is the reverse of removal. Tighten all fasteners to specifications at the end of the chapter. Use new cotter pins in the tie rod ends.

Steering Gear Removal/ Installation (1979-1982 Prelude)

This procedure applies to non-power steering models only. Removal of the steering gear on models equipped with power steering requires special tools and should be done by a Honda dealer or other qualified specialist.

Refer to **Figure 61** for this procedure.

1. Set the handbrake. Securely block both rear wheels so the car will not roll in either direction.
2. Loosen the front wheel nuts. Jack up the front end of the car, place it on jackstands and remove the front wheels.
3. Remove the cotter pin from each tie rod end. Loosen the tie rod castle nut halfway along the tie rod stud. Push the tie rod stud loose from the knuckle with Honda ball-joint remover part No. 07941-69200000 (**Figure 62**). Remove the tool and castle nut, then separate the tie rod stud from the knuckle.
4. Remove the pinch bolt attaching the bottom universal joint to the pinion shaft. See **Figure 61**.
5. Lower the steering gear straight downward until the pinion shaft separates from the bottom universal joint. Rotate the steering gear 180°, so the pinion shaft points straight down, then pull the steering gear out through the left side.
6. Installation is the reverse of removal, plus the following:
   a. Tighten all fasteners to specifications at the end of the chapter.
   b. Use new cotter pins in the tie rod studs.

Steering Gear Removal/ Installation (1983-on Prelude)

This procedure applies to non-power steering gears only. Power steering gear removal and

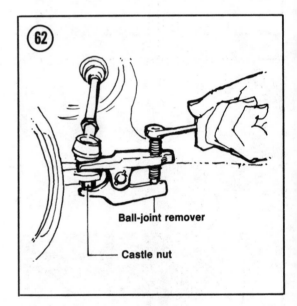

62

Ball-joint remover

Castle nut

installation should be done by a Honda dealer or other qualified specialist.

Refer to **Figure 63** for this procedure.

1. Set the handbrake. Securely block both rear wheels so the car will not roll in either direction.
2. Working inside the car, remove the bottom bolt from the steering shaft connector. See **Figure 64**. Pull the connector off the pinion shaft.
3. Loosen the front wheel nuts. Jack up the front end of the car, place it on jackstands and remove the front wheels.
4. Remove the cotter pin from each tie rod end. Loosen the tie rod castle nut halfway along the tie rod stud. Push the tie rod stud loose from the knuckle with Honda ball-joint remover part No. 07941-69200001 (**Figure 62**). Remove the tool and castle nut, then separate the tie rod stud from the knuckle.
5. Disconnect the exhaust pipe from the manifold. Disconnect the exhaust pipe bracket from the engine.

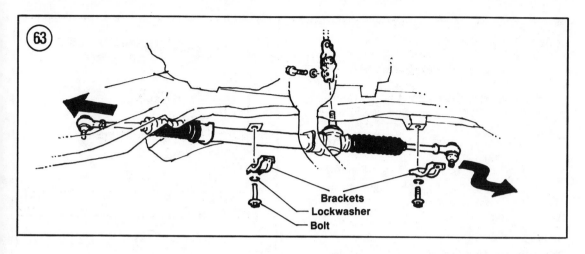

Brackets
Lockwasher
Bolt

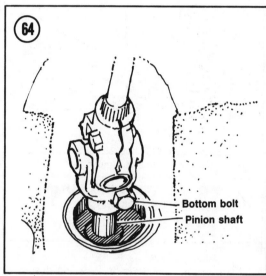

Bottom bolt
Pinion shaft

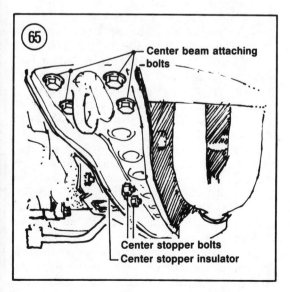

Center beam attaching bolts

Center stopper bolts
Center stopper insulator

6. Unbolt the center beam from the crossmembers. See **Figure 65** and **Figure 66**. Take the center beam out.

7A. *Manual transaxle:* Detach the shift rod and extension from the transaxle. See **Figure 67**.

7B. *Automatic transaxle:* Detach the shift cable guide from the floor, then pull the shift cable down by hand.

8. Move the rack all the way to the right (the full left turn position). Remove the steering gear mounting bolts and brackets (**Figure 63**).

9. Lower the rack until the pinion shaft clears the body. Rotate the rack forward until the pinion shaft comes around and points to the rear. Move the gearbox to the right until the left tie rod is clear of the exhaust pipe, then lower the gearbox and take it out through the left side of the car.

10. Installation is the reverse of removal. Tighten all fasteners to specifications at the end of the chapter. Use new cotter pins in the tie rod ends.

POWER STEERING

Fluid Check

Fluid level in the power steering reservoir should be checked at the intervals specified in Chapter Three. On 1976-1981 Accords and 1979-1982 Preludes, check level on the reservoir dipstick. On 1982-on Accords and 1983-on Preludes, make sure fluid level is up to the upper line on the reservoir.

If the fluid level is low, add only genuine Honda power steering fluid. Honda states that the use of automatic transmission fluid or other brands of power steering fluid will damage the power steering system.

Belt Adjustment

To check belt tension, push down on the power steering pump belt midway between pulleys with

10

an approximate force of 10 kg (22 lb.). A properly adjusted belt should deflect as follows:

   a. 1976-1981 Accord—12-14 mm (9/16 in.).

   b. 1982-on Accord, all Prelude—18-22 mm (3/4-7/8 in.).

To adjust belt tension, loosen the adjusting bolt and pivot bolt. Refer to the following illustrations:

   a. 1976-1981 Accord (**Figure 68**).

   b. 1982-1983 Accord, 1981-1982 Prelude (**Figure 69**).

   c. 1984 Accord, 1983-on Prelude—**Figure 70**).

Pull the pump away from the engine to tighten the belt or push it toward the engine to loosen. When tension is set properly, tighten the adjusting bolt and pivot bolt.

Pump Removal/Installation

Refer to the following illustrations:

   a. 1976-1981 Accord (**Figure 68**).

   b. 1982-1983 Accord, 1981-1982 Prelude (**Figure 69**).

   c. 1984 Accord, 1983-on Prelude (**Figure 70**).

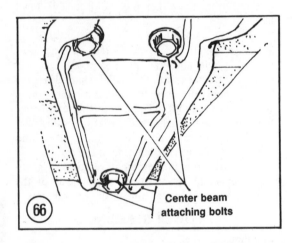

Center beam attaching bolts

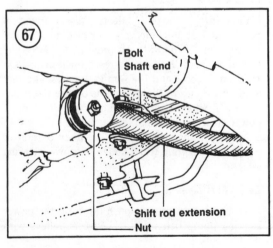

Bolt
Shaft end
Shift rod extension
Nut

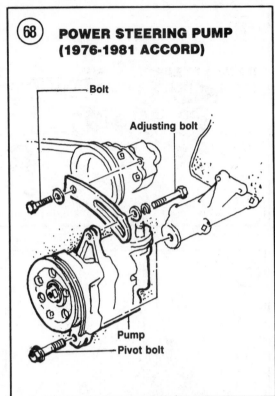

POWER STEERING PUMP (1976-1981 ACCORD)

Bolt
Adjusting bolt
Pump
Pivot bolt

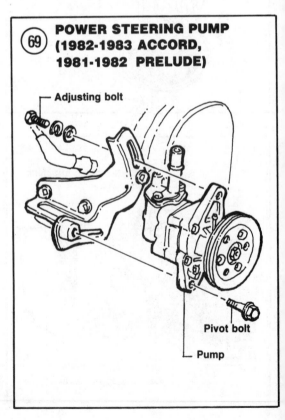

POWER STEERING PUMP (1982-1983 ACCORD, 1981-1982 PRELUDE)

Adjusting bolt
Pivot bolt
Pump

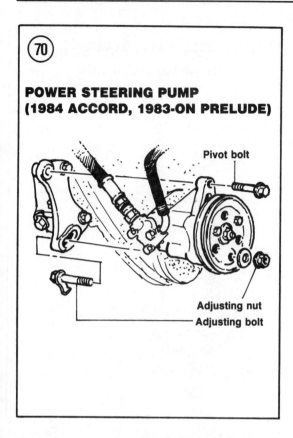

**POWER STEERING PUMP
(1984 ACCORD, 1983-ON PRELUDE)**

Pivot bolt

Adjusting nut

Adjusting bolt

1. Disconnect the fluid return hose at the reservoir. See **Figure 71** (1976-1981 Accord and 1979-1982 Prelude) or **Figure 72** (1982-on Accord, 1983-on Prelude). Put the end of the hose in a container.

2. Have an assistant start the engine and run it at a fast idle. Turn the steering wheel from left to right several times to force fluid out of the hose into the container. When the fluid stops flowing out of the hose, turn the engine off. Uncap the fitting and reconnect the hose to the reservoir.

3. Loosen the pump adjusting and pivot bolts as described under *Drive Belt Adjustment* in this chapter. Push the pump toward the engine to loosen the belt, then take it off.

4. Label and disconnect the fluid hoses at the pump.

5. Remove the pump adjusting and pivot bolts, then take the pump off.

6. Installation is the reverse of removal, plus the following:

   a. Fill the fluid reservoir to the "FULL" mark on the dipstick or to the upper level line on the reservoir. Use only genuine Honda power steering fluid. Do not use automatic transmission fluid or any other brand of power steering fluid.

   b. Adjust drive belt tension as described in this chapter.

   c. Start the engine and turn the steering wheel from side to side to bleed air out of the power steering system.

   d. Check power steering fluid level as described in this chapter. Top up as needed, but do not overfill.

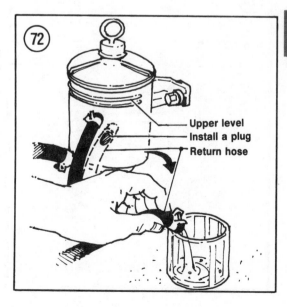

Upper level

Install a plug

Return hose

10

**Fluid and Filter Replacement
(1976-1981 Accord, 1979-1982 Prelude)**

The power steering fluid and filter should be changed whenever the system is repaired or if the fluid is contaminated with dirt or water.

1. Disconnect the fluid return hose at the pump. See **Figure 71**. Put the end of the hose in a container.

2. Have an assistant start the engine and run it at a fast idle. Turn the steering wheel from left to right several times to force fluid out of the hose into the container. When the fluid stops flowing out, turn the engine off.

3. Fill the reservoir to the "FULL" mark on the dipstick with genuine Honda power steering fluid (do not use any other fluid) and repeat Step 2 to flush the system.

4. Label and disconnect the remaining hoses at the reservoir. See **Figure 71**. Remove the reservoir retaining bolt and take the reservoir off.

5. Loosen the reservoir center guide bolt with a 12 mm socket. See **Figure 73**. When the bolt is free, remove it from the reservoir together with the filter assembly.

6. Remove the clip at the bottom of the guide bolt (**Figure 74**) and disassemble the filter assembly. Discard the filter.

7. Check all seals for deterioration and distortion. Also check the springs for weakness. Replace as needed.

8. Using a new filter, install the assembly onto the guide bolt in the order shown in **Figure 74**. Be sure

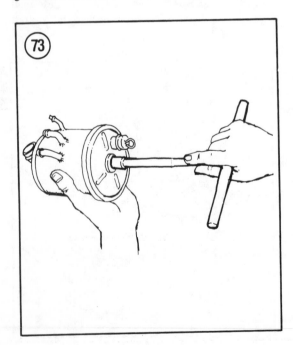

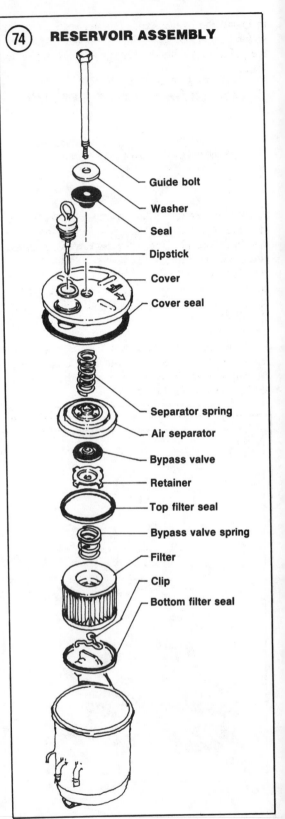

RESERVOIR ASSEMBLY

Guide bolt
Washer
Seal
Dipstick
Cover
Cover seal
Separator spring
Air separator
Bypass valve
Retainer
Top filter seal
Bypass valve spring
Filter
Clip
Bottom filter seal

to install the bypass valve retainer with the arms facing toward the filter. Secure the assembly onto the guide bolt with the bottom clip as shown in **Figure 75**.

> *CAUTION*
> *The top filter seal must seat evenly under the air/oil outer edge or fluid will bypass the filter.*

9. Place the bottom filter seal in the reservoir and seat evenly all the way around. Install the guide bolt/filter assembly into the reservoir. Tighten the guide bolt until the bolt bottoms.

10. Reinstall the reservoir in the car and secure it with the retaining bolt. Connect the hoses to the reservoir. Fill the reservoir to the "FULL" mark on the dipstick, using only genuine Honda power steering fluid.

11. Start the engine and turn the steering wheel from side to side to bleed air out of the power steering system. As required, top up the reservoir to the dipstick "FULL" mark.

Fluid Replacement
(1982-on Accord, 1983-on Prelude

1. Disconnect the fluid return hose from the reservoir and put the end in a container. Cap the opened fitting as shown in **Figure 72**.

2. Start the engine and let it idle. Turn the steering wheel from lock to lock several times to force fluid out of the hose. When fluid stops flowing, turn off the engine.

> *NOTE*
> *If water or dirt in the fluid has contaminated the filter inside the fluid reservoir, replace the reservoir and filter as an assembly.*

3. Uncap the fitting and reconnect the hose to the reservoir.

4. Fill the reservoir to the upper mark with genuine Honda power steering fluid. Do not use automatic transmission fluid or any other brand of power steering fluid.

5. Start the engine and run it at a fast idle. Turn the steering wheel from lock to lock several times to bleed air from the system.

6. Recheck the fluid level and top up as needed. Do not overfill.

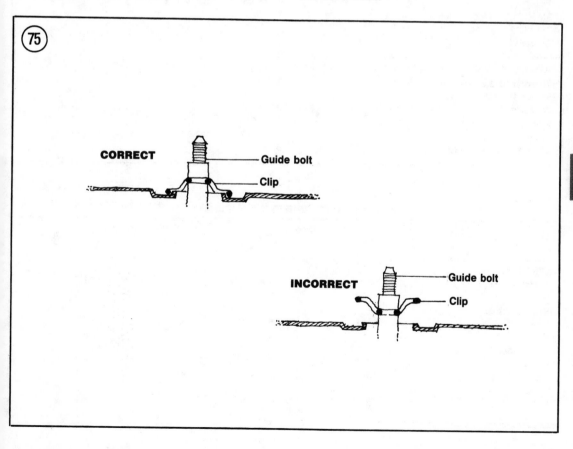

75

CORRECT — Guide bolt — Clip

INCORRECT — Guide bolt — Clip

10

Table 1 WHEEL ALIGNMENT SPECIFICATIONS

1976-1977	
Caster	1° 50'
Camber	0° 40'
Toe-out	1 mm (1/32 in.)
Steering axis inclination	12° 10'
1978	
Caster	2°
Camber	0.75°
Toe-out	1 mm (1/32 in.)
Steering axis inclination	12° 10'
1979-1981 Accord	
Caster	1° 20'
Camber	
1979	0° 40'
1980	0° 20'
1981	0° 40'
Toe-out	1 mm (1/32 in.)
Steering axis inclination (1979)	12° 10'
Steering axis inclination (1980-1981)	12° 30'
1982-1983 Accord	
Caster	1° 25'
Camber	0°
Toe-out	0 mm (0 in.)
Steering axis inclination	12° 30'
1984 Accord	
Caster	1° 25' ±1°
Camber	0°
Toe-in	0 ±3 mm (0 ±0.012 in.)
Steering axis inclination	12° 30'
1979-1982 Prelude	
Caster	1° 30'
Camber	0°
Toe-out	0 mm
Steering axis inclination	12° 50'
1983-on Prelude	
Caster	0° ±30'
Camber	0° ±1°
Toe-in	0 ±3 mm (0 ±0.12 in.)
Steering axis inclination	6° 51'

Table 2 SPRING HEIGHT SPECIFICATIONS

Model	Standard		Service limit	
	mm	in.	mm	in.
1976-1978				
Front	625	24.6	610	24.0
Rear	660	26	645	25.4
1979 hatchback				
Front	637	25	622	24.4
Rear	667	26.2	652	25.6
1979 4-door				
Front	632	24.8	617	24.2
Rear	662	26	647	25.4

(continued)

Table 2 SPRING HEIGHT SPECIFICATIONS (continued)

Model	Standard		Service limit	
	mm	in.	mm	in.
1980-1981 Accord hatchback standard				
Front	666	26.2	651	25.6
Rear	618	24.3	603	23.7
1980-1981 Accord hatchback LX				
Front	654	25.7	639	24.2
Rear	618	24.3	603	23.7
1980-1981 Accord 4-door				
Front	661	26	646	25.4
Rear	618	24.3	603	23.7
1982-1983 Accord hatchback				
Front	673	26.5	658	25.9
Rear	654	25.7	639	25.2
1982-1983 Accord 4-door				
Front	672	26.5	657	25.9
Rear	651	25.6	636	25.0
1984 Accord				
Front	675	26.6	655	25.8
Rear	652	25.7	637	25.1
1979-1982 Prelude				
Front	635	25	620	25.37
Rear	630	24.826	615	24.25
1983-on Prelude				
Front	665	26.2	650	25.6
Rear	657	25.8	642	25.3

Table 3 TIGHTENING TORQUES (ACCORD)

Part	N•m	ft.lb
1976-1978		
Hub nut	12-18 mkg	87-130
Radius rod to frame	40-48	29-34
Radius rod to lower arm	50-60	36-43
Stabilizer bar	19-25	14-18
Lower arm ball-joint	40-50	29-36
Front brake caliper	50-60	36-43
Wheel hub to disc	50-60	36-43
Lower arm pivot bolt	35-50	25-36
Knuckle to shock absorber	60-70	43-51
Upper shock mounting	27-35	20-25
1979-1981		
Hub nut	15 mkg	110
Radius rod to frame*	44	32
Radius rod to lower arm	55	40
Stabilizer bar (all)	22	16
Lower arm ball-joint	45	33
Front brake caliper	55	40
Wheel hub to disc	55	40
Lower arm pivot bolt	50	36
Knuckle to shock absorber	65	47
Upper shock mounting	31	22

10

(continued)

Table 3 TIGHTENING TORQUES (ACCORD) (continued)

Part	N•m	ft.-lb.
1982-on		
Hub nut	190	137
Radius rod to frame	44	32
Radius rod to lower arm	55	40
Stabilizer bar (all)	22	16
Lower arm ball-joint	55	40
Front brake caliper		
Mounting bolts	78	56
Guide bolts	27	20
Lower arm to knuckle	55	40
Lower arm pivot bolt	50	36
Knuckle to shock absorber	65	47
Upper shock mounting	39	28

* Always replace this nut. Do not reuse the old nut.

Table 4 TIGHTENING TORQUES (PRELUDE)

Part	N•m	ft.-lb.
1979-1982		
Hub nut	150	108
Lower arm to knuckle	45	33
Stabilizer bar to lower arm	44	32
Stabilizer bar bracket nuts	39	28
Stabilizer bar lateral stop		
(1982 only)	42	30
Lower arm pivot bolt	55	40
Shock absorber pinch bolt	65	47
Shock absorber upper nut		
1979-1982	45	33
1983-on		
Shock absorber upper nuts	40	29
Shock absorber pinch bolt	44	32
Damper fork bolt	65	47
Upper suspension arm to frame	83	60
Upper suspension arm pivot	55	40
Upper ball-joint to suspension arm	55	40
Upper ball-joint to knuckle		
Castle nut	44	32
Shield bolt	18	13
Lower ball-joint castle nut	55	40
Caliper bracket bolts	78	56
Caliper lower pin bolt	18	13
Radius rod to frame	44	32
Lower arm pivot bolt	44	32
Spindle nut		
1983	190	137
1984	185	134

REAR SUSPENSION

The Accord and Prelude use a MacPherson strut rear suspension. The shock absorbers and springs are combined into single units. The struts are attached to the body at the top and to the hub carriers at the bottom.

The hub carriers are attached to the outer ends of the suspension arms. The inner ends of the suspension arms are attached to the body.

Front-rear movement of the suspension arms is controlled by radius rods or radius arms. On Preludes and 1984 Accord hatchbacks, body lean is controlled by a stabilizer bar.

Table 1 is at the end of the chapter.

CAUTION
*All fasteners used in the rear suspension must be replaced with parts of the same type. Do **not** use a replacement part of lesser quality or substitute design, as it may affect the performance of vital components and systems or result in major repair expenses.*

NOTE
Many of the fasteners used in the rear suspension are self-locking, i.e., the fastener has some type of locking feature built into the threads. When installing a self-locking bolt or nut, it should not turn freely on the mating thread. A wrench or socket will be required to remove and tighten the fastener. The self-locking design prevents the fastener from working loose due to vibration during vehicle operation. If a self-locking fastener can be threaded easily, it should be replaced.

SUSPENSION STRUTS

The suspension struts must be removed to replace rear shock absorbers or coil springs. While the struts can be removed and installed by home mechanics, the disassembly necessary to replace shock absorbers or springs requires special tools and skills. Part of the expense can be saved by removing the strut assemblies yourself and taking them to a dealer for service.

NOTE
Before removing the struts, check with local shops to find out how much of the labor charge will be saved by removing them yourself. It may be more practical to take the car to a shop and have the whole job done there.

11

**Strut Removal/Installation
(1976-1981 Accord)**

1. Place the transaxle in FIRST (manual) or PARK (automatic). Securely block both front wheels so the car will not roll in either direction.
2. Loosen the rear wheel nuts. Jack up the rear end of the car, place it on jackstands and remove the rear wheels.
3. Disconnect the metal brake line from the brake hose at the strut. See **Figure 1**. Use a flare nut wrench to unscrew the nut. These are available inexpensively from auto parts stores. Pull out the brake hose clip and detach the brake hose from the bracket on the strut.

> *CAUTION*
> *Immediately cap the disconnected line and hose to keep dirt out. Plastic vacuum caps, available from auto parts stores, work well for this.*

4. Disconnect the handbrake cable from the arm on the backing plate. See **Figure 2**.
5. Remove the shock mounting bolt from the bottom bracket. See **Figure 3**.
6. Remove the cotter pin from the castle nut on the hub carrier bolt. See **Figure 4**. Support the hub carrier with a jack, then remove the nut and bolt. Lower the carrier with the jack and let it hang on the radius rod.

> *NOTE*
> *Have an assistant support the strut during the next steps.*

7. Remove the rear interior panels to gain access to the strut upper mounting nuts.

> *WARNING*
> *During the next step, do not remove the center nut from the top of the strut. This could allow the coil spring to fly out and cause serious injury.*

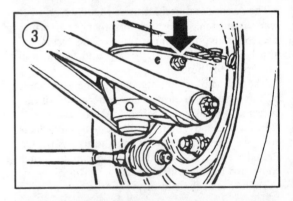

8. Remove the strut upper mounting nuts. Lower the strut and take it out from under the car.
9. Take the strut assembly to a Honda dealer or other qualified specialist for disassembly and inspection.
10. Installation is the reverse of removal, plus the following:
   a. Be sure the bottom end of the strut mates properly with the hub carrier as shown in **Figure 5**.
   b. Tighten all nuts and bolts to specifications in **Table 1**.
   c. Use a new cotter pin to secure the castle nut and hub carrier bolt.

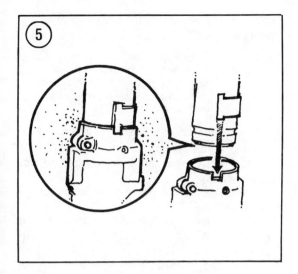

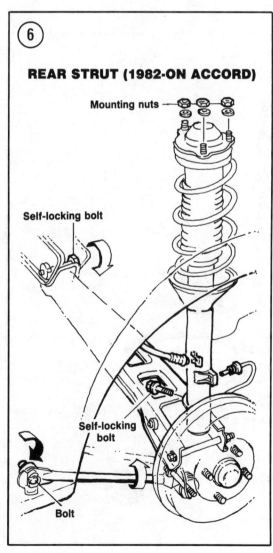

REAR STRUT (1982-ON ACCORD)

Mounting nuts

Self-locking bolt

Self-locking bolt

Bolt

d. Bleed the brakes and adjust the handbrake as described in Chapter Twelve.

Strut Removal/Installation
(1982-on Accord)

Refer to **Figure 6** for this procedure.
1. Place the transaxle in FIRST (manual) or PARK (automatic). Securely block both front wheels so the car will not roll in either direction.
2. Loosen the rear wheel nuts. Jack up the rear end of the car, place it on jackstands and remove the rear wheels.
3. Disconnect the metal brake line from the brake hose at the strut. See **Figure 6**. Use a flare nut wrench to unscrew the nut. These are available inexpensively from auto parts stores. Pull out the brake hose clip and detach the brake hose from the bracket on the strut.

> *CAUTION*
> *Immediately cap the disconnected line and hose to keep dirt out. Plastic vacuum caps, available from auto parts stores, work well for this.*

4. Loosen, but do not remove, the nut at the front end of the radius rod.
5. Loosen, but do not remove, the nut and bolt at the inboard end of the suspension arm.
6. Remove the brake drum as described under *Hubs and Wheel Bearings* in this chapter.
7. Disconnect the handbrake cable from the rear brake assembly.
8. Support the hub carrier with a jack. Remove the self-locking bolt that secures the strut to the hub carrier.

> *WARNING*
> *During the next step, do not remove the center nuts at the top of the strut. This could allow the coil spring to fly out and cause serious injury.*

9. Remove the strut upper mounting nuts. Detach the strut from the hub carrier, lower the strut and take it out from under the car.
10. Take the strut to a Honda dealer or other qualified specialist for disassembly and inspection.
11. Installation is the reverse of removal, plus the following:
   a. Align the tab on the strut with the slot in the hub carrier as shown in **Figure 5**.
   b. Raise the jack beneath the hub just enough so the car is lifted off the jackstand on the side nearest you. Tighten all nuts and bolts to specifications in **Table 1**, then lower the car so its weight is resting on the jackstand again.

11

c. Install the brake drum as described under *Hubs and Wheel Bearings* in this chapter.

d. Bleed the brakes as described in Chapter Twelve.

Removal/Installation (1979-1982 Prelude)

Refer to **Figure 7** for this procedure.

1. Place the transaxle in FIRST (manual) or PARK (automatic). Securely block both front wheels so the car will not roll in either direction.

2. Loosen the rear wheel nuts. Jack up the rear end of the car, place it on jackstands and remove the rear wheels.

3. Disconnect the metal brake line from the brake hose at the strut. See **Figure 7**. Use a flare nut wrench to unscrew the nut. These are available inexpensively from auto parts stores. Pull out the brake hose clip and detach the brake hose from the bracket on the strut.

> *CAUTION*
> *Immediately cap the disconnected line and hose to keep dirt out. Plastic vacuum caps, available from auto parts stores, work well for this.*

4. Remove the brake drum as described under *Hubs and Wheel Bearings* in this chapter.

5. Disconnect the handbrake cable from the rear brake assembly.

6. Loosen, but do not remove, the lower control arm inboard bolt.

7. Loosen and remove the stabilizer bar connecting link bolt at the underside of the radius arm.

8. Loosen the forward radius arm bolt. Do not remove the bolt.

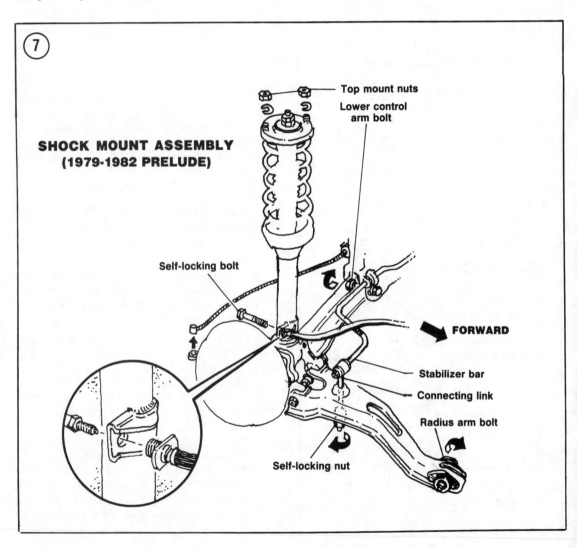

SHOCK MOUNT ASSEMBLY (1979-1982 PRELUDE)

Top mount nuts
Lower control arm bolt
Self-locking bolt
FORWARD
Stabilizer bar
Connecting link
Radius arm bolt
Self-locking nut

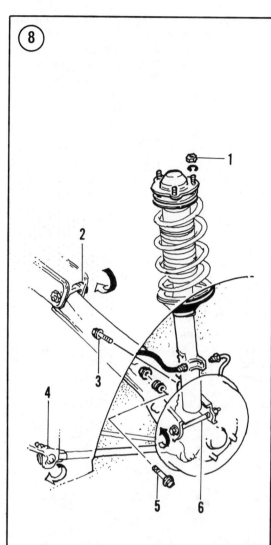

REAR STRUT (1983-ON PRELUDE)

1. Mounting nuts
2. Suspension arm pivot bolt
3. Strut lockbolt
4. Radius rod nut
5. Stabilizer attaching bolt
6. Hub carrier bolt

9. Remove the strut mounting bolt at the hub carrier. Discard the bolt.

NOTE
Support the strut with a jack during the next step.

10. Remove the rear interior panels. Unscrew the upper mounting nuts from the strut, then separate the strut from the hub carrier and take it out.
11. Take the strut assembly to a Honda dealer or other qualified specialist for disassembly and inspection.
12. Installation is the reverse of removal, plus the following:
   a. Be sure the tab on the strut aligns with the slot in the hub carrier as shown in **Figure 5**.
   b. Use a new strut mounting bolt at the hub carrier.
   c. Raise the jack beneath the hub carrier just enough so the car is raised off the jackstand on the side nearest you. Tighten the suspension arm inboard pivot bolt and forward radius arm bolt to specificiations in **Table 1**, then lower the car back onto the jackstand.
   d. Tighten all nuts and bolts to specifications in **Table 1**.
   e. Install the brake drum as described under *Hubs and Wheel Bearings* in this chapter.
   f. Bleed the brakes as described in Chapter Twelve.

Removal/Installation
(1983-on Prelude)

Refer to **Figure 8** for this procedure.
1. Place the transaxle in FIRST (manual) or PARK (automatic). Securely block both front wheels so the car will not roll in either direction.
2. Loosen the rear wheel nuts. Jack up the rear end of the car, place it on jackstands and remove the rear wheels.
3. Disconnect the metal brake line from the brake hose at the strut. See **Figure 8**. Use a flare nut wrench to unscrew the nut. These are available inexpensively from auto parts stores. Pull out the brake hose clip and detach the brake hose from the bracket on the strut.

CAUTION
Immediately cap the disconnected line and hose to keep dirt out. Plastic vacuum caps, available from auto parts stores, work well for this.

4. Remove the brake drum as described under *Hubs and Wheel Bearings* in this chapter.

11

5. Disconnect the handbrake cable from the rear brake assembly.

6. Detach the stabilizer bar from the suspension arm.

7. Loosen, but do not remove, the suspension arm pivot bolt.

8. Loosen, but do not remove, the radius rod nut.

9. Loosen, but do not remove, the hub carrier bolt.

10. Remove the strut lockbolt. Detach the bottom end of the strut from the hub carrier.

> *WARNING*
> *Do not remove the center nuts at the top of the strut. This could allow the coil spring to fly out and cause serious injury.*

11. Remove the mounting nuts at the top of the strut. Lower the strut and take it out from under the car.

12. Take the strut to a Honda dealer or other qualified specialist for strut disassembly and inspection.

13. Installation is the reverse of removal, plus the following:

a. Be sure the tab on the strut aligns with the slot in the hub carrier as shown in **Figure 5**.

b. Raise the jack beneath the hub carrier just enough so the car lifts off the jackstand on the side nearest you. Tighten the suspension arm bolt to specifications in **Table 1**. Install the stabilizer bar, then tighten the radius rod bolt to specifications in **Table 1**. Lower the car back onto the jackstand.

c. Tighten all remaining nuts and bolts to specifications in **Table 1**.

d. Install the brake drum as described under *Hubs and Wheel Bearings* in this chapter.

e. Bleed the brakes as described in Chapter Twelve.

SUSPENSION ARMS/ RADIUS RODS

Removal/Installation (1976-1981 Accord)

Refer to **Figure 9** for this procedure.

1. Place the transaxle in FIRST (manual) or PARK (automatic). Securely block both front wheels so the car will not roll in either direction.

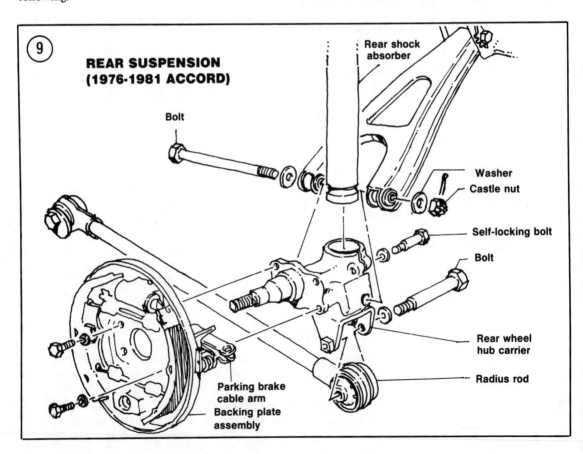

REAR SUSPENSION (1976-1981 ACCORD)

- Bolt
- Rear shock absorber
- Washer
- Castle nut
- Self-locking bolt
- Bolt
- Rear wheel hub carrier
- Radius rod
- Parking brake cable arm
- Backing plate assembly

2. Loosen the rear wheel nuts. Jack up the rear end of the car, place it on jackstands and remove the rear wheels.

3. Remove the brake drum as described under *Hubs and Wheel Bearings* in this chapter.

4. Disconnect the metal brake line from the brake hose at the strut. See **Figure 1**. Use a flare nut wrench to unscrew the nut. These are available inexpensively from auto parts stores. Pull out the brake hose clip and detach the brake hose from the bracket on the strut.

CAUTION

Immediately cap the disconnected line and hose to keep dirt out. Plastic vacuum caps, available from auto parts stores, work well for this.

5. Disconnect the handbrake cable from the arm on the backing plate. See **Figure 2**.

6. Remove the backing plate mounting bolts. Take off the backing plate, together with the assembled rear brake components.

7. Remove the cotter pin securing the lower arm castle nut (**Figure 4**). Remove the castle nut and washer.

8. Remove the lower arm pivot bolt and separate the lower arm from the hub carrier. If the lower arm is to be removed completely, remove the self-locking bolt and nut that secure the inboard end of the lower arm to the frame. Then take the lower arm out.

9. Remove the bolts from front and rear ends of the radius rod, then take the radius rod out.

10. Check all parts for wear or damage. Replace worn or damaged parts.

11. Check bushings for melting, cracks, wear or deterioration. See **Figure 10**. Have a machine shop replace bushings that show these conditions.

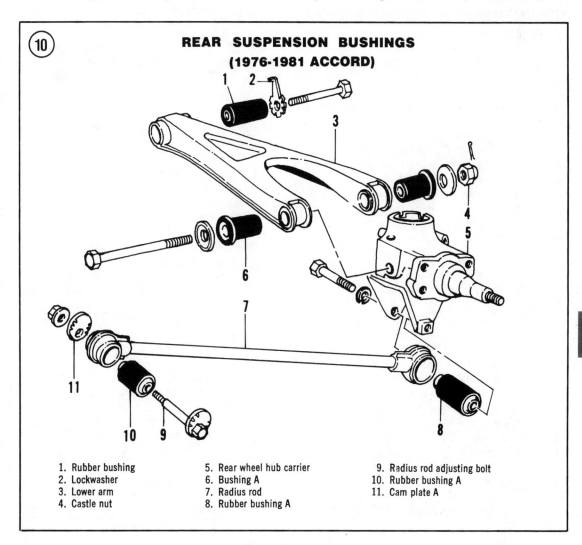

REAR SUSPENSION BUSHINGS (1976-1981 ACCORD)

1. Rubber bushing
2. Lockwasher
3. Lower arm
4. Castle nut
5. Rear wheel hub carrier
6. Bushing A
7. Radius rod
8. Rubber bushing A
9. Radius rod adjusting bolt
10. Rubber bushing A
11. Cam plate A

11

12. Installation is the reverse of removal, plus the following:

   a. Install all parts and tighten the fasteners slightly. Do not tighten the fasteners to specifications at this time.

   b. When all parts are installed, place a jack under the hub and raise it just enough to lift the car off the jackstand on the side nearest you. Tighten all fasteners to specifications in **Table 1**, then lower the car back onto the jackstand.

   c. Make sure to bend the lower arm pivot bolt locktab (**Figure 11**) as shown in **Figure 12**.

   d. Bleed the brakes and adjust the handbrake as described in Chapter Twelve.

   e. Have rear wheel toe-in adjusted by a Honda dealer or other qualified specialist.

Removal/Installation (1979-1982 Prelude)

Refer to **Figure 13** for this procedure.

1. Place the transaxle in FIRST (manual) or PARK (automatic). Securely block both front wheels so the car will not roll in either direction.

2. Loosen the rear wheel nuts. Jack up the rear end of the car, place it on jackstands and remove the rear wheels.

3. Remove the brake drum as described under *Hubs and Wheel Bearings* in this chapter.

4. Disconnect the metal brake line from the brake hose at the strut. See **Figure 7**. Use a flare nut wrench to unscrew the nut. These are available inexpensively from auto parts stores. Pull out the brake hose clip and detach the brake hose from the bracket on the strut.

> *CAUTION*
> *Immediately cap the disconnected line and hose to keep dirt out. Plastic vacuum caps, available from auto parts stores, work well for this.*

5. Disconnect the handbrake cable from the rear brake assembly.

6. Remove the backing plate mounting bolts. Take the backing plate off the hub carrier, together with the assembled brake components.

7. Remove the stabilizer mounting bolts at the radius arm and lower suspension arm. Take the stabilizer bar out.

8. Remove the nuts and bolts that secure the radius arm to the hub carrier and to the car's frame. Take the radius arm out.

9. Remove the strut pinch bolt from the hub carrier. See **Figure 13**. Separate the strut from the hub.

10. Remove the suspension arm attaching bolts and nuts. Detach the suspension arm from the frame and take it out.

11. Separate the hub carrier from the suspension arm.

12. Check all parts for wear or damage. Replace worn or damaged parts.

13. Check bushings for melting, cracks, wear or deterioration. See **Figure 14**. Have a machine shop replace bushings that show these conditions.

14. Installation is the reverse of removal, plus the following:

   a. Install all parts and tighten the fasteners slightly. Do not tighten the fasteners to specifications at this time.

   b. When all parts are installed, place a jack under the hub and raise it just enough to lift the car of the jackstand on the side nearest you. Tighten all fasteners to specifications in **Table 1**, then lower the car back onto the jackstand.

   c. Bleed the brakes and adjust the handbrake as described in Chapter Twelve.

   d. Have rear wheel toe-in adjusted by a Honda dealer or other qualified specialist.

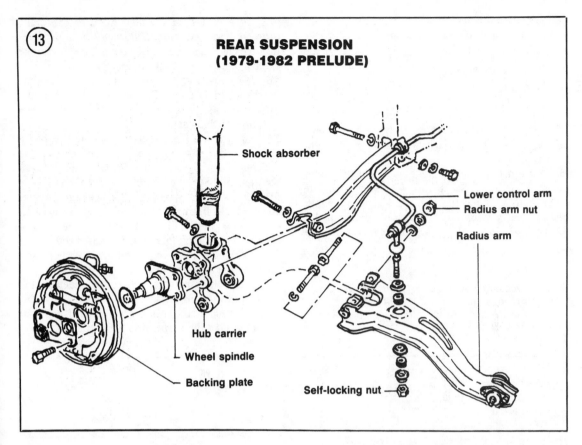

(13)

REAR SUSPENSION
(1979-1982 PRELUDE)

Shock absorber

Lower control arm

Radius arm nut

Radius arm

Hub carrier

Wheel spindle

Backing plate

Self-locking nut

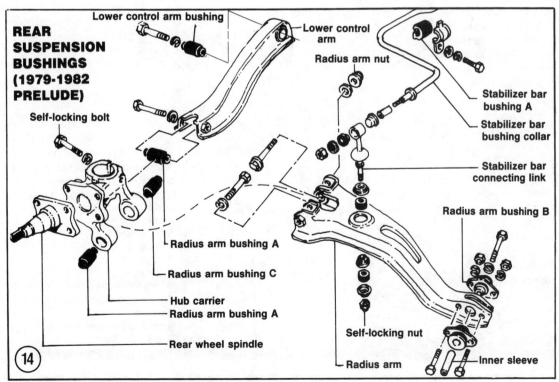

REAR SUSPENSION BUSHINGS (1979-1982 PRELUDE)

Lower control arm bushing

Lower control arm

Radius arm nut

Self-locking bolt

Stabilizer bar bushing A

Stabilizer bar bushing collar

Stabilizer bar connecting link

Radius arm bushing B

Radius arm bushing A

Radius arm bushing C

Hub carrier

Radius arm bushing A

Rear wheel spindle

Self-locking nut

Radius arm

Inner sleeve

11

(14)

**Removal/Installation
(1982-on Accord, 1983-on Prelude)**

Refer to **Figure 15** (all except 1984 Prelude) or **Figure 16** (1984 Prelude).

1. Place the transaxle in FIRST (manual) or PARK (automatic). Securely block both front wheels so the car will not roll in either direction.

2. Loosen the rear wheel nuts. Jack up the rear end of the car, place it on jackstands and remove the rear wheels.

3. Disconnect the metal brake line from the brake hose at the strut. See **Figure 6**. Use a flare nut wrench to unscrew the nut. These are available inexpensively from auto parts stores. Pull out the brake hose clip and detach the brake hose from the bracket on the strut.

> *CAUTION*
> *Immediately cap the disconnected line and hose to keep dirt out. Plastic vacuum caps, available from auto parts stores, work well for this.*

4A. *All except 1984 Prelude:* Remove the brake drum as described under *Hubs and Wheel Bearings* in this chapter. Then disconnect the handbrake cable from the rear brake assembly.

4B. *1984 Prelude:* Remove the brake caliper as described in Chapter Twelve. Then remove the brake disc as described under *Hubs and Wheel Bearings* in this chapter.

5A. *All except 1984 Prelude:* Remove the brake backing plate mounting bolts, then remove the backing plate together with the assembled brake components. See **Figure 15**.

5B. *1984 Prelude:* Remove the caliper bracket and splash shield from the hub carrier. See **Figure 16**.

6. Remove the radius rod bolt and radius rod adjusting bolt, then take out the radius rod.

7. On Preludes, remove the stabilizer bar bolts and take out the stabilizer bar.

8. Loosen the strut pinch bolt, then detach the strut from the hub carrier.

9. Remove the suspension arm inboard bolt and nut, then take the suspension arm out.

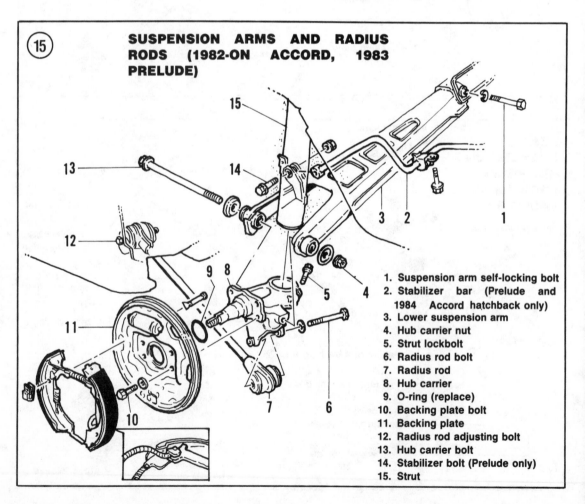

⑮ SUSPENSION ARMS AND RADIUS RODS (1982-ON ACCORD, 1983 PRELUDE)

1. Suspension arm self-locking bolt
2. Stabilizer bar (Prelude and 1984 Accord hatchback only)
3. Lower suspension arm
4. Hub carrier nut
5. Strut lockbolt
6. Radius rod bolt
7. Radius rod
8. Hub carrier
9. O-ring (replace)
10. Backing plate bolt
11. Backing plate
12. Radius rod adjusting bolt
13. Hub carrier bolt
14. Stabilizer bolt (Prelude only)
15. Strut

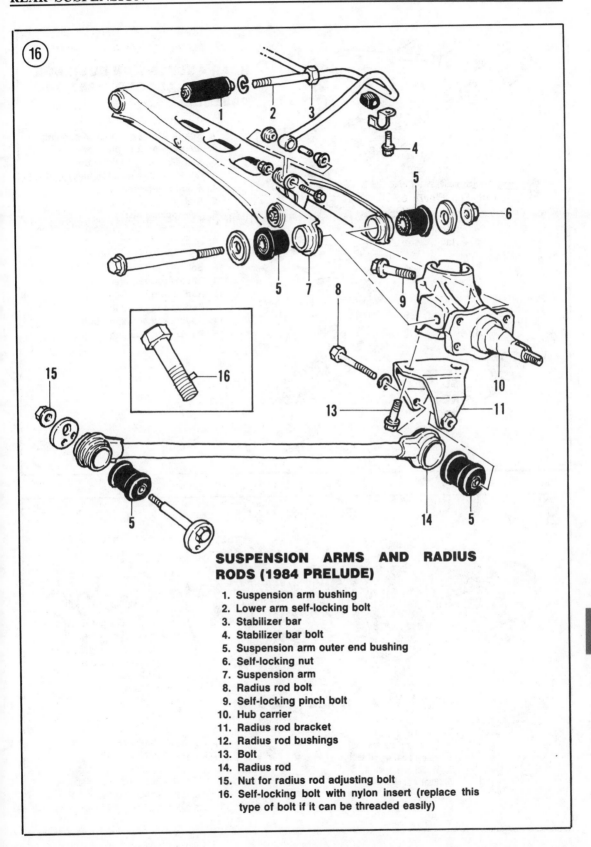

SUSPENSION ARMS AND RADIUS RODS (1984 PRELUDE)

1. Suspension arm bushing
2. Lower arm self-locking bolt
3. Stabilizer bar
4. Stabilizer bar bolt
5. Suspension arm outer end bushing
6. Self-locking nut
7. Suspension arm
8. Radius rod bolt
9. Self-locking pinch bolt
10. Hub carrier
11. Radius rod bracket
12. Radius rod bushings
13. Bolt
14. Radius rod
15. Nut for radius rod adjusting bolt
16. Self-locking bolt with nylon insert (replace this type of bolt if it can be threaded easily)

11

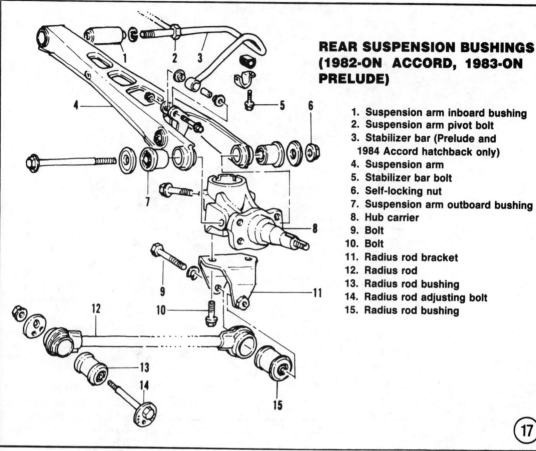

REAR SUSPENSION BUSHINGS (1982-ON ACCORD, 1983-ON PRELUDE)

1. Suspension arm inboard bushing
2. Suspension arm pivot bolt
3. Stabilizer bar (Prelude and 1984 Accord hatchback only)
4. Suspension arm
5. Stabilizer bar bolt
6. Self-locking nut
7. Suspension arm outboard bushing
8. Hub carrier
9. Bolt
10. Bolt
11. Radius rod bracket
12. Radius rod
13. Radius rod bushing
14. Radius rod adjusting bolt
15. Radius rod bushing

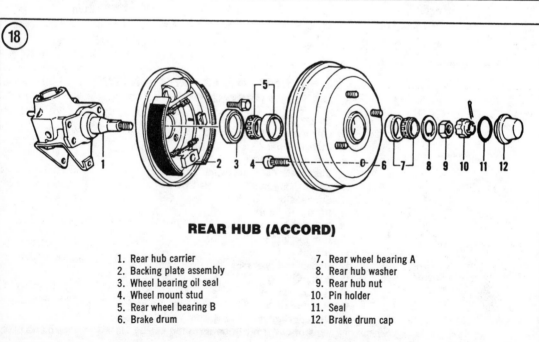

REAR HUB (ACCORD)

1. Rear hub carrier
2. Backing plate assembly
3. Wheel bearing oil seal
4. Wheel mount stud
5. Rear wheel bearing B
6. Brake drum
7. Rear wheel bearing A
8. Rear hub washer
9. Rear hub nut
10. Pin holder
11. Seal
12. Brake drum cap

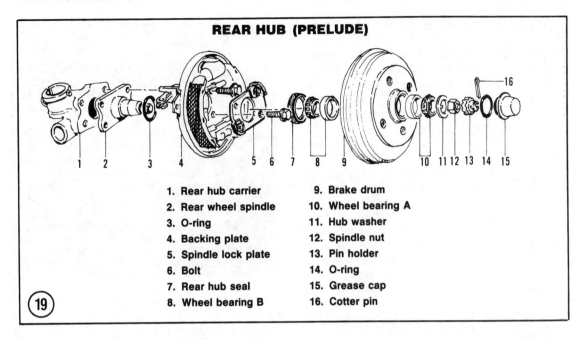

REAR HUB (PRELUDE)

1. Rear hub carrier
2. Rear wheel spindle
3. O-ring
4. Backing plate
5. Spindle lock plate
6. Bolt
7. Rear hub seal
8. Wheel bearing B
9. Brake drum
10. Wheel bearing A
11. Hub washer
12. Spindle nut
13. Pin holder
14. O-ring
15. Grease cap
16. Cotter pin

⑲

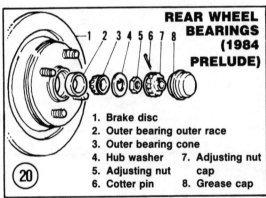

REAR WHEEL BEARINGS (1984 PRELUDE)

1. Brake disc
2. Outer bearing outer race
3. Outer bearing cone
4. Hub washer
5. Adjusting nut
6. Cotter pin
7. Adjusting nut cap
8. Grease cap

⑳

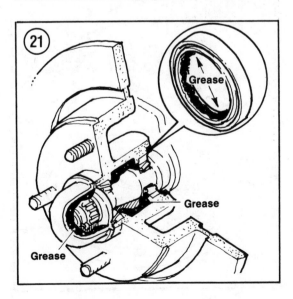

㉑

Grease

Grease

Grease

10. Detach the hub carrier from the suspension arm.

11. Check all parts for wear or damage. Replace worn or damaged parts.

12. Check bushings for melting, cracks, wear or deterioration. See **Figure 17**. Have a machine shop replace bushings that show these conditions.

13. Installation is the reverse of removal, plus the following:

   a. Install all parts and tighten the fasteners slightly. Do not tighten the fasteners to specifications at this time.

   b. When all parts are installed, place a jack under the hub and raise it just enough to lift the car off the jackstand on the side nearest you. Tighten all fasteners to specifications in **Table 1**, then lower the car back onto the jackstand.

   c. Bleed the brakes and adjust the handbrake as described in Chapter Twelve.

   d. Have rear wheel toe-in adjusted by a Honda dealer or other qualified specialist.

HUBS AND WHEEL BEARINGS

Figure 18 shows a hub and wheel bearings for the 1976-1981 Accord. Later Accord models are basically the same.

Figure 19 shows a hub and wheel bearings for the 1979-1982 Prelude. The 1983 Prelude is basically the same.

Figure 20 and **Figure 21** show the hub and wheel bearings for the 1984 Prelude.

11

1. Place the transaxle in FIRST (manual) or PARK (automatic). Securely block both front wheels so the car will not roll in either direction.

2. Loosen the rear wheel nuts. Jack up the rear end of the car, place it on jackstands and remove the rear wheels.

3. On 1984 Preludes, remove the brake caliper as described in Chapter Twelve.

4. Remove the wheel bearing grease cap (**Figure 22**).

5. Remove the cotter pin from the adjusting cap (**Figure 23**). Remove the adjusting cap and hub washer.

6. Pull the brake drum or disc out about one inch, then push it back in. This will expose the outer bearing cone so it can be removed with fingers.

7. Take the brake drum or disc off the hub spindle.

8. Tap the outer bearing's outer race out of the hub as shown in **Figure 24**. Tap evenly around the race so it doesn't tilt sideways and jam.

9. Turn the disc or drum over. Pry out the grease seal and remove the inner bearing cone. Tap out the inner race as shown in **Figure 24**.

Inspection

1. Thoroughly clean the wheel bearings and hub in solvent, then let them dry.

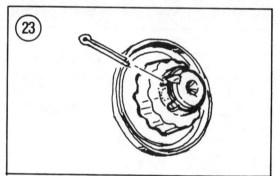

> *WARNING*
> *If the bearings are blown dry with compressed air, do not use the air jet to spin the bearings. This can cause them to fly apart and inflict serious injury.*

2. Check inner and outer races for rust, galling and the bluish tint that indicates overheating. Rotate the bearings and check for roughness or excessive noise. Compare the races and rollers to the defective bearing parts shown in **Figure 25**. Replace any bearings which have similar defects.

3. Check the inside of the hub for wear or damage. Replace the hub if wear or damage can be seen. Since the hub is manufactured in one piece with the brake drum or disc, the drum or disc must also be replaced.

4. If brake drum or disc inspection procedures in Chapter Twelve indicated that the drum or disc must be replaced, the hub must be replaced as well.

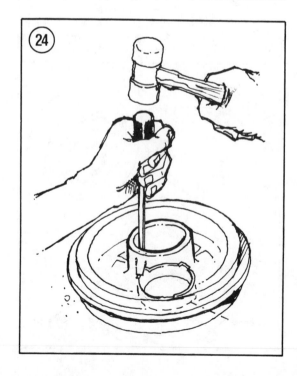

Installation

1. Tap the outer bearing races into place with a bearing driver such as the one shown in **Figure 26**.

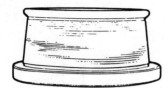

a) Inner race flaking

b) Roller flaking

c) Chipped inner race

d) Chipped roller

e) Recess on inner race

f) Recess on outer race

g) Recess on roller

h) Rust on outer race

11

Bearing drivers are available at auto parts stores. Make sure the races seat evenly when installed.

CAUTION
If you don't have the proper tool, have the races pressed in by a machine shop. An improvised tool may damage the outer races.

2. Pack the hub and grease cap (shaded areas in **Figure 27**). Use multipurpose lithium grease.

3. Work as much grease as possible between the wheel bearing rollers.

4. Install the inner wheel bearing in the hub, then tap in the grease seal. Use a block of wood to spread the hammer's force so the seal won't tip sideways and jam. Coat the grease seal lips with grease.

5. Apply a light coat of grease to the bearing spindle, including the threaded area. Install the hub and brake drum or disc.

6. Install the outer wheel bearing. Lightly grease the bearing washer and the spindle nut threads. Install the washer and nut.

7. On 1984 Preludes, install the brake caliper.

8. Adjust wheel bearings as described in this chapter.

Adjustment

1. Tighten the wheel bearing nut to 25 ±5 N•m (18 ±4 ft.-lb.). See **Figure 28**.

2. Rotate the hub several turns in both directions to seat the bearings.

3. Back off the locknut until it can be turned with fingers. Then retighten it to 5 N•m (4 ft.-lb.).

4. Rotate the hub. Check for noise or rough movement. If these are present, remove the wheel bearings and check for foreign material.

5. If the hub rotates smoothly, install the adjusting cap. Position the adjusting cap so its cotter pin holes align with the cotter pin hole in the spindle. If necessary, tighten the wheel bearing nut just enough to align the holes.

6. Attach a spring scale (**Figure 29**) and measure the force necessary to turn the hub:

   a. On 1976-1981 Accords, this should be 0.33-1.5 kg (0.73-3.3 lb.).

   b. On all except 1976-1981 Accords, this should be 4-18 N (0.9-4.0 lb.).

7. If rotating force is not within specifications, check for a damaged spindle, damaged bearings or dragging brakes. If these are good, repeat the adjustment procedure and recheck turning force.

8. Install a *new* cotter pin and spread it. See **Figure 30**. Install the grease cap.

9. Install the wheels, lower the car and tighten the wheel nuts.

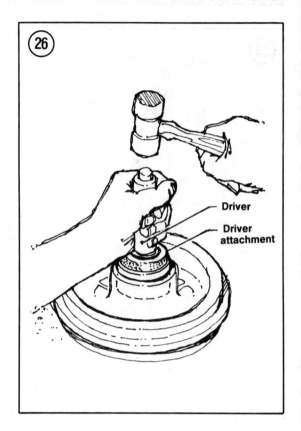

Driver

Driver attachment

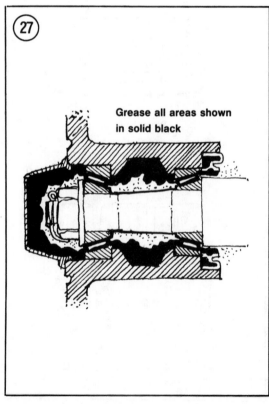

Grease all areas shown in solid black

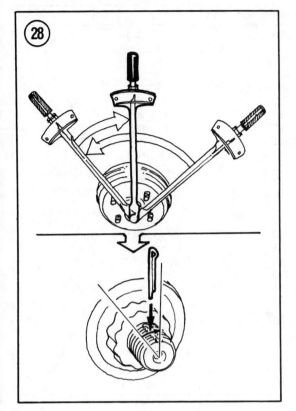

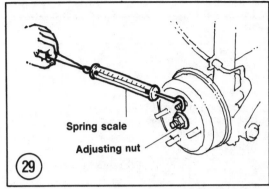

Spring scale

Adjusting nut

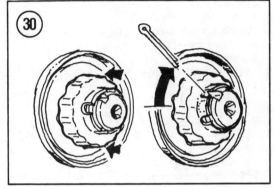

Table is on the following page.

11

Table 1 TIGHTENING TORQUES

Part	N•m	ft.-lb.
1976-1981 Accord		
Top strut nuts		
1976-1978	16	12
1979-81	22	16
Suspension arm pivot bolt	50	36
Suspension arm to hub	83	60
Hub shock mount bolt	55	40
Radius rod to hub	70	51
Radius rod adjustment bolt	65	47
Brake backing plate to hub	22	16
Wheel spindle nut	See text	
1982-on Accord		
Top strut nuts	22	16
Suspension arm pivot bolt	55	40
Suspension arm to hub	83	60
Hub shock mount bolt	55	40
Radius rod to hub	70	51
Radius rod adjustment bolt	65	47
Brake backing plate to hub	30	22
Wheel spindle nut	See text	
Stabilizer bar*	22	16
1979-1982 Prelude		
Top strut nuts		
Center nut	33	24
Outside nuts	22	16
Lower suspension arm		
Pivot bolt	55	40
At hub	55	40
Stabilizer bar		
At suspension arm	22	16
At radius arm	22	16
Hub shock mount bolt	55	40
Radius arm		
Toe adjustment bolt	55	40
At hub	102	74
Pivot bolt	85	64
Bushing mount bolts	22	16
Brake backing plate to hub	55	40
Wheel spindle nut	See text	
1983-on Prelude		
Top strut nuts (outer 3 only)	22	16
Suspension arm pivot bolt	55	40
Suspension arm to hub	83	60
Hub shock mount bolt	55	40
Radius rod to hub	70	51
Radius rod adjustment bolt	65	47
Brake backing plate to hub**	30	22
Wheel spindle nut	See text	
Stabilizer bar	22	16

* 1984 hatchback only.
** Drum brakes only.

CHAPTER TWELVE

BRAKES

All models use disc brakes at the front. All except the 1984 Prelude use drum brakes at the rear. The 1984 Prelude uses disc brakes at the rear.

This chapter provides service procedures for the front and rear brakes, parking brake, master cylinder and brake booster. **Table 1** and **Table 2** are at the end of the chapter.

FRONT DISC BRAKES
(1976-1981 ACCORD)

Refer to **Figure 1** for the following procedures.

Pad Replacement

The brake pads should be replaced whenever the friction material is worn to less than specified in **Table 1**.

1. Set the handbrake. Securely block both rear wheels so the car will not roll in either direction.
2. Loosen the front wheel nuts. Jack up the front end of the car, place it on jackstands and remove the front wheels.
3. Pull the clips out of the caliper locking blocks. See **Figure 2**.
4. Tap the upper caliper locking block (**Figure 3**) sideways with a hammer and screwdriver. Pull it

out with pliers. Remove the lower locking block in the same manner.

CAUTION
During the next step, do not let the caliper hang by the brake hose.

5. Lift the caliper body off the mounting bracket. See **Figure 4**. Tie the caliper up out of the way.

CAUTION
Do not press the brake pedal with the pads removed or the piston will fall out.

6. Take the shim and pads off the mounting bracket, then remove the anti-rattle spring and clip from the mounting bracket. See **Figure 5**.
7. Inspect the pads. Light surface grease or oil stains may be sanded off. Pads must be replaced under the following conditions:
   a. If oil or grease has penetrated the surface.
   b. If any brake fluid has touched the pad friction material.
   c. If the friction material is worn to less than specified in **Table 1**. This measurement does not include the metal backs of the pads.
   d. If thickness of the 4 pads varies by more than specified in **Table 1**.

NOTE
Always replace pads in complete sets.

12

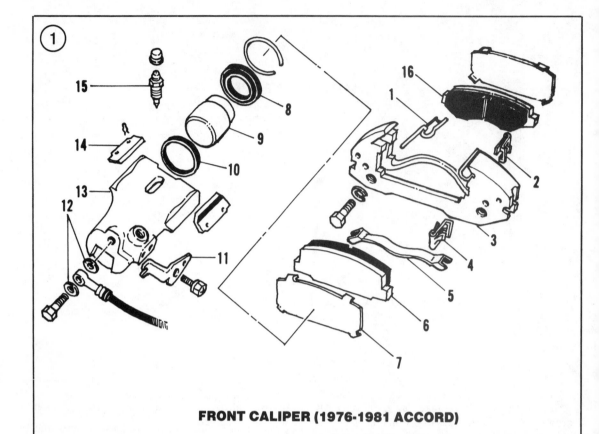

FRONT CALIPER (1976-1981 ACCORD)

1. Anti-rattle spring
2. Anti-rattle pad clip B
3. Mounting support
4. Anti-rattle pad clip
5. Anti-rattle pad clip A
6. Inner pad
7. Shim
8. Piston boot
9. Piston
10. Piston seal
11. Hose bracket
12. Aluminum washer
13. Caliper
14. Side plate
15. Bleeder screw
16. Outer pad

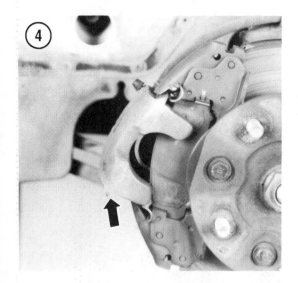

8. Check the cylinder body for brake fluid leaks. If fluid has leaked from the cylinder, have the caliper overhauled.

9. Check the anti-rattle spring and clip for wear, damage or corrosion. Replace them if these conditions are found.

10. Carefully clean the space which holds the brake pads. Use alcohol or aerosol brake cleaner. Do not use gasoline, kerosene or solvent. These leave residues which can cause rubber parts to soften and swell.

NOTE
The next step is not necessary if the old pads are being reused.

11. Remove a small amount of brake fluid from the master cylinder with a turkey baster or similar tool.

CAUTION
Brake fluid can damage paint. Place rags beneath the master cylinder to catch spilled fluid. If brake fluid spills, wipe it up immediately and clean the spill area with soap and water.

12A. If installing new pads, open the bleed valve (**Figure 6**). Place a pan beneath the caliper to catch spilled brake fluid. Press the piston into the cylinder just far enough to make room for the new pads, then close the bleed valve.

12B. If reusing the old brake pads and shim, clean the pad face and shim with a wire brush.

13. Apply high-temperature disc brake grease (General Electric G-622, Dow Corning DC No. 5 or equivalent) to the red side of the pad shim. This is the side that goes next to the outer pad.

14. Install the anti-rattle spring and clip on the mounting bracket. Position the pads and shim on the mounting bracket. See **Figure 5**. The red side of the shim goes next to the outer pad.

15. Untie the caliper and install it over the pads.

16. Make sure the locking blocks are clean. Coat the locking blocks with high-temperature disc brake grease, then install them. Secure the locking blocks with the clips.

17. Press the brake pedal several times to seat the pads.

18. Install the wheels, lower the car and tighten the wheel nuts. If a bleed valve was opened, bleed the brakes as described in this chapter.

Caliper Removal/Installation

1. Perform Steps 1-4 of *Pad Replacement* in this chapter.

12

2. Disconnect the caliper brake hose and lift the caliper off.

> *CAUTION*
> *Immediately cap the end of the hose and the union bolt hole in the caliper to keep out dirt.*

3. If necessary, unbolt the caliper mounting bracket and take it off.

4. Installation is the reverse of removal, plus the following:

   a. Tighten the mounting bracket bolts (if removed) to specifications in **Table 2**.

   b. Coat the locking blocks with high-temperature disc brake grease.

   c. Use new washers at the brake hose connection.

   d. Bleed the brakes as described in this chapter.

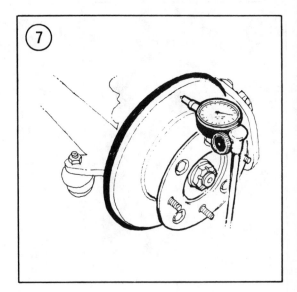

Disc Inspection

1. Perform Steps 1-5 of *Pad Replacement* in this chapter.

2. Check wheel bearing adjustment as described in Chapter Ten.

3. Check the disc for rust, scratches or cracks. If cracks are visible, replace the disc. If rust is visible or if scratches are deep enough to snag a fingernail, have the disc turned by a machine shop.

4. Set up a dial indicator so its pointer contacts the disc's swept area as shown in **Figure 7**. Rotate the disc one full turn and measure runout. If it exceeds specifications (**Table 1**), have the disc turned by a machine shop.

5. Measure disc thickness with a micrometer or vernier caliper at 8 equally spaced locations around the disc, 19 mm (3/4 in.) from the edge. See **Figure 8**. If any of the measurements are not within specifications (**Table 1**), replace the disc.

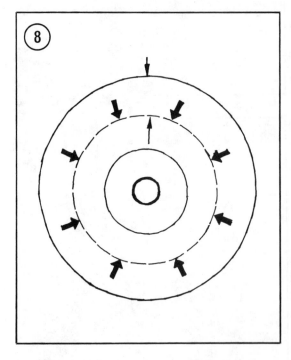

Disc Removal/Installation

To remove and install a brake disc, refer to the *Front Wheel Bearings* section of Chapter Ten.

FRONT DISC BRAKES
(1982-ON ACCORD, ALL PRELUDE)

Refer to the following illustrations:

   a. **Figure 9** — 1982-1983 Accord.

   b. **Figure 10** — 1984 Accord.

   c. **Figure 11** — 1979-1982 Prelude.

   d. **Figure 12** — 1983 and later Prelude.

Pad Replacement

The brake pads should be replaced whenever the friction material is worn to less than specified in **Table 1**.

1. Set the handbrake. Securely block both rear wheels so the car will not roll in either direction.

2. Loosen the front wheel nuts. Jack up the front end of the car, place it on jackstands and remove the front wheels.

3. Remove the lower guide bolt (Accord) or lower caliper pin (Prelude).

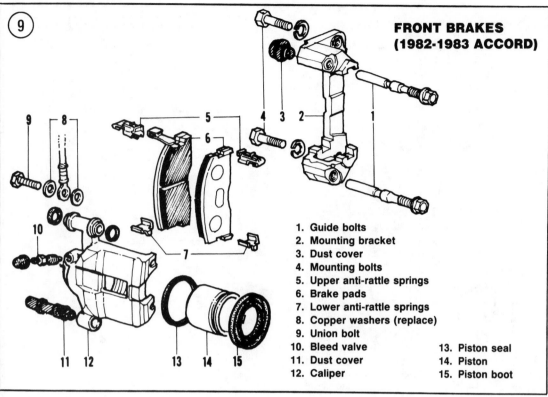

**FRONT BRAKES
(1982-1983 ACCORD)**

1. Guide bolts
2. Mounting bracket
3. Dust cover
4. Mounting bolts
5. Upper anti-rattle springs
6. Brake pads
7. Lower anti-rattle springs
8. Copper washers (replace)
9. Union bolt
10. Bleed valve
11. Dust cover
12. Caliper
13. Piston seal
14. Piston
15. Piston boot

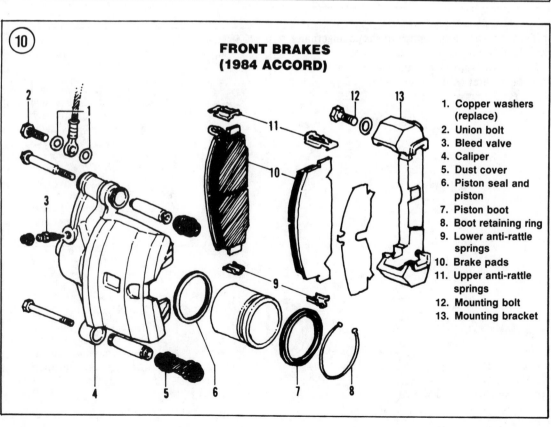

**FRONT BRAKES
(1984 ACCORD)**

1. Copper washers
   (replace)
2. Union bolt
3. Bleed valve
4. Caliper
5. Dust cover
6. Piston seal and
   piston
7. Piston boot
8. Boot retaining ring
9. Lower anti-rattle
   springs
10. Brake pads
11. Upper anti-rattle
    springs
12. Mounting bolt
13. Mounting bracket

12

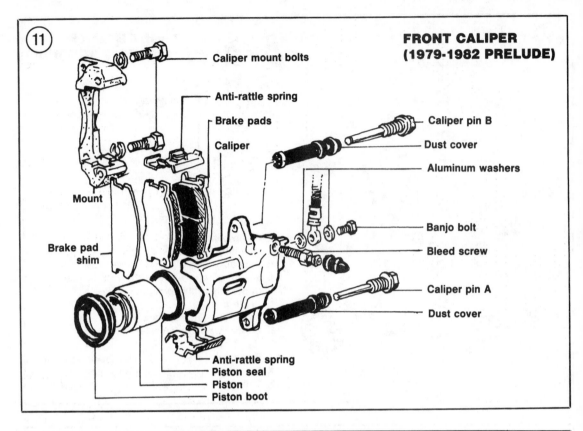

⑪ **FRONT CALIPER (1979-1982 PRELUDE)**

- Caliper mount bolts
- Anti-rattle spring
- Brake pads
- Caliper
- Mount
- Brake pad shim
- Caliper pin B
- Dust cover
- Aluminum washers
- Banjo bolt
- Bleed screw
- Caliper pin A
- Dust cover
- Anti-rattle spring
- Piston seal
- Piston
- Piston boot

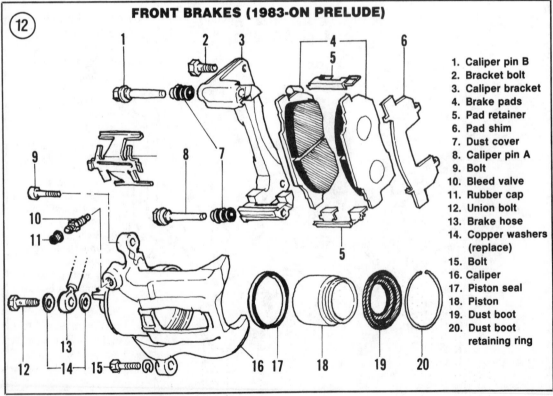

⑫ **FRONT BRAKES (1983-ON PRELUDE)**

1. Caliper pin B
2. Bracket bolt
3. Caliper bracket
4. Brake pads
5. Pad retainer
6. Pad shim
7. Dust cover
8. Caliper pin A
9. Bolt
10. Bleed valve
11. Rubber cap
12. Union bolt
13. Brake hose
14. Copper washers (replace)
15. Bolt
16. Caliper
17. Piston seal
18. Piston
19. Dust boot
20. Dust boot retaining ring

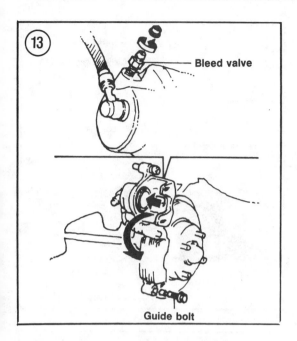

Bleed valve

Guide bolt

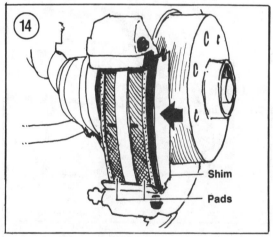

Shim

Pads

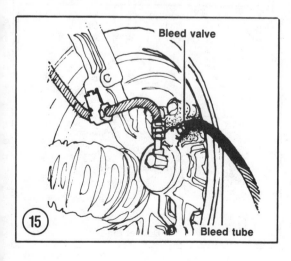

Bleed valve

Bleed tube

4. Pivot the caliper upward to expose the pads. See **Figure 13**.

5. Take the pads off the mounting bracket. See **Figure 14**. On 1984 Accords and all Preludes, remove the shim from the outer pad.

CAUTION
Do not press the brake pedal with the pads removed or the piston will fall out.

6. Inspect the pads. Light surface grease or oil stains may be sanded off. Pads must be replaced under the following conditions:
    a. If oil or grease has penetrated the surface.
    b. If any brake fluid has touched the pad friction material.
    c. If the friction material is worn to less than specified in **Table 1**. This measurement does not include the metal backs of the pads.
    d. If thickness of the 4 pads varies by more than specified in **Table 1**.

NOTE
Always replace pads in complete sets.

7. Check the cylinder body for brake fluid leaks. If fluid has leaked from the cylinder, have the caliper overhauled.

8. Check the anti-rattle spring and clip for wear, damage or corrosion. Replace them if these conditions are found.

9. Carefully clean the space which holds the brake pads. Use alcohol or aerosol brake cleaner. Do not use gasoline, kerosene or solvent. These leave residues which can cause rubber parts to soften and swell.

NOTE
The next step is not necessary if the old pads are being reused.

10. Remove a small amount of brake fluid from the master cylinder with a turkey baster or similar tool.

CAUTION
Brake fluid can damage paint. Place rags . beneath the master cylinder to catch spilled fluid. If brake fluid spills, wipe it up immediately and clean the spill area with soap and water.

11A. If installing new pads, open the bleed valve (**Figure 15**). Place a pan beneath the caliper to catch spilled brake fluid. Press the piston into the cylinder just far enough to make room for the new pads, then close the bleed valve.

11B. If the brake pads and shim (1984 Accords and all Preludes) are to be reused, clean the pad

12

face and shim with a wire brush. Apply silicone grease to all cleaned areas and to the *backs* of the pads.

12. On 1984 Accords and all Preludes, apply high-temperature disc brake grease (General Electric G-622, Dow Corning DC No. 5 or equivalent) between the outer pad and pad shim.

13. Install the anti-rattle spring and clip on the mounting bracket. Position the pads and shim (if so equipped) on the mounting bracket. See **Figure 14**.

> *NOTE*
> *If the pads are equipped with wear indicators, install the inner pad with its wear indicator inboard. See **Figure 16**.*

14. Pivot the caliper downward over the pads.

15. Make sure the lower guide bolt or caliper pin is clean. Apply silicone grease to the guide bolt or caliper pin, then install it and tighten to specifications in **Table 2**.

16. Press the brake pedal several times to seat the pads.

17. Install the wheels, lower the car and tighten the wheel nuts. If a bleed valve was opened, bleed the brakes as described in this chapter.

Caliper Removal/Installation

1. Set the handbrake. Securely block both rear wheels so the car will not roll in either direction.

2. Loosen the front wheel nuts. Jack up the front end of the car, place it on jackstands and remove the front wheels.

> *CAUTION*
> *After the next steps, immediately cap the end of the hose and the union bolt hole in the caliper to keep out dirt.*

3A. *Accord models:* Disconnect the caliper brake hose and remove the guide bolts. See **Figure 17**. Take the caliper off.

3B. *Prelude models:* Disconnect the caliper brake hose and remove the caliper pins. See **Figure 18**. Take the caliper off.

4. If necessary, unbolt the caliper mounting bracket and take it off.

5. Installation is the reverse of removal, plus the following:

   a. Tighten the mounting bracket bolts (if removed) to specifications in **Table 2**.

   b. Apply silicone grease to the guide bolts or caliper pins. Tighten the guide bolts or caliper pins to specifications in **Table 2**.

   c. Use new washers at the brake hose connection.

   d. Bleed the brakes as described in this chapter.

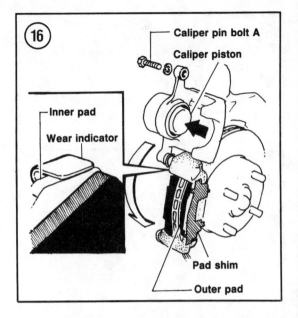

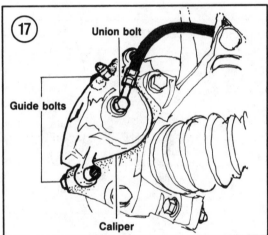

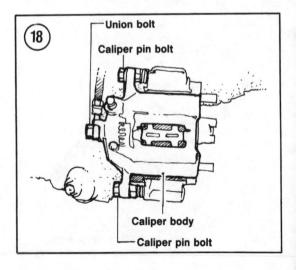

Disc Inspection

This is the same as for 1976-1981 Accords, described in this chapter.

REAR DRUM BRAKES
(1976-1981 ACCORD)

Removal

Refer to **Figure 19** for the following procedures.

WARNING
Do not inhale brake dust. It contains asbestos, which can cause lung injury.

1. Securely block both front wheels so the car will not roll in either direction. Place the transaxle in FIRST (manual) or PARK (automatic).
2. Loosen the rear wheel nuts. Jack up the rear end of the car, place on jackstands and remove the front wheels.
3. Make sure the handbrake is off.
4. Remove the brake drum as described under *Wheel Bearings* in Chapter Ten.
5. Grasp the shoe retaining pins with pliers. Rotate the pins to align with the slots in the shoe clamp springs, then remove the shoe clamp springs.
6. Remove the shoe return springs. Take off the shoes, parking brake lever and parking brake lever spring.
7. Detach the brake adjuster assembly from the backing plate and take it off.
8. If backing plate removal is necessary, remove the wheel cylinder as described in Step 9 and Step 10, then unbolt the backing plate and take it off. Backing plate removal is not necessary for normal brake service.
9. Disconnect the brake line from the cylinder.
10. Remove the wheel cylinder mounting nuts and lockwashers. Take off the wheel cylinder and gasket.

Inspection

1. Clean all parts with aerosol brake cleaner or new brake fluid. Do not clean with gasoline, kerosene or solvent. These leave residues which can cause rubber parts to soften and swell.

CAUTION
If cleaning with brake fluid, keep it off the linings. Brake fluid will ruin the linings and they will have to be replaced.

2. Check drums for visible scoring, excessive or uneven wear and rust. If you have precision measuring equipment, measure the drums for wear and out-of-roundness. If you don't have the equipment, this can be done by a machine shop. If the drum has surface damage or excessive runout, it can be turned by a machine shop. However, the inside diameter must not exceed specifications (**Table 1**, end of chapter). If the drum would have to be cut larger than this to correct it, it must be replaced.
3. Check brake shoes for the following:

  a. Excessive wear. If the friction material is worn to less than specified in **Table 1**, replace the shoes.
  b. Cracked, unevenly worn or separated friction material. Replace the shoes if these conditions are found.
  c. Oil or grease. Light surface stains may be sanded off. If oil or grease has penetrated the surface, replace the shoes.
  d. Brake fluid stains. Since brake fluid can cause the friction material to crumble, replace the shoes if brake fluid has touched the linings.

4. Check the springs, adjuster parts and shoe clamp springs and pins for wear or damage. Replace as needed.
5. Pull back the wheel cylinder boots. Slight moisture inside the wheel cylinder is normal. If fluid runs out, have the wheel cylinder overhauled.

Installation

Installation is the reverse of removal, plus the following.
1. If the backing plate was removed, apply a thin layer of silicone sealer to the contact points of backing plate and spindle.
2. Lubricate the adjuster ramps and adjuster bolt threads with high-temperature brake grease.
3. Apply small amounts of high-temperature brake grease to the metal-to-metal friction points of brake shoes and backing plate, as well as to the ends of the brake shoes that fit into the wheel cylinders and adjuster slots.

WARNING
Do not use ordinary multipurpose grease, since it may melt and contaminate the brake linings.

12

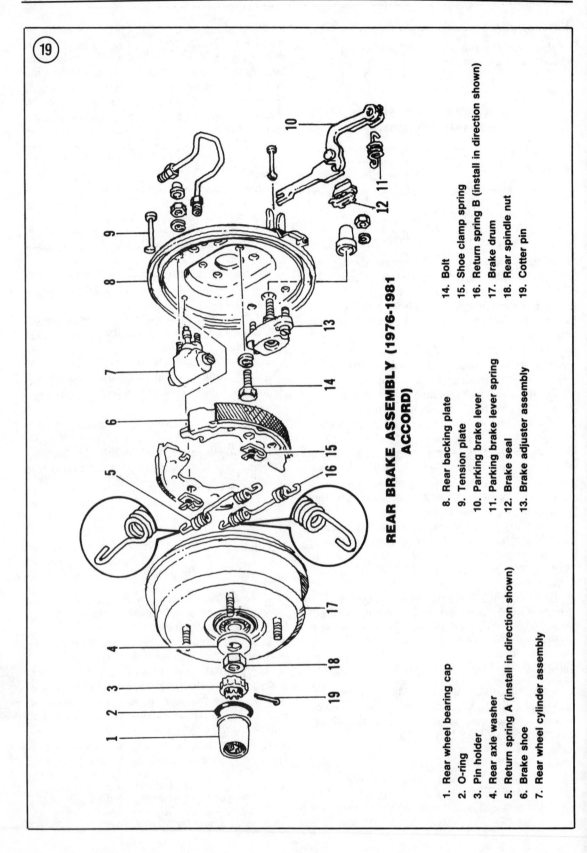

REAR BRAKE ASSEMBLY (1976-1981 ACCORD)

1. Rear wheel bearing cap
2. O-ring
3. Pin holder
4. Rear axle washer
5. Return spring A (install in direction shown)
6. Brake shoe
7. Rear wheel cylinder assembly
8. Rear backing plate
9. Tension plate
10. Parking brake lever
11. Parking brake lever spring
12. Brake seal
13. Brake adjuster assembly
14. Bolt
15. Shoe clamp spring
16. Return spring B (install in direction shown)
17. Brake drum
18. Rear spindle nut
19. Cotter pin

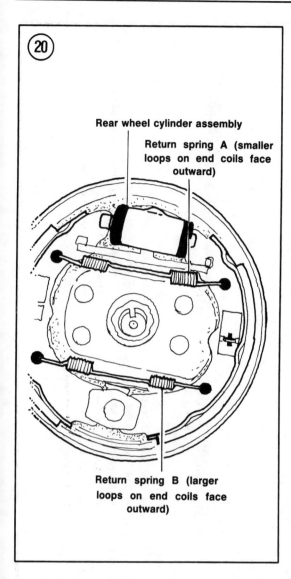

Rear wheel cylinder assembly

Return spring A (smaller loops on end coils face outward)

Return spring B (larger loops on end coils face outward)

4. Install the return springs as shown in **Figure 20**. The upper return spring has smaller coils, which face outward when installed. The lower return spring has larger coils, which face inward when installed.

5. Install the brake drum as described under *Wheel Bearings* in Chapter Eleven.

6. Adjust the rear brakes and handbrake as described in this chapter.

7. If a brake line was disconnected, bleed the brakes as described in this chapter.

WARNING
Do not drive the car unless the brake pedal feels firm. If the brake pedal feels soft, bleed the brakes. Check for brake fluid leaks and worn hydraulic system parts.

REAR DRUM BRAKES
(1979-1982 PRELUDE)

Removal

Refer to **Figure 21** for the following procedures.

WARNING
Do not inhale brake dust. It contains asbestos, which can cause lung injury.

1. Securely block both front wheels so the car will not roll in either direction. Place the transaxle in FIRST (manual) or PARK (automatic).

2. Loosen the rear wheel nuts. Jack up the rear end of the car, place in jackstands and remove the front wheels.

3. Make sure the handbrake is off.

4. Remove the brake drum as described under *Wheel Bearings* in Chapter Eleven.

5. Grasp the shoe retaining pins with pliers. Rotate the pins to align with the slots in the shoe clamp springs, then remove the shoe clamp springs.

6. Remove the shoe return springs. Take off the shoes, parking brake lever and parking brake lever spring.

7. If backing plate removal is necessary, remove the wheel cylinder as decribed under *Wheel Cylinder Replacement,* then unbolt the backing plate and take it off. Backing plate removal is not necessary for normal brake service.

Inspection

1. Clean all parts with aerosol brake cleaner or new brake fluid. Do not clean with gasoline, kerosene or solvent. These leave residues which can cause rubber parts to soften and swell.

CAUTION
If cleaning with brake fluid, keep it off the linings. Brake fluid will ruin the linings and they will have to be replaced.

2. Check drums for visible scoring, excessive or uneven wear and rust. If you have precision measuring equipment, measure the drums for wear and out-of-roundness. If you don't have the equipment, this can be done by a machine shop. If the drum has surface damage or excessive runout, it can be turned by a machine shop. However, the inside diameter must not exceed specifications (**Table 1**, end of chapter). If the drum would have to be cut larger than this to correct it, it must be replaced.

12

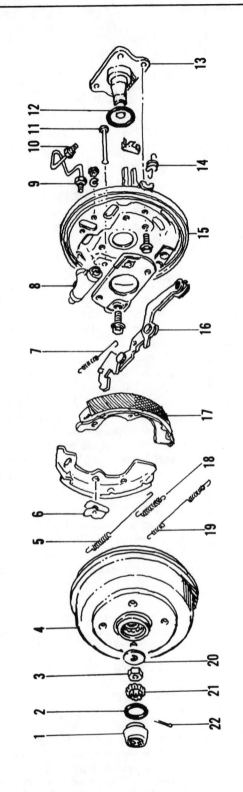

REAR BRAKE ASSEMBLY (1979-1982 PRELUDE)

1. Rear wheel bearing cap
2. O-ring
3. Spindle nut
4. Rear brake drum
5. Return spring A
6. Shoe clamp spring
7. Quadrant ratchet/parking brake lever spring
8. Wheel cylinder
9. Flare nut
10. Flare nut
11. Tension pin
12. O-ring
13. Wheel spindle
14. Return spring
15. Backing plate
16. Quadrant ratchet/parking brake lever
17. Brake shoe
18. Rod spring
19. Return spring B
20. Rear axle washer
21. Pin holder
22. Cotter pin

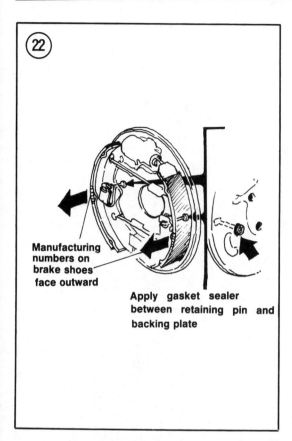

Manufacturing numbers on brake shoes face outward

Apply gasket sealer between retaining pin and backing plate

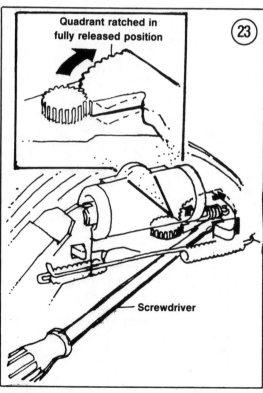

Quadrant ratched in fully released position

Screwdriver

3. Check brake shoes for the following:
   a. Excessive wear. If the friction material is worn to less than specified in **Table 1**, replace the shoes.
   b. Cracked, unevenly worn or separated friction material. Replace the shoes if these conditions are found.
   c. Oil or grease. Light surface stains may be sanded off. If oil or grease has penetrated the surface, replace the shoes.
   d. Brake fluid stains. Since brake fluid can cause the friction material to crumble, replace the shoes if brake fluid has touched the linings.

4. Check the springs, adjuster parts and shoe clamp springs and pins for wear or damage. Replace as needed.

5. Pull back the wheel cylinder boots. Slight moisture inside the wheel cylinder is normal. If fluid runs out, have the wheel cylinder overhauled.

Installation

Installation is the reverse of removal, plus the following.

1. If the backing plate was removed, apply a thin layer of silicone sealer to the contact points of backing plate and mounting point.

2. Apply small amounts of silicone sealer between the shoe retaining pins and backing plate.

3. Apply small amounts of high-temperature brake grease to the metal-to-metal friction points of brake shoes and backing plate, as well as to the ends of the brake shoes that fit into the wheel cylinders and anchor block.

> *WARNING*
> *Do not use ordinary multipurpose grease, since it may melt and contaminate the brake linings.*

4. Install the return springs and shoes as shown in **Figure 22**.

> *CAUTION*
> *Be sure to position the springs as shown. If they are installed backwards, they will rub on the hub.*

5. Move the quadrant to the released position with a screwdriver. See **Figure 23**.

6. Install the brake drum as described under *Wheel Bearings* in Chapter Eleven.

7. Install the brake drum and spindle nut. If the wheel cylinder has been overhauled, bleed the brakes as described in this chapter to restore hydraulic pressure to the rear wheels.

8. Press the brake pedal. Remove the spindle nut and brake drum, then check to make sure the

12

quadrant has moved to the position shown in **Figure 24**. If not, repeat the test. If the quadrant still doesn't move, check the parking brake lever, quadrant and ratchet for wear or damage.

9. Adjust the handbrake as described in this chapter.

10. If a brake line was disconnected, bleed the brakes as described in this chapter.

> *WARNING*
> *Do not drive the car unless the brake pedal feels firm. If the brake pedal feels soft, bleed the brakes. Check for brake fluid leaks and worn hydraulic system parts.*

REAR DRUM BRAKES
(1982-ON ACCORD, 1983 PRELUDE)

Refer to **Figure 25** for the following procedures.

> *WARNING*
> *Do not inhale brake dust. It contains asbestos, which can cause lung injury.*

Removal

1. Securely block both front wheels so the car will not roll in either direction. Place the transaxle in FIRST (manual) or PARK (automatic).

2. Loosen the rear wheel nuts. Jack up the rear end of the car, place on jackstands and remove the front wheels.

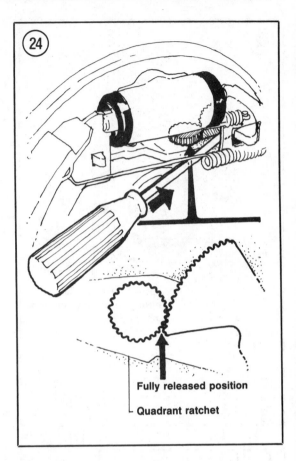

Fully released position

Quadrant ratchet

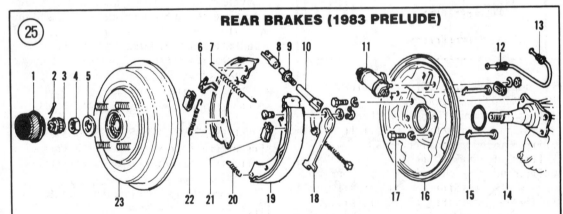

REAR BRAKES (1983 PRELUDE)

1. Rear wheel bearing grease cap
2. Cotter pin (replace)
3. Wheel bearing adjusting cap
4. Wheel bearing adjusting nut
5. Wheel bearing washer
6. Self-adjuster lever
7. Upper return spring
8. Self-adjuster bolt clevis
9. Self-adjuster bolt
10. Self-adjuster bolt
11. Wheel cylinder
12. Brake line
13. Flare nut
14. Wheel bearing spindle
15. Brake shoe hold-down pin
16. Brake backing plate
17. Backing plate bolt
18. Handbrake lever
19. Brake shoe
20. Return spring
21. Hold-down spring
22. Self-adjuster spring
23. Brake drum

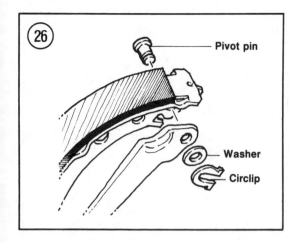

(26)

Pivot pin

Washer

Circlip

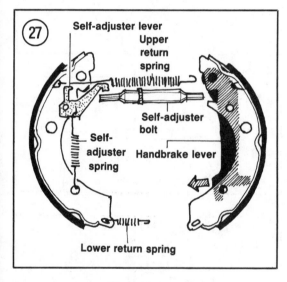

(27)

Self-adjuster lever
Upper
return
spring

Self-adjuster
bolt

Self-
adjuster
spring

Handbrake lever

Lower return spring

3. Remove the brake drum as described under *Wheel Bearings* in Chapter Eleven.

4. Grasp the retainer pins with pliers and twist them so they align with the slots in the retainer springs. Take off the retainer springs.

5. Lower the brake shoes, together with the springs, until they clear the wheel cylinder and anchor block. Detach the handbrake cable from the parking brake lever, then take the shoes off.

6. Separate the shoes, springs, self-adjuster bolt and parking brake lever.

7. Pry off the clip and remove the washer, pivot pin and parking brake lever from the secondary brake shoe. See **Figure 26**.

8. If backing plate removal is necessary, remove the wheel cylinder as described under *Wheel Cylinder Replacement* in this chapter. Then unbolt the backing plate from the spindle and take it off. Backing plate removal is not necessary for normal brake service.

Inspection

1. Clean all parts with aerosol brake cleaner or new brake fluid. Do not clean with gasoline, kerosene or solvent. These leave residues which can cause rubber parts to soften and swell.

> *CAUTION*
> *If cleaning with brake fluid, keep it off the linings. Brake fluid will ruin the linings and they will have to be replaced.*

2. Check drums for visible scoring, excessive or uneven wear and rust. If you have precision measuring equipment, measure the drums for wear and out-of-roundness. If you don't have the equipment, this can be done by a machine shop. If the drum has surface damage or excessive runout, it can be turned by a machine shop. However, the inside diameter must not exceed specifications (**Table 1**, end of chapter). If the drum would have to be cut larger than this to correct it, it must be replaced.

3. Check brake shoes for the following:
   a. Excessive wear. If the friction material is worn to less than specified in **Table 1**, replace the shoes.
   b. Cracked, unevenly worn or separated friction material. Replace the shoes if these conditions are found.
   c. Oil or grease. Light surface stains may be sanded off. If oil or grease has penetrated the surface, replace the shoes.
   d. Brake fluid stains. Since brake fluid can cause the friction material to crumble, replace the shoes if brake fluid has touched the linings.

4. Check the springs, adjuster parts and shoe retainer pins for wear or damage. Replace as needed.

5. Pull back the wheel cylinder boots. Slight moisture inside the wheel cylinder is normal. If fluid runs out, have the wheel cylinder overhauled.

Installation

Installation is the reverse of removal, plus the following.

1. If the backing plate was removed, apply a small amount of silicone sealer to the contact points of backing plate and spindle. Install the backing plate on the spindle and tighten its mounting bolts to specifications in **Table 2**.

2. Assemble the shoes, springs and self-adjuster mechanism as shown in **Figure 27** and **Figure 28**. Screw the adjuster bolt in all the way.

12

3. Apply small amounts of high-temperature brake grease to the friction points shown in **Figure 29**.

> *WARNING*
> *Do not use ordinary multipurpose grease, since it may melt and contaminate the brake linings.*

4. Connect the handbrake cable to the secondary shoe, then install the assembled shoes, springs and adjuster mechanism on the backing plate.
5. Apply small amounts of silicone sealer between the tension pins and backing plate.
6. Install the brake drum as described under *Wheel Bearings* in Chapter Eleven.
7. Bleed the brakes as described in this chapter.
8. Press the brake pedal several times to operate the self-adjuster mechanisms, then adjust the handbrake as described in this chapter.

REAR DISC BRAKES

Rear disc brakes are used on 1984 Preludes. Refer to **Figure 30** for the following procedures.

Pad Replacement

1. Place the transaxle in FIRST (manual) or PARK (automatic). Securely block both front wheels so the car will not roll in either direction.
2. Loosen the rear wheel nuts. Jack up the rear end of the car, place it on jackstands and remove the rear wheels.
3. Remove the caliper shield (**Figure 31**).
4. Disconnect the handbrake cable from the caliper. See **Figure 32**.
5. Remove the caliper mounting bolts (**Figure 33**), then take the caliper off.

> *CAUTION*
> *Do not let the caliper hang by the brake hose. Tie it up out of the way.*

6. Remove the pads (**Figure 34**) and pad guides (**Figure 35**).
7. Inspect the pads. Light surface grease or oil stains may be sanded off. Pads must be replaced under the following conditions:
   a. If oil or grease has penetrated the surface.
   b. If any brake fluid has touched the pad friction material.
   c. If the friction material is worn to less than specified in **Table 1**. This measurement does not include the metal backs of the pads.

> *NOTE*
> *Always replace pads in complete sets.*

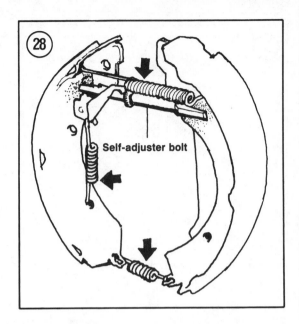

Self-adjuster bolt

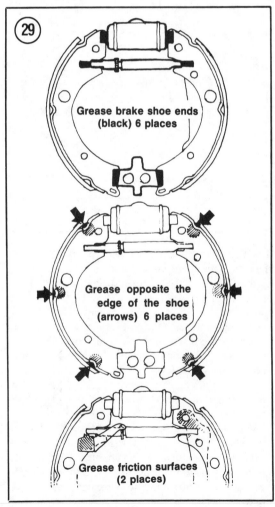

Grease brake shoe ends (black) 6 places

Grease opposite the edge of the shoe (arrows) 6 places

Grease friction surfaces (2 places)

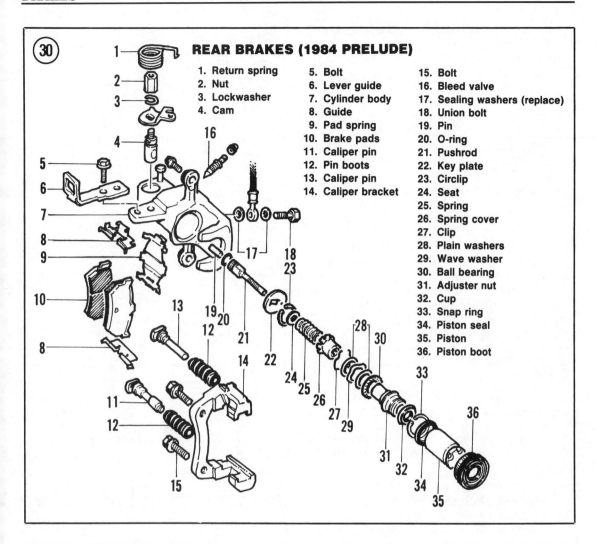

(30) **REAR BRAKES (1984 PRELUDE)**

1. Return spring
2. Nut
3. Lockwasher
4. Cam

5. Bolt
6. Lever guide
7. Cylinder body
8. Guide
9. Pad spring
10. Brake pads
11. Caliper pin
12. Pin boots
13. Caliper pin
14. Caliper bracket

15. Bolt
16. Bleed valve
17. Sealing washers (replace)
18. Union bolt
19. Pin
20. O-ring
21. Pushrod
22. Key plate
23. Circlip
24. Seat
25. Spring
26. Spring cover
27. Clip
28. Plain washers
29. Wave washer
30. Ball bearing
31. Adjuster nut
32. Cup
33. Snap ring
34. Piston seal
35. Piston
36. Piston boot

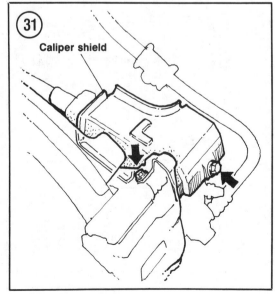

(31) Caliper shield

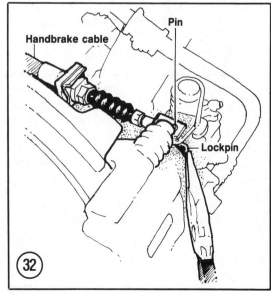

(32) Handbrake cable — Pin — Lockpin

12

8. Check the cylinder body for brake fluid leaks. If fluid has leaked from the cylinder, have the caliper overhauled.

9. Check the pad guides for wear, damage or corrosion. Replace them if these conditions are found.

10. Carefully clean the space which holds the brake pads. Use alcohol or aerosol brake cleaner. Do not use gasoline, kerosene or solvent. These leave residues which can cause rubber parts to soften and swell.

11. Install the pad guides (**Figure 35**).

CAUTION
During the next step, do not twist the piston boot.

12. Rotate the piston clockwise as shown in **Figure 36**, so it retracts into the cylinder to make room for the new pads. Make sure one piston notch is positioned so it will align with the tab on the back of the inner pad when the pads are installed.

13. Install the pads on the mounting bracket. Position the caliper over the pads, install the caliper mounting bolts and tighten to specifications in **Table 2**.

14. Connect the handbrake cable.

Caliper Removal/Installation

1. Perform Steps 1-5 of *Pad Replacement*.

2. Disconnect the caliper brake hose (**Figure 33**). Take the caliper off.

CAUTION
Immediately plug the brake hose end to keep dirt out. Make sure no dirt enters the brake hose hole in the caliper.

3. Installation is the reverse of removal. Use new washers at the brake hose connection. Tighten the union bolt and caliper mounting bolts to specifications in **Table 2**.

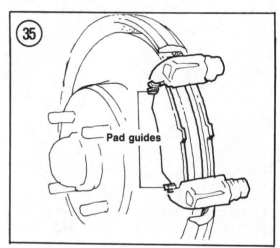

Pad guides

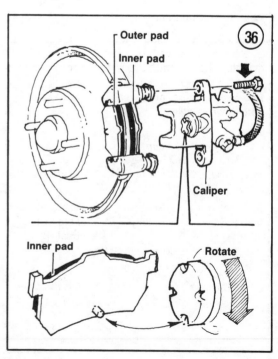

Outer pad
Inner pad
Caliper
Inner pad
Rotate

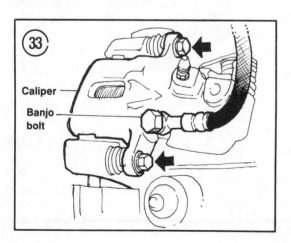

Caliper

Banjo bolt

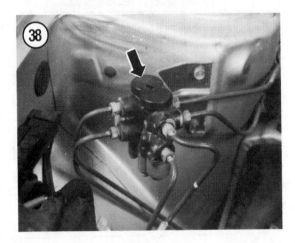

BRAKE BOOSTER

Service to the brake booster is limited to removal and installation. While the booster is rebuildable, special tools and experience are required. Overhaul should be done by a Honda dealer or qualified brake specialist.

NOTE
The price of booster overhaul should be compared to the price of a new or rebuilt booster before having the overhaul done.

Removal/Installation

Refer to **Figure 37** for this procedure.
1. Remove the master cylinder as described in this chapter.
2. Disconnect the booster vacuum line.
3. Working in the passenger compartment, detach the booster pushrod from the brake pedal. Remove the booster mounting nuts.
4. Lift the booster out into the engine compartment.
5. Installation is the reverse of removal. Bleed the brakes as described in this chapter.

PROPORTIONING VALVE

The proportioning valve prevents premature rear wheel lockup. On 1976-1979 models, 2 proportioning valves are used: primary and secondary. On 1980 and later models, one proportioning valve combining these functions is used. See **Figure 38**.

To replace the valve(s), label and disconnect the brake lines. Remove the mounting bolts and take the valve(s) out. Install in the reverse order and bleed the brakes as described in this chapter.

BRAKE LINE INSPECTION

Check the brake lines for the following:
a. Cracks, dents or wear. Replace lines that show these conditions.
b. Leaks at connections (have an assistant hold the pedal down while you check this). Tighten leaky connections. If tightening doesn't help, replace the connecting parts.
c. Deteriorated or twisted flexible brake hoses. Replace deteriorated hoses. Reposition twisted hoses to remove the twist.

Removal/Installation

1. Disconnect the fluid level sensor wires.
2. Place a rag beneath the master cylinder to catch dripping brake fluid. Disconnect the brake lines from the master cylinder with a flare nut wrench. Inexpensive flare nut wrenches are available at auto parts stores.

CAUTION
Immediately cap the ends of the brake lines to keep dirt out. Plastic vacuum caps, available from auto parts stores, work well for this.

3. Remove the master cylinder mounting nuts and take the master cylinder off the brake booster.
4. Installation is the reverse of removal. Bleed the brakes as described in this chapter.

WARNING
Do not drive the car unless the brake pedal feels firm. If the pedal feels soft, bleed the brakes again. If this doesn't help, check for worn hydraulic system parts and leaks in brake fluid lines.

12

BRAKE BLEEDING

The hydraulic system should be bled whenever air enters it. This is because air in the brake lines will compress, rather than transmitting pedal pressure to the brake operating parts. If the pedal feels spongy or if pedal travel increases considerably, brake bleeding is usually called for. Bleeding is also necessary whenever a brake line is disconnected.

This procedure requires handling brake fluid. Be careful not to get any fluid on brake discs, pads, shoes or drums. Clean all dirt from bleed valves before beginning. Two people are needed: one to operate the brake pedal and the other to open and close the bleed valves.

Bleeding should be done in the following order: left front, right rear, right front, left rear.

1. Clean away any dirt around the master cylinder reservoir. Top up the master cylinder with brake fluid marked DOT 3.

> *NOTE*
> *DOT 3 means the brake fluid meets current Department of Transportation quality standards. If the fluid doesn't say DOT 3 somewhere on the label, buy a brand that does.*

2. Attach a plastic tube to the bleed valve (**Figure 39**). Immerse the other end of the tube in a jar containing several inches of clean brake fluid.

> *NOTE*
> *Do not allow the end of the tube to come out of the brake fluid during bleeding. This could allow air into the system, requiring that the bleeding procedure be done over.*

3. Slowly press the brake pedal 2 or 3 times, then hold it down.

4. With the brake pedal down, open the bleed valve 1/3-1/2 turn. Let the brake pedal sink to the floor, then close the bleed valve. Do not let the pedal up until the bleed valve is closed.

5. Let the pedal back up slowly.

6. Repeat Steps 3-5 until the fluid entering the jar is free of air bubbles.

7. Repeat the process for the other bleed valves.

> *NOTE*
> *Keep an eye on the brake fluid level in the master cylinder during bleeding. If the fluid level is too low, air will enter the brake lines and the entire bleeding procedure will have to be repeated.*

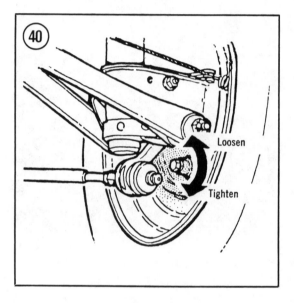

ADJUSTMENTS

Front Disc Brakes

The front disc brakes are adjusted automatically by the piston seals. No means of manual adjustment is necessary or provided.

Rear Drum Brakes (1976-1981 Accord)

Rear drum brakes on 1976-1981 Accords are adjusted manually.

1. Place the transaxle in FIRST (manual) or PARK (automatic). Securely block both front wheels so the car will not roll in either direction.

2. Make sure the handbrake is off.

3. Press the brake pedal 2 or 3 times and release it.

4. Jack up the rear end of the car and place it on jackstands.

5. Turn the brake adjuster (**Figure 40**) clockwise until the wheel is locked. Then back off the adjuster 2 clicks (1/2 turn).

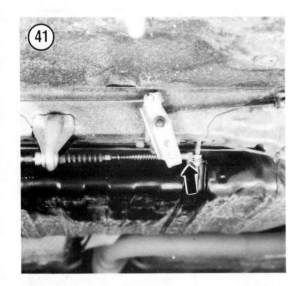

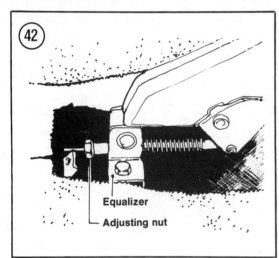

Equalizer

Adjusting nut

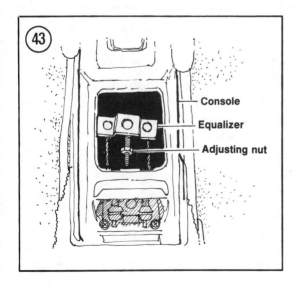

Console

Equalizer

Adjusting nut

6. Turn the wheel by hand and check for dragging brakes. If the brakes drag, back off the adjuster one more click.

7. Repeat Step 5 and Step 6 on the opposite rear wheel.

8. Remove the jackstands and lower the car.

Rear Drum Brakes
(1982-on Accord, 1979-1983 Prelude)

The rear drum brakes on these models are self-adjusting. No adjustment is required during normal operation. After shoe replacement or other brake service, press the brake pedal several times to set the self-adjusting mechanism.

Rear Disc Brakes (1984 Prelude)

The rear disc brakes are self-adjusting. No adjustment is required during normal operation. After pad replacement or other brake service, press the brake pedal several times to set the self-adjusting mechanism.

Handbrake Adjustment

1. Place the transaxle in FIRST (manual) or PARK (automatic). Securely block both front wheels so the car will not roll in either direction.

2. *1976-1981 Accord:* Adjust the rear brakes as described in this chapter.

3. *All except 1976-1981 Accord:* Press the brake pedal several times to make sure the self-adjuster mechanism sets itself.

4. If you haven't already done so, jack up the rear end of the car and place it on jackstands.

5. Loosen the handbrake equalizer nut:

   a. On 1976-1981 Accords and 1979-1982 Preludes, the equalizer nut is located under the car. See **Figure 41**.

   b. On 1982-on Accords and 1983-on Preludes, the nut is located inside the car. See **Figure 42** (1984 Accord, 1983-on Prelude) or **Figure 43** (1982-1983 Accord).

6. Raise the handbrake lever one notch.

7. Turn the equalizer nut clockwise until the rear wheels just begin to drag slightly. Turn the rear wheels by hand so you can tell when they begin to drag.

8. Release the handbrake lever. Turn the rear wheels by hand again and make sure they no longer drag. If they do, repeat Step 6 and Step 7.

9. Raise the handbrake lever slowly, counting the notches, until the rear wheels are locked. Compare the number of notches with **Table 1** at the end of the chapter:

   a. If the rear wheels lock when the lever is raised the specified number of notches, the procedure

12

is done. Remove the jackstands, lower the car and unblock the front wheels.

b. If the rear wheels do not lock when the lever is raised the specified number of notches, repeat Steps 6-9. If this doesn't work, check the handbrake linkage and rear brakes for wear or damage.

Brake Pedal Height

Refer to **Figure 44** (Prelude) or **Figure 45** (Accord).

1. Disconnect the brake light switch wiring.
2. Loosen the brake light switch locknuts and back off the switch until it no longer contacts the pad on the brake pedal.
3. Measure pedal height from the floor. **Figure 44** shows the Prelude measurement. The Accord measurement is similar. Compare with specifications in **Table 1**.
4. If pedal height is incorrect, loosen the pedal pushrod locknut (**Figure 46**). Rotate the pushrod to change pedal height, then tighten the locknut securely.
5. Turn the brake light switch in until its plunger is completely pressed in and the threaded end of the switch contacts the brake pedal. Then back off the switch 1/2 turn and tighten its locknuts.
6. Reconnect the brake light switch wiring.
7. Have an assistant press the brake pedal. Make sure the brake lights come on when the pedal is pressed and go off when the pedal is released. If they don't perform as described, readjust the brake light switch.

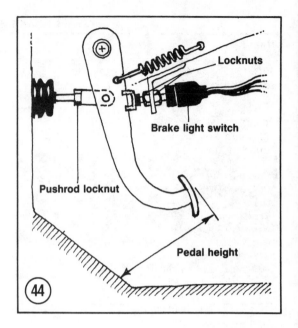

Locknuts

Brake light switch

Pushrod locknut

Pedal height

44

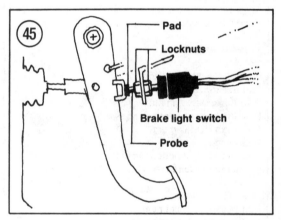

45

Pad

Locknuts

Brake light switch

Probe

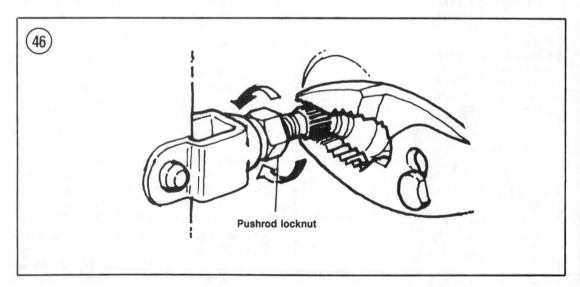

46

Pushrod locknut

Table 1 BRAKE SPECIFICATIONS

Item	mm	in.
1976-1981 Accord		
Pad thickness, minimum		
1976-1978	1.0	0.04
1979-1981	1.6	0.06
Pad thickness variation	2.0	0.08
Disc thickness, minimum		
1976-1978	11	0.43
1979-1981	10.5	0.41
Disc thickness variation, maximum	0.015	0.0006
Disc runout, maximum	0.15	0.006
Drum inside diameter, maximum	181	7.126
Shoe lining thickness, minimum	2.0	0.079
Handbrake notches	3-7	—
Pedal height	184	7.24
1982-1983 Accord		
Pad thickness, minimum	1.6	0.06
Pad thickness variation	2.0	0.08
Disc thickness, minimum	15	0.60
Disc thickness variation, maximum	0.015	0.0006
Disc runout, maximum	0.15	0.006
Drum inside diameter, maximum	201	7.91
Shoe lining thickness, minimum	2.0	0.079
Handbrake notches	4-8	—
Pedal height	187	7.36
1984 Accord		
Pad thickness, minimum	1.5	0.059
Pad thickness variation	2.0	0.08
Disc thickness, minimum	17	0.67
Disc thickness variation, maximum	0.015	0.0006
Disc runout, maximum	0.15	0.006
Drum inside diameter, maximum	201	7.91
Shoe lining thickness, minimum	2.0	0.079
Handbrake notches	4-8	—
Pedal height	187	7.36
1979-1982 Prelude		
Pad thickness, minimum	1.6	0.063
Pad thickness variation	2.0	0.079
Disc thickness, minimum		
1979-1981	10.5	0.413
1982	10.0	0.394
Disc thickness variation, maximum	0.015	0.0006
Disc runout, maximum	0.15	0.006
Drum inside diameter, maximum	181	7.13
Shoe lining thickness, minimum	2.0	0.079
Handbrake notches		
1979-1981	3-7	—
1982	4-8	—
Pedal height	184	7.25

(continued)

12

Table 1 BRAKE SPECIFICATIONS (continued)

Item	mm	in.
1983 Prelude		
Pad thickness, minimum	3.0	0.118
Disc thickness, minimum	15	0.59
Disc thickness variation, maximum	0.015	0.0006
Disc runout, maximum	0.15	0.006
Drum inside diameter, maximum	201	7.91
Shoe lining thickness, minimum	2.0	0.08
Handbrake notches	4-8	—
Pedal height	176	7
1984 Prelude		
Front disc brakes		
Pad thickness, minimum	3.0	0.12
Disc thickness, minimum	17	0.67
Disc thickness variation, maximum	0.015	0.0006
Disc runout, maximum	0.10	0.004
Rear disc brakes		
Pad thickness, minimum	1.6	0.06
Disc thickness, minimum	8.0	0.31
Disc thickness variation, maximum	0.015	0.0006
Disc runout maximum	0.15	0.0006
Handbrake notches	4-8	—
Pedal height	176	7

Table 2 TIGHTENING TORQUES

Part	N•m	ft.-lb.
1976-1978 Accord		
Caliper mounting bolts	80-90	58-66
Caliper brake hose union bolt	10-14	7-10
Caliper bleed valve	9-13	6.5-9.5
Disc-to-hub bolts	50-60	36-43
Disc backing plate bolts	4-6	2.9-4.3
Rear wheel cylinder nuts	5-7	3.6-5.1
Rear backing plate bolts	19-25	14-18
Master cylinder mounting nuts	15-20	11-15
Brake booster mounting nuts	7-12	5-9
1979-1981 Accord		
Caliper mounting bolts	80	56
Caliper brake hose union bolt	35	25
Caliper bleed valve	9	6.5
Disc-to-hub bolts	55	40
Disc backing plate bolts	5	4
Rear wheel cylinder nuts	6	4.5
Rear backing plate bolts	22	16
Master cylinder mounting nuts		
1979	18	13
1980-1981	14	10
Brake booster mounting nuts	10	7

(continued)

Table 2 TIGHTENING TORQUES (continued)

Part	N•m	ft.-lb.
1982-on Accord		
Caliper mounting bolts	78	56
Caliper guide bolts	27	20
Caliper brake hose union bolt	35	25
Caliper bleed valve	9	7
Rear backing plate bolts	30	22
Master cylinder mounting nuts	7	5
Master cylinder stop bolt	7	5
Brake booster mounting nuts	13	9
1979-1982 Prelude		
Caliper mounting bolts	77	56
Caliper pin bolts	18	13
Caliper brake hose union bolt	35	25
Caliper bleed valve	9	6
Disc-to-hub screws	9	6
Disc backing plate screws	5	4
Rear backing plate bolts	55	40
Master cylinder mounting nuts	14	10
Master cylinder stop bolt	9	6
Brake booster mounting nuts	10	7
1983 Prelude		
Caliper mounting bolts	78	56
Caliper upper guide bolt	19	14
Caliper lower guide bolt	18	13
Caliper brake hose union bolt	35	25
Caliper bleed valve	9	7
Rear backing plate bolts	30	22
Master cylinder mounting nuts	7	5
Master cylinder stop bolt	9	6
Brake booster mounting nuts	13	9
1984 Prelude		
Front calipers		
Caliper mounting bolts	78	56
Caliper upper pin bolt	19	14
Caliper lower pin bolt	18	13
Caliper brake hose union bolt	35	25
Caliper bleed valve	9	6
Rear calipers		
Caliper bracket bolts	39	28
Caliper mounting bolts	30	22
Handbrake lever guide bolt	27	20
Caliper brake hose union bolt	35	25
Caliper bleed valve	9	6
Master cylinder mounting nuts	14	10
Master cylinder stop bolt	9	6

12

1985 SERVICE INFORMATION

The following supplement provides procedures unique to all models since 1985.

The 1985 Accord SEi model is equipped with fuel injection. The top end (cylinder head and related items and both manifolds) on the SEi engine is unique while the lower end (cylinder block and related items) are the same as on the carburetted Accord models. On the fuel injected models, unless otherwise noted, follow the service procedures relating to carburetted Accord models.

The chapter headings in this supplement correspond to those in the main body of this book. If a change is not included in the supplement, there are no changes affecting models since 1985.

CHAPTER THREE

SCHEDULED MAINTENANCE

Refer to **Table 1** for the factory suggested maintenance schedule. Refer to **Table 2** for tune-up specifications which differ for 1984 models.

Fuel Filter (Fuel Injected Accord)

> *WARNING*
> *Whenever disconnecting any fuel lines on the fuel injection system, wear eye protection and have a fire extinguisher, rated for gasoline fires, handy. Work in a well ventilated area, away from open flames (including home appliance pilot lights) and do not allow anyone to smoke in the work area.*

> *NOTE*
> *If the engine loses power or "stumbles" at high speed or when accelerating or climbing hills, the problem may be caused by a clogged fuel filter.*

The fuel filter should be replaced at the intervals specified in **Table 1**.

Refer to **Figure 1** for this procedure.

1. Place the transaxle in FIRST (manual) or PARK (automatic).

2. Open the hood and disconnect the battery negative lead.

3. Place a small flat pan (pie tin) under the fuel filter to catch as much fuel as possible.

> *WARNING*
> *The fuel injection system is under pressure. Do not loosen any of the union bolts on the fuel filter until the fuel system is depressurized.*

4. Hold the special union bolt with an open end wrench and attach a 6 mm box wrench onto the service bolt as shown in **Figure 2**.

5. Place a shop cloth over the service bolt and slowly loosen the service bolt one full turn with the wrench. This will relieve the pressure within the fuel system. Discard any spilled fuel properly.

6. Remove the union bolts and sealing washers on each side of both fuel hose fittings. Discard the sealing washers as they cannot be reused.

7. Remove the fuel filter clamp bolt and clamp.

8. Remove the fuel filter from mounting bracket on the firewall.

9. Install the new fuel filter into the mounting bracket with the fuel line locating tabs facing away from the firewall.

10. Install the clamp and clamp bolt. Do not completely tighten the clamp bolt at this time.

11. Refer to **Figure 2** and install the union bolts and new sealing washers. Be sure to install a new sealing washer on each side of both fuel line fittings.

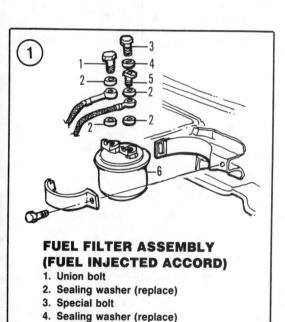

**FUEL FILTER ASSEMBLY
(FUEL INJECTED ACCORD)**
1. Union bolt
2. Sealing washer (replace)
3. Special bolt
4. Sealing washer (replace)
5. Special union bolt
6. Fuel filter

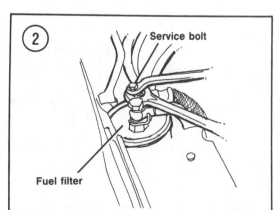

Service bolt

Fuel filter

13

12. Make sure the fuel lines are indexed properly into the locating tabs on the fuel filter and tighten the union bolts to 25 N•m (18 ft.-lb.).

13. Tighten the clamp bolts securely.

14. Remove the service bolt and sealing washer from the top of the special union bolt. Discard the sealing washer and install a new sealing washer.

15. Hold the special union bolt with an open end wrench and tighten the 6 mm service bolt, with a box wrench, to 12 N•m (9 ft.-lb.).

16. Attach the battery negative lead. Test drive the car a short distance and check the fuel filter for fuel leakage.

Drive Belts

The drive belts drive the water pump, alternator, air conditioner compressor and power steering pump. A belt in poor condition or improperly adjusted can cause serious cooling or battery charging problems.

1. At the specified time or mileage, check the belts for wear, fraying or cracking. If any of these conditions exist, replace the belt as described in this supplement.

NOTE
On models equipped with air conditioning or power steering, the air conditioning compressor belt and power steering pump belt must be removed before the alternator belt can be removed.

2. If the belts are in good condition, check belt tension and adjust if necessary. To check tension, press on the belt midway between pulleys and note how far the belt deflects. If belt tension is not within specifications, adjust it as described in this supplement.

Alternator and water pump belt
(Fuel injected Accord)

1. Loosen the alternator adjusting bolt and mounting nut (**Figure 3**).

2. Push the alternator toward the engine to loosen the belt, then take the belt off the pulleys.

3. Install a new belt on the pulleys. Pry the alternator away from the engine until belt tension is 3-6 mm (0.12-0.24 in.). On initial adjustment of a new belt the tension is 3 mm (0.12 in.).

4. Tighten the mounting nut and adjusting bolt.

Air conditioner belt
(Accord-Nippondenso type)

Refer to **Figure 4** for this procedure.

1. Loosen the compressor mounting and adjusting bolts.

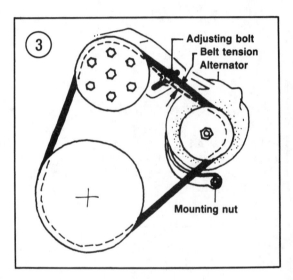

Adjusting bolt
Belt tension
Alternator
Mounting nut

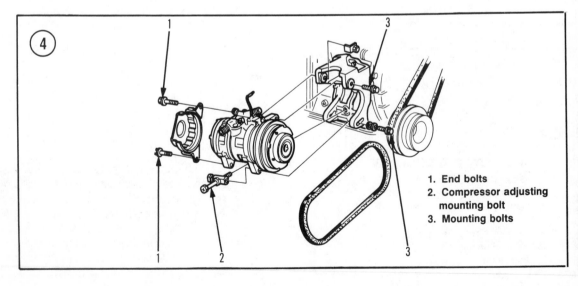

1. End bolts
2. Compressor adjusting mounting bolt
3. Mounting bolts

2. Push the compressor toward the engine to loosen the belt, then take the belt off the pulleys.

3. Install a new belt on the pulleys. Pry the compressor away from the engine until belt tension is 8-10 mm (0.31-0.40 in.).

4. Tighten the adjusting and mounting bolts.

Crankcase Emission Controls

Fuel injected Accord

1. Check the system hoses for cracks, deterioration, clogging or looseness. Replace, clean or tighten as needed.

2. Remove the PCV valve from the chamber cover on the backside of the engine.

3. Start the engine and let it idle. While the engine idles, plug the bottom of the PCV valve with a finger as shown in **Figure 5**. A click should be heard as the valve is plugged:

   a. If a click is heard, the valve is good.

   b. If there is no click, replace the valve and repeat Step 3.

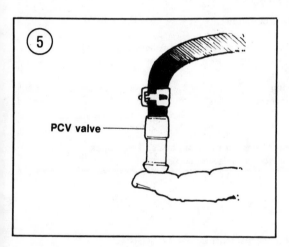

PCV valve

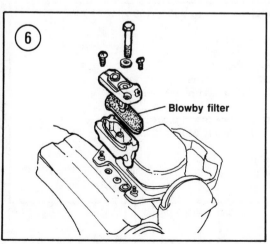

Blowby filter

4. Check the PCV valve's grommet in the chamber cover for cracks or deterioration. Replace it if conditions are found.

5. Reinstall the PCV valve in the chamber cover.

6. Remove the air cleaner cover as described in this supplement.

7. Remove the bolt and washer and the Phillips screws securing the blow-by housing to the valve cover (**Figure 6**).

8. Inspect the blow-by filter and replace it if it is contaminated with dirt or oil.

TUNE-UP

Valve Clearance Adjustment

Fuel injected Accord models

The valve clearance procedure is the same as on *1984 Accord, 1983-on Prelude* as described in Chapter Three in the main body of this book with the following exceptions. This engine is not equipped with the auxiliary valves.

1. Remove the air cleaner cover as described in this supplement.

2. Refer to **Figure 7** for valve identification and locations.

3. Refer to **Table 2** for valve clearance dimensions.

Spark Plugs

Spark plug service is the same as on earlier models with the exception of the heat range for the fuel injected Accord models. Refer to **Table 2** for spark plug recommendations.

Ignition Timing

The ignition timing procedure is the same as on earlier models with the exception of the crankshaft timing degrees. Refer to **Table 2** for timing degrees.

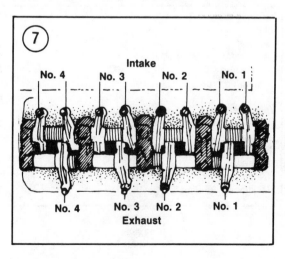

Intake
No. 4   No. 3   No. 2   No. 1

No. 4   No. 3 No. 2   No. 1
Exhaust

13

Table 1 MAINTENANCE SCHEDULE (FUEL INJECTED ACCORD)

Every 7,500 miles	• Change engine oil and filter • Inspect front brake pads and discs • Check clutch pedal and release arm • Inspect power steering system and check power steering fluid
Every 15,000 miles	• Check automatic transaxle fluid • Check suspension mounting bolt tightness[1] • Inspect exhaust system[1] • Inspect brake lines and hoses[1] • Adjust valve clearance[2] • Check front wheel alignment
Every 30,000 miles	• Check manual transaxle oil • Inspect rear brake linings • Inspect parking brake[1] • Inspect steering system and check operation • Change brake fluid • Inspect cooling system hoses and connections • Inspect and adjust alternator belt • Inspect and adjust power steering pump belt • Inspect crankcase emission control system • Replace spark plugs[2] • Replace air cleaner element
Every 60,000 miles	• Lubricate rear wheel bearings • Inspect fuel lines and connections • Replace fuel filter and engine compartment hoses • Inspect distributor cap and rotor[2] • Inspect ignition wiring • Check ignition timing • Inspect emission control systems[3]

1. First inspection @ 7,500 miles
2. Described under Tune-up in this supplement and Chapter Three in the main body of this book.
3. Have done by a Honda dealer or mechanic familiar with Honda emission controls.

Table 2 TUNE-UP SPECIFICATIONS (FUEL INJECTED ACCORD)

Ignition timing	18 BTDC ±2° at 750 ±100 rpm
Idle speed	
Manual	750 ±100 rpm
Automatic	700 ±100 rpm
Idle mixture CO%	See dealer
Spark plug type	NGK BPR6EY-11 or BPR6ES-11 ND W20EXR-U11 or W20EPR-11
Valve clearance	
Intake	0.12-0.17 mm (0.005-0.007 in.)
Exhaust	0.25-0.30 mm (0.010-0.012 in.)
Compression	
Normal	184 psi
Minimum	156 psi
Maximum variation	28 psi

CHAPTER FIVE

12-VALVE ENGINE

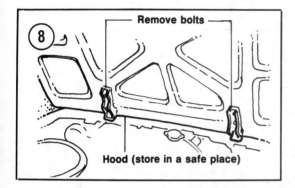

Remove bolts

Hood (store in a safe place)

Oil drain plug

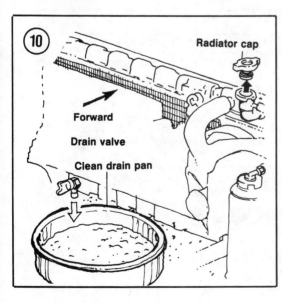

Radiator cap

Forward

Drain valve

Clean drain pan

The service procedures in this portion of the supplement are the only ones unique to the 1985 fuel injected Accord models. Service procedures not listed are identical to 1984 carburetted Accord models and are covered in Chapter Five in the main body of this book.

The cylinder head on the 1985 fuel injected Accord is the same as used on 1984-on Prelude models.

ENGINE REMOVAL
(FUEL INJECTED ACCORD MODELS)

WARNING
At all times during this procedure, keep the rear wheels securely blocked so the car will not roll in either direction.

1. Disconnect the negative cable from the battery, then the positive cable.
2. Unbolt the hood hinges and remove the hood. See **Figure 8**.
3. Remove the splash shield from under the car.
4. Remove the oil filler cap. Place pan under the oil drain plug (**Figure 9**) and drain the oil. Once the oil is drained, reinstall the drain plug, using a new gasket.
5. Remove the radiator cap. Place a pan beneath the radiator drain valve (**Figure 10**) and drain the radiator.

WARNING
Ethylene glycol is poisonous and may attract animals. Do not store the drained antifreeze where it is accessible to children or pets.

6. Remove the transaxle filler plug (manual) or filler plug/dipstick (automatic). See **Figure 11**. Place a pan beneath the transaxle and remove the drain plug. Use a 3/8 in. drive ratchet without a socket to remove the drain plug. Let the transaxle oil or fluid drain, then reinstall the drain plug.
7. Disconnect the resonator tube (A, **Figure 12**) and the cruise control vacuum hose (B, **Figure 12**) from the air intake duct. Remove the air intake duct (C, **Figure 12**).

13

8. Disconnect the engine secondary ground cable.

9. Disconnect the emission tubes (A, **Figure 13**) and remove the connecting tube bolt (B, **Figure 13**). Remove the connecting tube (C, **Figure 13**).

10. Remove the nuts securing the air cleaner case and remove the air cleaner case (**Figure 14**).

11. Loosen the throttle cable locknut and adjust nut. Carefully disconnect the throttle cable from the throttle linkage wheel. Do not use pliers as the cable may get kinked in the process. If the cable is kinked, it must be replaced.

12. Disconnect the ground cable from the fuse box on the right-hand fender panel.

13. Disconnect the engine compartment sub-harness electrical connector located between the battery and the fuse box. Remove the sub-harness clamp.

14. Disconnect the ignition coil electrical wires (**Figure 15**).

15. Disconnect the radio condenser electrical connector.

16. Depressurize the fuel system as follows:

a. Place a small flat pan (pie tin) under the fuel filter to catch as much fuel as possible.

WARNING
The fuel injection system is under pressure. Do not loosen any of the union bolts on the fuel system until the fuel system is de-pressurized.

b. Hold the special union bolt with an open end wrench and attach a 6 mm box wrench onto the service bolt as shown in **Figure 2**.

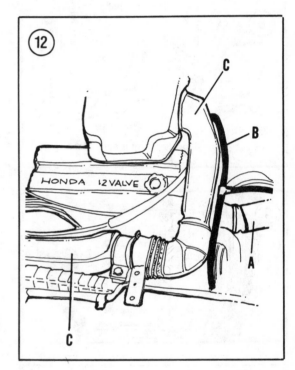

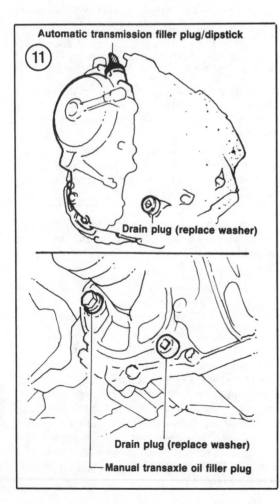

Automatic transmission filler plug/dipstick

Drain plug (replace washer)

Drain plug (replace washer)

Manual transaxle oil filler plug

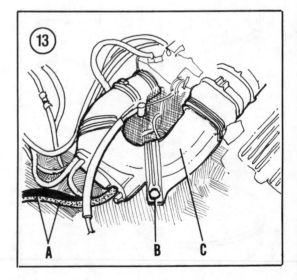

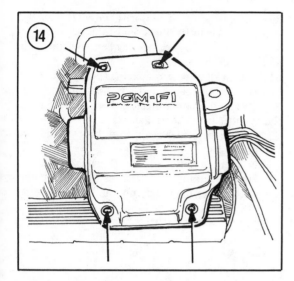

c. Place a shop cloth over the service bolt and slowly loosen the service bolt one full turn with the wrench. This will relieve the pressure within the fuel system. Discard any spilled fuel properly.

17. Disconnect the fuel return hose (A, **Figure 16**) from the pressure regulator.

18. Remove the special nut (B, **Figure 16**) and remove the fuel hose (C, **Figure 16**) from fuel pipe.

19. Disconnect the emission hoses from the tubing manifold.

20. Disconnect the electrical connectors (A, **Figure 17**) then remove the bolts (B, **Figure 17**) securing

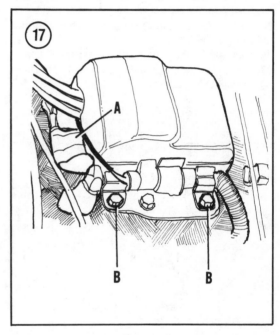

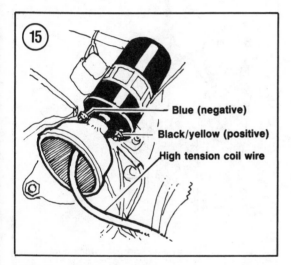

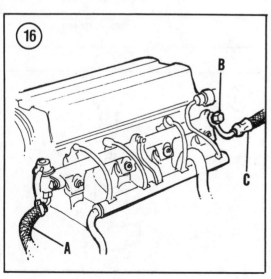

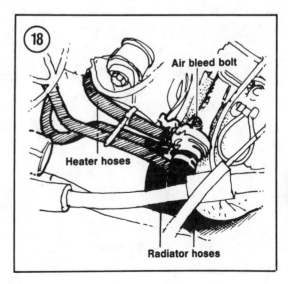

13

the No. 2 control box to the left-hand fender well. Let the control box hang down next to the engine.

21. Disconnect the vacuum hose from the master cylinder vacuum booster.

22. Disconnect the radiator and heater hoses from the engine (**Figure 18**). Mark the hoses so they will be reinstalled correctly.

23. If equipped with a manual transaxle, disconnect the clutch cable from the release fork. See Chapter Nine in the main body of this book for details.

24. If equipped with an automatic transaxle, disconnect the fluid cooler hoses (**Figure 19**). Cap or plug the hoses and their fittings to keep out dirt, then hang the hoses out of the way.

25. Disconnect the battery negative cable from the attaching point on the transaxle.

26. Disconnect the starter cable from the starter.

27. Unplug the engine electrical harness connectors (**Figure 20**).

> *CAUTION*
> *In the next step, do not remove the speedometer cable holder or the speedometer gear may fall into the transaxle housing.*

28. On cars without power steering, remove the speedometer cable clip. Pull the speedometer cable out of the holder. See **Figure 21**.

> *NOTE*
> *Steps 29-32 apply to cars with power steering.*

> *CAUTION*
> *During the next step, do not disconnect the hoses from the speed sensor on the power steering pump.*

29. Detach the speed sensor (**Figure 22**). Lay the speed sensor and its hoses out of the way.

30. Remove the power steering belt adjusting bolt and take off the belt.

31. Detach the power steering pump from its bracket. Lay the pump and hoses out of the way.

32. Detach the power steering hose bracket from the cylinder head. See **Figure 23**.

33. Detach the center beam from beneath the car. See **Figure 24**.

34. Loosen the radius rod nut (**Figure 24**).

35. Spray pentrating oil such as WD-40 on the exhaust pipe-to-manifold nuts and exhaust pipe

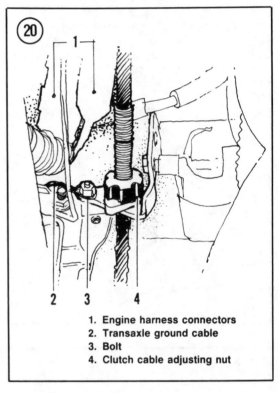

1. Engine harness connectors
2. Transaxle ground cable
3. Bolt
4. Clutch cable adjusting nut

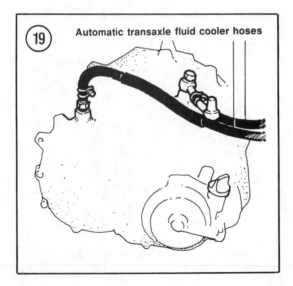

Automatic transaxle fluid cooler hoses

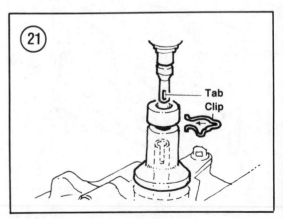

Tab
Clip

bracket bolts. See **Figure 25**. Remove the nuts and bolts, then remove the exhaust pipe.

NOTE
Steps 36-38 apply to cars with air conditioning.

WARNING
In the next steps, do not disconnect the air conditioning hoses. They contain refrigerant under high pressure which can cause frostbite if it touches skin and blindness if it touches the eyes.

36. Disconnect the compressor clutch wire (**Figure 26**).

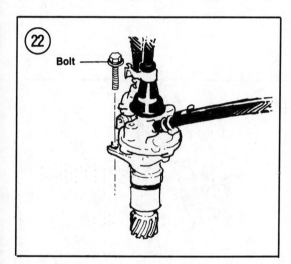

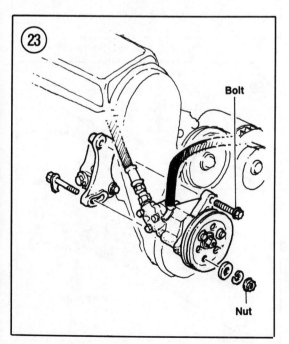

37. Loosen the compressor drive belt adjusting bolt. See **Figure 27**. Take the drive belt off.
38. Remove the compressor mounting bolts. Lift the compressor off the engine with hoses attached, then tie it to the front bulkhead.

NOTE
Step 39 and Step 40 apply to cars with a manual transaxle.

39. Remove the shift yoke rod attaching bolt (**Figure 28**).
40. Detach the shift lever torque rod from the clutch housing (**Figure 29**).

NOTE
Steps 41-44 apply to cars with an automatic transaxle.

41. Remove the center console.
42. Place the shift lever in REVERSE. Remove the lockpin assembly from the end of the shift cable. See **Figure 30**.
43. Remove the shift cable mounting bolts (**Figure 31**). Remove the cable holder.

CAUTION
During the next step, do not loosen the upper locknut or the transaxle shift points will change.

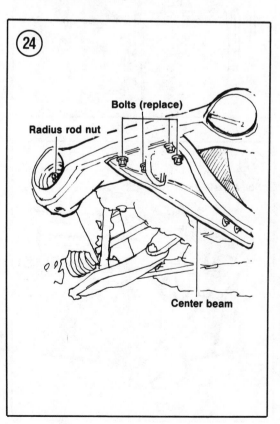

13

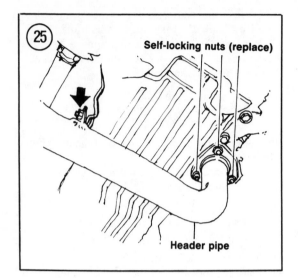

(25) Self-locking nuts (replace)

Header pipe

(28) Shift rod yoke attaching bolt

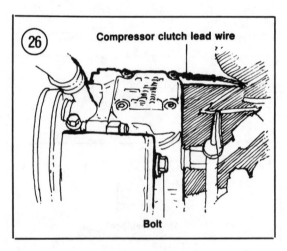

(26) Compressor clutch lead wire

Bolt

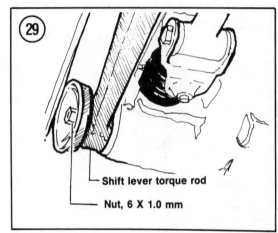

(29)

Shift lever torque rod

Nut, 6 X 1.0 mm

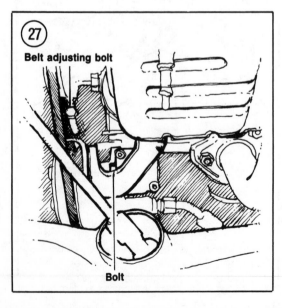

(27)

Belt adjusting bolt

Bolt

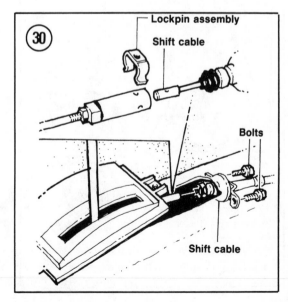

(30)

Lockpin assembly

Shift cable

Bolts

Shift cable

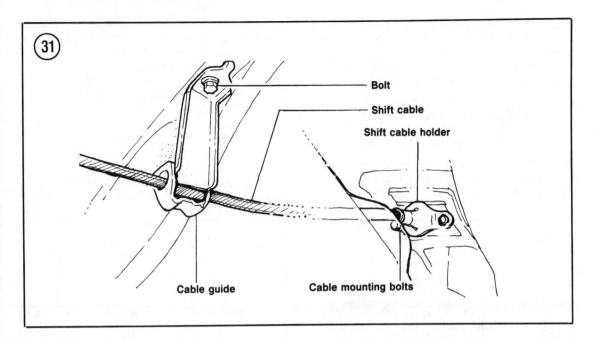

(31)

Bolt

Shift cable

Shift cable holder

Cable guide

Cable mounting bolts

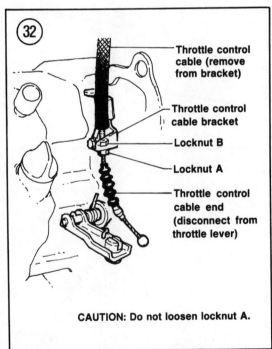

(32)

Throttle control cable (remove from bracket)

Throttle control cable bracket

Locknut B

Locknut A

Throttle control cable end (disconnect from throttle lever)

CAUTION: Do not loosen locknut A.

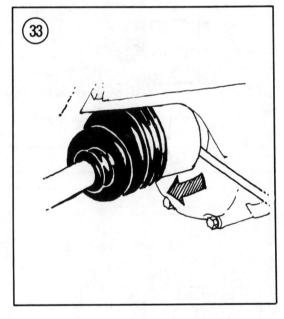

(33)

44. Disconnect the end of the throttle control cable from the transaxle throttle lever. See **Figure 32**. Loosen the lower locknut, but not the upper locknut and detach the throttle control cable from the bracket.

45. Turn each steering knuckle as far outboard as it will go. Gently pry the inner end of each axle shaft out of the transaxle as shown in **Figure 33**, then pull each axle shaft out of the transaxle. Discard the axle shaft spring clips (**Figure 34**). They must not be reused.

46. Remove the nuts that secure the exhaust pipe to the manifold. See **Figure 35**.

47. Detach the exhaust pipe bracket from the transaxle (**Figure 36**), then pull the exhaust pipe out of the way. Discard the exhaust pipe gasket and self-locking nuts. They must not be reused.

48. Disconnect the sub-harness electrical connector next to the brake master cylinder.

13

49. If equipped with cruise control, label and disconnect the cruise control vacuum lines at the intake manifold.

50. Remove the drive shafts as described in Chapter Ten in the main body of this book.

NOTE
For the next step, a portable hydraulic crane type hoist is easiest to use. These are available from tool rental dealers.

51. Attach a hoist to the engine lifting brackets. See **Figure 37**. Raise the hoist just enough to take the slack out of the chain.

52. If equipped with ari onditioing, unplug the idle control solenoid valve wire. See **Figure 38**. Detach the solenoid from the body and lay it out of the way with the tubes attached.

53. Remove the engine mounting bolts shown in **Figure 39**. Push the engine mount into the tower as shown in **Figure 40**.

54. Remove the front and rear engine mounting nuts. See **Figure 41** and **Figure 42**.

55. Remove the alternator as described in Chapter Eight.

56. Unbolt the rear torque rod from the engine. See **Figure 43**. Loosen the bolt that secures the

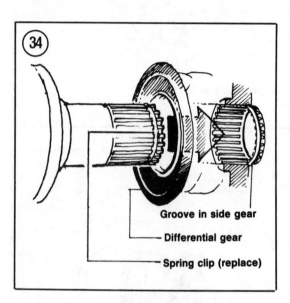

Groove in side gear

Differential gear

Spring clip (replace)

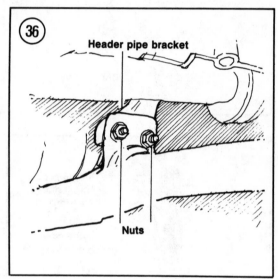

Header pipe bracket

Nuts

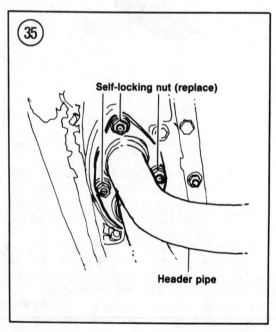

Self-locking nut (replace)

Header pipe

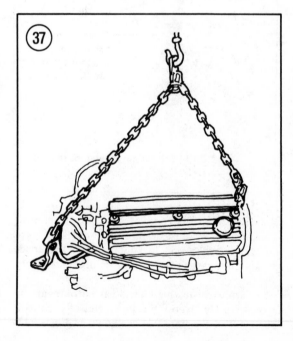

torque rod to the frame and pivot the torque rod up and out of the way.

CAUTION
At this point, all linkage, wires and hoses should be disconnected. Recheck this to make sure nothing can hamper engine removal.

57. Slowly raise the engine and transaxle approximately 6 inches. See **Figure 44**. Stop raising at this point and make sure the engine and transaxle are completely disconnected from the car.

58. Pull the engine and transaxle up and out of the engine compartment, then move them away from the car. Remove the transaxle from the engine and transfer the engine to a suitable stand or work surface.

CAUTION
To prevent damage or deterioration, tie plastic bags over the ends of the drive shafts. Coat all precision-finished surfaces with clean engine oil or grease.

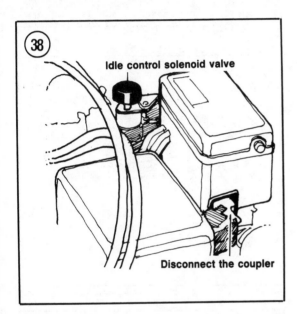

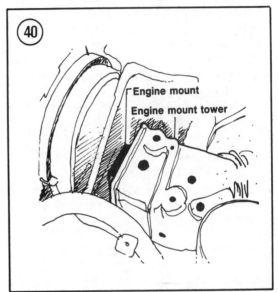

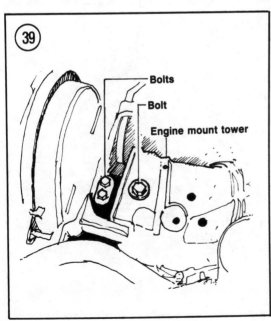

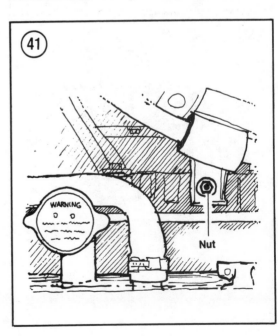

13

ENGINE INSTALLATION
(FUEL INJECTED ACCORD MODELS)

Installation is the reverse of removal, plus the following.

1. Tighten the engine mountings in the order shown in **Figure 45**. Tightening torques are listed in **Table 3** in this supplement.

2. Fill the engine and transaxle with oils recommended in Chapter Three in the main body of this book.

3. Fill and bleed the cooling system as described in Chapter Seven in the main body of this book.

4. Install the drive shafts as described in Chapter Ten in the main body of this book.

5. Adjust the throttle cable as described in Chapter Six in the main body of this book.

6. If equipped with a manual transaxle, check clutch pedal free play as described in Chapter Nine in the main body of this book.

7. If equipped with an automatic transaxle, have the throttle control cable adjustment checked by a Honda dealer or other qualified specialist.

CYLINDER HEAD REMOVAL
(FUEL INJECTED ACCORD)

The cylinder head design is basically the same as used on the 1984-on Prelude. Refer to **Figure 46** for this procedure.

1. Make sure the coolant temperature is below 38° C (100° F) before removing the cylinder head.

2. Open the hood and disconnect the battery negative lead.

3. Place a drain pan beneath the radiator drain valve and drain the cooling system. If the coolant is clean and kept clean, save it for reuse.

WARNING
Ethylene glycol is poisonous and may attract animals. Do not leave the drained coolant where it is accessible to children or pets.

4. Turn the engine so No. 1 piston is at top dead center (TDC) on its compression stroke. When this

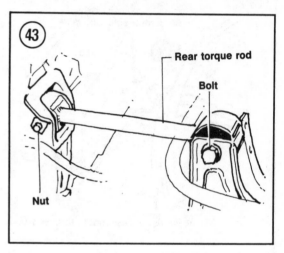

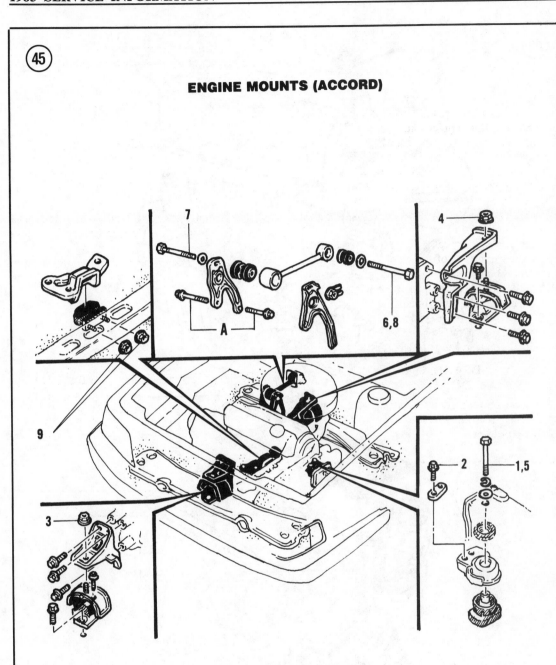

ENGINE MOUNTS (ACCORD)

Tighten numbered bolts in the order shown.
See Table 3 at the end of the chapter for
tightening torques. Make sure the rubber
damper on the center beam is centered in
its mount on the transaxle. If not, loosen
the damper and center beam fasteners (9),
center the damper and retighten the fasteners.

13

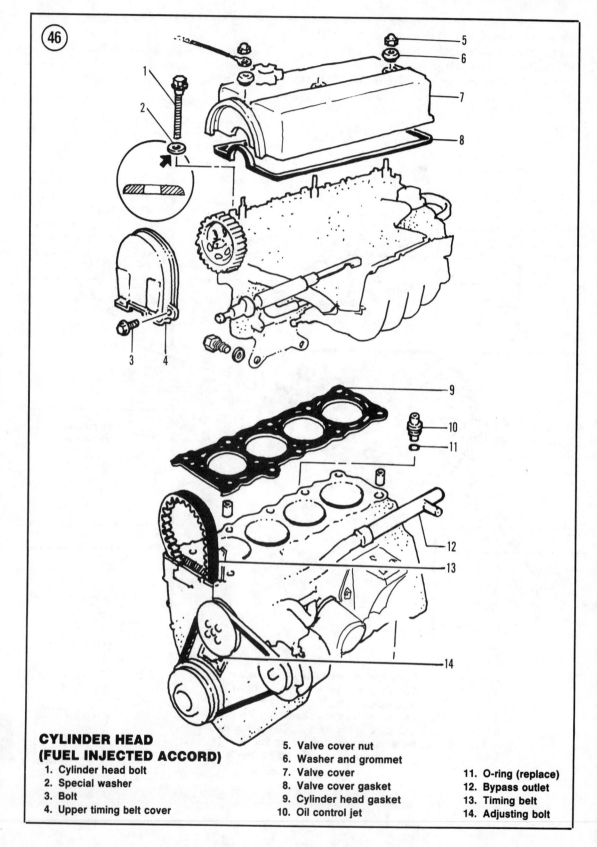

**CYLINDER HEAD
(FUEL INJECTED ACCORD)**

1. Cylinder head bolt
2. Special washer
3. Bolt
4. Upper timing belt cover
5. Valve cover nut
6. Washer and grommet
7. Valve cover
8. Valve cover gasket
9. Cylinder head gasket
10. Oil control jet
11. O-ring (replace)
12. Bypass outlet
13. Timing belt
14. Adjusting bolt

occurs, the camshaft "UP" mark will be at the top and its timing mark will be aligned with the valve cover surface as shown in **Figure 47**. In addition, the crankcase pointer will point to the top dead center mark. See **Figure 48** (manual) or **Figure 49** (automatic).

5. Disconnect the brake booster vacuum hose (**Figure 50**).

6. Disconnect the resonator tube (A, **Figure 12**) and the cruise control vacuum hose (B, **Figure 12**) from the air intake duct. Remove the air intake duct (C, **Figure 12**).

7. Disconnect the emission tubes (A, **Figure 13**) and remove the connecting tube bolt (B, **Figure 13**). Remove the connecting tube (C, **Figure 13**).

8. Remove the nuts securing the air cleaner case and remove the air cleaner case (**Figure 14**).

9. Remove the distributor as described in this supplement.

10. Depressurize the fuel system as follows:
   a. Place a small flat pan (pie tin) under the fuel filter to catch as much fuel as possible.

WARNING
The fuel injection system is under pressure. Do not loosen any of the union bolts on the fuel filter until the fuel system is de-pressurized.

   b. Hold the special union bolt with an open end wrench and attach a 6 mm box wrench onto the service bolt as shown in **Figure 2**.
   c. Place a shop cloth over the service bolt and slowly loosen the service bolt one full turn with the wrench. This will relieve the pressure

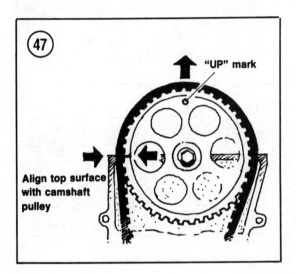

47. "UP" mark
Align top surface with camshaft pulley

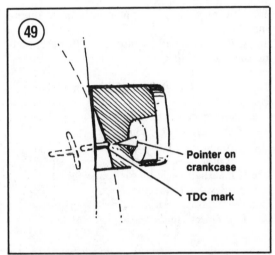

49. Pointer on crankcase
TDC mark

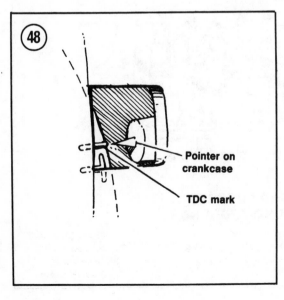

48. Pointer on crankcase
TDC mark

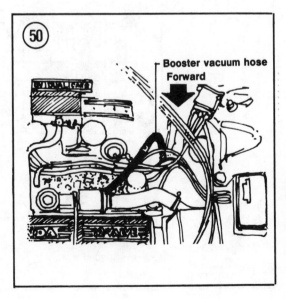

50. Booster vacuum hose
Forward

13

within the fuel system. Discard any spilled fuel properly.

11. Disconnect the fuel return hose (A, **Figure 16**) from the pressure regulator.

12. Remove the special nut (B, **Figure 16**) and remove the fuel hose (C, **Figure 16**) from fuel pipe.

13. Loosen the throttle cable locknut and adjust nut. Carefully disconnect the throttle cable from the throttle linkage wheel. Do not use pliers as the cable may get kinked in the process. If the cable is kinked, it must be replaced.

14. Disconnect the engine secondary ground cable (**Figure 51**).

15. Disconnect the charcoal canister tube at the throttle valve.

16. Disconnect the ignition coil wires (**Figure 15**).

17. Disconnect the radio condenser electrical connector.

18. Disconnect the emission hoses from the tubing manifold.

19. On models with cruise control, label and detach the cruise control vacuum hoses at the intake manifold.

20. Disconnect the following sub-harness electrical connectors:

    a. Fuel injector connectors.

    b. Temperature unit connector.

    c. Ground terminals on the fuel pipe.

    d. Throttle sensor connector.

    e. Crankshaft angle sensor connector.

    f. EGR valve connector.

    g. Wire harness clamps (4).

21. Disconnect the oxygen sensor coupler.

22. Disconnect the radiator and heater hoses from the engine (**Figure 18**). Mark the hoses so they will be reinstalled correctly.

23. Disconnect the hose between the thermostat housing and the intake manifold.

24. Detach the connecting pipe-to-valve body hose and the bypass outlet hose.

NOTE
Steps 25-28 apply to cars with power steering.

CAUTION
During the next step, do not disconnect the hoses from the speed sensor on the power steering pump.

25. Detach the speed sensor (**Figure 22**). Lay the speed sensor and its hoses out of the way.

26. Remove the power steering belt adjusting bolt and take the belt off.

27. Detach the power steering pump from its bracket. Lay the pump and hoses out of the way.

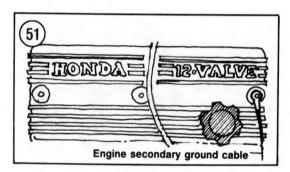

Engine secondary ground cable

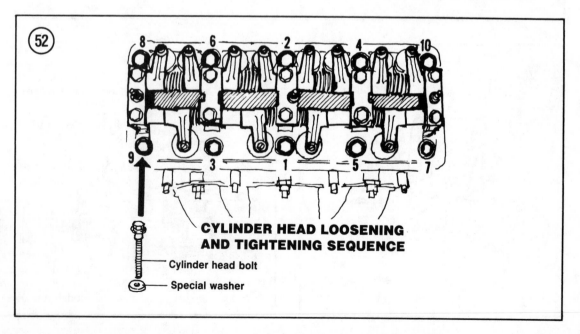

CYLINDER HEAD LOOSENING AND TIGHTENING SEQUENCE

Cylinder head bolt

Special washer

28. Detach the power steering hose bracket from the cylinder head. See **Figure 23**.

29. Remove the nuts and washers securing the valve cover and remove the cover and gasket.

30. Remove the engine splash guard.

31. Spray penetrating oil such as WD-40 on the exhaust pipe-to-manifold nuts and exhaust pipe bracket bolts. See **Figure 25**. Remove the nuts and bolts, then remove the exhaust pipe and bracket.

32. Disconnect the hose from the intake manifold to the breather chamber on the cylinder block.

33. Remove the timing belt and its camshaft pulley as described in Chapter Five in the main body of this book.

34. Loosen the cylinder head bolts in the order shown in **Figure 52**. Loosen the bolts in several stages, 1/3 turn at a time, until all bolts are loose. This is necessary to prevent warping the cylinder head.

35. Once the head bolts are loose, remove them and lift the cylinder head off the block. If this is difficult, tap gently with a rubber mallet.

CAUTION
Do not pry the cylinder head off. This will damage the gasket surface.

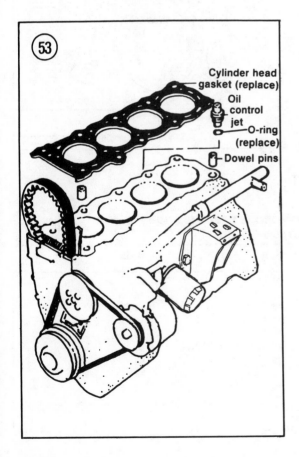

Cylinder head gasket (replace)
Oil control jet
O-ring (replace)
Dowel pins

Rocker Arm and Camshaft Inspection

Rocker arm and camshaft inspection is the same as on previous models with the exception of the camshaft lobe height specifications as follows:

   a. Intake A: 38.855 mm (1.5297 in.).
   b. Intake B: 38.608 mm (1.5200 in.).
   c. Exhaust: 38.796 mm (1.5274 in.).

CYLINDER HEAD INSTALLATION (FUEL INJECTED ACCORD MODELS)

Installation is the reverse of removal, plus the following.

1. Be sure the cylinder head, block and cylinder bores are clean. Check all visible oil passages for cleanliness.

2. Install a new cylinder head gasket. Never reuse an old head gasket. Make sure the cylinder block dowels and oil control jet are in their proper positions. See **Figure 53**.

CAUTION
During the next step, do not let the cylinder block dowels scratch the cylinder head surface.

3. Position the cylinder head on the block.

4. Install the cylinder head bolts and special washers. See **Figure 52**. Tighten the cylinder head bolts in 2 stages. Follow the sequence in **Figure 52**. Tighten the bolts to 30 N•m (22 ft.-lb.) in the first stage. Tighen them to 68 N•m (49 ft.-lb.) in the second stage.

5. Change the engine oil as described in Chapter Three in the main body of this book. This is necessary to remove any water that may have leaked into oil passages when the cylinder head was removed.

6. Fill and bleed the cooling system as described in Chapter Seven in the main body of this book.

VALVES AND VALVE SEATS (ACCORD MODELS)

Valve service is the same as on previous models with the exception of the valve spring free length specifications as follows:

   a. Exhaust inner: 39.8 mm (1.57 in.).
   b. Intake outer: 49.15 mm (1.935 in.).
   c. Exhaust outer: 49.78 mm (1.960 in.) (fuel injected).
   d. Exhaust outer: 51.0 mm (2.01 in.) (carburetted).
   e. Intake (auxiliary, carburetted models only): 31.73 mm (1.25 in.).

13

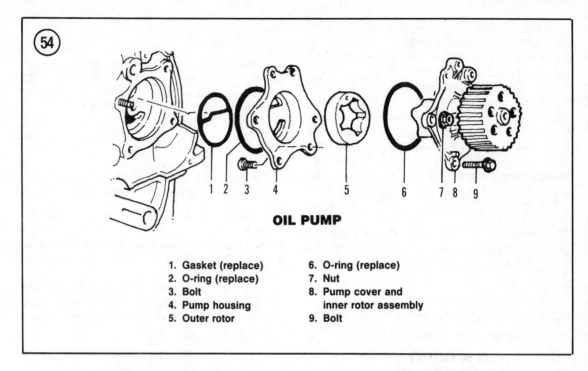

OIL PUMP

1. Gasket (replace)
2. O-ring (replace)
3. Bolt
4. Pump housing
5. Outer rotor
6. O-ring (replace)
7. Nut
8. Pump cover and
   inner rotor assembly
9. Bolt

OIL PAN, OIL PUMP AND PRESSURE RELIEF VALVE

Oil Pump Removal/Installation

1. Remove the timing belt as described in Chapter Five in the main body of this book.
2. Remove the oil pump bolts and nut (**Figure 54**). Take off the oil pump.
3. Installation is the reverse of removal. Use a new gasket and O-ring. Apply gasket sealer around the O-ring groove as shown in **Figure 55**.

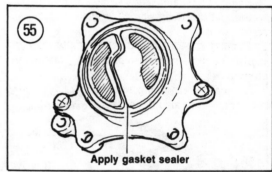

Apply gasket sealer

Table 3 ENGINE MOUNTING TORQUE SPECIFICATIONS*
FUEL INJECTED ACCORD

Fastener	Thread size	N·m	ft.-lb.
No. 1	10×1.25	39	28
No. 2	10×1.25	55	40
No. 3	10×1.25	20	14
No. 4	10×1.25	20	14
No. 5	10×1.25	39	28
No. 6	12×1.25	75	54
No. 7	12×1.25	75	54
No. 8	12×1.25	75	54
No. 9	10×1.25	20	14

* Tighten numbered bolts in order shown in text.

CHAPTER SIX

FUEL, EXHAUST AND EMISSION CONTROL SYSTEMS

AIR CLEANER
(FUEL INJECTED ACCORD)

Element Replacement

Refer to **Figure 56** for this procedure.
1. Remove the nuts and washers and the bolts securing the air cleaner cover and remove the cover.
2. Remove and discard the air cleaner element. If the inside of the housing is dirty, wipe it clean with a damp cloth.
3. Install a new element. Make sure the element is correctly seated into the air inlet connecting tube.

Housing Removal/Installation

Refer to **Figure 56** for this procedure.
1. Remove the nuts and washers and the bolts securing the air cleaner cover and remove the cover.
2. Remove the air cleaner element. If the element is dirty or it is time for replacement, discard the element.
3. Loosen the clamping screw on the air intake tube and on the air inlet connecting tube.

4. Remove the air cleaner base from the air intake tube and the air inlet connecting tube.
5. Install in the reverse order.

FUEL PUMP
(FUEL INJECTED ACCORD)

The Honda is equipped with an electric fuel pump located next to the fuel tank. The fuel pump assembly is shown in **Figure 57**.

If the fuel pump is suspected of being faulty (see *Troubleshooting*, Chapter Two), check the line connections to make certain the mounting bolts and the fuel pump body screws are tight.

Fuel Pump Testing

1. Turn the ignition switch OFF.
2. Remove the fuel pump cover and disconnect the black/yellow and black wires.
3. Connect a voltmeter to the chassis harness side of the disconnected electrical wires. Attach the positive test lead to the black/yellow wire and negative test lead to the black wire.
4. Turn the ignition switch ON. If there is battery voltage (12V), replace the fuel pump.
5. If there is no battery voltage, inspect the main relay and/or wiring harness.

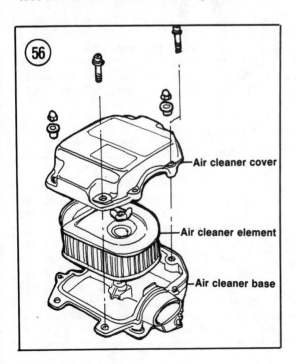

(56)

Air cleaner cover

Air cleaner element

Air cleaner base

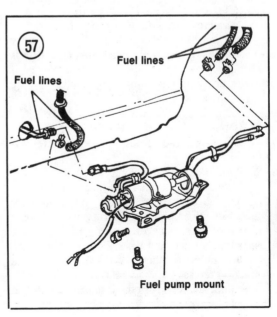

(57)

Fuel lines

Fuel lines

Fuel pump mount

13

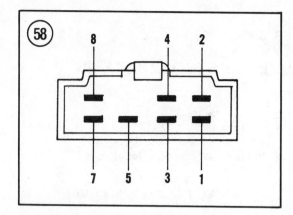

Main Relay Testing

Refer to **Figure 58** for this procedure.

Locate the fuse panel underneath the dashboard and remove the main relay from the fuse panel.

Test no. 1

1. Connect the leads from a 12-volt battery as follows:
   a. Positive lead to the No. 4 terminal.
   b. Negative lead to the No. 8 terminal.
2. Using an ohmmeter, check for continuity between the No. 5 and No. 7 terminals. If there is continuity (low resistance), go to Test No. 2. If there is no continuity (infinite resistance) replace the main relay.

Test no. 2

1. Connect the leads from a 12-volt battery as follows:
   a. Positive lead to the No. 5 terminal.
   b. Negative lead to the No. 2 terminal.
2. Using an ohmmeter, check for continuity between the No. 1 and No. 3 terminals. If there is continuity (low resistance), go to Test No. 3. If there is no continuity (infinite resistance) replace the main relay.

Test no. 3

1. Connect the leads from a 12-volt battery as follows:
   a. Positive lead to the No. 3 terminal.
   b. Negative lead to the No. 8 terminal.
2. Using an ohmmeter, check for continuity between the No. 5 and No. 7 terminals. If there is continuity (low resistance), the relay is okay. If the fuel pump still does not work, there is an open in the wiring harness. If there is no continuity (infinite resistance) replace the main relay.

Install the main relay in the fuse panel under the dashboard.

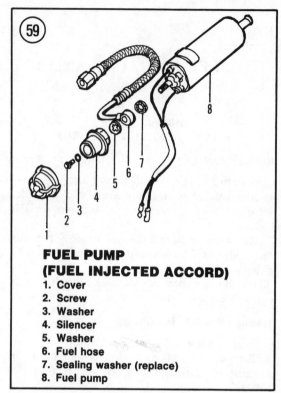

**FUEL PUMP
(FUEL INJECTED ACCORD)**
1. Cover
2. Screw
3. Washer
4. Silencer
5. Washer
6. Fuel hose
7. Sealing washer (replace)
8. Fuel pump

**Fuel Pump
Removal/Installation**

1. Securely block the front wheels so the car will no roll in either direction.
2. Jack up the rear end of the car and place it on jackstands.
3. Disconnect the battery negative lead.
4. Depressurize the fuel system as follows:
   a. Place a small flat pan (pie tin) under the fuel filter to catch as much fuel as possible.

*WARNING
The fuel injection system is under pressure. Do not loosen any of the union bolts on the fuel filter until the fuel system is depressurized.*

   b. Hold the special union bolt with an open end wrench and attach a 6 mm box wrench onto the service bolt as shown in **Figure 2**.
   c. Place a shop cloth over the 6 mm service bolt and slowly loosen the service bolt one full turn with the wrench. This will relieve the pressure within the fuel system. Discard any spilled fuel properly.
5. Remove the bolts that hold the fuel pump in place and lower the pump to provide access to the fuel lines.

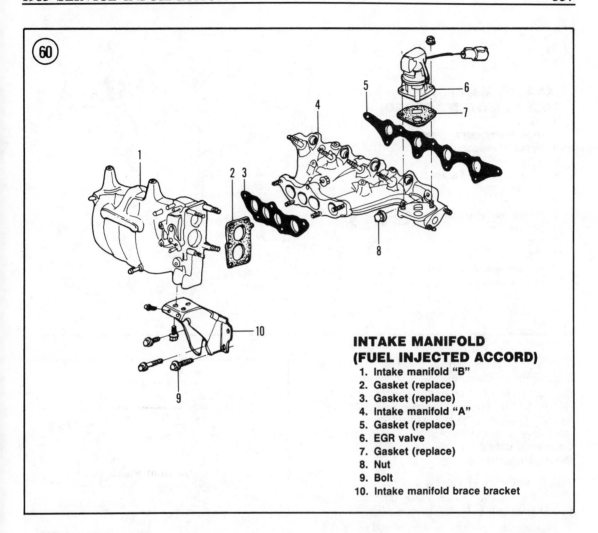

⑥⓪

**INTAKE MANIFOLD
(FUEL INJECTED ACCORD)**
  1. Intake manifold "B"
  2. Gasket (replace)
  3. Gasket (replace)
  4. Intake manifold "A"
  5. Gasket (replace)
  6. EGR valve
  7. Gasket (replace)
  8. Nut
  9. Bolt
10. Intake manifold brace bracket

6. Unplug the electrical leads from the fuel pump.
7. Disconnect the fuel lines from the pump and remove it.
8. Remove the bolt and clamp and remove the fuel pump from the mounting bracket.
9. Remove the fuel line and silencer from the end of the fuel pump (**Figure 59**).
10. Installation is the reverse of removal, plus the following:

   a. Carefully clean the sealing surface of the flared fuel line, then reinstall it onto the fuel line on the car. Tighten the flare nut to 38 N•m (27 ft.-lb.).

   b. Attach the other end of the fuel line and new sealing washer onto the fuel pump. Install the silencer and tighten to 28 N•m (20 ft.-lb.).

   c. Connect the battery negative cable.

   d. Turn the ignition switch ON and check for and correct any fuel leaks in the lines and connections.

EXHAUST AND INTAKE MANIFOLDS (FUEL INJECTED ACCORD MODELS)

Intake Manifold
Removal/Installation

Refer to **Figure 60** for this procedure.
1. Perform Steps 3, 5-24 and 32 of *Cylinder Head Removal (Fuel Injected Accord)* in this supplement.
2. Remove the fuel pipe and fuel injectors as described in this supplement.
3. Remove the intake manifold brace bracket.

CAUTION
The manifold should come off easily during the next step. If not, check to be sure all fasteners have been removed. Do not pry the manifold off.

4. Remove the manifold fasteners and take the manifold off.
5. Remove all traces of old gasket material from the engine and the manifold.

13

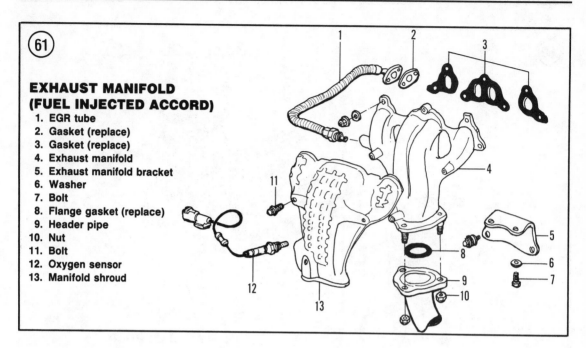

**EXHAUST MANIFOLD
(FUEL INJECTED ACCORD)**
1. EGR tube
2. Gasket (replace)
3. Gasket (replace)
4. Exhaust manifold
5. Exhaust manifold bracket
6. Washer
7. Bolt
8. Flange gasket (replace)
9. Header pipe
10. Nut
11. Bolt
12. Oxygen sensor
13. Manifold shroud

6. Install by reversing Steps 1-4. Use new gaskets. Tighten the intake manifold "A"-to-cylinder head fasteners evenly in a crisscross pattern, to 22 N•m (16 ft.-lb.). Tighten the intake manifold brace bracket fasteners to 22 N•m (16 ft.-lb.).

**Exhaust Manifold
Removal/Installation**

Refer to **Figure 61** for this procedure.
1. Set the parking brake. Place the transaxle in FIRST (manual) or PARK (automatic).
2. Jack up the front end of the car and place it on jackstands.
3. Disconnect the exhaust pipe from the manifold (**Figure 62**). Detach the exhaust pipe bracket (**Figure 63**), then pull the pipe downward away from the manifold.
4. Remove the exhaust manifold bracket.
5. Disconnect the oxygen sensor wire and remove the EGR tube from the manifold.
6. Remove the exhaust manifold shroud.

CAUTION
The manifold should come off easily during the next step. If not, check to be sure all fasteners have been removed. Do not pry the manifold off.

7. Remove the manifold fasteners and take the manifold off.
8. Remove all traces of old gasket material from the engine and the manifold.
9. Install by reversing Steps 3-7. Use new gaskets. Tighten the exhaust manifold fasteners evenly in a

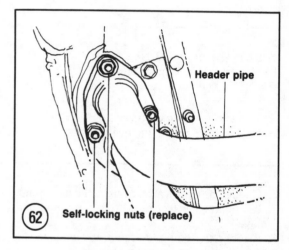

Header pipe

Self-locking nuts (replace)

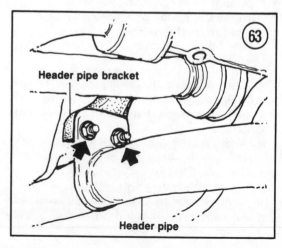

Header pipe bracket

Header pipe

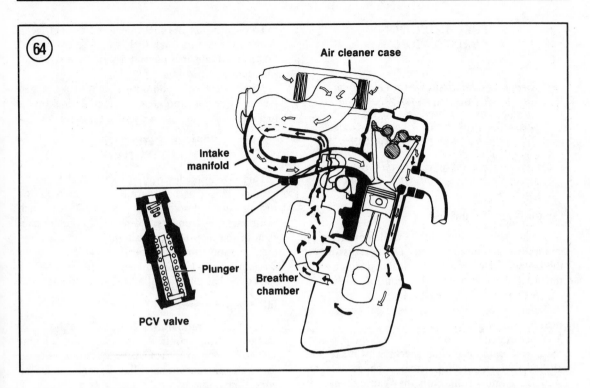

PCV valve

Air cleaner case

Intake manifold

Plunger

Breather chamber

crisscross pattern, to 32 N•m (22 ft.-lb.). Tighten the exhaust manifold brace bracket fasteners to 22 N•m (16 ft.-lb.).

CRANKCASE EMISSION CONTROL SYSTEM (FUEL INJECTED ACCORD MODELS)

The crankcase emission control system (**Figure 64**) used on the fuel injected Accord models is equipped with a positive crankcase ventilation (PCV) valve. The valve regulates the flow of blowby gases into the intake manifold according to engine conditions.

EXHAUST EMISSION CONTROLS (FUEL INJECTED ACCORD MODELS)

The exhaust emission control system is actually a group of subsystems designed to control emissions when the engine is idling, accelerating, cruising and declerating. The sub systems are:

a. Ignition timing control.
b. Exhaust gas recirculation.

Because the fuel injected engine runs more efficiently, it is cleaner and requires fewer emission control subsystems. The same subsystems are used on all models whether the car is sold in California, in the high-altitude states or any remaining states.

A brief description of these systems is located in Chapter Six in the main body of this book.

FUEL INJECTION SYSTEM (ACCORD MODELS)

The electronic fuel injection system consists of a fuel pump, fuel filter, 4 fuel injectors, fuel delivery pipe assembly, throttle body assembly, intake manifold, air cleaner and all of the electronic support hardware.

This section describes how the fuel injection system works. Almost all of the components must be serviced by a Honda dealer either due to any applicable warranty or because they require complicated electronic troubleshooting equipment and a thorough knowledge of the fuel injection system. Some of these components are very expensive and could be damaged by someone unfamiliar with them or the test equipment. Also typical of complex electronic systems, most parts cannot be repaired, only replaced.

CAUTION
Servicing an automobile with electronic fuel injection requires special precautions to prevent damage to the expensive electronic control unit. Common electrical system service procedures acceptable on other automobiles may cause damage to several parts of the fuel injection system. Be sure to read **Fuel Injection Precautions** *in this section of the supplement.*

13

FUEL INJECTION
PRECAUTIONS

CAUTION
Servicing an automobile with electronic fuel injection requires special precautions to prevent damage to the expensive electronic control unit (computer). Common electrical system service procedures acceptable on other automobiles may cause damage to several parts of the fuel injection system.

Control Unit Precautions

1. Do not start the automobile while any electrical connectors are disconnected. Do not disconnect the battery cables or any electrical connector while the ignition switch is ON. The control unit will be damaged and must be replaced.
2. Before disconnecting any electrical connectors, turn the ignition switch OFF.
3. When repairs are completed, do not try to start the engine without double checking to make sure all fuel injection electrical connectors are connected; faulty connectors may cause damage to the control unit and its related components.
4. Do not disconnect the battery while the engine is running.
5. Do not apply anything other than a 12-volt battery to the automobile's electrical system. The automobile's battery must be removed before attaching a battery charger.

Fuel System Precautions

1. The fuel system is pressurized, so wear eye protection whenever working on the fuel system, especially when disconnecting fuel lines.
2. The fuel pump is cooled and its bearings are lubricated by the fuel it is pumping. Refill the fuel tank when there is a minimum of 1/4 tank remaining. If the pump is operated without fuel, its bearings will be damaged. The fuel pump cannot be disassembled; if damaged it must be replaced.
3. Do not add any lubricants, preservatives or additives to the gasoline; fuel system corrosion or clogging may result.

FUEL INJECTION OPERATION

The fuel injection system consists of the air intake system, fuel system and the control system. The sensors of the control system monitor coolant and air temperature, atmospheric and intake manifold pressures, throttle opening, piston location from top dead center (TDC), engine speed, etc.

To ensure that the fuel injectors are kept clean from fuel contaminants, fuel is filtered two times, first at the main fuel filter and then by a screen at each fuel injector unit.

The control unit (computer) computes the best fuel mixture for smooth performance, maximum fuel economy and lowest exhaust emissions.

FUEL INJECTION
SYSTEM COMPONENTS

This is a brief description of the fuel injection system. This will help familiarize you with the system and describe the function of each component. An understanding of the function of each of the fuel injection system components and their relation to one another is a valuable aid for pinpointing fuel injection problems. **Figure 65** shows the basic layout of all the components.

Idle Control System

The fuel/air ratio during engine idle is controlled by the electronic control unit and various solenoid valves (idle control, fast idle, automatic transaxle idle and air conditioner idle). Except for the air conditioner idle control, these valves change the amounts of air bypassing into the air intake manifold. The air conditioner valve opens the throttle when the air conditioner is turned on to achieve a higher idle.

Idle Adjuster (Bypass Circuit)

Fuel cutoff takes place at a set position or angle of the throttle valve. This circuit is designed to control the amount of air bypassing into the intake manifold without changing the position of the throttle valve.

Fast Idle Mechanism

When the engine is cold, it is necessary to raise idle speed. The air bypass valve is controlled by a thermowax plunger similar to the thermostat in the cooling system. Additional air is bypassed into the intake manifold when the engine is cold so the engine will idle faster than normal.

Control Unit (Computer)

The control unit does the following:
a. Receives signals from all of the support sensors to inject fuel into the cylinders in the correct amount and at the correct time. The control unit signals the injectors to one of their two basic discharge memories; one for small throttle openings and the other for large throttle openings. The fuel injector opening is fixed in the full open position. The fuel

FUEL INJECTION MAJOR COMPONENTS

1. Cold advance solenoid valve
2. Fast idle control solenoid valve
3. Idle mixture adjuster solenoid
4. Manifold air pressure sensor
5. Automatic transaxle idle control solenoid valve
6. Throttle angle sensor
7. Intake air temperature sensor
8. EGR control solenoid valve
9. Air conditioner idle control solenoid valve
10. Resistor
11. EGR valve lift sensor
12. Oxygen sensor
13. Coolant temperature sensor
14. Crankshaft angle sensor
15. Idle control solenoid valve

mixture is controlled by the length of time the injector is open.

b. Controls the fuel pump.

c. Determines the optimum ignition timing based on the signals it receives from the various sensors.

d. Indicates what systems or components are faulty through a self-diagnosis system and offers a fail-safe function in the event one or more of the components in the fuel injection system breaks down. If a sensor has a problem, the self-diagnosis lights (LED's) on the side of the control unit will come on. These lights will flash in a sequence to indicate what the problem is.

Crankshaft Angle Sensor

This sensor and rotor are part of the distributor assembly. As the camshaft and distributor rotate, the sensors detect the specific angular position of the crankshaft. This information is used to detect engine speed to determine the discharge duration of the fuel injectors.

Manifold Air Pressure Sensor

This sensor converts intake manifold pressure into electrical signals that are sent to the control unit. This information, along with signals from the crankshaft angle sensor, is used to determine the discharge duration of the fuel injectors.

13

Atmospheric Pressure Sensor

Similar to the manifold air pressure sensor, this sensor converts atmospheric manifold pressure into electrical signals that are sent to the control unit. This information then modifies the discharge duration of the fuel injectors to compensate for changes in atmospheric pressure.

Coolant Temperature Sensor

This sensor is located on the coolant thermostat housing. It measures the coolant temperature in the engine and sends information signals to the control unit.

Inlet Air Temperature Sensor

This sensor is located on the intake manifold. It measures the incoming air temperature and sends information signals to the control unit.

Throttle Angle Sensor

This sensor is attached to the throttle body. It is an electric rheostat that measures the throttle opening in degrees and sends information to the control unit.

Oxygen Sensor

This sensor is located in the exhaust manifold. It measures the oxygen content of the exhaust gases and sends information signals to the control unit.

Idle Mixture Adjust Sensor

This sensor is located in control box No. 1. It maintains the correct fuel/air mixture at all times under all conditions.

Starter Switch

During engine cranking, the starter switch receives signals from the control unit and increases the amount of fuel going into the intake manifold according to engine temperature.

Pressure Regulator

The pressure regulator maintains a constant fuel pressure to the fuel injectors at all times.

Resistor

In order for the fuel injectors to operate at their maximum efficiency and reliability, the number of electrical wire coils in each injector is kept to a minimum to reduce the electrical inductance in the coil. This type of winding offers very little resistance and allows high current flow. To add resistance to the circuit (and decrease heat buildup) the resistor is added in series to the circuit. It is located between the electrical power source and the injector coil.

Main Relay

This relay controls the power to the control unit depending on the position of the ignition switch or battery voltage or starter signal. The entire fuel injection system is shut down when the electrical supply to the control unit is turned off.

BASIC TROUBLESHOOTING

Control Unit Self-diagnosis

If trouble occurs in the fuel injection system while the engine is running, the trouble is diagnosed by the control unit. The control unit sends a message and the "PMG-FI" warning light on the instrument panel tells the driver of a system problem. The control unit is mounted under the driver's seat.

There are 4 LED's (light emitting diodes) on the control unit and these lights are visible under the side of the driver's seat. If a problem exists, the LED's will blink ON or OFF. These pulses indicate what problem exists within the fuel injection system. If the "PMG-FI" warning light come on, take the car to a Honda dealer for service immediately.

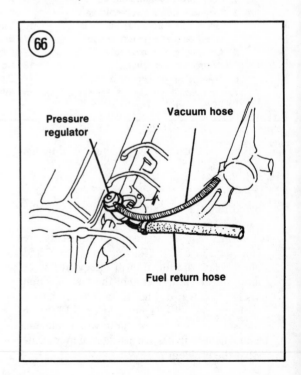

FUEL INJECTORS

The fuel injectors are a solenoid-activated, constant stroke pintle type. Each one consists of a housing with a solenoid, plunger and needle valve within the housing. When current is applied, the solenoid lifts the needle valve and fuel is injected. The fuel injector's opening is fixed in the open position and fuel pressure is constant at all times. The amount of fuel injected is controlled by the length of time the injector is open.

Injector Testing

For a quick check to see if the fuel injectors are operating, perform the following.

Engine will not run

1. Disconnect the electrical connector from the fuel injector.
2. Use an ohmmeter and measure the resistance between the terminals on the injector. The specified resistance is 1.5-2.5 ohms. If the reading is not within the specification, replace the injector.
3. Repeat Steps 1-2 for all injectors.
4. If the resistance is within specification, perform the following:
   a. Check the electrical connector for each injector for corrosion or damage.
   b. Have the circuit resistor checked and the fuel injector circuit checked for an open or short.

Engine will start

1. Start the engine and let it idle.
2. Disconnect the electrical connector from one injector at a time. If the idle drop is almost the same for each cylinder, the fuel injectors are operating properly.
3. To make sure the injector is opening, place the tip of a long screwdriver against the injector body with the grip against your ear. If the injector fails to make the typical clicking sound, the injector or its circuit is faulty. Have the electrical circuit between the control unit and the fuel injectors checked out for an open or short, then repair the circuit or replace the injector as necessary.

Fuel Pipe and Fuel Injector Removal/Installation

1. Disconnect the battery negative cable.
2. Depressurize the fuel system as follows:

a. Place a small flat pan (pie tin) under the fuel filter to catch as much fuel as possible.

WARNING
The fuel injection system is under pressure. Do not loosen any of the union bolts on the fuel filter until the fuel system is depressurized.

b. Hold the special union bolt with an open end wrench and attach a 6 mm box wrench onto the service bolt as shown in **Figure 2**.
c. Place a shop cloth over the service bolt and slowly loosen the service bolt one full turn with the wrench. This will relieve the pressure within the fuel system. Discard any spilled fuel properly.
3. Remove the air cleaner case as described in this supplement.
4. Disconnect the electrical connector from the fuel injector.
5. Place a shop cloth over the fittings while disconnecting them. Disconnect the vacuum hose and fuel return hose from the pressure regulator (**Figure 66**).
6. Detach the 2 electrical ground cables from the intake manifold.
7. Detach the fuel lines from the fuel pipe.
8. Remove the nuts securing the fuel pipe and remove the fuel pipe.
9. Remove the fuel injector and discard the O-ring seal, cushion ring and seal ring. They must not be reused.
10. Install by reversing these removal steps, noting the following.
11. Install a new O-ring seal on the end of the injector cap where it attaches to the fuel pipe. Apply a light coat of clean engine oil to the O-ring seal.
12. Install a new cushion ring and seal ring (**Figure 67**) and install the injector into the intake manifold.
13. Align the centerline mark on the fuel injector and the index mark on the intake manifold (**Figure 68**).
14. Perform Steps 9-13 for the other fuel injectors if necessary.
15. Turn the ignition switch ON, but do not start the engine. Let the fuel pump run for about 2 seconds to fill the fuel pipe and hoses with fuel. Turn the ignition switch OFF. Repeat this step 2-3 times prior to starting the engine.

Check and repair any fuel leaks.

13

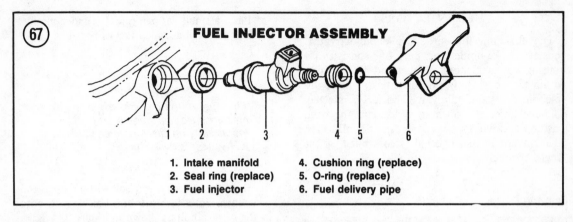

FUEL INJECTOR ASSEMBLY

1. Intake manifold
2. Seal ring (replace)
3. Fuel injector
4. Cushion ring (replace)
5. O-ring (replace)
6. Fuel delivery pipe

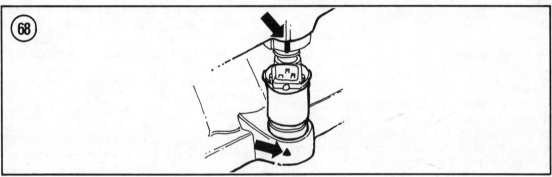

CHAPTER SEVEN

COOLING, HEATING AND
AIR CONDITIONING SYSTEMS

RADIATOR

Removal/Installation
(Fuel Injected Accord Models)

The removal and installation procedures are the same as on previous carburetted Accord models. Refer to **Figure 69** for parts locations.

COOLING FAN

Removal/Installation
(Fuel Injected Accord Models)

The removal and installation procedures are the same as on previous Accord models. Refer to **Figure 69** for parts locations.

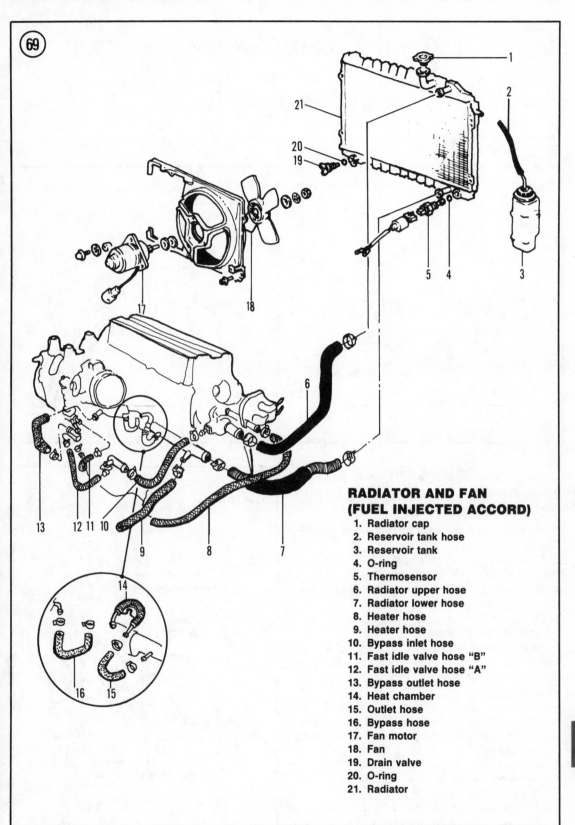

**RADIATOR AND FAN
(FUEL INJECTED ACCORD)**
1. Radiator cap
2. Reservoir tank hose
3. Reservoir tank
4. O-ring
5. Thermosensor
6. Radiator upper hose
7. Radiator lower hose
8. Heater hose
9. Heater hose
10. Bypass inlet hose
11. Fast idle valve hose "B"
12. Fast idle valve hose "A"
13. Bypass outlet hose
14. Heat chamber
15. Outlet hose
16. Bypass hose
17. Fan motor
18. Fan
19. Drain valve
20. O-ring
21. Radiator

13

CHAPTER EIGHT

ELECTRICAL SYSTEMS

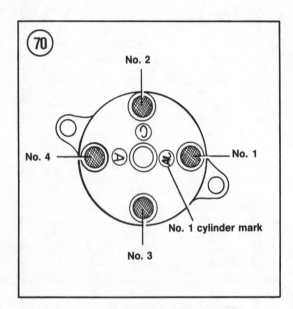

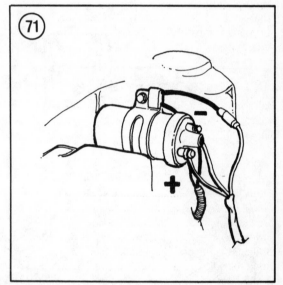

DISTRIBUTOR

Removal/Installation
(Fuel Injected Accord Models)

1. Label the spark plug wires as shown in **Figure 70**.
2. Disconnect the primary and secondary wires from the ignition coil. See **Figure 71**.
3. Disconnect the distributor vacuum lines (**Figure 72**).
4. Disconnect the 4-pin electrical connector from the crankshaft angle sensor.
5. Remove the distributor hold down bolts and take the distributor out of the cylinder head.
6. Installation is the reverse of removal, plus the following:
   a. Note that the distributor drive lug and the slot in the end of the camshaft are both offset so the distributor can be installed only one way (**Figure 72**).
   b. Use a new O-ring on the distributor base.
   c. Connect the spark plug wires in the order shown in **Figure 70**.
   d. Adjust the ignition timing as described in Chapter Three in the main body of this book.

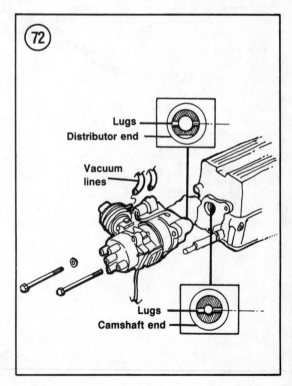

INDEX

14